S0-AKX-011

Not Enough Tears

by

Dave Wright

authorHOUSE®

AuthorHouse™
1663 Liberty Drive
Bloomington, IN 47403
www.authorhouse.com
Phone: 1 (800) 839-8640

Published by AuthorHouse 06/14/2016

ISBN: 978-1-4184-3682-7 (sc)
ISBN: 978-1-4184-3683-4 (e)

Library of Congress Control Number: 2004093548

Print information available on the last page.

This book is printed on acid-free paper.

CONTENTS

DEDICATION

A DETOUR IN LIFE

* * *

I've heard it said that life's a journey. If that's true, there's a story I need to tell about one of those detours off the main highway of life. Though the story describes my experiences, they were written down for my wife, Janet, my son Jonathan and his friends. Each week, we read one story to capture the kid's attention as part of a Bible study. Through each chapter, we saw God's faithful work in a different light. It's my hope that some of the examples of His unbounded grace get put on the back-shelf of your mind, where the Holy Spirit can grab and use them when the timing is right. Since recording these stories I've found peace and have no desire to search for a way back to the main road of life. After realizing, and seeing God's repeated faithfulness, now I'm beginning to trust the pathway He's laying out for me.

These stories were written with thirty years of hindsight. I returned home from Vietnam as a very cynical young man. For years, the experiences of that war clashed with my beliefs of what was right and fair. Though I've been a "Christian" from age eleven, these stories, and the last thirty years were filled with the struggle between my understanding and God's. Most of those years were darkened by Post Traumatic Stress and consumed with anger, bitterness and frustration directed at myself and those around me. I became deeply depressed, feeling there may be no hope of change for myself or the world that created these attitudes.

I've recently found that God ***is*** changing things. He's healing me! I believe He will heal as much as I can release to Him. It's been a little more than ten years since I've been able to thank God for my year in Vietnam. Though the healing story continues, I want to let other Vets, their families, and any who are still curious, watch that year of hell turn into a day-by-day healing and blessing. These stories reveal a love that is more gracious and patient than I can imagine. It's taken all this time to finally see and believe that when we let God, He can use all things, in all people, for our good. "So, even now Lord, this is your story, and anything good that comes out of it, is for your glory alone."

Author's note: The experiences in these stories are true to the best of my knowledge. * Names of individuals have been change to preserve their privacy.

PREFACE

There were not enough tears in the whole of Southeast Asia to wash away the guilt Dave felt for having survived the Vietnam War when so many good young men next to him did not. Tears were not shed for our soldiers by those who blamed them for fighting and killing instead of loving our enemies to peace. Tears couldn't cleanse our government for not allowing those they sent to fight in Vietnam to win, but expected that we should merely stop the Communist from taking over the country until the South Vietnamese were strong enough to win the war for themselves. There were no tears that could possibly absolve our national embarrassment and shame that these same young soldiers couldn't achieve the glory in Vietnam that past generations had brought home from the Good War, (WWII)

Some say healing comes in the process of understanding. The young men who fought the Vietnam War were perhaps the most misunderstood combatants in our nation's history. Many veterans still cannot, or will not verbalize what they went through. Their lives changed forever, but they couldn't understand or explain why or what happened during their tour that brought on so much frustration, anger and despair.

Not Enough Tears takes you on the roll-a-coaster ride of emotions felt by a young infantryman walking point in the steaming jungles and rice paddies of South Vietnam.

It was like stepping into another reality. Everything Dave had learned growing up was challenged. Life was not sacred or precious, and it certainly wasn't fair in that foreign culture ten thousand miles from home. New survival skills became intensely important; reactions had to be quick and without thought. Emotions became distractions that had to be suppressed, sleep was deadly and getting home was the hope he tried to cling to, but too often, present reality exploded and "home" felt like an unreachable fantasy.

Many did get home, some without a scratch like Dave, but he was no longer in tune with his fantasy. The "American Dream" somehow turned shallow and empty. What had changed so much? Why couldn't he simply return to life as it was before the war?

As a young man, Dave admits he couldn't commit 100% of himself to any one thing. Thirty years of hard lessons after the war drove him to seek all that's good and true, and that hope finally rescued him from his most difficult times.

PROLOGUE

The jungle was as dense as I'd ever seen. Wait-a-minute bamboo, lush broad-leafed plants as tall as we were, tangles of vines, and huge trees reduced visibility to inches. About seventy-five yards into the mess, sunlight appeared through an opening in the canopy over the top of a bamboo thicket to my left. Bamboo might be easier to negotiate than the wall we were facing, so I broke my way through and popped into a tiny clearing in front of a termite mound at the edge of a bomb crater. Bamboo lay back around the crater at the angle of the explosion and another opening was just beyond this one, probably another crater. Skirting around the edge looked better than trying to work back into the twisted jungle. Slowly I walked up beside the termite mound, which was about four feet high and six feet across at the bottom, not really big compared to others I'd seen.

One more step put me on top of the soft dirt piled up at the rim of the empty cone. The walls were steep but stable enough to walk on. The air was still heavy with the smell of burnt powder from the explosion. My squad stacked up as we inched around the twenty foot diameter hole. Now lined up in a semicircle, we froze in unison, all eyes locked onto a two-foot diameter, turquoise dish at the beginning of the opening to the next crater. An electrical wire led through the space between clumps of bamboo to the next splash of sunlight.

The face of the large Chinese claymore pointing towards us was filled with bits of shrapnel that would be blasted into our bodies as soon as the detonator was pushed. The electrical wire meant it was command-detonated, and the VC were watching, waiting for the greatest number of us to walk into their kill zone. At any second the explosion would rip us apart.

As a group, my squad all turned around and ran back to the termite mound. I was left standing, still frozen. Why wasn't I running with them? An invisible hand pushed me to the ground where I was. The claymore was no more than twelve feet to my left with nothing between its crushing blast and me. I tucked my hands under my throat, hoping my steel helmet would protect them, and my forearms would protect my shoulders. There was just enough time to think this is another really dumb thing to do, then everything exploded.

- 1 -

THE DRAFT/INDUCTION

A deep sucking breath filled my lungs with cool midmorning air. My eyes fixed on a crevice just a few feet ahead, and my breathing fell silent. Every muscle tensed, then I sprang to the next foothold in the newly cut rock face. My boots caught the narrow seam, but my body was tilting helplessly away from the near vertical slope. While in midair, the tip of my Philly rod struck a protruding boulder and glanced into open space threatening to carry me with it. "Off balance" alarms flashed in my mind, and my right hand sank a rock hammer into another crevice I'd selected earlier just for that purpose. Exhaling slowly, I eased myself back to an upright position.

Safe for the moment, my eyes searched for the survey crew a hundred and twenty feet below. Switching hands, I gently placed the tip of the rod into the same crack my toes clung to, then strained to hold it as vertical as possible while looking for directions from the instrument man. His flag waved to the left. I pulled the rod closer until the flag waved back and forth. Noting the spot, I placed the rod on the top of my boot and leaned it back against the abutment. With my free hand I grabbed a can of red spray paint from the tool bag on my belt and continued marking the diagonal line I'd begun an hour earlier at the base of the fill. The red painted line indicated the point of separation between a clay core and rock backfill as layer upon layer merged and climbed the mountain face just recently blasted and cut to form one side of the dam we were building.

I loved this job. At twenty-two, I got to do all the things the older members of the survey crew were too smart to do. I'd dropped out of the engineering program at Sacramento State a year and a half earlier. My grades and incentive to study had dipped to the point where continuing would only have led to flunking out. It felt like the right decision. Everything was going my way. I was having fun, making good money, taking care of myself, dating my girlfriend Janet Brown, and Mom still did my laundry and gave me CARE packages when I decided to bless her with a visit. Life was all about me and it was good.

College wasn't that difficult, but I didn't have and didn't want to develop the self-discipline to do well. My circle of friends suffered a similar lack of commitment, and we always found something more interesting to do than homework. The final incentive – to please my parents, was also waning. It was becoming more important to satisfy myself. I even bought halfway into the universal excuse, "I need to find out who I am and what I want to do with my life." I still don't know what that means, other than it opens a door to an endless journey of self-pursuit.

The real problem was I needed to grow up. At the time, I couldn't see that all these things were going to be used as pieces in the process of building my life. I didn't understand how God worked with everything, even self-centeredness, to bring about what's best when we let him. How much easier it would have been had I submitted to His love, mercy, and grace at that point. I didn't, so He used the decisions I made and we went forward.

My decision to work instead of going to school meant I lost my student deferment and was now eligible for the upcoming lottery/draft. The Vietnam War was beginning to chew up a lot of young kids, which left vacancies Uncle Sam wanted filled immediately. I worried about the draft and the possibility it might disrupt my newly found independence and life of self-involved choices. My logic may have been different from some, but I didn't want to spend more anxious months wondering when or if I would get my invitation from Uncle Sam. So, I went down to the post office to see where my name fell on the list; the W's were coming up in just a few months. There wasn't enough time to get back into college and I wasn't ready to buckle down anyway.

It was hard to visualize giving up two full years of my life to the military. It wasn't part of my career plan and seemed to be a total waste of time. My dad fortunately missed WWII because a horse had broken his foot, which never healed properly. My brother was three years older and married. None of my family had been in the military for generations. I had no one to talk with.

It seemed inevitable that the draft would pick me up shortly, so I decided to get it over with. The earlier I went in, the quicker I'd get out. Maybe my engineering training, three years of college, and "volunteering" for the draft would land me a better job than just waiting for my number to come up. Things brightened a little when a good friend, Chip Davis, decided to join me. At least we would go to basic training at the same place and might end up doing the same thing for our short "military careers."

We rode with a whole busload of kids from Sacramento down to Oakland, California. This was the "big city" to us. The bus driver wove his way gracefully through the crowded streets and pulled up to a curb alongside the building where most of our lives would change forever. The Induction Center was an old, gray building sitting back about a hundred feet from the street. We stepped off the bus and looked for the main entrance. The lawn and trees were well kept, but it was difficult to see the surroundings or the front door with all the people milling about. For a brief moment I wondered if the large crowd had come to congratulate us for serving our country and wanted to see us off. As I have found many times since, my logic didn't always line up with reality.

My eyes began to notice a lot of long hair and hippie garb when it dawned on me: we had arrived in the middle of a Vietnam War protest. I'd seen the demonstrations on the news but never thought I would end up in the middle of one, and the idea of becoming a focal point for our national conscience regarding this undeclared war was totally foreign. Demonstrators lined both sides of the sidewalk all the way to the main entrance, yelling and handing out antiwar literature.

"Stand up for your rights, burn your draft card, refuse to go to Vietnam, don't be a baby killer!" It was easy enough for them to say; they'd already turned their back on everything "normal." I wasn't ready to give up my middle-class life style just yet. The thought of going to jail or leaving home and country to avoid Vietnam didn't balance in my mind. I couldn't quite see myself as a dropout with long hair, beads, and a tie-dyed T-shirt.

I had conflicting ideas about Vietnam and the war. I was afraid of being put into that ultimate situation of kill or be killed, but at the same time, like many young men, I was secretly curious to know how I'd measure up in the face of death. Would I be a hero or a coward?

Vietnam seemed small and far away. If the Communists did take over, it would probably pose little threat to my way of life in spite of the "domino theory." From the little I knew about Communism, it seemed to allow an oppressive and maybe even brutal form of government whether in Russia, China, or North Vietnam. I'd seen news reports of atrocities committed by the Communists, but that foreign culture seemed to tolerate even those actions a little. I didn't like what was shown on TV, but I didn't want to kill anyone over it either.

I couldn't say that our society was perfect, but in all our previous wars we were the "good guys" riding to the rescue. It appeared that North Vietnam was trying to take over the South, and maybe they did need some protection from their aggressive neighbor. We had already sent a couple hundred thousand kids over there to "fight for freedom." I guessed if they could do it, I could do it.

Anyway, I did have my "ace in the hole." If for some reason I did end up in Vietnam, they would certainly put me on a construction or survey crew. I had valuable experience and training, and was volunteering for the draft. The Army was going to treat me differently. Surely, they wouldn't waste my talents by sending me to Vietnam as just another warm body to replace the ones they brought home in bags. Ah, my impeccable logic!

One of the best things the military does is create lines. Once through the gauntlet of protesters and inside the Induction Center, there were lines going everywhere. Chip and I handed our papers to the clerk at the front desk, who nodded for us to follow the other new arrivals into a classroom. A pencil and something resembling an aptitude test had already been placed on each desk. It quickly became apparent that our answers to the questions could result in extremely different placements within the multiple "opportunities" the Army had available. One went something like, "Would you rather be marooned on a deserted island with adequate supplies for a year, or would you be more comfortable working in a very crowded city for a year." It was easy to tell where that was headed, but I decided to answer truthfully. I picked the desert island and hoped honesty would be better than trying to second-guess everything. They should have asked, "Would you rather live in a steamy, bug-infested jungle where people you can't see are trying everything they can to kill you, or would you rather be totally bored out of your skull for an entire year doing mountains of meaningless paperwork?"

After completing the questions, we lined up behind the growing numbers following a red line painted on the floor. It zigzagged between desks, eventually joining other colored lines heading straight up a long stairway.

The longhaired kid in front grabbed the handrail tightly and slowly ascended. At the top of the stairs he crumpled to the floor without warning. Two medics ran over to examine him. After checking his vital signs and asking a few questions they propped him up and pronounced him fit, as if it were an everyday occurrence, which it probably was! Flunking the physical meant you were classified 4-F and no longer subject to the draft. The stakes were high, and some figured this was an acceptable way to avoid the draft and stay out of jail at the same time. Some produced written excuses from doctors, one failed his eye test by hiding his glasses, another pretended aggressive hostility and insanity—all to get out of going to Vietnam. Most attempts were laughable and given the same treatment as the kid who had passed out. The excuses continued as we trudged around the building following the red line from station to station. My nerves were on edge, and I felt sick and a little frightened. This was an alien world, a place where familiar things like home, family and a good job were being stripped away.

Somehow, Chip flunked his physical without trying. He apologized as he picked up his paperwork and headed for the exit line. I knew he was sincere, but it didn't alleviate my shock at being left alone. We were supposed to be together when things got tough, and now he was walking away. A knot formed in my stomach as I turned to shuffle along with the others still following the red line. Shortly after the old "bend over" physical, we were led to the doorway of a small office. Only six people could enter the office at a time. I was lost somewhere in the middle of a group, and when it was our turn, we entered and sat on a bench next to the wall.

My body slumped against the old wainscoted paneling while my mind tried to make sense of what was happening. In the middle of thousands of people, I felt abandoned. Alone. Everything seemed to be in chaos. There were countless people following red, blue, green, and yellow lines to unknown destinations, all set on their courses by indifferent people and an unfathomable system. Overwhelmed, I sensed a turning point in my life, but which direction would it turn? I'd passed the point of backing out weeks before. Committed now, I had to follow through. My little piece of reality began to crumble, and was replaced by growing anxiety. My future was not in my control.

The floor of the ten by ten office was covered in ancient brown linoleum, and everything else was painted green. The desk was green, the clerk's uniform was green, the unit patches on his uniform were green with black insignias. He melted into a background of the nameless processing line. This must be how cattle feel as they're herded through the chutes and pens in a stockyard. While moving closer and closer to their final destination, they have no control of whether they'll end up at the slaughterhouse or in green pastures. The green clerk took the top six folders from a stack on his desk and opened the covers. His right hand picked up a stamp. Thump, thump, thump in rapid succession. A pause to change stamps. Thump, thump, thump! He handed our folders back with a large "A" or "M" stamped in red ink at the top of each. The M's were supposed to follow the blue line, the A's followed the green. This was my first peek into military logic. There is none! The bored-to-tears, low-ranking clerk at the desk in that small green office had the awesome responsibility of filling the draft quota for both the Army and the Marines. There was no evaluation or screening to determine who might make a better Marine or who would do well in the Army. Instead, this function was carried out by arbitrarily picking the first three folders and stamping them "M" for Marine and sending the remaining three to the Army.

It went completely over my head at the time, but I was seeing God's grace in my life. I missed being drafted into the U.S. Marines by a single folder. The Marines I've met are wonderful people, but at the age of twenty-two, I probably wasn't quite as moldable as the Marines would have liked. My independence allowed me to sidestep what I felt was the Army's attempt at brainwashing, and focus on those things that might keep me alive. The Marines wouldn't have let me get away with that—they wanted 110 percent commitment. I needed to hold something back; I couldn't have given myself totally to the Marines.

- 2 -

BASIC TRAINING

The red line at the Oakland Induction Center finally led to a large room where we swore an oath to officially become members of the elite fighting force known as the U.S. Army. Actually, I never did officially complete the ceremony. At one point we were supposed to step forward to indicate our concurrence with the proceedings. Just for the heck of it, I stayed put. Safely hidden in the mass of bodies, I knew no one would notice, so I initiated my own little act of defiance, a weakness that persisted throughout my short, but illustrious career. It allowed me to feel like an individual with some control and not just an insignificant part of a huge uncaring machine.

Processing wasn't completed until early evening. What happened to lunch? What happened to dinner? What kind of outfit was this? A booming voice broke our roster into bus-sized groups headed for the airport.

We flew north to Seattle and were then bused back to Tacoma, arriving at the main gate of Fort Lewis, Washington about 1:30 in the morning. We were deposited in the middle of row after row of white, two-story wooden barracks that had served out their useful life during World War II.

Tired, hungry, and disoriented, we became fresh meat for the training cadre. They seemed to take a special delight in our misery and didn't finish until 3:00 A.M. We split into platoons and "marched" to our new barracks where we'd spend the next eight glorious weeks in basic training. We picked our bunks and fell into them. My body sighed; finally a chance to rest. They'll let us catch up on our sleep and maybe start training after lunch. The amplified strains of reveille jolted us awake promptly at 5:30!

The following days and weeks were a continuous comedy of the military mind versus kids who were home with Mom just a few days earlier. We lost our hair, got our OD (Olive Drab) uniforms, OD underwear, even OD socks. It was surprising how much everyone looked alike. Of course, that was part of the psychology of our training; no one was an individual. Everyone was equal, reduced to a homogeneous blob that ate, slept, and suffered together. The military strategy was to get everyone to act as a cohesive unit while learning a range of basic skills from how to brush our teeth to shooting, bludgeoning, and bayoneting the enemy.

Most of our training was administered by that common enemy of the new recruit, the drill sergeant. What a job! They got paid to be bullies. The more they scared us, the better they were doing their job. A scared recruit paid a lot more attention than one who was allowed to daydream. They did have important things to teach, so I put up with the "occasional" over exuberant outburst. For the first few weeks nobody could do anything right. They yelled at us for not being able to march, for not being strong enough to endure the daily physical training, for not moving fast enough, for not eating fast enough, for not doing just about anything we were told to do in the way we were supposed to do it. We were new recruits! What'd they expect? That wasn't the point, of course. The Army just wanted us to give up thinking and automatically do what we were told.

A drill instructor would try to motivate us into trying harder by stepping up nose to nose, yell in our face, and poke the brim of his hat into our foreheads. Unfortunately, there were a few souls who took the insults very personally. They were marked and harassed even more than the rest of us, both as an example, and to see if they would break and become compliant. If not, they had to be "recycled." If they didn't understand it was just a game (a serious one), they were destined to start basic training all over again with a new company. No one wanted to repeat this hell a second time! Most learned to give the required performance. Some enjoyed being made into men and honestly worked to excel.

Others were not quite as smitten by the Army's ideal man and put forth a tad less effort. Most of my platoon fell into the latter category.

To embarrass us into doing better, the drill sergeants would grade each of the four platoons in our training company on how well we did the preceding week. The platoon with the lowest score got special recognition in the form of a big black rock painted to resemble an "eight ball." This rock stayed in front of the substandard barracks for the entire week, and that platoon would be ridiculed until the next evaluation. Military logic was, "Everyone will work harder to avoid getting the eight ball." It worked for the other three platoons, but my platoon was the proud owner of the eight ball for nearly the entire training program. We were a little less enthusiastic than the Army wanted, but we were acting as a unit!

When it was our platoon's turn to provide volunteers for a "special" job, I jumped for a chance to escape whatever boring class we were scheduled for that day. I stepped out and was told to report to the mess hall. Oh well, I enjoyed cooking. Several five-gallon buckets of potatoes and an oversized cook were waiting for me at the back door.

He held out a knife and grumbled, "Do these and I'll bring sum-mor." Did you know they still peel potatoes by hand in the Army? After a morning of sticky potato peelings and hot sun, I decided it really wasn't fun. A mental note validated that age-old maxim of the military: "Don't ever volunteer for anything." To counterbalance my feelings of being duped into peeling a mountain of potatoes, I put my mind to payback. It took a little while to pick something that would be worthy of a member of the eight ball platoon. It came to me as we served lunch that afternoon.

As usual, the new recruits had to slam down their food in the shortest possible time while constantly being yelled at for chewing too slowly. To my surprise, the training cadre sat down for a leisurely meal, enjoying each other's jokes and stories after the mess hall was cleared of recruits. That was it! I worked out my plan with the other three volunteers, and we swung into action that afternoon. There were several watermelons left in the cooler from lunch. The two volunteers washing dishes let me know when the cook was occupied. Too scared to even glance into the dining hall, I tucked a melon under each arm and exited the back door to our hiding spot behind the dumpster. After dark, we recovered our booty and shared the fun of stolen watermelon and good company at our leisure. If the lifers could have fun, so could we!

My finest individual contribution came when a young second lieutenant was inspecting our early-morning formation, and spotted the fact that I'd forgotten to shave. He gleamed, then did the best he could to intimidate and berate me for appearing so untidy. For my punishment, I had to return to the barracks, get my razor, and dry shave in front of everyone. I saluted, turned on my heels, ran into the barracks, grabbed my razor, stopped by the restroom for a moment to moisten my beard, then ran back to face the gloating little second lieutenant. I looked him squarely in the eyes, put the razor to my cheek and began to carefully draw it down my face. I grimaced appropriately several times as I finished the job. The lieutenant smiled with smug assurance that he had taught me a lesson I would never forget. Plus, he now had a story to tell at lunch that afternoon. He didn't laugh as much as we did though. He didn't know I was too cheap to buy shaving foam and had been dry shaving for the past three or four years. It was one more unseen strike for the eight ball platoon and individualism.

Tyrrell Brown got transferred to our platoon about mid-cycle. He was one of the unfortunate ones who got marked for having an attitude. He was black; we were white. What were they thinking? I guess we were supposed to be his punishment. The eight balls weren't going to break him; we kind of admired him. He was as strong as an ox, but he refused to participate in P.T. (Physical Training). It was his way of showing he was still in control.

One rare evening we were in the barracks without much to do, and some of the guys were getting acquainted with Tyrrell. He came from a rough background down South and was used to being put down and having to fight for what he wanted. He said he really could do the physical training if he wanted to and he'd show us. He was lying on his back looking up at the rafters in our barracks, which were about ten feet apart. Tyrrell said, "I bet I can swing from one of those rafters to the next one without touching the floor." None of us would have attempted it, and we scoffed at his bragging. He jumped up and grabbed the bottom cross beam of the nearest rafter and started swinging back and forth. As he swung almost horizontally, he let go, twisted his body in midair, and caught the next rafter with room to spare! We gasped in astonishment. Nobody in the eight ball platoon could match that. He had our respect and what little protection we could give him, and he continued his protest with our approval. Sadly, they didn't let him stay very long. We were too immature ourselves to explain, and he never could understand that it was just a game. You could survive with some integrity if you could play the game.

Graduation day was approaching. The most significant thing about finishing basic training was the arrival of orders for our next training assignment. This was the point when we'd know if we were going to

Vietnam or not, or at least what we'd be doing when we got there. The next twelve-week period would be used for training in our primary MOS (**M**ilitary **O**ccupational **S**pecialty), i.e., mechanic, construction, communications, artillery, truck driver, clerk, medic, and … infantry.

We lined up alphabetically. The captain of our training company sat behind a table with a stack of sealed envelopes. Recruits marched up to the table and saluted. The captain snapped a return salute and handed each an envelope containing his orders—all very formal and military. It meant we couldn't open our orders until we had walked back behind the line. I was practically at the end of the line so my ears perked up hearing, "Wow! Georgia for Communications School," or," I can't believe, I'm going to Texas to a tank division." Germany was even mentioned a couple of times. When it was over, out of nearly fifty graduates in my platoon, only three had the misfortune to get orders for Infantry Training, Thor Peterson, Rob Hendrix, and I. My heart sank. I knew where I was going and what I would be doing when I got there. Maybe the worst part of it was that the Infantry Training Center was located just across the parade ground. The orders said to report immediately after the graduation ceremony. There would be no leave to go home to see my family or fiancée. There wasn't even a chance to see another part of the country.

Fort Lewis is on the northern Washington coast. It was late summer. Graduation morning turned out cold, windy, and drizzly. I needed to pack my gear to haul it across the parade field after we marched for the crowd and listened to a few speeches. A deep depression made it hard to move. Why didn't I lie on those aptitude test questions? Other kids were sent to training schools where I could have done better. Why did just three out of fifty get Infantry Training? I was trying to be a nice guy, but life was not being fair!

The only thing that made me finish packing was the fact that Mom and Dad had promised to be there to see me graduate. I was humbled by the effort they made just to show they loved me. It was a sixteen-hour drive, and we couldn't spend more than a couple of hours together. We couldn't even go off base. But they made the trip anyway.

As we marched, my eyes turned to the grandstands. There weren't more than twenty-five people sitting there in the rain. Most were wives and families of officers, who had to be there to support careers. That meant, among other things, they had to clap appropriately during the post commander's speech. A little off to one side, huddled under an umbrella, I recognized the familiar outline of my parents. They were there, just as they said they would be. I marched proudly, not for me, but for them.

After the speeches, everyone was dismissed. Most talked and joked happily as they headed back to the barracks to call a taxi or catch a bus to the airport. I did my best to hold back the tears as I walked toward the grandstands. My happiness was overshadowed by the apprehension and fear that I couldn't share. Of course Mom cried a little but tried to be brave. Dad was more somber than usual in a tender sort of way. I could tell he was filled with emotion, but didn't know what to say to ease the moment. We all knew what Infantry Training meant and it weighed heavily on our short visit. We drove to the barracks with my duffle bag stuffed into the trunk, and we shared the trip back around the parade grounds to my new home in near silence. We got out and shared hugs. "Thanks, Mom and Dad, for coming." I choked and wanted to say more, but that would have broken the dam of tears I was holding back. I could only think to myself, "You'll never know how much this meant to me."

I've never felt more lonely than watching them drive away.

- 3 -

AIT (Advanced Individual Training)

Their car disappeared, swallowed up in merging traffic. Aching with loneliness, I forced myself to turn away and swing the heavy duffle bag onto my shoulder. Slowly, reluctantly, my feet headed towards our next temporary home and climbed the steps. My hand turned the knob and pushed the door open with a long squeak. No one stirred. Good, being first to arrive meant there'd be time to myself.

The new barracks were identical to the one I just left. The same aisle separated familiar rows of bunks lining the walls. I walked passed the first three and rolled onto my back into the fourth bottom bunk to the right. One arm shut out the world by covering my eyes, and black emptiness permeated my attempt to focus. "This is why they wouldn't let us off base after graduating. They knew we wouldn't have come back." In just three short months all the unknowns of the Vietnam War would swallow me up. The thought made a knot in my stomach. I could always push it aside in basic, hoping to go somewhere else, but like Jonah trapped in the belly of the whale, there was no running away now.

I was going and there wouldn't be a job for me other than fighting for my life. Never very aggressive, the thought of having to kill someone moved from childhood fantasy to sickening reality. How could I do it? An image flashed of standing frozen with indecision for a crucial moment in front of a VC (Viet Cong) who passed that crisis long before. I was dead or at least wounded. Scenes from old war movies of soldiers dying in agony and pain flickered through my mind. What if I came home maimed or crippled? My stomach was nauseous, and there seemed to be no limit to my imagination. I wanted to get up and occupy my mind with something else, but there was nothing to do except wait for the rest of the unfortunate few to arrive so we could begin our training to take other men's lives.

A squeak from the opening door brought a thankful end to my morbid thoughts. Rob and Thor walked into the barracks and managed a half-hearted greeting. Rob took the upper bunk above mine. Thor preferred the next bottom bunk. We knew and liked each other from basic and drew together now because we didn't have to go through that uncomfortable stage that total strangers do. We were the remnant of the eight balls, but the fun was over. It was time to get serious.

The yelling from our instructors slowed down with time. Now, to get our attention they would just say, "If you don't listen up, you're not going to last ten seconds in the 'Nam!" They were career men, and a lot of them looked close to retirement. To most, it was just a job.

There were a few others who spoke with real passion. Those few were young men who had just returned from Vietnam. They burned to teach us anything they could that might keep us from repeating some of their nightmares. I could see it behind their eyes, the unwanted wisdom of soldiers back from combat, wanting to give as much as they could to anyone who would accept it. There was pain behind those eyes, and fear, and urgency. How could they give us lifesaving knowledge when it came from such awful experiences? The only tools they had were a half-dozen specialized classes in jungle warfare. I could see their frustration when we joked and refused to listen. They were so sincere! They had been there. They had seen the bodies of their friends. They had gone through the, "If only I had just . . . my friends might still be alive." I tried to listen maybe more than most, but I couldn't catch it all—all that stuff behind their eyes that they wanted to give. It was too much for me at times.

One exercise involved looking for the telltale signs of an enemy soldier who was somewhere in the stubble rows of a harvested cornfield. The object was to see the signs early enough to keep out of trouble. We stood in a line with our backs to the field. The order came, "Turn around and look for an obvious sign that VC are here. As soon as you see it, turn back around."

My eyes stared at the empty field and saw nothing. Everything appeared normal, just black furrows between rows of cut corn stalks. What else was there? A few kids smiled with a knowing look and turned around.

"OK, all of you turn back around now. We're going to set up another clue for those who didn't see the first one. Look back at the field now."

This time I strained to see something different or out of place. More kids indicated they saw the VC and turned their backs.

"OK, some of you didn't catch that one either. Turn back around and we'll set up another clue." My stomach churned in anticipation.

"Those of you who still didn't see anything, turn back to the field now."

In near panic, I spun around a third time but still saw nothing. Disappointed and embarrassed, I didn't want to fake it and turn around just because everyone else did. In the jungle, it might mean the difference between life and death. Finally! The cone shape of a coolie hat appeared about fifty feet away. "Thank you," I sighed and quickly turned back. There were just twenty kids out of more than one hundred who missed it.

"OK, for those of you who are as blind as bats, turn around and we'll give you one more chance. OK, turn back now!"

Gratefully, I remained facing the parking lot and felt sorry for those who had to turn around. Glancing over my shoulder, I saw a man in black pajamas lying on the ground with his head under the coolie hat. All but one of the remaining kids turned away.

"OK? You! Turn around. You're so stupid, see if you get this one! Turn around now!"

The "VC" in his black pajamas was standing right in front of the kid, with a huge knife at his throat. "Do you see that?" yelled the instructor? We all laughed, but I was uncomfortable about how long it took to see the clues. The first missed clue had been a foxhole dug in the middle of the field. There was no excess dirt piled around the hole like the foxholes we dug as kids. The second clue was cigarette smoke rising out of the foxhole. The third was a coolie hat sticking just out of the hole (the one I finally saw). Fear tugged at my confidence. If it took that long to see the clues, what would happen in the real war?

One of the highlights of our training consisted of running through a survival course. The instructors gave it a lot of hype. Supposedly, there was an authentic Viet Cong prisoner of war camp and another company of veterans trying to capture us before we reached the other side of the course. It all took place at night, heightening the mystery and suspense of who was friend or foe. Rumors circulated about the tortures the VC had waiting if we were unlucky enough to be captured. My mind knew they weren't VC, and they couldn't hurt us too badly, so I discounted the stories about the poisonous snake pit and the hot coals. When captured, the prisoner's field jacket was turned around with the hood covering his face, then they'd work on his imagination. It would be as uncomfortable as possible, but there were limits. Just the humiliation of not being smart enough to avoid capture was a great motivator for me.

We were shown a large map of the course, given the rules and a little more hype on the POW camp. Then we waited for dusk to be released. A half dozen of us decided we would get through it together, and might even attack the prisoner camp and release those who had fallen into captivity. It was a great picture. We were invincible. Time came to go, and our small group headed out. We made a quarter of a mile before stumbling through the dark became a real problem. The terrain turned to hills and ravines with fallen trees between piles of boulders. There was no way to stay quiet, and it was impossible to know if we were walking into an ambush. Someone snapped a twig and stumbled. The whole group "shushed" him.

"Which way should we go?"

"Stay right, we'll avoid the lake."

"No, there's not enough room to run between the lake and the paved road, they'll catch us."

"If we go around the other end, it'll take too long."

"Nobody's going that way."

"It's best to stay in the middle."

"But that's where everybody else is going!"

"You don't know that."

"Aw, you're full of it!" So much for cooperation! Our group effort quickly disintegrated into every man for himself. That was OK with me; I felt comfortable in the woods.

Halfway through the course was a dirt road leading to the POW camp. The fantasy of sneaking in and breaking out some prisoners tantalized me. What a hero! They certainly wouldn't expect that kind of action from a new recruit. The sky above the trees started to glow as I stumbled on. It looked like an area about a quarter mile ahead was lighted. It must be the prisoner camp. I crept to the edge of the forest and saw the long dirt road stretching in both directions as far as I could see. There were floodlights every hundred yards, and the VC camp was nowhere in sight. Also missing from the landscape were, brush, trees, boulders, or any other form of concealment for a hundred yards on either side of the road. At best, it would be a two hundred-yard dash across the well lighted clearing. Those trying to capture us might have observers with radios at the far edge of the trees. That's what I'd do.

This was looking pretty risky. The prisoners could fend for themselves, there would be enough trouble just getting myself across. So much for being a hero! I settled down just back from the clearing and watched. Nothing happened. I took a chance and sprinted forward in a crouch to some ferns surrounding an old tree stump. The muffled roar of a diesel engine made me drop to the ground. An OD truck heavily tinged with red emerged from a cloud of dust about three hundred yards down the road to my left. There were dead ferns and debris on the ground. There might be enough time to camouflage myself. The driver downshifted and the brakes squealed to slow the big deuce-and-a-half (2 ½ ton truck) to a stop.

Did they see me diving for cover? Maybe they had cameras hidden in the trees. I stuck my head up just high enough to see about ten soldiers jump out and start yelling while running through the clearing in all directions. I dropped back to the ground and buried my face in the mossy dirt. Footsteps approached my hiding place. "Don't run, don't run!

They'll have to step on me before they see me in these ferns." The boots were walking now. Closer, closer. They stopped ten feet away. My heart pounded in my ears. It was too late to get up and run. The soldier remained motionless. This must be how quail and pheasants feel before exploding into the air. A few more seconds passed, then the tension was broken by a blast from the truck's horn signaling everyone to return.

Whew! Good thing it was only a game. My body lay shivering on the damp earth for another thirty seconds while everyone ran back to the idling truck. Still shaking, I rose to my knees. The truck had turned around and lumbered back down the road in a whirl of dust. They must drive up and down the road in somewhat regular intervals, so there shouldn't be another one for a few minutes. This would be my best chance. As soon as the dust disappeared, my feet began to churn, eating up ground as quickly as possible. Through the clearing, across the road and up the other side until tree branches started tearing at my face and clothes. Just in case the retreating truck wasn't alone, I kept running until the lights faded into darkness again. It wasn't real, but to make it without being captured would be a small validation of myself. It would be something to look back on and draw confidence from.

The thick growth of fir and pines made it difficult to move in a straight line. Trying to keep the moon behind and over my left shoulder caused me to make a huge arc through the course as the moon traveled across the sky. It took another hour to reach the far side where buses were waiting to take us back to our barracks. I looked around for Rob, but Thor said he got caught and taken to the prisoner camp. It would be a blow to his ego, just as it would have been to mine. Sure enough, he wouldn't talk about it when he came back the next morning.

Summer was fading, and the temperatures were falling at night. We ran to most of our training areas now and were in good shape. Our skills were improving along with our confidence. Nearly all of our training was completed. The last big hurdle was the twenty mile march with full gear, rain, or snow—like it or not. We were herded back into our "cattle trucks" and driven away from the main fort. Finally we got to see a little stretch of ocean between fog banks and the biting wind. There would be little if any sleep tonight. I tried to concentrate on getting through this with a little dignity. It was still only a game. No one was really going die from any of this, but it would be a long exhausting march. We were in the best shape of our lives, and we'd just have to go for it.

The trucks pulled up in a large turnaround, then we marched a short distance to an area sprinkled with a mixture of evergreen and hardwood trees. There were lots of ferns, and everything was damp and dripping from the fog. We dug our defensive positions in a large circle, two men to a foxhole about thirty feet apart. It was muddy, cold, and soggy. We would be probed all night long to see if anyone fell asleep on guard duty. If the "enemy" found any weak points, they would sneak in to take the foxhole and then try to overrun the entire position. We had blank ammo to add to the realism, and they told us to only fire on sure targets—the muzzle blast was easy to see and would give away the location of our foxholes. It would be as close to the real thing as we would get until we landed in Vietnam.

Darkness fell all too quickly. Rob and I were still digging out the bench in our foxhole. We may have gone a little overboard. We draped our poncho over a few branches for protection from the drizzle then covered it with ferns for camouflage. Cedar boughs on the floor and seat kept our feet out of the mud and our tails off the cold ground. Finally done! Rob crawled into our only sleeping bag, and I took the first two-hour watch. We were so nervous, it was hard to sleep. Rob woke up every time my body shifted. My ears strained for any sound, any sign of movement. Our foxhole wouldn't be the one to let down the company. The cold air was penetrating, but we couldn't move around for warmth so I buried myself under all the clothing we had. The little warmth it generated brought on drowsiness. It was miserable and exciting at the same time.

"There! Rob, someone's moving over there!" A moment later, with our ears strained, the damp silence was broken by the crack of a half dozen blanks somewhere down the line. Thank God they're not in front of us! Maybe they are. That might have been a decoy; maybe the main body was just out there a few feet from our foxhole! Where will they try next? "I hear something!" The CO's radio squelched, followed by low muttering.

We could hear a faint "thunk . . . thunk" a long way off, then "pop . . . pop" right over our heads. The forest lit up in an eerie yellow-green as flares ignited and slowly descended through the fog then sank, suspended by their parachutes, among the trees. The movement of the flares made shadows stream from every tree and branch. The mixture of pale green light and dark shadows danced and rotated in unison like characters in some gruesome ballet. I couldn't see anything moving, yet everything was moving! It was too weird! How would I survive in Vietnam? The night continued in much the same way. Finally, the drippy blackness started to melt into a dark gray band along the eastern horizon. Our world grew lighter in increments of gray as the sun rose but stayed hidden by the shroud of fog and overcast. We had made it! There was only one thing left now. We had to pack up our gear, grab a quick bite from the chow line, and find our place for the last march back to our barracks, some twenty miles away.

Almost everyone threw their rain gear onto a truck so they wouldn't have to carry the extra weight. Being smarter than most, I decided to wear all my gear including my boots to ward off the miserable dampness and provide protection from the bone-chilling wind now blowing off the ocean. I was getting the hang of this stuff and smiled to myself as we lined up for the march. There would be no individual breaks. We had to stay with our unit and do everything together.

Crafty, that was me. The march turned brutal within an hour. The fog burned off, and the sun warmed a beautiful autumn morning. The wind slowed to a mild breeze, and I was overheated and sweating by 9:30 in the morning. My rubberized rain suit wouldn't let any air in or out. My fatigues were drenched in sweat, and my face was burning up as my body tried to lose excess heat. I was the poster child of what not to wear on a twenty-mile hike. Some of this stuff had to come off.

Have you ever tried to take rain gear off and pack it while you're marching? It looked hilarious as I hopped along trying to pull off my boots and pants, and I almost did it without complaining. It was my own dumb decision. Taking responsibility for myself was new!

Reaching out to others was something new also. We were about halfway through the march, coming up to a long 6 percent upgrade. This was going to be a killer. My legs downshifted into "granny gear" as Rob pulled away then disappeared in the long line of blistering feet and exhausted, sweaty, green uniforms. Thor, on the other hand, was falling behind even my slow pace. His eyes were nearly closed in his red wilted face, and he looked like he was ready to drop from heat exhaustion. I pulled up beside him. "How are you doing?" No answer. "Thor, stop for a minute." No response. "Thor, let me carry this for a while." I tried to lift the rifle off his shoulder. There was a weak protest of pride, but I continued to lift and he finally gave it up. We went on together. I didn't want to lose him in the crowd too! How could I return his rifle if it turned out to be too much for me? Oh well, so much for my Christian attitude!

The company took a break about halfway up the hill. Thank God! We collapsed on a mound of dirt beside the road. Everyone was flat on his back from exhaustion except for one irritably cheery individual. He walked back and forth between the groups of gasping, footsore bodies asking how everyone was doing. Who was this guy? It turned out that he was our very own training company captain, and he was walking around with a huge pack still on his back. Were officers really trained that much better than we were? He finally sat down and released his pack. One of the grunts (that's what we called ourselves) bumped the pack while getting out a canteen. It turned out that our leader's pack was stuffed with wadded up newspapers. It weighed about ten ounces. What a great example! I didn't blame him for being human, but what he would have to fall back on if things really did get tough.

I discovered there was a little extra in me to give during the really hard times, and that someone else would fall out before I would. These weren't big things to anyone else, but looking back, I'm grateful that God put them into my life; they sustained me many times on the brink of giving up.

Bob Sphar (left), Thore* Pierson (middle), Dave Wright (right) after graduation from Advance Infantry Training, heading home before going to Vietnam. All three of us were drafted from the Sacramento area and flew home together after AIT, then flew to Vietnam together and finally back home again after our 365 day tour. We all came home without a physical scratch, but the three of us still suffer from PTSD to this day.

- 4 -

ANOTHER WARM BODY IN VIETNAM

Training was over. Our orders gave us just enough time to be home for Thanksgiving before reporting to Oakland for transport to Vietnam. The holidays were so reserved and somber that they faded quickly from memory. Janet and I drove to the Oakland Naval Yard in the early morning of November 26th, 1968. The cold air made me shiver, or maybe it was the loss that hit me while stepping out of her old '56 Chevy wagon. Life as we had known it was about to change forever. The coming year wouldn't wait, and would be more difficult than anything we had faced. We hugged and kissed our goodbyes until we could bear it no longer. I tried to walk away without looking back but turned and waved one last time before disappearing into the confusion.

Rob, Thor, and I somehow found each other in the mass of bewildered young soldiers. When the time came we managed to get on the same bus, then the same plane debarking for beautiful Southeast Asia. Sitting side by side in a row of seats directly over the right wing of a Pan Am jetliner, we tried to settle in for the long flight ahead. Travis AFB to Anchorage, Japan, Guam and finally to Vietnam took twenty-two hours. There were flight attendants, snacks, and airplane food—everything seemed almost normal. As one of the stewardesses passed by, I wondered out loud why there was no first class section on the plane. It was a matter of economics. The price for each plane was fixed, and the Army wanted to be as efficient as they could. Taking out the first class section meant another eighteen boys could fit onto the plane. My mind leapt to the thoughts of a desperate young man. How inspiring! We could funnel more boys into the war while still keeping costs to a minimum. Our taxpayers should be most grateful.

The flight was uneventful and would have been deathly boring if not for the fear looming at the end of our journey. Small talk could only be sustained for a limited time. Men are not good at maintaining trivial discussions when something important is weighing on their minds. But then, most men can't discuss the really important things either. Eating, napping and reading travel magazines occupied a few long hours. Daydreaming was acceptable, but that often led to visions of things that would be on us all too quickly. Our trio started fantasizing about the things we wanted to do when we came back home. It seemed harmless enough to treat the fear as if it were all behind us by jumping a year into the future. We talked as if nothing had changed and we would pick the same seats coming home. The cynicism in the jargon we heard at Oakland went over our heads, but we wanted to believe, "it would just be three hundred sixty-four days and a wake-up." Our minds were incapable of understanding how much the coming year would change us.

It was around 11:00 A.M. when our plane flew over the coast of Vietnam. We pressed our heads together (as close as men will allow) staring out the tiny window. Maybe we'd see machine guns spewing tracers across the jungle, or shells exploding and tanks breaking down trees as they crawled over the hills. That's what we saw in the war movies. Even dinnertime back home was filled with eye-catching news clips of what real soldiers were doing in Vietnam. We weren't real soldiers yet. We were just kids flying into a real war, and we didn't know what to expect. Maybe a MIG would fly out of the clouds and strafe us! Maybe we'd have to run from the plane to the safety of bunkers while mortars exploded around us!

Our angle of descent increased as we continued inland toward the airport at Bien Hoe. It became apparent from the lack of activity on the ground that our arrival summoned little interest. The countryside was peaceful, a quilt-work of emerald green jungle, red unpaved roads, shimmering rice paddies, and an occasional cluster of white stucco houses. On the final leg, I saw a farmer bent at the waist working in his rice field. He didn't even bother to look up as we thundered overhead.

A shudder and screech of tires hitting the tarmac signaled the beginning of our three hundred and sixty-four days. The plane turned from the runway and rolled to a stop. We sat in motionless apprehension, not wanting to be expelled from our protective cocoon into an unknown and hostile world. The side door swung open with a bang, and a commanding voice instructed us to line up on the ground and wait for our duffle bags to be unloaded. We obediently stood and pressed each other down the aisle. A blast of heat hit me like a wall twenty feet from the open doorway. The outside temperature was 100° plus. My eyes squinted and my head turned from the blinding sun while we crowded onto the old-fashioned stairway that descended to the ground. Halfway down, a sickening odor crept into my nostrils while I still tried to collect myself. It was filled with stagnant water, musty vegetation, fine powdery dust, and what turned out to be the very distinctive odor of a burning mixture of diesel fuel and human feces. I was uncomfortable and nauseated. "Could I just turn around and get back on the plane?"

We sorted out our gear and trudged to an assembly area. This was certainly different from Fort Lewis. There were no melodious calls of the DI marching clean-cut platoons of new recruits from one point to another. No grandeur, no pretense of the strict military discipline that had constrained us for the last five months, not even a welcoming speech from General So-and-So. At least that was a grateful relief in this foul-smelling midday oven.

Our names were read from a roster that sorted us onto buses. Rob, Thor, and I were being sent to the First Division headquarters at Di An. Great! We struggled to get ourselves and our heavy bags loaded onto the same bus. The door closed and the driver spun the wheel to head for the main gate. Once outside the barbed wire perimeter, we were engulfed by the surrounding city. Just like the movies, people in oriental costumes were going in every direction: on foot, bicycles, mopeds, rickshaws, cars, trucks, and buses. The city was thriving, alive with people buying, selling, and doing their normal business. There was no war here! Driving along with the stream of traffic gave me time to watch these exotic people and wonder why I was here? I felt like a tourist. The urge rose to snap pictures, buy souvenirs, and discover something about this foreign place and its people.

The heavy screens over the bus windows caught my attention. Similar buses were used to transport prisoners back home. Then it dawned on me that the screens were not there to protect the people outside, but to protect us on the inside. Paranoia sounded a warning from basic training that anyone, even kids, might throw a grenade into a busload of GIs. How could you tell who the enemy was and who was friendly? In training, the Viet Cong wore black pajamas and coolie hats. Here, *everyone* wore black pajamas and coolie hats!

Buildings and people thinned as the city's outskirts fell behind. I felt vulnerable as the jungle closed in and had to remind myself that everything must be OK because they haven't issued us any weapons yet. The dense green foliage gave way to open countryside, and French architecture mixed with mud and thatched roof huts. This part of the world had been managed by farmers for centuries. There were manicured canals, freshwater ponds, clean footpaths of red compacted dirt leading between green, well-kept fields and clusters of huts. Occasionally, there'd be a driveway lined with palms or pampas grass leading to an old French villa. It was a beautiful country. How did this peaceful scene out of an art gallery end up being the center of the world's latest struggle between good and evil? The thought was inconsistent in this third-world agricultural setting. I could see nothing in this land as valuable as the tremendous sacrifices being made for it.

The only thing of value other than the land, were the people. Why were they worth all this effort? Why should we care how these people chose to live? Were we mobilizing billions of dollars worth of men and material just to allow these people a free choice? Their own culture allowed them to commit horrid acts of terrorism in support of an ideology that was not working well in other places. Why not let them find out on their own that Communism was flawed?

The real answers, of course, were obscured in multi-national politics, treaties, different cultures, and economic alliances . . . and spiritual forces. What was God's view of this whole thing? Would He rally forces to postpone a change in government? Could He do anything in the face of such powerful military forces? Did He care that I was here in a place that was hazardous to my health? I wondered if my understanding would increase enough to shed light on any of these questions.

The sign said Di An as we drove through another gate and barbed-wire perimeter. It was a small, apparently prosperous community somewhere northwest of Saigon. It was also the First Division headquarters and where our group of three got sent to different battalions. We weren't shipped out that day. They held us at Di An for another week so our bodies could adjust to the sudden climate change from late fall in the American Northwest to the dry season in Vietnam. There were only two seasons in the tropics—wet and dry. Dry meant anything from 100° to 120° days with ninety percent plus humidity. At night it would cool all the way down to 80° or 85°, and there were mosquitoes by the billions!

The break provided one more opportunity to participate in training classes all day then practice guard duty all night. I was sick from the heat. Gallons of water didn't help; they just soaked my wilted uniform, but the nearby trees stayed well watered. My head swirled from information overload. My feet felt disconnected as they stumbled through the mine and tripwire class. The tiny wires were invisible and the flares they set off were always hidden behind a tree or shrub. If they'd been real, I wouldn't have made it. What waited for me out in the jungle?

Explosives, on the other hand, were fascinating. They gave us a whole stick of C-4 (plastic explosive). It looked like a white brick of Play-Doh. We learned to clear a landing zone (LZ) instantly. The bigger trees took a half or whole stick of C-4, while the smaller ones were wrapped with a few coils of det-cord (small plastic tubing filled with explosives—the ends were connected to detonating caps and stuck into the C-4). Press the electrical detonator and . . . Blam! Everything toppled over simultaneously.

No one seemed nervous about the war in these big rear-area base camps. Men worked in spacious tents that may or may not have sandbagged walls depending on the importance and nerve of the occupants. The encampment was so large that everyone drove jeeps and deuce-and-a-halves. The only sign of danger seemed to be the string of bunkers, guard towers, and barbed wire fencing surrounding the perimeter.

The war did seem a little distant, but it was getting closer. All of the new guys had to pull guard duty somewhere on the bunker line every night. It was pitch black inside the bunkers, and the air was sticky and motionless. Rumors were that rats and snakes considered the line bunkers acceptable substitutes for the homes we destroyed while building these fortifications. At least outside the bunkers an occasional breeze swept by, and the light from the moon and stars softened the blackness.

Even at night our bodies were soaked and sticky with sweat, then it was time to cover every patch of exposed dirty skin with an oily film of Army-issued bug repellent. Lord knows what it was made of, but that was of little concern when the feasting hordes of mosquitoes came whining in from the adjacent rice paddies. There were no beds or cots.

A few of the short-timers had air mattresses, but they weren't standard issue, especially for the new guys. It turned out they were too hot, too heavy, and too noisy for the jungle anyway. The trick was to find a place on the sandbagged top of a bunker that allowed a few hours of sleep before the pain in your back or neck woke you up.

It was one of those hot but peaceful nights with another new kid and a short-timer who had gotten himself into some sort of trouble. A necklace of sparkling lights from surrounding villages hung just below the black horizon. My attention suddenly riveted on a string of green tracers that started arcing across the horizon about two miles away. The VC were kind enough to use different colored tracers from ours. In such a crazy war, why would this one thing make any sense? Anyway, some red tracers started arcing back. There were more exchanges of green, then red. Artillery started lighting up the distant sky . . .four, five, then six flashes with no sound. It was like watching lightning storms back home. The thunder of the artillery finally swept over us. We couldn't see the terror of bullets whizzing inches from heads, or ripping bodies apart, nor could we see the agony of a soldier missing the lower half of his body from the last explosion. It was really quite beautiful and impersonal from a distance.

There was no fire from our base. I asked the short-timer why nobody seemed worried that some fairly serious fighting was going on not that far away. He responded that except for Tet, the VC really didn't mess around with the big bases or rear echelon areas; the odds were too much in our favor. They would send in a couple of rockets each month or probe a perimeter just to let us know they were around, but they liked to wait until the odds were tipped more to their side before getting serious. Great! This wasn't going to be an "all or nothing fight," but a "pick and choose your best chance to win kind of fight." After the fireworks, I settled down to a fitful sleep knowing that things were going to be a lot more complicated than I wanted them to be.

- 5 -

FIRST DAY IN THE FIELD

The airframe and floor of the cargo bay vibrated in harmony with the roar of the turboprop engines. The barren interior of the Caribou (a small transport plane) held thirty of us sitting on nylon benches facing one another, backs against the humming fuselage.

My orders said to report to "Alpha" Company of the 1st Battalion, 26th Regiment of the 1st Infantry Division in Lai Khe. We carried our gear down the rear ramp directly into a thick cloud of swirling red dust. Squinting and holding onto my cap, I headed for a crowd at the edge of the runway. Luckily there was a clerk with a radio who looked at my orders and called for limousine service. Five minutes later a jeep drove up. The driver yelled,

"First and twenty sixth, over here." I was the only one in the crowd to respond. The driver explained that "Alpha" company was somewhere out in the jungle and wouldn't be back for a day or two. He dropped me in front of several tents that apparently belonged to the company, then drove away in the dust. It was like walking into a ghost town.

Lifting the flap of the nearest tent, I stepped into the shade. The presence of someone in the darkness caused me to stand a moment and let my eyes adjust. Another fresh replacement was lying on a bunk just past the entry. The nametag on his shirt identified him as "Woods." Everybody had only one name in Vietnam. Until you were in country long enough to get a nickname, you were simply known by your last name which was conveniently stenciled above your right shirt pocket. Anyway, Woods and I had some time to pass so we settled down to get acquainted.

He was skinny, short, fair-complexioned, and wore glasses. In high school he'd be labeled an "egghead," probably more comfortable in college than camping here in Southeast Asia. It turned out he was talkative and friendly; he could have been typecast as one of the neighborhood kids in "Leave it to Beaver." After graduating from high school his application for a college deferral was beaten by the draft. Unfortunate timing landed him here on this hot November day.

It was lunchtime so we followed our noses to the mess hall, not an entirely pleasant experience. We sat next to a short-timer (anyone with less than three hundred and fifty days was a short to us), who told us "A" company had taken it pretty hard since Tet (the Buddhist New Year celebration). We shouldn't expect them to be real open when they arrived. Our sheltered lives were jolted when he explained that nobody wants to get to know the new guys, because they may not make it. I realize we weren't just new guys; we were replacements for close friends with whom they had been living and struggling with for several months. There was no way we could replace those people. We didn't have their experiences. We'd be reminders of their laughing and crying, living and dying. There was no way to fill the gap or fit in. We could expect nothing from these who were grieving without crying.

About 4:00 in the afternoon of the following day, our tent flap flew open and in came the real-life John Waynes and Audie Murphys of this war. They handled themselves and their equipment with the comfort that comes from using those weapons to save their own lives by taking the lives of the enemy. There was no shock in their faces about the brutality of war. It was a fact of life, and the fact was, they were the ones who were alive right now. One stood out a little more than the others.

They called him "A-hoe." It probably wasn't the nickname he would have chosen, but that's what he was stuck with. The unspoken rule was, you can't change your own nickname. It was something given to you by those who were close. It might be good or bad, but it represented something they saw in you, and you couldn't change it.

A-hoe was short, blond, and stocky unlike Audic Murphy but what caught my attention was the fifty-foot rope slung around his neck and shoulder. Why did he carry a rope in this day of modern warfare? Maybe he was a sniper and used it to climb trees, or there could be cliffs we'd have to rappel down. My desire to ask was checked by not wanting to appear like a total nerd. My curiosity would have to be satisfied somewhere out in the jungle.

I wanted to explain my presence in their world and not get in the way or take someone else's bunk, especially one of those we came to replace. I stammered, "Is it OK for me to take this one?" No one seemed to care. One or two introduced themselves, but no one tried to explain how or where we were supposed to fit in. Some gave a brief look then turned back to a familiar face to complain about the dust, the heat, or how bad their feet hurt after humping the jungle for a week.

A-hoe and Taylor seemed to be the acknowledged leaders in our tent. Leadership wasn't something that necessarily came with rank. It was a form of respect given to the few who were able to think in a situation where most would panic. It belonged to those who could make good decisions when they were needed most. I'm sure we spent a few days in base camp with our company, but they were a blur. My mind was trying to understand these guys we were supposed to be working with, people who wouldn't pay any attention to Woods or me. Oh well, we had each other.

A-hoe told us to see the supply sergeant and get our field equipment. Fortunately the supply tent had a sign over the door. We knocked and entered. An amused voice came from behind the desk. "You boys new? First thing you got to do is get rid of your underwear."

"Huh? Why?"

"It'll make you sweat too much".

"You mean you don't wear underwear under your uniform?"

"That's right, get rid of it." So Woods and I dumped our underwear in a pile, never to be seen or worn again.

"What do we need next?"

"Pick what you want." He waved his arm toward racks of used and discarded equipment.

"You'll need lots of water."

I knew that, but why wasn't he helping us pick out what we needed? Wasn't there some standard issue or something? Maybe it was some kind of stupid test to see what we'd pick by ourselves. If we did well, that said something about how we would fit in with the rest of the guys. If not, we would be considered just more dead weight. Or maybe the guy just didn't care, which turned out to be the case. Anyway, from my knowledge of camping, hunting, and basic training I picked up four canteens, a canteen cup, and a web belt with a harness. Four old World War II ammo pouches just fit in front – three for M16 ammo and one for grenades. I grabbed a rifle that seemed in pretty good shape, a claymore, and blanket. There I was, a fully equipped nameless grunt ready to step into a real war.

We packed up the next morning and ate breakfast on paper plates. Thank God the Army got smart enough to use paper plates. The old aluminum mess kits were noisy, took up space, had to be washed, and added extra weight. In the jungle we ate directly from C-ration cans.

Our cases of Cs had already been opened, which meant the officers had gotten first choice. Watching everyone else, I could see there was an art in finding appetizing combinations among the OD cans and plastic bags with various non-descriptive names like B-1, B-2, and B-3 units. Entrees wore labels allowing each of us to avoid personal gut busters like "Ham & Eggs" and "Spaghetti." The "B" units had fruit, crackers, and other side dishes and were only identifiable by size, weight, and sound (or lack of) when shaken. Skills were finely honed to produce at least one can of peaches and a can of pound cake. With the passage of time, these treasures grew in value as trading stock or for the ruckus and fun they'd cause when simply eaten slowly in front of everyone.

We didn't carry regular packs or rucksacks like some units. They were too bulky and held too much. When hugging the ground in a firefight the big packs looked like a camel's hump and gave away your position as well as making a pretty big target. Without packs, carrying enough food for three to five days might have been difficult if the Army hadn't designed the perfect can carrier. Wool socks stretched two or three feet when stuffed with cans, they'd stay quiet and were easy to reach. Half a stick of C-4 was all the heat needed to cook for a week, and empty cans served as stoves.

Packed, fed, supplied and ready to go within forty-five minutes, deuce-and-a-halves delivered us to the helipad and waiting choppers. I grabbed a seat in the middle that looked safe. A-hoe didn't hurry to find the best seat, but walked up after everyone else was loaded and calmly sat on the floor in the open doorway, his feet resting on the skids. There were five to six of us per chopper (not including the four man crew), but they lifted effortlessly and flew off toward the jungle with their load of destruction and disaster. The rapid-fire beat of the rotor blade was deafening, its rhythm burned into my memory (It still turns my head from miles away, holding the promise of extraction from the jungle to the safety of a firebase). Rice paddies, farmers, roads, trails, and thick jungle whizzed by at eighty miles an hour and two hundred feet below. Hey, we could get shot flying this low! It dawned on me why some were sitting on their upturned steel helmets—not a bad idea— but it turned out not to be very comfortable or stable.

My eyes darted between the open doors and the Plexiglas between the two pilots trying to take in as much as I could. There were four or five choppers chasing each other over the rolling hills and across an occasional small river valley. They began to line up, heading towards a long clearing where a thin column of purple smoke was drifting skyward. Treetops flashed by as we descended and slowed with a nose-up flare, then settled briefly to the ground. We burst out and ran to form a protective perimeter while the pilot nosed forward and lifted off in a single motion. It was a well-rehearsed ballet; in less than thirty seconds our entire platoon was on the ground and in position to provide cover for the next wave. The second flight was lining up for their approach less than a minute behind and already gliding in over the treetops.

The radio broke squelch. "Incoming! Incoming! We're taking hits!" Someone threw a red smoke meaning the LZ (Landing Zone) was hot! A crackle of small arms fire seemed to come from the far end of the clearing about two hundred yards away. The second lift continued undeterred, but now every door gunner was rattling the tree line with his M-60 as they swooped into the meadow. I hugged the ground wondering when the VC would attack en masse. No one around me fired a shot, so I figured we weren't in big trouble yet. The second platoon quickly joined our perimeter. The third and final flight followed with no incoming, and our entire company made it in without a casualty. My feared attack turned out to be a single VC. When his ammo ran out, so did he.

A-hoe barked instructions as we arose from the knee-high grass and checked our gear. "All right, line up over there, we're the lead platoon today. Woods, you take point, and Wright, you take flank."

"Great!" I thought to myself, "What's flank?" It was time to be stupid.

"Ah, where do I go?"

"You walk parallel with the column about twenty-five to fifty feet to the side and back from point. If you run into anything, you come and tell us, OK?"

Somehow I knew this wasn't one of the Army's best decisions. If I got into trouble, they would probably know it by the chatter of AK fire as I got blown away. I knew why A-hoe put me on flank. I wasn't one of the older guys yet. Having no experience, and being placed in one of the two most vulnerable positions gave me little chance of becoming one.

It didn't make sense, but I couldn't change it.

It was hard to keep pace and sight of the rest of the column while pushing through the lush exotic plants and trees of the jungle. Unlike the movies led us to believe, most of the greenery had thorns or razor-sharp edges that cut, scraped, or grabbed arms and legs. Even the bamboo had little claws on the ends of long, drooping runners that would hook your clothes and rip your flesh if you didn't stop to remove them. I quickly discovered why they were called "wait-a-minute" vines. Tripping as much as walking, falling down as much as standing up, I became more and more exhausted as the morning wore on.

Finally I gave up. The jungle was growing thicker, and it was getting the best of me. Every inch of my uniform was drenched in sweat while my skin turned dry. Close to becoming a heat stroke casualty, I made my way back to the column and plodded along behind some else. No one said anything. They knew what it was like. Somehow, in this strange war, it was OK. All I could focus on was the person in front of me. Three canteens of water were gone in less than three hours. My condition improved from total exhaustion to mere extreme fatigue.

Kak, kak, kak! Everyone hit the ground as incoming AK fire tore the thick noon air. Tat,tat,tat,tat. Outgoing M-16 fire! I dove for the ground and looked wildly for movement.

I couldn't see anything but jungle! All the shooting seemed to be up front, about fifteen people and thirty yards away. My mind raced, but action was frozen by confusion. More fire from both directions, then our lieutenant yelled for Taylor to bring up his squad. Hearing no movement, I decided to crawl up to be of some help. Everyone in front was firing blindly into the jungle. I still couldn't see anything but added a few magazines to the group effort. Kak, kak, kak, right passed my ear! The soldier next to me rolled his head and said in a slow high-pitched voice, "They're shootin' at you, sucker!" My response came without thinking. "They're not very good shots." He stared and shook his head in disbelief.

The machine gun moved up and started hammering the brush and bamboo in front of us. Five hundred rounds later, nothing was standing within a thirty-foot arc. What an awesome weapon. The lieutenant was yelling now, not even using his radio. "Taylor, get your ass up here!"

Glancing over my left shoulder, I saw him leaning against a tree trunk, holding his right forearm in his left hand. He was in severe pain but still yelled for support. His right elbow had been hit. There was a small piece of skin and flesh holding the muscle above his elbow to the forearm below it – everything in between was gone. Fifteen minutes later, Taylor finally showed up with a couple of men. He said he couldn't get the rest of them to budge. A-hoe came up and asked what happened to Woods. Someone said, "He's out there someplace," pointing in the general direction of the incoming rounds.

"I think he's down."

"Wounded or dead?"

"Don't know?"

"Well, shit, somebody's got to go out and get him".

A-hoe turned to me and said he was going after Woods and not to shoot him by mistake. He crawled back a couple of minutes later holding one end of his rope. He and the fellow next to me slowly pulled in Woods tied to the other end. I couldn't tell how badly he was wounded. Someone laid out a blanket and rolled Woods onto it. As they carried him by, l peeked over the blanket and saw his dead body. He'd been shot in the head and chest.

Somehow my mind couldn't believe his life had ended so quickly. This was his first morning! Wasn't it supposed to be like when we were kids? We played army and shot each other and acted out agonizing deaths. But everybody got up afterwards and laughed. Then we went off to play some more. I had killed deer and small game and knew death was final, but I wasn't ready for it here, now. In my struggle, I tried to comfort his dead body saying, "You'll be OK, Woods." Realizing what I'd said, I felt embarrassed and foolish about being so out of touch with reality.

There hadn't been incoming fire for several minutes so I looked to see if anyone else needed help. I pitched in to drag another wounded kid back to a clearing where he could be picked up by the medevac. We crawled far enough towards the rear to stand and put him on a poncho liner. Four of us each grabbed a corner and started back down the trail. 105s whooshed over our heads and exploded about a hundred yards up the line. There were men still lying on the ground doing nothing this far back.

My mind was thinking, "They need help up front," but words hadn't formed yet. WHAM! The ground erupted not more than ten feet behind me. I remained standing, hanging onto one corner of the blanket. Everyone else was on the ground. Dazed, I couldn't understand why they were on the ground and I wasn't; maybe my reaction time was too slow. They began moving slowly with groans of pain. Blood started seeping from little rips and holes in their fatigues.

Someone yelled, "Short round." Then I realized that one of the 105s going over our heads didn't make it. 105 casings are still hand-loaded with bags of powder before the explosive head is set in place and the entire shell is rammed into the cannon ready to fire. The more bags of powder, the farther the round will go. The fewer bags, the shorter. Someone had put one too few bags of powder in a round from the last volley. As I stood there collecting myself, one of the soldiers protecting the edge of the trail glanced at my belt, then looked up at me and said, "You are one lucky SOB." In keeping with my stupidity for the day, I just stared and didn't respond. Later that evening I realized the full extent of what he'd said.

Our medic ran up and started to work on the three new casualties. Groans changed to frantic screams as one of the wounded noticed blood stains around his groin.

"Oh God, why me, why me God? I'll never have kids. Doc, tell me everything's still there!" In frustration, the medic turned his attention to the screams and curses.

"Shut up and stop thrashing around, you're going to make it worse!" With less than six months of training, he skillfully applied bandages and tried to quiet the man before turning back to another who rolled slowly in agony.

The medevac flew in, and we loaded our latest casualties. With the exertion of the morning and the firefight that lasted into the afternoon, I decided to save my last canteen of water and drink it that evening when all was quiet. It was finally cooling down, the sun had set, my bedroll was laid out, my rifle and ammo were there in front of me, and my claymore was set. All I had left to do was enjoy the evening and that last canteen of water. I reached down and pulled it out . . . all too easily. The water was gone, but there was something inside that rattled when I turned it over. A crease near the bottom caused me to pick up my belt and inspect the canvas cover. There were slits in two of the holders where a piece of shrapnel from the 105 round had first hit the cover with my canteen cup then ricocheted into the next canteen – the one I'd been saving. An inch one-way or the other would have put the chunk of iron in my back, and I'd have joined the rest on the ground for my first day in combat.

I spent the rest of the evening lying on my back watching the stars come out and reflecting. That soldier on the ground extolling my luck after the short round hit must have been watching water leak from my canteen while I just stood there in a daze. There were still three hundred and fifty-two days to go. How would I possibly survive? Was it just dumb luck or had God intervened? I wasn't anybody special, no different from Woods. Why did A-hoe pick him to walk point? And why did I fall back into the column just before the firefight started? More questions came to my foggy mind than answers as exhaustion drove me to sleep at the end of my first day in the field.

- 6 -

A TRUE GRUNT

After that first day, the rest of our outing seemed fairly subdued, with the exception of being volunteered for my first night ambush. The more experienced men didn't want the new guy to fall asleep on guard duty, so they told stories about the VC who could sneak into a squad at night and slit their throats without waking anyone. Then there was the one about the tiger that leaped on a soldier and strangled him by biting his throat. He couldn't make a sound and was found half-eaten the next morning.

I suspected the stories weren't true but let the point sink in. Out of fear, my body learned to wake up when anyone came within two feet of any part of me. Sleep in Vietnam really meant staying half-awake all night ready to react instantly, at any moment. Fear kept adrenaline high, and reactions came quickly but at a price still being paid for today.

Swirling clouds of mosquitoes magnified our misery after sunset. Trying to hide inside my poncho liner was impossible because the heat was unbearable. A few weeks in the field brought a revelation. Mosquitoes couldn't penetrate a good, thick, terry cloth towel. Dampened with a little water, it doubled as an evaporative cooler on my face, neck, and shoulders. In the line company, we wore steel helmets; later in Recon, our boonie hats on top of the towel kept the whining beggars far enough away to allow some sleep.

Towels turned out to be the Swiss Army knife of clothing. Daytime temperatures soared into triple digits, but a wet towel on the neck cooled the whole body. Part of our function in life was to walk through bombed-out sections of jungle and assess damage to whatever the B-52s were trying to hit. Bomb bursts created a great deal of dust and debris that settled from the trees and tall shrubs as we passed below. There's nothing quite like being sweaty and gritty at the same time, knowing showers only happened back at the firebase, usually several days away. A good old terry cloth towel around the neck saved the day again.

Then there were fire ants. They made colonies by wrapping several rubber tree leaves together with a silk like thread. They would enter and exit the nest through a hole in the bottom, kind of like bees except they didn't fly. One of the short-timers showed me how aggressive they were. He lit a cigarette and held the red-hot end under the hole of the nest. Soldier ants dropped down and bit the burning tobacco, then died with ashes still clutched in their pinchers. Large numbers would drop several feet onto anything below their nest that resembled a threat. That's what we looked like, I guess.

A live demonstration of this principle occurred when a new kid unknowingly stood under a nest. It took a few seconds to realize he was the subject of attack. As the soldier ants started to work, he dropped to the ground, swatting, screaming, and trying to strip his clothes off, all at the same time. They kept biting until killed or swept away. Again, a towel around the neck gave that extra layer of protection and an instant brush when needed. These irritating pests were one more thing no one told us about, and we never see in the jungle movies.

My learning curve was tough, filled with ups and downs. I borrowed some C-4 from our top sergeant. C-4 is a high-grade explosive, but it won't go off without a detonating cap. You could hit it with a hammer, even shoot it and nothing happened. It burned like a fuel pellet when lit with a match. It was great stuff to heat food. Anyway, the guy next to me wanted some, and the next, and the next, until everyone in the squad had ripped off a piece of Top's C-4. Sheepishly, I tossed a small piece back to him. He just glared. Learning to say no became important. Unfortunately, it came too late to stop a long downhill slide in my relationship with Top.

My education included how to create culinary delights in five minutes or less out of mere cans of Cs (a few spices went a long way). Spaghetti and Ham & Eggs quickly ended up on my list of gut busters because C-4 burned so hot it always scorched the bottoms of the cans, making them inedible. Then there were the basics of learning to crap anywhere, in front of just about anybody. A dozen steps off the trail was far enough, and always keep your rifle close by. Not getting caught with your pants down had real meaning.

Out in the jungle, my body was getting more acclimated to the heat. Most of our "maneuvers" consisted of plodding along in one or two columns, waiting to see if the guys up front ran into anything. One particularly hot, stuffy morning, our battalion commander was watching our progress from his helicopter hovering directly over our heads. The jungle was thick, and apparently we weren't moving fast enough. There was some sort of trail up ahead beside a large stand of reeds or tall grass. He wanted us to quickly move up to that point. Maybe he saw something from the air that we couldn't.

Finally, the point man of the lead platoon burst out onto the trail from heavy cover, and into an instantaneous firefight. The VC weren't as stupid as we were. They probably watched that helicopter and figured out just about where we would hit the trail. All they had to do was wait. As usual, they ran after they fired up most of their ammo, and we moved up the trail without further contact. I stepped onto the trail where everyone was moving slowly, all eyes focused on something just up ahead.

Like a parade of ants we followed one another in a half-circle around the point man who was leaning against a small tree. A bullet had creased his abdomen, and he sat there holding his intestines in both hands, trying not to let them spill out farther. He looked bewildered and stared back as we walked by. It was my turn to pass; I glanced into his eyes then looked straight ahead. If it had been me, I wouldn't want everyone to stare. We secured an LZ down the trail and medics came back with a stretcher to carry the point man out.

The flying colonel was convinced we had wounded some VC in the firefight. His chopper landed, and a thin, gray-haired old man dismounted to be with his troops. He drew his .45 and looked like a kid with a new toy. We lined up to sweep through the tall grass between our trail and adjoining jungle. He wanted to shoot a VC in the worst way and seemed genuinely disappointed when the sweep produced nothing. The guy must have been in a different world to enjoy this stuff. How could he be so oblivious to the point man who followed orders, just to end up with his guts in his lap after the colonel marked our position with his own helicopter?

Our company (of about one hundred) would walk in one or two columns, depending on how rough the terrain was. Each column had a point man. There were three platoons per company, and two rifle squads per platoon. The point platoon would rotate each day. So, the two point men (one from each rifle squad in the platoon) would walk point every third day. Walking point was the least desirable job in the platoon.

It was about my second week in the field when the kid who was walking point for our squad approached me. He had been in-country for three months and had walked point for maybe a month (which really boiled down to about ten actual days on point). He was getting really nervous and convinced me that if everyone took their turn walking point, it wouldn't be that bad for anyone. It was logical. He was afraid his luck was running out. Point men were the first to walk into trouble, like my friend Woods and the recently wounded point man from the second platoon. This kid had put in his time on point and I hadn't, so I decided to do it and get it over with (not the clearest thinking I'd ever done). Working with a compass was easy. I walked our night obstacle course at basic and hit my designated station after a mile of pacing, twisting, turning, and falling into a huge hole dug for a tank trap. I could do this for a month, and after that it would be someone else's turn.

I knew but didn't quite realize the importance of not following someone else. Instead, I'd be the one who got to where we were going first. Our outings were arranged to check areas of reported activity (usually around VC base camps or supply depots), or we'd check bombed base camps for damage and body counts. That meant every third day guess who got to be the first man to walk into an area of high activity or an enemy base camp! My adrenaline was pegged all the time. I was so green and inexperienced that I walked onto a mound of dirt one day before realizing it was a VC bunker. The shock knocked me to the ground right on top of the thing. My squad leader radioed back that we were approaching a base camp. The captain asked how close we were?

"Wright's lying on top of a bunker!" "Why? Any activity?

"It looks OK, sir."

"Well, get him moving then."

I quieted my terror and stood up, trying to act like walking across the tops of enemy bunkers was an everyday experience. It didn't stop my knees from shaking as I whispered, "Thank you God." The VC usually saw us coming and left before we walked into their camp. This time it had only been a matter of minutes. Fresh bunkers were already being dug. Food was still cooking in front of another bunker. Bodies, if there were any, had already been buried. We walked through the camp knowing we were being watched. We set our ambushes that night, but as usual, the VC knew where we were and managed to avoid us. They never seemed to go out of their way to attack if they had time to run away, unless we had killed one of them, then they'd retaliate.

Walking point beat the boredom of plodding behind someone else, but it was a little more excitement than I wanted at times. After crossing a maze of craters and fallen trees from a recent B-52 strike, I headed for a small trail that led back into the jungle. I stepped around a vine-covered tree and took two steps onto the trail. The jungle pulled away in thirty-foot pie shapes on both sides of the trail. A few logs were stacked at the notch of the "V" to my left. There was a square hole in the middle, kind of like the forts we wish we could have made as kids. Panic struck as I turned to the right and saw a similar set of logs and a firing hole on the other side of the trail. I was standing at the edge of the kill zone of two opposing bunkers. There were no visible gun barrels in the firing ports, but I wasn't enough of a gambler to just walk out into the clearing. Hugging the edge of the jungle, I inched up to the first bunker. No one was home! The second wasn't quite as terrifying; if anyone was watching they would have tried to shoot me while creeping up on the first one.

The next test came as I broke out of the jungle into a large grassy meadow and onto the usual footpath between the trees and the edge of the clearing. We were moving westerly around the meadow when my eyes focused on something between two small trees a hundred yards up the trail. It turned out to be a tarp strung up for shade, but no one seemed to be around. Cautiously, slowly moving forward, I saw what appeared to be a package wrapped in brown paper and string on the ground with an NVA pith helmet next to it. We must have surprised a VC lookout, and he fled without his belongings. NVA pith helmets were prized souvenirs, and what was in that package? It was too easy, too tempting. I walked past and told those behind that it was probably booby-trapped, leave it alone. I'll never know what might have happened, but it was the right thing to do. No souvenir, especially a really obvious one was worth the risk of someone getting killed or maimed.

Christmas came at the end of my first month. It was a disaster. Janet, my fiancée, bless her heart, had mailed an entire *live* Christmas tree, with ornaments, lights, and the works. Peeking into a ripped corner of the package, my heart sank. It wasn't Christmas here. It was probably the hottest time of the year. There was no excitement in the air, no malls to shop, no decorations, no Christmas spirit. There was a disjoint in reality. Friends were getting killed here. This was not the festive holiday it was back home. I couldn't put the tree up. This was not a place to honor Christmas, and I didn't want to go through a fight with some jerk making a callous joke about such a sweet sentiment. There were none of the tender scenes from the old war movies about GIs getting misty-eyed at Christmas time. Maybe in Germany, or back home, but not here in this place! Janet didn't understand this was a place where people let out the worst of themselves and got hard to survive. Walking point didn't allow the luxury of being distracted by homesickness. How could she ever understand?

We were out in the jungle again on New Year's Day. The third platoon was up front. Their point man kept stopping to say he could hear someone, then he'd ask permission to fire. First time I'd heard that! He must have been a new guy. I would have started blazing away if I thought the VC were close enough to hear. He fired a few rounds without a response. We moved on, then stopped again at the report of movement. We started again. At about 2:00 P.M., the firefight erupted. We did the normal thing: hit the ground and stayed where we were. After a ten-minute firefight, we moved up to help pick up the pieces. The point man who had been so careful was KIA (Killed In Action).

Ironically, the same hour we lost a man in some unknown piece of the jungle in Vietnam, the whole world was focused on the Apollo 8 space mission. The capsule was going around the backside of the moon, and contact with earth would be lost for a couple of hours. They had to fire their rocket for the return flight while behind the moon and people around the world held their breaths not knowing if the astronauts would make it. If they miscalculated, they might keep circling the moon or they might overshoot the earth and just kept going.

My mind couldn't reconcile how people could focus so intently on the astronauts and not seem to care that there was a young point man from the third platoon who gave his life in service of his country that day. It was one of those "life isn't fair" lessons. The injustice haunted me. We often joked that if the politicians on both sides of this war were given weapons and told they had to fight it out, peace would have been negotiated very quickly. I didn't like the discrepancies I saw in people's hearts.

The dry season was blowing by. Day after hot day we walked, and night after night we pulled ambushes. The routine was broken only by the terror of each new firefight. My first month and a half in Vietnam was boiling down to one grinding reality: nearly every time we went out into the jungle, we killed one or two VC, and we'd lose a man or two of our own. There were no decisive battles and no loss or gain on either side.

Losing a couple of kids per mission wasn't as important to the guys with more time in country. They were jaded and smart enough to stay away from the front of the column. One or two men out of a hundred were pretty good odds. The odds were further improved when they hit the ground during a firefight and wouldn't move. Those in the front ended up doing all the fighting, which often meant we lost the point man and/or someone near him during the average firefight. The odds for point men were about one in six. The kid who talked me into walking point might have been right; each of us might only have a certain amount of luck. When it ran out, your number was up. Walking point was using up a lot of luck. But another part of me could hear a small voice saying God had been taking care of me since that first day in the field. Which was right? Which one should I trust?

Walking point wasn't the only risk. Our company manned a small firebase next to a road north of Ben Cat. It was getting dark and time came to set out our claymores. Some ARVNs (Army of the Republic of Viet Nam) down the road in Ben Cat decided to test fire their .50 caliber machine gun the same moment I stepped towards the roadway with my claymore in hand. Dust billowed from my body hitting the ground. Red tracers streaked down the center of the road just three feet in the air. A second burst followed the same line. Shooting down the center of the road was OK, heck that was five or six feet away. With tracers still flashing, I set my claymore, then crawled back to our bunker. Fifteen minutes later explosions started erupting everywhere. Like Tarzan, I dove for the bunker, grabbed the edge of a metal stake above the doorway, swung my feet inside, and let go in a single motion. The stake was notched on the edges to hold up concertina wire, and the end of my finger ripped off in one of the notches. It hurt like crazy, but was a small price worth paying to get away from the shrapnel flying outside.

Our mortars started popping out volleys in all directions while the 105s cranked up and fired at predetermined targets where VC might concentrate for an attack. The bleeding finger was wrapped in my towel as I prepared for the onslaught. Flashes from continuing explosions and muzzle blasts from our own 105s lit up the inside of our bunker like a strobe. With the pulses of light I checked the rest of my body for unexpected holes. Finding nothing new, I grabbed my M-16 and laid it in one of the firing ports, straining to see the VC who must be hitting the wire by now.

Incoming explosions had stopped, and our own guns quieted thirty seconds later. A tirade of cursing and confusion erupted from the command bunker. Apparently the ARVNs used the wrong coordinates to test fire their 105s that evening. We were supposed to be on the same side! I wasn't the only one who wondered how the coordinates of our firebase ended up being used for the ARVN test fire. VC had infiltrated all levels of the ARVN units, and we didn't trust them much, for good reason. Fortunately, that was the last time we operated close enough to Ben Cat to receive "friendly" fire.

- 7-

THE POINT MAN

After two months in-country the routine hadn't changed, but I was beginning to. Six weeks of walking point with no direct contact made me a lucky charm for our platoon, but the voices of reason were whispering in my ear, "You have over three hundred days to go, you can't push your luck any more. The odds are getting worse every time you walk point. Who gets shot nearly every time we go out? You were only supposed to walk point for a month, remember?"

That's it! Just the feeling that everything would be OK couldn't override the logic anymore. Walking point in our platoon didn't seem to be an assigned position. After a month it was time for someone else to step up and take over for a while. It seemed that no one wanted the responsibility for that decision. "Volunteers" caused less guilt when they got waxed. That meant I'd have to recruit my own replacement. The older guys knew the odds well enough, and they weren't going to volunteer. It would have to be someone new, someone who didn't understand how dangerous it was and who didn't know they could simply refuse. Now I understood how the new kids ended up on point. It had nothing to do with making a good decision; it boiled down to who wouldn't refuse to do it. And now, out of fear, I was eager to convince someone else to take it on. The next new kid into the company looked like he could handle the job. He was alert, strong, and seemed as though he could keep his senses about him.

"Hey, you're new here. You look like you can handle yourself."

"Yeah, so?"

"Well, look, everybody has to learn from the bottom up around here, and we all take turns doing most of the jobs. When we all put in our time at each job, nobody gets stuck doing one thing too long, and we can fill in for each other when needed."

"Ah . . . what do you want me to do?"

"Well, I've been walking point for over six weeks now. That's longer than I was supposed to, and I'm afraid my luck is running out. If you take point for a month or so, you can pass it on to someone else. What do you think?

A thoughtful pause ended with, "Man, are you kidding? Find someone else!" Rats, smarter than I thought.

Two days later, we took our new replacements out to the jungle. My turn came to lead the column, and the morning nearly passed without incident. It was maybe 10:00 when we started moving onto a jungle plateau set above a shallow river valley. The undergrowth was sparse and tall rubber trees provided plenty of shade, a welcome relief from the sweltering 100 degree temperature on the open slope we just crossed. The jungle floor was covered with dry leaves and little else. The crunching leaves reminded me of walking through walnut orchards in the fall back home. Nothing seemed remotely dangerous, so I dropped my guard a little and continued another three hundred yards into the trees. There were no foot trails or disturbance in the leaves on the ground. It was hot, it was in the middle of the day, and the leaves made so much noise my mind slipped back to similar times while hunting—we weren't going to see anything here. We approached an old trench line and what looked like a small bomb shelter covering a fifteen-foot section. By this time, old trenches were old news. The VC probably used this one fighting the French. Most had been abandoned and overgrown for years. This one looked no different and I barely glanced as we continued.

A voice behind me sputtered, "There's someone in there! What should I do?"

I turned and followed his eyes into the darkness under the shelter. He must have been seeing things, but just in case and half-joking I said, "Throw in a grenade." He was new, and I thought he was just reacting from the tension of seeing this old VC fighting position. He would probably think twice before throwing a grenade and realize it must have been a bird or small animal moving in the shadows. This complex had been abandoned years ago.

To my surprise, he reached for his web belt, grabbed a grenade, pulled the pin, and tossed it gingerly into the blackness. All I could do was yell, "Fire-in-the-hole!"

Everyone dropped to the ground knowing it would be just seconds before the explosion. Somewhere in the transition from vertical to horizontal and from blissful ignorance to brutal fear, there was a brief glimpse of someone running out the other end of the shelter. BLAM! I flinched and the image was gone. We were so dumbfounded, no one fired a shot.

The rest of the afternoon was spent searching a large tunnel complex I would have passed by. Our CO even called in Tunnel Rats, who would actually crawl into these things and dig out any VC in there. Not me. I'd heard the stories about VC hanging snakes in tunnels so you'd get bitten crawling underneath, or they tied explosives to trap doors that exploded when opened. One of the Tunnel Rats walked up. He was barely five feet tall. With a flashlight in one hand and his .45 in the other, he crouched and disappeared under the shelter. I wasn't claustrophobic, but the thought of shooting it out with someone at close range in such a confined space gave me the creeps.

Nearly an hour later, the Tunnel Rat emerged to say there was a body way back in the complex. He'd been dead a couple of days. He went through nearly a mile of empty tunnels with no end in sight. While waiting, we discovered an underground storage room filled with bicycles, rice, and a few old weapons. We filled it with C-4 and blew it up. The escapee must have just been a caretaker. The site was currently used as a supply point and wasn't an active base camp. Thank God.

It was late afternoon when we started moving again. After another thousand yards, the platoons split out to look for their own defensive positions for the night. My platoon found another relic left by the VC when they fought the French here. It was a fifty-foot diameter circular trench with a bench or seat on the inside of the arc. Young rubber trees had taken over, but it would still serve as a formidable defense if necessary. The trench was too small to sleep in, so we set up like spokes around the outside where we could slip back into it if we had to. We set claymores and ate before darkness descended. It was pitch black in the thicket of twenty-foot-tall rubber trees. At 1:00 or 2:00 in the morning my eyes popped open. I lay frozen on my back, listening for sounds in the darkness, knowing someone was out there. A slight rustle some distance away confirmed my suspicion. It was time to roll over onto my rifle. Dry leaves crunched loudly under my poncho liner. Well, he knows someone is awake! Sights were useless, so I aimed instinctively into the inky blackness. My left hand flipped the safety off my claymore detonator. The muscles in my fingers tightened but hesitated to squeeze fully, waiting without breathing until one more sign gave that final focus before shattering the night.

Five minutes crept by, nothing! The presence left and something inside said the danger was over. Relax, and go back to sleep. The next morning I thought it may have all been in my imagination so I didn't say anything. We went out to pick up our claymores, and the guy next to me found that his had been turned around to face towards us. The story of what happened the night before poured out. Our eyes locked as the willies hit.

If I hadn't woke and made so much noise rolling over, many more claymores would have been turned around. We would have annihilated ourselves when tricked into a false ambush. If I'd blown my claymore, the grunt next to me would have set his off, and several of us would have been wounded or killed. An unexplained impulse woke me, then lulled me back to sleep. It was the first time direction came so strongly. God had intervened again.

Another week and another mission ended. Desperate feelings to get off point clawed at me as we trudged into the protection of our firebase. Gambling or taking risks was not part of my nature. Always the average kid, never running the odds on anything, and never better than average at any sport, what was I doing out here? Even my grades were no better than average until halfway through high school, but this was entirely different. Why was I out here in front of everyone, the first person to walk into trouble, the first person the VC saw, and likely the first person to get shot? Who in their right mind would take this job? My refusal to walk point would force the lieutenant to make a decision, but I wasn't quite ready to go to jail if he ordered me to continue. On the other hand, there was a feeling that somehow I'd get through this. For now I was torn between logic and something deep inside that said, "It'll be OK."

Don Thompson, a new replacement, was assigned to our platoon while we were out camping in the jungle. He was in my bunker when we came through the perimeter of concertina wire surrounding the fire base we were currently working out of. Lord, he reminded me of myself. He didn't want to be here. In fact, he'd gotten married between AIT and coming to Vietnam. But he was willing to do his share of what needed to be done.

He didn't even question my pitch that everyone should walk point for a while. I broke a rule of the old-timers by liking him immediately. That brought on a huge load of guilt, so I decided to level with him and began to explain some of the difficulties.

"The worst part about walking point is when you get tired. If you're not alert, you start to miss things and that's when it gets dicey. So, this is what we'll do, we'll walk point together and I'll pass on everything I can. When you're getting tired, I'll take over for a while, then you can take over for me when I'm tired. Each of us will only have to walk point half the time."

That was the best I could do. The job wasn't dumped on him the way it was on Woods and me. Don knew nothing about being in the jungle. It would take weeks to start seeing more than a few feet into the green wall, and we would share the odds together. I offered one more thing, to be a friend in a club that didn't take on new friends.

Mail call came the day we headed back out. Don got a small package from his new bride, with a short note and a cassette tape inside. We were in a firebase with one company of mortars, one company of 105s, and one rotating company of infantry surrounded by razor wire and completely isolated in the middle of the jungle. There wasn't even a gate where Mama-san could run down the road to a nearby village for us. Our only contact with the outside was by helicopter. There wasn't time to track down a tape player, so I told Don to put it in his pack and we'd find some way for him to listen to it when we got back.

We threw on our equipment and headed to the helipad. A-hoe had made it back to the world, and now I was one of the last getting on the chopper. I really enjoyed riding the skids and seeing the country slide beneath my feet. The deafening rhythm of the rotor blades faded behind the excitement of flying, which had been a dream from childhood. Sitting in the doorway with my feet riding on the skids was close to the freedom birds must feel as they glided over the countryside. My fantasy came to a halt when three black pajamas caught my eye walking a trail in the jungle below my feet. Reflexes were quicker than the brain, my safety clicked, and half a magazine emptied before the door gunner yelled, “What are you doing? You can’t do that!”

“They’re VC!”

“It don’t matter, no one shoots from the chopper ‘cept the door gunner.”

He told the pilot, who was bellowing for a situation report, “It wasn’t incoming, just some fool grunt.” I wanted them to swing around to see if there were bodies, but to my disappointment, we had to stay in formation with the rest of the choppers.

We landed at the edge of some rice paddies and jumped out. It was a pretty, but narrow little valley. A brown river snaked through it with well-kept rice paddies on either side that gave way to thick jungle on the rising slopes. An alarm bell should have rung, but it looked so typical of the country. I should have asked myself, “Who maintains these rice paddies so far away from any village.” Don started on point with me trailing to give him tips if anything seemed unusual. He was doing fine, and the bearing took us right out into the rice with water up to our knees and thick muck clinging to our boots. The water was warm and felt crawly . . . leeches! It would have been much easier to walk on the levees between the paddies, but that’s where the booby traps would be.

We slogged through an upcoming tree line and continued into the paddies on the other side. Halfway to the next tree line, the unmistakable thump of a mortar tube came from behind us. We automatically dove into the water and mud before the round exploded. We lay in the muck for a couple of minutes while our rear platoon tried to spot the VC, but there were no shots and no movement. We decided nothing else was going to happen, got up, and just kept moving in the same direction.

The valley narrowed more and the river tightened its curves into alternating U's following each other upstream. "What's that?" I yelled to Don. Out of the corner of my eye there was a flash of something white behind a tree. Someone or something was hiding in the trees along the riverbank. We stopped while Don and I started walking in the general direction. A figure ran from behind a tree and dropped down the riverbank about forty yards away. He didn't have a weapon and seemed more out of place than a threat. There was no coolie hat, and his long-sleeved white shirt didn't belong to the typical farmer or VC, but there might be others. It took a minute or two to reach the edge of the high bank overlooking the river. He was gone of course. Probably had a boat waiting along the shore and disappeared around the next corner in the swift current. He looked like a merchant out selling his wares to the VC. Well, I didn't miss that clue. They were here and somewhere close.

It was getting spooky. Don started leading the company across the mouth of the next U in the river. He stepped out of the paddies onto a trail that curved to the right twenty yards ahead towards the tree-covered riverbank at the bottom of the U. A dog barked, then yipped in pain, then silence. They're here, hiding in the brush under the protection of those overhanging trees, and they were watching. Fortunately, our compass heading took us across the opening and not down the trail.

Halfway across, compulsion caused me to peel off the track Don was following and head down the pathway toward the river. In the middle of the U, I dropped to one knee with my M-16 pointing at the tree line. I asked myself, "What are you doing? This is stupid!

Are you going to take on the VC by yourself?" After a couple of high-adrenalin minutes, most of the column had passed. It was OK to get up and trot back to my position. Why? These weird impulses were coming more regularly, but inside I trusted and acted on them before trying to figure them out. It must have been as confusing to the VC as it was to me. Maybe that's all it was supposed to do, just confuse them for a while and stare them down. They might have blown us away in the open without that bit of stupidity. Don had done a good job that morning. I'd take over for a while. He sighed in relief and gratefully handed me the compass and dropped behind.

We received a new heading as soon as I took over. It turned us ninety degrees from the river, straight into the jungle. It was a relief to be moving away from the VC, my mind relaxed, the danger was behind us. Hindsight is always better than foresight, and I've often wished I'd been a little more frightened and alert at this point. Maybe things would have been different. Many of our missions included checking damage to bombed base camps. We had just walked by a group of VC, and there were no bomb craters. Now we're headed straight into triple-canopy forest. Might there be a base camp nearby?

The jungle was as dense as I'd ever seen. Wait-a-minute bamboo, lush broad-leafed plants as tall as we were, tangles of vines, and huge trees reduced visibility to inches. About seventy-five yards into the mess, sunlight appeared through an opening in the canopy over the top of a bamboo thicket to my left. Bamboo might be easier to negotiate than the wall we were facing, so I broke my way through and popped into a tiny clearing in front of a termite mound at the edge of a bomb crater. Bamboo lay back around the crater at the angle of the explosion and another opening was just beyond this one, probably another crater. Skirting around the edge looked better than trying to work back into the twisted jungle. Slowly I walked up beside the termite mound, which was about four feet high and six feet across at the bottom, not really big compared to others I'd seen.

One more step put me on top of the soft dirt piled up at the rim of the empty cone. The walls were steep but stable enough to walk on. The air was still heavy with the smell of burnt powder from the explosion. My squad stacked up as we inched around the twenty foot diameter hole. Now lined up in a semicircle, we froze in unison, all eyes locked onto a two-foot diameter, turquoise dish at the beginning of the opening to the next crater. An electrical wire led through the space between clumps of bamboo to the next splash of sunlight.

The face of the large Chinese claymore pointing towards us was filled with bits of shrapnel that would be blasted into our bodies as soon as the detonator was pushed. The electrical wire meant it was command-detonated, and the VC were watching, waiting for the greatest number of us to walk into their kill zone. At any second the explosion would rip us apart.

As a group, they all turned and ran back around the crater towards the termite mound.

I was left standing, still frozen. Why wasn't I running with them? An invisible hand pushed me to the ground where I was. The claymore was no more than twelve feet to my left with nothing between its crushing blast and me. I tucked my hands under my throat, hoping my steel helmet would protect them, and my forearms would protect my shoulders. There was just enough time to think this is another really dumb thing to do, then everything exploded.

Dirt, dust, and leaves filled the air for the next thirty seconds. A fast check for wounds . . . nothing, not even touched! How? A quick glance to where the claymore used to be confirmed it had exploded. There was no time to figure out what happened, only time to get ready for what would come next. The open mouth of the crater would be too easy to toss a grenade into, and there'd be no protection on its steep flat walls. The only cover within a few feet was a small three-inch diameter tree, it would have to do! Vietnamese voices began to chatter on the other side of the bamboo. They should be coming right through the opening where the electrical wire had been. My rifle was braced against the tiny tree to keep it stable when firing, and I pulled a couple grenades from my web gear. My temples throbbed from the explosion and the adrenaline pumping through my body. Ten seconds, thirty seconds, a minute passed but no one came. I should pitch a grenade over the bamboo where the voices came from, but limbs were hanging right above me, the grenade would fall back in my lap if it hit one.

The VC stayed behind the bamboo wall and ran down the length of our column throwing grenades over the top. Explosions erupted all down the line, followed by moans and then screams of pain far back in the column. Alone, vulnerable, and hearing no rifle fire, there was no way to tell where the enemy was. My M-16 was pretty useless in the dense bamboo. No more voices or footsteps meant they either left, or were waiting for us to break through to the next bomb crater. Where was John Wayne when you needed him? Charging the enemy single-handedly wasn't in my script, so I waited for someone to join me.

Finally, our machine gun team moved up to a large dead tree just behind the termite mound. They were about thirty feet behind. Dust and leaves from the explosion covered my body, and they opened fire assuming there were only VC in front of them. I held my breath and gritted my teeth, anticipating bullets slamming into my body. Red flashes zipped by just inches off the ground keeping me petrified until the gunner stopped to hook up another belt. It was time to get their attention. I lifted my foot and shook it, better to have my foot shot by mistake than try to stand up in their line of fire. It worked! The gunner waved his arm to move back. Crawling backwards wasn't easy, but I wouldn't take my eyes off the opening where the VC would likely come through. He motioned to turn one way, then another in a crazy zigzag pattern.

Back under the dead tree, I puffed and tried to catch my breath. The scene around me started to sink in. There was a scramble of shiny, brown, thin plastic tape strewn over the tops of the bamboo to our right. After several seconds my brain flashed, "That's Don's cassette tape." How did it come out of his pack and end up strewn all over the bamboo? My heart sank into my stomach. The message from his new bride was strung out, unraveled, and now exposed to the world, but he never got to hear her. Someone should take it down, but it was too high and too dangerous.

If that was his tape, where was he? Everything looked different. The termite mound had vanished. In its place was a new clearing with green, dust-covered lumps lying in front of the M-60. The gunner had steered me around them while I was crawling backwards.

My mind started to focus a little better and then recoiled as the lumps turned into the bodies of my squad members. They made it back to the termite mound, only to be killed by a booby trap buried inside it. They must have all been looking for me, wondering why I didn't follow them when the claymore detonated. The booby trap had been buried just about the height of their shoulders, because it took the heads off three of them. My mind went numb. I tried to identify which body was which, but couldn't tell the difference without their heads. My thoughts wrenched away to a burning pain in the middle of my back. Was I hit? I reached back between my shoulders and could feel nothing. A minute later another burning spot made me reach quickly to the middle of my back. This time I turned over and looked into the tree. There, hanging from a limb about fifteen feet in the air and still smoking was an arm and a claymore bag. The shirtsleeve was still smoldering and burning pieces of fabric were dropping onto my back.

There were no targets for the machine gun. When they shut down, so did my mind.

The damage was bad . . . worse than I imagined. Intellectually overwhelmed by the loss and in emotional shock, I wanted to acknowledge the impact but felt nothing. It was too soon to grieve, and I didn't want to sweep it aside by telling myself, "It don't mean nothin'." This was important. It was huge, but losing control wasn't an option either. The enemy was too close. I crumpled to a sitting position, wrapped my arms around my knees, buried my face, and forced myself to cry, then ended with a vow to never forget. That's all I could do before the remnants of our company began pulling back and reorganizing.

Medevacs were taking out our dead and wounded, so I stumbled back to the rear. Someone asked if I was OK. It was my chance to head in. The loud ringing in my ears was a ticket to get out of the field for a few days, but only silence followed my blank stare.

My squad was dead. There wasn't much of the platoon left either, but somehow I was alive and didn't have a scratch. How could I go in? It would have been disrespectful to those who gave everything just a few minutes earlier.

The last chopper rose, dipped its nose, and carried away the final load of blood and pain. My eyes turned to a pile of abandoned weapons now lying in the dust. They were a fitting monument to the shattered bodies and minds that left them behind. How many did we lose? About half. Some of those who were too scared to stay, or couldn't "hear" or had some other excuse, but still, we were hit hard that day in the middle of January. What happened to me? Nothing. But I still have difficulty dealing with the images and numbed emotions.

Our captain refused to withdraw from the field. He couldn't run away either. It meant something to stay, even with half of our company gone. We pulled back and walked into the jungle a few hundred yards down river from the ambush site. It was late afternoon, so we set up a single perimeter for the night. A mountainous thundercloud blotted out the setting sun and cast its shadow over our tiny patch of jungle. Lightning flashed under its darkened face. In the fading light, the cloud glowed and pulsed from inside with each new bolt of lightning. It was going to rain. No one carried a poncho. The rainy season hadn't started and the extra weight was unnecessary, we thought. My poncho liner went under my steel pot to stay dry until the rain stopped. Most of the night was spent leaning against a small tree; the VC were close. Each new lightning strike momentarily lit up the jungle, and a part of me expected and even hoped to see them coming for us.

My mind whirled from the terror of the day. I led my squad to their deaths and felt terribly alone. Don didn't get to hear the comfort of his wife's voice in this unforgiving land. It was his first day in the field, just like Woods. My squad leader had made it halfway through his tour. Someone said he was married and had kids at home. My mind went numb with questions that had no answers. About 3:00 or 4:00 in the morning the rain stopped and I dug out my poncho liner. It felt warm and soothing as exhaustion swallowed up my ability to think or feel.

The VC had gotten lucky and done a lot of damage, maybe more than they expected. Now they just let us go. We walked out the next morning without further contact. This wasn't the kind of war our fathers had been involved in. There were no front lines, no battles to win, no territory to hold, and hardly any direct confrontation. Not that I wanted a conventional war, but we just walked away and let the VC have everything back the way it was before we arrived. It seemed the only contribution that the deaths of my friends made were some bloodstains on the ground. This wasn't the way it was supposed to be. How could we win a war doing this?

The non-logical, spiritual part of me knew that nothing under my control had saved my life. The invisible hand that pushed me to the ground was more than just an impulse.

Impulses don't stop shrapnel from ripping your body apart when there's nothing between you and a Chinese claymore. I recognize the owner of the invisible hand better today than I did thirty years ago on that dark, angry, rainy night with over 300 days to go!

Back in Lai Khe, our main base camp, life was pretty easy. We didn't even have to pull bunker guard. There were enough REMF's (Rear Echelon Mother F_______s) to cover the perimeter so they let us rest for a few days.

I was skinny and scared- making me a perfect point man. I couldn't ask another young kid to take point after walking my company into an ambush, so I just continued doing the job as long as I could.

- 8 -

X-RAY VISION

Two months in-country and twenty-three years old, I became the "old man," a legend in my own time. The new guys would point and whisper as I walked by. Well, maybe it wasn't quite like that. Nobody wanted to talk about the day we lost half of our company or how I survived walking point, which suited me just fine. It would have been uncomfortable—a "man thing," I guess. The expression, "It don't mean nothin'," now meant something. Kids would hold back their tears and anger by repeating it to one another like some mantra in an attempt to dismiss or trivialize the impact of such life changing events. The phrase was born from the frustration of not being able to find an explanation that made sense out of all the senseless destruction.

Still in shock and numb from the loss of my squad, moving past the incident didn't seem possible or respectful. Someone should give tribute or at least acknowledge the men who died. There was no ceremony, no time or place to grieve. It was impossible to pretend they were here one day and the next day they were simply gone. Our lives were entangled with each other, and they were ripped apart. The physical pieces were sent home in body bags while their images stayed in my mind. Someone had to acknowledge the tragedy. No one else was left, so the responsibility to honor and give meaning to what happened fell to me. Something was wrong with the world that didn't seem to care, but I didn't know how to deal with the world. All I could do was swear not forget them. Even that turned out to be an empty promise. My mind went numb and blocked out names, dates and even the unit I was in, not long after coming home.

The drug culture had never been attractive to me; the hippies and "flower children" were a little too far out. There were no flower children here. There were a lot of kids laughing and joking and smoking something that seemed to help them forget what was going on. I needed to forget. Unfortunately, it wasn't a frame of mind that led to mere recreational use. I smoked with a vengeance. There was pain to escape and questions that needed answers. If the war didn't make sense being straight, maybe expanding my mind would help. It didn't.

At best, I wasn't isolated and in pain alone. It was easy to slip into one of the two major social groups in Vietnam . . . dopers and alcoholics. Both used their drug of choice to cope with the extremes of military life. One moment you were in the jungle pumped with adrenalin, looking for any sign of the enemy or fighting for your life. The next moment you were fighting total boredom, sitting around a bunker at some firebase trying to figure out what to do with your downtime. Desk jockeys in the rear areas had it worse. They didn't even get the adrenalin rush.

So there we were, a bunch of emotional cripples supporting and medicating one another, trying to stay alive for three hundred and sixty four days until we could exit the stage of this bizarre play.

At the same time, another part of me suspected pot and the world system in general would never give the correct answer to what was happening. After all, the world system had created this mess. If the world had answers that worked, we wouldn't even be here! In my spare time or when it was too early to get loaded, I'd pick up a copy of the New Testament and read about Jesus. I knew the Bible stories from childhood. It was still hard to believe Jesus was a real person, even if He was, how could His two-thousand-yearold words help me now? I loved Jesus' total honesty and His ability to see straight through the smoke and mirrors of the most respected and powerful men of His day. They claimed to be God's representatives, but He told them they were blind leaders of the blind. They had to get rid of Him and thought they'd succeeded, but ended up playing a part in the plan of making God's grace and forgiveness available to all of us.

From the outside my life looked pretty schizophrenic; the guys even gave me a new nickname, "Father Wright." It represented the times I'd ramble on about how Jesus had it together to go through what He did and continue loving people instead of hating them. A real hatred was brewing in my heart for a world that was responsible for this. I needed to find out how Jesus did it, loved instead of hated.

After the ambush it was impossible to ask anyone to walk point again. I couldn't look into their eyes and tell them it would be better if we all shared the load. There was no assurance that after a month the job could be passed on to someone else. And how could my presence be explained against all odds? Maybe it was supposed to be my job. Another new kid might end up like Woods or Don on their first day. Better me than someone else.

The voice of reason screamed, "How can you continue walking point? What are the odds now?" Vietnam was becoming as much of a battleground inside my mind as it was in the jungle. The conflict seemed unsolvable, and it depressed me to think that life might be just screwed up. God knew my feelings and allowed some light to shine through my discouragement and gloom.

One of those lights was Farley, a little blond-haired kid with a deep Southern drawl. His goal in life was to have everyone around him laughing and talking together. What a godsend! He could find laughter in the weirdest situations. Like the time we were out touring the countryside and set up for a quick rest and lunch break. Farley was the "new guy," and I was starting to take on that grizzled, hardened look of an old timer. But Farley wasn't afraid to ask questions. He came over with a puzzled look when we stopped, so I told him we were going to set up under a clump of bamboo for lunch. He should set out his claymore on the other side of the clump; you never know what might happen. He did as instructed then walked back around the bamboo and connected the wire to his detonator. The bamboo was thirty feet long, ten feet wide and about fifteen feet high. It provided shade and concealed us from the surrounding open meadow and heavily used trail at its edge.

No one talked in a normal voice in the jungle; the sound carried too far. We whispered or used hand signals to keep from broadcasting our location to nearby VC. Farley didn't have the fear yet. He was making disparaging remarks about his lunch when I froze. One of those impulses caused me to look over my shoulder into the bamboo behind us. Two feet of mature bamboo is close to a solid wall, much less ten. But as I looked, God gave me x-ray vision. The bamboo became like a backlit screen showing the shadow of a man sneaking up from behind. Our rifles wouldn't penetrate the bamboo, so I grabbed Farley's shoulder and whispered, "Blow your claymore, NOW!" He knew I was dead serious and started looking for the detonator. Unable to locate it, he gave me a desperate glance with his hands raised in the air. "*Find it*," I mouthed in silence! He fell on his stomach and started crawling in circles until he ran across the wire. He grabbed the plunger and squeezed . . . BLAM! No one had a clue what was going on, but they instantly hit the ground. There was no more shadow behind the bamboo, just dust and smoke. We fired a few rounds then slowly went to investigate. No one else had seen a thing; I had my own doubts of what we'd find. Maybe my mind was just playing tricks.

There was a big trail behind the bamboo with several "spider holes" on either side.

The VC didn't dig foxholes like we did. They carefully cut perfectly square holes with straight walls and a flat bottom. The excess dirt was carried off and deposited out of sight. They were all exactly the same size and too small for most of us. When they were unoccupied they made a great place for spiders. About thirty feet up the trail an AK with a rifle grenade attached was sticking out the top of one of the spider holes.

We looked at each other waiting for someone to decide what to do. Everyone quickly stepped behind the "old man." My heart pounded in my throat while watching the AK for any sign of movement. I prayed the VC at the other end of the rifle was either dead or so badly wounded he couldn't move. It stayed perfectly still. There were two spider holes between the AK and us. The first was close enough to tell it was empty but the next was a little too far. I tossed a grenade fifteen feet and made a bulls-eye into the second hole. No one threw it back, but it took forever to detonate. I crept forward with my still eyes glued on the AK. My hands reached another grenade and pulled the pin. After the handle popped off I started counting . . . two-one thousand, three-one thousand, four-one thousand, five-one thousand then tossed it in with the AK. Still no movement, . . . seven, . . . eight, . . . nine, . . . wham! I inched forward as the smoke cleared and peeked over the edge. There was a young, black-pajama'd body smashed into the bottom, his hand still on the trigger of his rifle. It was a grotesque picture; I hoped he was dead before the grenade landed in his lap. We found one more body up the trail. He must have been hit from our wild fire. These two couldn't run or crawl away. How many others were there? What would have been the results of their ambush on us? God only knew. He gave another gift that day that saved Farley and me.

Well, Farley couldn't just leave it at that. He had to make a funny story out of it. Everyone knew basically what had happened already. It wasn't a story to brag, or a story to scare anyone. The two dead VC weren't even mentioned. That wasn't the point. As we sat around in a firebase one evening where it was safe, Farley started to spin his tail. It was kind of like watching the Korean War series, Mash. In his best Southern drawl, Farley started from back when he first came into our company and went on to paint a hilarious picture of the bumbling new kid who was scared and didn't know which end was up.

"I thought y'all was crazy when ya'd hold those little green cans of Cs up to yur ear and shake um like they'z spozed ta talk to ya or sumthin'. Then you'd rip off a piece of explosive an' put it under the can. I thought ya was pissed off an' go'na blow it up! I tell ya this is a loony place over here . . ."He went on, and everyone held their sides and cried from laughter as he led up to the description of himself spinning around on the ground like a turtle on its belly looking for that lost detonator. Laughter really is a medicine, and Farley was the doctor.

Farlcy* and I taking a break. His Southern drawl and quick wit was a breath of fresh air. It wasn't long before our CO recognized his silver tongue and put him on radio/telephone where he shined and moved up to battalion radio communications.

Another shining light came through an amazing act of heroism that will always be an example of the kind of courage and self-sacrifice that surfaced in some men's hearts. It happened one night as VC walked into our night defensive perimeter. Our company was set up on a main trail in an area of bomb craters. A small group of VC got caught that night walking the trail. Claymores went off, and the firefight erupted with several exchanges of red and green tracers. Artillery was called and flares began to pop between the H.E. rounds (high explosive). We had wounded, so the CO called for a medevac after things began to quiet down.

Even though it was pitch black and about 10:00 P.M., the chopper was willing to come and carry out our wounded. The terrain was covered with bomb craters, trees, brush, and occasional bursts of fire from both sides. The wounded were carried to a small clearing about fifty feet behind me. Rotor blades began beating the air about a mile away. They were trying to find us, but it was difficult in the dark. More flares popped, pinpointing our position. The pilot flew in as low as he could without lights, then at thirty feet he briefly flicked on a spotlight. He sank to twenty-five feet, then at twenty feet he slowed a little to get down between a couple trees and miss a bomb crater. Pow! A single green tracer came from the edge of our perimeter and streaked upwards like a laser. The machine quivered for a moment like an animal when shot. The spotlight went out, but the slick continued to settle down into the tiny landing zone. Our wounded were loaded and the chopper took off. Ten minutes later when they landed at the hospital, we found out the pilot was dead, shot by the green tracer. The co-pilot continued the landing and took out our wounded men with his pilot dead in the seat beside him. I haven't seen such bravery since.

- 9 -

THE BRIDGE

Everyone tried to get along in the jungle. The stakes were too high to argue among ourselves. In spite of that, two people really pushed my buttons. One was a new lieutenant with the third platoon. He showed up the morning God gave me the gift of "X-ray vision." Shortly after the dust settled, he and a few of his people pulled the dead VC out of the spider hole and stripped his body. They were delighted to find a few North Vietnamese dollars, while family pictures and personal items were thrown on the ground because they had no souvenir value. It was like watching vultures fight over a carcass. My revulsion at their treatment of this dead enemy soldier was answered by, "We're looking for important papers." They didn't care about papers. These were spoils of war, and they were going to get their share. They didn't understand that one or more of us might be lying there if God hadn't intervened.

Disgust filled my heart while walking up the trail to the second body. He had no papers so I put what little he had back together and propped him up against a tree with a live grenade between the tree and his back. The third platoon was told not to touch him. He was booby-trapped.

Later that afternoon the young lieutenant got his revenge for my impudence. I was on point, and our Cambodian scout was trying to explain in excited gestures and language I couldn't understand that something or someone was in front of us. He made signs and sounds like a mortar firing. I wasn't going to lead us into a mortar barrage, so we stayed put until someone could determine what he was trying to tell us. Where we saw nothing but bushes and trees in the jungle, these Cambodians could see bunkers from fifty feet.

Anyway, I couldn't understand, and he couldn't explain well enough, so we sat there for ten minutes trying to figure it out.

The boys in back (the third platoon) got mad and started a brushfire so we'd be forced to move ahead. I was furious. What kind of idiot would push us into a situation we didn't understand? Finally, the little lieutenant came up and asked if we wanted his help. We tried to explain there was something in front of us, but we couldn't make out what it was. He walked up the trail about twenty five yards and found a couple of mortar casings—no mortars, and no barrage. He was lucky, and I was left feeling humiliated. He grinned as I took over point and moved out again.

I felt foolish for not being able to understand our scout and embarrassed for holding up the entire company because of two mortar casings. Instead of thanking the lieutenant for discovering there was no danger, I felt he had challenged my position. The one good thing about walking point, there was a little bit of control over what we did, and this new lieutenant didn't respect that. He might have pushed us into an ambush, and his people would have stayed in the rear until the shooting was over. I'd show him who was in control! It's always harder to keep up when you are in the back of a quickly moving column. My body had fully acclimated, but his hadn't. "OK, you want to move, I'll show you how to move." I hit the afterburner. A half hour later, his tongue must have been dragging. He was red-haired, fair-skinned, and looked like he'd sweat gallons as I imagined him running, trying to keep up. Finally, my squad leader caught me and said everyone needed a break.

I sat down and tried to calm down. What a stupid thing to do. The column was strung out for a half mile. Very few had kept up with me. It took ten minutes for the rest of the column to catch up. It was a childish thing to do. Fortunately, we were moving across what looked like miles of open rice fields where there was little chance of running into an ambush. I think the captain knew what was happening, but he didn't call me on it. He did, however, transfer the lieutenant before the week was through.

The second person who troubled me was our top sergeant. He was a "lifer," a twenty year man, and wanted to live long enough to get his pension check, not go home in a body bag. He even stopped going out into the jungle with us. I didn't understand at the time, but I tried to live with it. What sent me over the edge was when Top jumped on a bunker in our firebase one morning as we were heading out into the jungle. He started yelling at us to get out of the firebase so he didn't have to miss his movie in Lai Khe that afternoon. He was probably kidding, but from that moment on, it was my goal to make that man's life as miserable as possible for acting like a jerk. Shooting a round over his head right then crossed my mind, but we were still inside the wire of the firebase and I'd probably get into trouble. As our column passed by the bunker, I glared at him then held up a bullet and said, "This one's for you, Top." Fortunately, it ended up being an idle threat, but I wanted him to realize he shouldn't just write us off.

Just before Christmas, our whole battalion was brought into Lai Khe for one of the traveling shows that were touring during the holidays. It wasn't Bob Hope, but no one cared because there were "round-eyed girls" in the act. Everyone wanted to see girls from home. It turned out they were actually from Australia. We were disarmed coming into camp. Of course, I thought it was Top's paranoia, but it turned out to be a base-wide policy. The mixture was already volatile with this many kids in from the jungle, drinking, doing drugs, and having hormones peaked from watching scantily clad dancers. Live ammo was an added risk the brass didn't want to take. It didn't deter me from my misguided mission to make life miserable for Top. There he was, standing on the outskirts of the large crowd already gathering around the stage. I reached into my pocket and pulled out a single bullet. "I saved this one for you Top." I thought it was hilarious, but he probably thought his widow would be the only one to see his retirement checks if he didn't get rid of this kid.

By three months I was sick of life as a grunt in a line company. Nobody in the rear of the column would come up front to fight, we'd lose a man every time we went out, and no one would take responsibility to assign the point position to someone else. The limits of luck had been exceeded long ago, and the inner voice saying I'd be OK was totally illogical and therefore difficult to trust.

Some guys knew they were going to make it and used the inner knowledge to become "cowboys." Several extended their tours because they liked the adrenaline rush and liked being "good" at something that terrified everyone else. I could have let myself do that, but it would have meant taking advantage of something that was beyond me. This was a very personal day-to-day gift which arrogance might jeopardize. Besides, one of the "cowboys" confided to me that he was afraid to go back home. What back in the world could compare to this? He looked forward to becoming a mercenary, a soldier for hire when he got out.

Our company was shipped north to guard a bridge over the Son Bay River located near the southern edge of the Michelin Rubber Plantation. The bridge itself was nothing spectacular. The engineers could have rebuilt it in a week, but it served as a vital link in a heavily traveled supply route. We were to stay in camp around the north end of the bridge for a couple of days, then move out to conduct the normal operations of walking all day and ambushing at night. Our second day brought the "opportunity" to dig a couple of new bunkers. It was hard work. Even under the late morning sun, sweat poured down our bodies and mixed with dirt and dust creating a sticky, gooey layer over every exposed portion of skin. Trying to wipe it off just produced red streaks of gritty mud and slimy hands. It was an excellent excuse to run down to the river to rinse and cool off.

Our arrival interrupted a group of local village women washing clothes on the rocks just downstream from the bridge. For them, it was a social event as much as work. They were all talking and laughing as they dipped clothes in the water and slapped them on the smooth black boulders. It was fascinating to watch another culture put a totally different meaning into such a common activity as washing clothes. A couple of the boys weren't quite as interested in the significance of the scene. As usual, in the presence of almost anything female they immediately wanted to exercise their manhood and began making cat-calls. The ladies quieted down and figured out the intent of the hand gestures and kissing sounds. Most seemed nervous and began leaving. I felt uncomfortable and got up with a few others to trudge back up to the bridge. It was another brush stroke in the picture of the ugly American. There was no respect for a culture that thrived without all the materialism we had or restraint from treating women as mere objects of lust.

Noon was approaching but there was time to grab a quick shave and relax before lunch. I collected a razor and balanced a mirror on top of the tire on the water trailer. The moment I bent down to shave, my back muscles locked and my body crumpled to the ground in agonizing pain. I couldn't move to get up and couldn't let others pick me up.

Medics finally eased me onto a stretcher and carried me off to a big empty bunker. There they deposited me onto a plywood bunk (minus the mattress). The problem was, my platoon was headed out after lunch. The medic handed me a bottle of pain pills and a canteen, saying he would have someone check on me later.

Two days went by in a blur of pain and boredom in the empty bunker. When the sun rose on the third day I was still flat on my back and couldn't sit up or even turn over. No one seemed to be looking for me and nobody moved into the bunker. That would have been OK, but I was getting hungry and didn't know how many days it would be before they discovered me. I'd been spacing the pain pills out to knock the edge off my pain and sleep a few hours. There were only six left. I took three and waited half an hour until my body could barely move. I downed the last three, pulled myself to my feet and staggered out of the bunker looking for the CO (Commanding Officer). He was in a tent by the mess hall with Top, who grumbled as soon as I walked in, "Wright! It's been reported that you lost your weapon. Is that true?"

"I've been in that bunker on the other side of the road for three days, and nobody even knew I was there. My rifle was leaning on the water trailer when my back went out. I couldn't move to pick up anything."

"Is this your rifle?" He pushed an M-16 towards me, expecting identification on the spot. "Yes, I think so." It looked like mine, but so did a million others!

"Don't you have the serial number memorized? Go get a note from your squad leader with your rifle's serial number on it."

"My platoon's out in the jungle. Don't you know where anybody's at?"

"Is this your serial number?"

"I don't know."

"Get me that note."

Glancing down, I memorized the serial number in a couple of seconds. It was some stupid game he wanted to play, and as long as I could write a note with the correct serial number on it, I could play. Back in the bunker, I found a pencil and paper and scribbled out my name and rifle serial number, then took it back to Top. I loathed him for not trying to understand and didn't make the connection between his behavior and my threats. He became the focus of my anger, and I really didn't want anything else. He tossed my rifle back and said nothing more.

I staggered over to the mess hall and carried some lunch back to the bunker to be by myself. The approach of a peaceful evening was interrupted when a new replacement stepped through the door. He introduced himself and said the two of us were supposed to pull guard duty at this bunker tonight. Guard duty didn't bother me anymore, and a little company would be OK after three days of isolation. We sat in the bunker for a while, but it was too hot and muggy. We grabbed up our poncho liners, rifles, and "widow makers" (ammo cans full of loaded M-16 magazines) then moved out to the top of the bunker. It bothered me that the two of us were supposed to secure the entire quadrant in front of this bunker by ourselves. If the VC decided to blow up the bridge, the two of us wouldn't be much opposition. Wait a minute. I was alone the last three nights, and no one pulled guard duty then. The new kid sat on the edge of the bunker for his first watch as I drifted off to sleep, confident there was no danger.

Pow! I bolted awake expecting to see VC coming through the wire in the moonlight. There was no movement and no other shots. The new kid was rolling in pain.

"Where'd that shot come from? Where'd it hit you?"

"In the knee."

"What happened?"

"I was holding my gun on top of my leg and it went off!"

The camp was stirring, so I yelled for a medic then went back to try and help. Two medics rushed over and gave him a quick check. One tried to apply a bandage, but screams of pain forced him to stop. The other rummaged through his bag and brought out a small tube (like a tiny tooth paste tube) and uncapped the attached syringe before plunging it into the mangled leg. The kid continued to scream and roll in pain, which caused the medics to put their heads together and decide the morphine should have been applied closer to his heart where it would take effect quickly.

"Should we give him another?"

"Why not, it won't hurt him."

The second injection was administered to his arm. Another minute passed before he calmed down, and they could load him onto a stretcher and off to a waiting chopper. I heard later that while under the influence of the two morphine shots, he confessed to shooting himself to keep from going out into the jungle. He'd held his rifle on top of his upper leg behind his knee and shot down through the bone out the back of his leg and into the calf. The energy of the bullet and muzzle blast shattered his knee. When he confessed, he lost all military benefits, and he'd be crippled for life. He didn't have to face the enemy in the jungle, but he got terribly wounded anyway and would have to live with the consequences of his decision for the rest of his life.

The enemy was tough and nearly invisible, but he wasn't the only thing to watch out for in the jungle. Rolled up in my poncho liner one night I heard something move in the dry leaves. It wasn't footsteps or someone crawling. It sounded like the belly of a large snake sliding over the leaves. Lying still seemed to quiet the noise. Rolling to my stomach for a better look started it again. Something wasn't right. Nothing visibly moved, and the sound didn't change position. There was a pinch on my chest, and the low rasping sound started again as my hand brushed across my fatigues. There was no thorn or twig poking me. I whispered for a flashlight and cupped the lens with my hand a few inches off the ground at the edge of my poncho liner. There was a line of army ants walking straight under my blanket. I moved and in unison, they started clacking their pinchers together making a rustling sound. I tried to brush them away, but they wouldn't deviate from their chosen route. They ate a pathway on the underside of my poncho liner as they passed beneath my body. Rather than risk more damage to my bedroll or my body, I decided to move and give them what they wanted.

Bugs got me again one afternoon on another mission. We were relaxing in the shade of a tree eating lunch when something crawled up the back of my leg inside my pants. I stood up to shake it out with no success. It continued to crawl past my calf up behind my knee and didn't show signs of slowing down. Not knowing what it was, I didn't want to just flatten it against my leg but didn't much like the direction it was headed either. I grabbed my pants and squeezed hard to crush it quickly. A second went by, then came a burning sting in the back of my thigh. I stripped my pants down and found a large centipede half crushed in the folds of my fatigues. The sting was about the same intensity as a wasp, but I didn't know if it was poisonous or not. The medic had no idea either. We needed some expert advice, so I suggested they fly me to the hospital to let the doctors inspect the centipede and my posterior. It would be a good two-day sham; maybe I could stretch it to three. The radio crackled with the reply from the hospital, "Wait and see what happens." That didn't sound like expert advice to me. I'd have to really get sick before they'd send me in. We sat around for another half hour to see if I'd go into a coma or something else worthy of requesting a dust-off (medevac). It turned out that the only damage seemed to be a little embarrassment and some difficulty pulling up my pants or sitting for a while. Sometimes you can't even depend on the bugs to do their part.

One thing we didn't have to worry about in the jungle was shaving. Water was too precious and resupply could be irregular. It didn't do any good to raise your hand and ask if you could go in to get cleaned up. Everyone smelled the same so we endured it along with the monsoon rains, billions of mosquitos, scorpions, snakes, ten inch centipedes, huge fire ants, leaches, knee deep stinking rice paddies, ten foot tall elephant grass, wait-a-minute vines and those other men hiding in the thick jungle trying to kill us.

- 10 -

R&R

The Army didn't want to totally wear us out, so they created something called R&R, (Rest and Relaxation). Grunts were allocated one R&R per tour. Eligibility came sometime after six months in-country. An opportunity came about a month early for me as the dry season was cooling slightly in transition to the wet season.

"Hey, Wright, you want an R&R to Hawaii?"

Uh, let me think. Hawaii is halfway home; what's to prevent me from catching a plane from Honolulu to San Francisco?

"Uh, yeah, I'll take Hawaii."

I wrote Janet to see if she could meet me in Honolulu. Neither of us had enough money to pay for the extra plane ticket and a week's worth of expensive accommodations and tourist attractions. We would meet in San Francisco, where Janet booked reservations at the Fairmont, then we'd drive to Sacramento for the remaining few days.

I jumped on a truck heading for Lai Khe. The thought of going home to see my fiancée was more than exciting. There'd be no worry about the next mission or walking point. The next week would be totally carefree! There was just enough time to pick up my orders and a few civilian clothes before the bus left Bien Hoa. We had to wear our uniforms to Hawaii. I'd change there before buying my ticket home. The entire trip was consumed with thoughts of getting back to the world, being with loved ones in a place that was completely safe from this war that wasn't a war.

When our plane landed in Honolulu, the military immediately told us we couldn't fly back to the mainland. With much regret about not being able to see the beautiful and historic state of Hawaii, about twenty of us disregarded those most recent instructions and set about searching for connecting flights back home.

Like Superman, I ducked into the restroom and did a quick change. My super powers ended when it came to portraying a civilian with my short hair and a guilty look. Even so, I tried to look casual strolling up to the ticket counter. It was almost a letdown when the ticket clerk didn't give me as much as a second glance. Obviously, this had been going on for as long as the war, and no one seemed to care. It was our responsibility to get back in time to catch our return flight to Vietnam. The earliest plane to San Francisco landed near midnight, so I called Janet to let her know when to pick me up.

She was ravishing. We fell into each others arms then headed back to town. It was after midnight when we arrived at the front desk of the Fairmont. The clerk behind the marble counter explained that he couldn't hold our reservation past 10:00 since there was a convention in town.

Janet put on her best pout. She told him the whole story of me flying in from Vietnam and how much we were counting on this time together in his beautiful hotel and how late it was to try and find somewhere else to stay. We hung our heads and looked very disappointed. He sighed as if he'd heard it all before. But then, with true compassion in his voice, he said, "We usually hold a room in reserve for special situations. How would you like to spend the night in the Presidential Suite?"

Unlike many experiences of Vietnam veterans, here was an unusually generous gesture. We were thrilled but a little nervous. How much do I tip? How do we act? A bellhop accompanied me to the parking garage to help with our luggage. Janet had brought along extra hangers because some hotels don't provide enough for all your clothes, and when I opened the rear door, all the hangers fell out with a clatter on the concrete. I laughed nervously about how "unsophisticated" this must seem. The bellhop chuckled and made me feel at ease.

The room(s) occupied nearly half the floor directly below the restaurant at the top of the building. The view was magnificent. We could see all the way around the eastern half of the city, from the Golden Gate to the Bay Bridge. The lights looked like a thousand jewels sparkling against the black velvet night. It was very romantic, and we lost ourselves in each other. The next morning we thanked the clerk and moved to another room, that wasn't quite as elaborate. It was close to ground level, small, something out of the 1940's.

The view was the wall of the building across the alley. We didn't care, we had each other. I suppose we did all the tourist things, but the main focus was each other, and all else faded into the background. When our two days in the big city were over, we drove back to Sacramento.

My fantasy of coming home didn't include the uneasy feeling that started gnawing at me. Everything was so "normal," yet there was another reality halfway around the world. There was a place where fear prevailed, and young kids were being shot at, maimed, and killed. The evening news didn't capture it nor did our nation understand that most of the young men fighting this war were really just trying to survive it. There was no underlying commitment to "save the world." The balance of good and evil wasn't tipped heavily in either direction. Most of us were there because we didn't want to go to Canada or jail. I found myself frustrated about how shallow people were on both sides of the issue. There were those who called us baby-killers and those who were determined this was the best chance of stopping Communism once and for all. Which side was right? I don't know, but there was enough right and wrong on both sides for anyone to argue. While everyone argued, nobody wanted to know what it was like being there in the middle of all the right, and all the wrong, trying to stay alive.

For the moment, I just wanted some peace. "Let's go for a drive in the country."

We drove to the American River and stopped to walk down the levee road. It was one of my favorite places. The sound of the water rushing down the gravel bar was soothing, and we walked past the spot where

I had poached salmon just a couple of years earlier. It was an early spring day with puffs of clouds skittering across the sky, and the forty degree temperature gave me goose bumps. It was much cooler than Vietnam, but I wanted to soak in as much as possible before going back. The river was peaceful and no one else was around. A red-tail hawk flew along the tree line and announced our presence with a screech.

I tried to absorb myself in all I was used to and loved, but it wasn't the same.

Something had changed. Even this experience couldn't replace the uneasiness inside. It had only been a few days earlier that I'd been watching for movement in the bushes and trees along a riverbank similar to this, and my adrenalin was pegged to react quickly to any sudden threat or danger. Then it hit me. The only thing that had changed in this picture was me.

That evening, lying in bed with my head on a pillow, my mind slipped back in time a few weeks. The soft bed turned into sand bags covering the top of a bunker, where several of us were listening to the communications radio tuned to the frequency of the 1/28th, one of our sister regiments. One of their companies was out on patrol and in trouble a few miles away. We could hear the supporting cannon fire from a nearby firebase, then the rounds exploding over the radio.

They walked into a base camp earlier that afternoon, just like we had done so many times. Some of the occupants chose not to leave and were stubbornly hanging onto their bunkers instead of running. Their captain insisted on taking the camp away from the VC, and the fight had already lasted three to four hours.

Situation reports were flashed from each platoon to the CP. Occasional cracks of rifle fire punctuated excited voices trying to give directions for artillery or to maneuver grunts into positions that would force the VC to abandon their bunkers. It was mean, nasty work, and no one liked sustained fighting against an enemy who was well dug in. They already had several casualties, and now evening was approaching. They had to make a move quickly or pull back for the night.

The radio crackled as one platoon leader reported he was sending his machine-gun squad up to a point where they could rain fire on a particularly resistant bunker. About five minutes later we heard a heartbroken voice call the CO and report they had casualties.

"How many?"

"Ah, we're trying to find out."

"Did the machine gun drive them out of the bunker?"

"No . . . ah, I don't think so."

"Sir . . . it sounds like the entire team is dead."

"What! How?"

"Ah . . . someone saw an AK pop out of the bunker . . . they just laid it on the ground and started firing. They killed everyone in our machine-gun squad, sir."

Our hearts sank. I held my eyes on the ground while others stared out into the coming darkness. We couldn't make eye contact. We didn't want to break into tears by looking into each others' eyes thinking it could have so easily been us out there.

Their captain finally gave the order to pull back a little and set up for the night. There was no more action. Morning came and it turned out the VC retreated under the cloak of darkness. What a waste of young men.

How could life be so different here from what is was just a short time ago? The miracle of flight didn't allow time to adjust to this totally different life. It was a life that was difficult to connect with because I hadn't disconnected from the reality of a few days earlier. My memories of home still seemed far away and long ago. I couldn't explain it to Janet, or even understand it myself, but there was a chasm between our two realities. Silence was the best way to protect those around me from the horror of Vietnam. They couldn't do anything about it, and it would only worry them more.

My innocence was gone. Maybe I'd never fit back into this lifestyle again. What would life in the World be like after six more months in Vietnam? I began to understand why some kids couldn't come home. They had been through too much. They'd changed too much. No one at home would understand them anymore, and they couldn't explain what had happened to them inside. With dread in my heart I prayed, "Please don't let me reach that point."

My few days of R&R were racing to an end. It was time to mentally prepare myself to go back. Thoughts of going to Canada were enticing, but my friends and my responsibilities were still in the jungle. Over six months of commitment still remained. I had to go back and finish what I started. There had to be some closure to this nightmare somehow. Running away would only add more confusion, and it was going to be hard enough to sort everything out as it was. There was no alternative but to enter hell again. Goodbyes were filed away with everything else that might become a painful distraction in a place where distractions could kill.

Sick with dread, like walking from life back into death, I boarded the plane back to Honolulu. Others must have struggled with the same decision, but I couldn't tell if any were missing. I could have been alone on the plane and not noticed.

Back in Vietnam it was time to let the fear and adrenalin rise again to make me quick enough to outshoot the VC who wanted to do the same to me. It was hard to psych myself up; my heart wasn't in it. Maybe it was time to try getting off point again.

There was an opening carrying ammo for the machine gun. The gunner and his team were less expendable than riflemen so they always walked last in the platoon. Ammo bearers carried two cans of ammo, two hundred rounds each at about fifteen pounds per can. My body weighed a hundred and forty-five pounds. The extra thirty pounds of ammo on top of my normal forty pounds of gear almost killed me. We were last in the column a few days later when I realized how far I was dragging behind. There was no way my body could keep up the pace. At thirty yards behind, I lost sight of the column when they disappeared around a bend in the trail. This was nuts! There was no fight left in me from the exhaustion of additional weight. VC could just step out of the jungle and take me prisoner before anyone knew it. Being wounded or killed was better than becoming a prisoner. I'd be better off walking point. Carrying the platoon radio was my final attempt, but the results were similar with the extra weight, and the lingo was difficult to learn quickly.

Farley, on the other hand, with his quick mind and smooth Southern accent, was a natural RTO (Radio Telephone Operator). His skills carried him to the inner circle of communications surrounding the battalion commander, and he no longer had to accompany us into the jungle. I missed his wonderful sense of humor and his ability to lift everyone up, but he was off line and I knew he'd do well.

- 11 -

THE SHAM

Farley didn't forget us. One dreary, rainy night back in our fire base, the tent flap opened and Farley yelled out, "Hey, I've been lookin' for y'all, I heard you were in. I started out 'bout an hour ago to find ya, but with all the rain and dark, I couldn't see and fell into a big ol' hole over there behind the mess tent. The rain filled it up to the top and I thought I was gonna drown. Then something floated by my nose, and it dawned on me that I must be in the hole where they burn shit from the outhouse! I was floating around there just like another big ol' turd! Well, I crawled out and smelled like somethin' that'd been dead 'bout four days. So I double-timed it over to the showers and hosed myself down. After I put on clean clothes, I started lookin' for my wallet. There was over $200 in it . . . I had to find it! It wasn't in the shower so I started to backtrack. I got all the way back to the pit I fell into.

I thought, "Oh Lord, it must be at the bottom. "What else could I do? I pulled off my shoes and socks and jumped right back in! I had to feel around with my toes until I found it. Man!

It's hard to pick up a wallet with your toes and keep your chin above water." He held up his thumb and forefinger with a little space between them. "My nose was this far from a big ol' floater! Well, I had to go take another shower before I could find ya' all. That's what took so long!"

We never knew if the story was true or not. It didn't matter. The picture of Farley jumping back in that pit for his wallet kept us laughing so hard we didn't remember the shithole we were in.

Maybe it was just coincidental that the next firebase we went to was the same place I'd met Don. When we flew into the clearing that served as the helipad, there was nothing left. The old firebase had been completely torn down. There was no wire, no bunkers, not even a leftover sand bag. We started from scratch building new bunkers, trenches, razor wire, everything including outhouses. It was hard work and it felt strange being back at this familiar place. After the 105s and mortar companies came, we were taken out to the jungle again.

The choppers flew into a clearing where tanks and APCs (Armored Personnel Carriers) were lined up facing a thick jungle wall. We assembled and were told that all we had to do was follow behind the mechanized units and clean up anyone they ran over. I got the idea that if the Army went to all the trouble to bring the big boys out here, there must be something serious in this plot of jungle. We lined up in squad-sized formations behind the iron coffins and waited a few minutes for them to finish getting organized. In unison, all their motors revved, and they lurched toward the tree line, crushing everything in their path. The small trees simply snapped or uprooted as they were pushed over, but even the tanks had to maneuver around the bigger trees. I stepped onto the churned ground from a track and followed it into the cool shade of the forest.

Everything ground to a halt within the first fifty feet. I stepped out beside an APC and walked forward until I saw a trench line parallel to the clearing we'd just left. The mech' units wanted us to check things out before moving on. Sometimes the VC would let them pass over, then pop up with RPGs hitting them from the rear. Tanks were most vulnerable from behind where their armor was thin.

We crept slowly along the trench to the next APC and chatted awhile until the section was declared clear. Smoke belched from twenty diesel engines, and we were off again. Thirty minutes into the operation, the undergrowth started to thin between the larger trees.

There didn't seem to be any opposition, and tired of eating diesel fumes, I stepped out and started moving through the shorter trees between the APCs and tanks. It felt pretty good walking through the jungle with a tank on one side and an APC on the other. My confidence led me to move out a little in front of the armor, and one of the tanker's didn't like it. There was no way he could get my attention so he fired his main cannon to let me know I was getting into his field of fire. Instinctively, I swung around and went to one knee with my rifle pointing at the source of the explosion. It was a ridiculous picture—facing down a tank with my M-16. The tanker laughed and shook his head.

Fortunately, the VC didn't stay to fight the heavy armor. The operation produced nothing but a little adrenaline and that vivid David and Goliath image.

That could have easily been the theme for the next operation. It was hot with no wind and a clear sky. I was on point, headed back from another uneventful excursion. I stumbled from the jungle into a huge opening cut by B-52s. Every tree had been blown apart for two hundred yards in front and a quarter of a mile to either side. It took a few minutes to sort out a route connecting the small openings between bomb craters and tangles of brush and trees.

About three-quarters of the way across, an F-4 Phantom streaked overhead. It arced upward, half-rolled, then snapped a 180-degree turn to the right. He'd spotted us and was going to make a run to see if we were VC. The plane became a motionless dot in blue sky as the nose turned directly toward me, and hung there, enlarging as it streaked closer.

My breathing stopped for a moment while I prayed he wouldn't open fire before making positive identification.

Just in case, I dropped to one knee, held my M-16 under my arm with my finger on the trigger and pointed it at the oncoming Phantom. I don't know what my mind was thinking—just survival instinct, I suppose. If he'd mistaken us for VC he would have eaten us in a second. The plane pulled up about forty feet off the ground, and the pilot smiled before rocketing by. He hit the afterburner, went straight up, rolled and wagged his wings, then flew off like a bird of prey continuing the hunt. Thank God the VC didn't have an air force!

Like a homing pigeon, I started heading back to the protection of our firebase. The CO sent up a bearing, which confirmed my internal map. I was a horse headed for the barn not wanting to spend another night outside the wire. We continued through the battered jungle until we encountered a large stand of elephant grass. I'd never seen anything like it before. Back home, Johnson grass might grow four or five feet tall, but this stuff was ten to twelve feet! Oh well, only one way to go. I started parting the grass with my left hand and my M-16 in my right. Dust and grit sifted down in clouds. The sharp edges were like saw grass. Ten to fifteen feet per minute turned out to be exhausting work. In desperation, I held my rifle over my head and began falling forward to mash a pathway a few feet at a time. It got hotter at the bottom of this sea of grass where no breeze could reach us. Forty five minutes later we broke through the other side. Back at the firebase, with cuts striping my hands and arms, covered in dust, soaked in sweat, spitting and snorting mud balls, I decided that was enough! I was going to get off line for a while, one way or another.

Others had faked injuries or found some "sham" that took them out of the jungle for a while. It was my turn, but how? Exhausted, I sat down on the wall of sandbags around the end of our bunker and pulled my boots off. My feet almost steamed as the sticky wet socks were rolled down my ankles and over my toes to reveal a little red spot on the middle toe of my left foot. It was like a tiny zit. "This might be it." I scratched off the skin and poured a handful of dirt on top of my foot then rubbed it into the small bloody spot.

With that done, I stripped down to my pants and set off in search of some hot water for a shower. There were no water heaters, but guys in the firebases had time to improvise. Strolling by an artillery bunker, I spotted a black plastic gas can and lifted it up. Perfect. Some poor gunner had put water in his black jeep can, set it in the sun by his bunker, and was expecting a warm shower that evening.

I walked off with the can and didn't look back. I was tired and mean enough to fight anyone for this water. He didn't need a shower as bad as I did (one look or whiff would have proven that). Besides, there was a million-to-one chance that this guy was the one who dropped a short round on me that first day in the field. The shower felt good. The ugly attitude washed down the drain along with the grit from my eyes, nose, mouth, ears, and hair. Feeling somewhat human again, clean clothes transformed me into a new man.

I filled up the gas can at the water trailer and took it back to where I'd "borrowed" it. A voice rose from thirty feet away, "Hey, what are you doing?"

I walked away and yelled back, "There are still a couple of hours before the sun goes down."

Given a few weeks of stability in a fire base, the cannon cockers (artillerymen) could devise a few of the comforts of home with empty ammo crates and G.I. ingenuity. We would come in to these fire bases for a couple days rest after a week or more out in the jungle. Showers were a heavenly treat after the accumulated dirt, dust, sweat and stink of a long patrol.

After six months in-country, sleeping on sandbags was like sleeping on a feather mattress. I settled down between the lumps and bumps and closed my eyes. Nothing was going to wake me. At 1:00 A.M. I sat straight up with an unbelievable pain in my left foot. I managed to pull my boot off (we never took our boots off to sleep in case we had to run or fight). My foot was swollen to the size of a small football and hurt so bad I couldn't touch it.

"Where's the medic?"

After what seemed like an hour, a groggy medic staggered over to my bunker.

"What happened?"

"I don't know, I just woke up and my foot was the size of a football. It really hurts. Can you do anything for me?"

"No, I can't give you any painkiller until we find out what did this."

"Can't you get me back to the hospital?"

"Not until the first chopper at 7:00 this morning."

"That's six hours away!"

"Sorry. Let me know if it gets any worse."

"How could it get any worse?"

"It could be something that'll make your whole body swell up, then I'll have to cut a hole in your throat and put a tube in your windpipe so you can breathe."

Great! This was a bad start for a little sham. It really hurt! Six agonizing hours later, the chopper arrived and someone helped me out to the helipad. Ten minutes later, I hopped into the receiving tent at some hospital. An orderly looked at the red, swollen foot, grabbed some crutches, and assigned me to a bunk a few tents away. The doctor showed up a couple hours later and poked at my toe until some pus came out. He wrote something on my chart, gave me some antibiotics, and told me to keep my foot up. The swelling went halfway down within a couple of days. With crutches, I managed to locate the mess tent, got something to eat, and returned to my bunk under my own power.

I relaxed and relished the calm. No jungle, no guard duty, no walking point, no ambushes. I could read outdated magazines, write a few letters, eat something other than Cs and sleep on a cot with a real mattress. Now this was turning into a sham! I wondered how long I could drag this out. My foot stayed elevated when the doctor or an orderly came around; somehow it just dangled to the floor the rest of the time.

An air raid siren went off about 8:00 one evening. Everyone jumped up and ran for the shelter of a bunker at the rear of our tent. There were no explosions, so I decided to remain in the comfort of my bed instead of hopping to the crowded bunker where I'd join others sitting in the cold on rows of sandbags for who knew how long. Some orderly ran through and said I had to get out of the tent and into the bunker.

"But nothing's happening."

"You've got to get up anyway. I'll get in trouble if you don't." Well, I didn't want him to get into trouble, so I struggled up and let him help me down the narrow aisle. Just as we arrived at the stairway, another siren signaled all clear. The orderly looked disgusted as we turned and headed back to my cot.

"You guys just don't care do you?"

"Yeah, I care if someone's shooting at me."

"Well, we had a dozen rockets in here last month. One of them landed right over there.

“He pointed just outside the tent.

I laughed and said, “It sounds pretty safe to me.”

He scowled and turned towards the door. “You guys are crazy.”

A couple more days of ease and the doctor came by for a checkup. “Hmmmm, it doesn’t look good. See this black stuff?” My toe was turning black and a little green. “If this isn’t better by tomorrow, I’m going to have to take it off! If that doesn’t do it, your foot may be next.”

Zoop! My foot went up on top of the raised end of my cot. The very next morning, the doctor came by and smiled, “Well, look at that, it’s a miracle. A few more days and you’ll be ready to go back to your unit.” He knew what I was doing but he gave me a couple extra days anyway.

This was a big hospital; medevacs were coming in and taking off constantly, all hours of the day and night. I didn’t even notice them after my first week. About 10:00 one morning, a chopper coming in about a half-mile away caught my attention. I was compelled to get up, take my crutches, and go out to watch it land. Why this chopper?

There’s been hundreds of others. It glided in, tipped its nose up to brake, and settled to the ground. Orderlies ran out and started carrying stretchers into a nearby tent. The first one passed and I saw why I needed to be there. It was my squad again! Like a parade, each of them passed in front of me, including our new lieutenant. The field bandages had been put on just minutes earlier and were already bright red with blood. No painkiller had been administered, but no one was crying out either. I crutched into the triage tent where they were tagged for priority before surgery.

One stretcher had only the upper half of a body on it. He was a farm boy from Minnesota who shared a little of his life with me a few weeks earlier. All he wanted to do was go home and work on the family farm. One evening he looked at the sky and said,

"It's going to rain tomorrow."

"How do you know that?"

He rattled off a jingle about red skies in the morning, sailor take warning. Red skies at night, sailor's delight. He could read the signs of the seasons, and none of the rest of us could. His lessons of caring for the land had probably been handed down from generations, and they would have gone to his children when it became their turn to work the land. But the chain had been broken here. The next morning, a jeep took me down to identify his body at the morgue. I imagined the letter his parents would be getting. They didn't even know yet. It felt awful.

There were broken legs, fragmentation wounds, and an arm with no hand. Stumping around the circle of stretchers, I tried to comfort everyone the best I could. Linnerman had a little blood coming out of his temple and no other apparent wounds. He opened his eyes when he heard the crutches, and in a shallow voice said, "Hey, Wright, what are you doing here?"

"I heard the chopper come in and wanted to come see who it was. "How are you doing?"

"Not good."

"It looks like you have a single wound."

"Stay with me awhile."

"I want to see the rest of the guys, then I'll come back."

Ten minutes passed before I completed the circle. Linnerman was dead. He had a small piece of shrapnel in his brain. I didn't realize he was dying when he asked me to stay with him.

One of the others told me what happened. They had spent the last three days setting up an ambush on a main trail less than a mile outside our current firebase. Each morning they'd pack up, move out, and were then told to return. The neighborhood VC didn't miss the repeating pattern.

On the third morning, they were waiting with an RPG (rocket propelled grenade, used as a tank killer). The squad was passing time playing cards since ambushes were seldom triggered in the daytime. The RPG was aimed at my Minnesota farmer friend and blew him in half. Everyone else in the circle was killed or had multiple shrapnel wounds. I visited the lieutenant the following day. He had been one of the first into surgery. He lay in bed with a cast from the top of his head to the bottoms of his feet. He couldn't talk or move a muscle, but somewhere underneath all the plaster he was alive. All of them were sent home. I never saw them again.

God had saved me once more, even while I was on a sham!

- 12 -

WOLFMAN

My infected foot healed quickly with the proper care. My sham was over. I appreciated the rest, but now it was time to face going back out to the jungle again. Without realizing it, my emotions had become totally numb. I survived the loss of my squad a second time but hardly noticed being alone. It made me look hard on the outside, but it was a skill necessary to keep functioning on the inside. The few who still knew me treated me differently. I was the mystery man. The one who outlives his squad. They respected the fact that something, someone, or some power was keeping me alive beyond just incredible luck. No one, including me, wanted to discuss how or why. It was a blessing to be alive, but there was a hidden curse: guilt for me and an eerie mistrust for new replacements. The odds were no longer relevant; whatever was going to happen would happen. There was little I could do about any of it.

Our company was to participate in a new program to win over the hearts and minds of the Vietnamese people. To accomplish this we were to simply walk through the village next to our firebase, be polite Americans checking for weapons, and make friends with the children. The kid part was easy. We just filled our pockets with candy, and they'd follow us around like the Pied Piper. Adults were more cautious; they'd peek out the doorway of their hooches and watch us go by probably hoping we wouldn't come in. One elderly man was different. He graciously invited us into his home and seemed genuinely pleased that we would take time to get acquainted (if you can call smiling, bowing, and saying hello in Vietnamese getting acquainted). His home was simple but beautiful, not one of the many thatched huts making up a majority of the village. There was a huge mahogany beam and rafters over the main living area containing a large mahogany table, chairs, and a simple china cabinet. He must have been one of the village elders but was a humble and gracious host. He brought out a bottle of rice wine and poured glasses for all five of us. Wow, white lightning! He filled our glasses again, and we drank up. I could barely walk out of there. We didn't find any weapons, but everyone in the village seemed more relaxed—I know I was! The kids loved the candy and the excitement of parading along the dusty road. Maybe we could make a difference. Maybe we could change our image from the "Ugly American" to the "Appropriate American" or even the "Kind American."

The next morning I jumped on a truck to go back into Lai Khe. As we drove through the middle of the village I saw four Vietnamese bodies hanging on a barbed wire fence. One of the bodies looked like the kindly old man who had treated us with such respect.

All of them had been hacked to death with machetes and hung on the fence as examples to the rest of the villagers. Pacification was abandoned. We couldn't fight like this.

The next time we got involved with an entire village was as part of a blocking force. Several companies were called out to surround a fairly large village thought to be sympathetic to the VC. We were strung out for a couple of miles on a perimeter just outside the hooches. My squad was assigned a section about two hundred feet wide. We were not supposed to let anyone in or out of the village and use force if necessary. There were no roads in our sector, so we set up between the huts and the adjacent jungle. The large trees had been cleared away years ago, so we cleared the remaining brush away as best we could and split into two groups. Each dug a shallow fighting position with sandbags making a low wall facing several thatched roof huts. There was a small ravine separating our two groups that neither could cover. That's where I'd go if I were a VC, so I set out to booby-trap the ravine to minimize the threat of someone sneaking up from that direction and throwing a grenade into one of our positions. Everything else was pretty clear.

For peace of mind I may have gone a little overboard, collecting several sticks of C-4, a couple claymores, hand grenades, smoke grenades, and tripwire. I carried my armload of goodies to a spot where we'd be protected from shrapnel and looked for hiding places to put explosives on both sides of the gully and connect them to the same wire. I removed the delayed fuses from the hand grenades and filled the holes with gunpowder from a few bullets. Next, I inserted the fuse from a smoke grenade into the hand grenade so there'd be no time delay. The grenades would now explode immediately after the pin was pulled. I molded C-4 around the grenades and set them behind the claymores. All that was needed to set the trigger was easing the hand grenade pin out until just a fraction of an inch held the handle in place. Unfortunately, there were two sides connected by the same wire; one was live while arming the other. My nerves were a little tight hoping no one would come out to investigate, or that I'd be clumsy enough to yank one of the pins out accidentally. To my relief, all went well and I retreated to the protection of our fighting position. Now, we just had to wait for nightfall and an unsuspecting VC to watch the fireworks. Even the pressure from a mild wind on the tripwire should have been enough to dislodge one of the grenade pins.

As night began to fall our nervous tension began to rise. The space between our two positions seemed to grow. Every small bush we hadn't cut down looked like a VC crawling towards us in the dark. There was little sleep that night. About 4:00 in the morning three VC did crawl out of the village and slowly sneak up within fifteen feet of a position about three hundred feet up the perimeter from our location. The slow moving branches in their hats were finally noticed and a firefight erupted. Two VC were killed outright. The third wasn't dead when our people started checking the bodies. He rolled over and shot one GI in the throat before he was dispatched. I went over early that morning to hear the story and decided that wasn't going to happen in my circle of influence. From that point on, if they weren't obviously dead, I'd shoot them in the head. There would be no wounded or faking VC after I did body checks. Gruesome as it was, it was just another necessary survival skill.

There were no fireworks from the booby trap. The thought of just leaving it crossed my mind, but the picture of some little kid walking through it drove me back to the gully to disarm the monster I'd created. Both explosives were still live, and who knows how much the safety pins had moved that night. My heart started pumping over how easily something might go wrong. What idiot set this thing up so there were two chances to get blown up? There was no delay in the fuses, so one mistake and it would be over in an instant!

I moved to the right side of the gully where the explosives were easiest to work. I gently cut the wire and turned my back to the explosive across the ravine then slowly reached for the handle of the first grenade. I made sure my palm and fingers were all the way around the grenade so I'd have a chance to squeeze it and maybe keep the hammer from firing if the pin dropped out. My adrenaline pumped as my hand gently depressed the handle and pushed the safety pin back to its normal position. I bent the ends back and slowly moved to the opposite side of the draw, keeping my eyes on the other half of the tripwire. This time the process had to be repeated in a position where the explosives were harder to handle. After it was over I sat back in the soft dirt and breathed deeply to calm down. That was a little too tense. No more booby traps like that, at least none that would have to be disarmed later. Coming to terms with being shot by an enemy who was quicker or "luckier" was one thing, but blowing myself up would be just plain stupid. This mission was over.

We flew back to our firebase where Top was waiting for me.

"You want to get out of this outfit, don't you?"

"Uh . . . you bet!"

"Here's your orders. Get on that truck, you're out of here."

"All I have is my field gear. What about the rest of my stuff?"

"We'll send it on the next truck."

I knew he was lying, but I didn't care. I ran and jumped on the open tailgate as the truck began driving off. He didn't even tell me what the orders were for or what I'd be doing, but it was enough to grab for a change, any change. The truck eventually drove up to a new tent behind our old company area at Lai Khe. There were ten to fifteen others standing around as I grabbed my rifle and pack and slid off the truck. No one looked familiar. I quizzed a big red-haired kid with a barrel chest and no front teeth. "Why are you here?"

"Oh, I kind of got in trouble in Delta Company. They transferred me here."

"How about you," someone asked.

"Well, I sort of threatened to shoot my Top Sergeant a couple of times. He didn't like that too much." Most were unhappy with previous situations and had "volunteered" to start a new outfit.

A young dark-haired lieutenant walked up the path and stopped in the middle of our group. He announced that he had been given the opportunity to start a Reconnaissance platoon for our battalion. We had been "handpicked" for this job (yeah, I knew how they picked us). I knew eight balls when I saw them, and I knew what they could do. I liked it already! We were the worst of the worst. The redhead with no front teeth was from New York. His nickname was Wolfman because he'd yelp like a wolf whenever he got drunk, which was most of the time back in base camp.

Our evenings were free. The Rear Echelon didn't trust us screw offs to protect them by pulling guard duty, so we quickly started running amuck. The first incident occurred when we crashed a movie at the engineering battalion camp across the road. We were a little more rowdy than these kids who didn't live out in the jungle. They may not have fired a shot except in basic training, and it didn't take much to convince them how tough it was out there and how mean and crazy we were.

"We even have a guy who, I swear, thinks he's Wolfman."

"Oh, come on. How dumb do you think we are? Where is he?"

"He's not here, but watch this." I leaned back, put my hands up to my mouth, and yelled as loud as I could, "Wolfman, Wolfman, where are you?" A couple of seconds went by, and off in the distance came this wolf howl. It sounded so good everybody broke up laughing. The tension from our bullying subsided, and we had a great time with our nervous new friends. Wolfman even showed up. He got right up on the stage and did a little dance while the movie was still playing. He wanted to pick a fight, but we got him down from the stage and convinced him he could thrash anyone in the place so he didn't have to prove anything.

It wasn't long before the eight balls got into mischief again. A half dozen were down at the bars and "tea" houses. They were too drunk to walk the mile back to camp, so they decided to commandeer a jeep and drive back. It wasn't just any old jeep either. For some reason the Navy had driven to Lai Khe and were a little upset about losing their transportation home. I found out about it when Wolfman started asking for paint to cover the identification numbers on the bumper. It was cleverly hidden in the tall weeds and brush behind our tent.

It was a little difficult to cover up the six-foot-wide swath broken down by the jeep while "hiding" it. Also, navy jeeps were *blue*, which made it a little more noticeable, since every other jeep in Lai Khe was OD green. It didn't take long for the MPs to track down the blue jeep with fresh paint covering the identification numbers. It was just a coincidence that they found it behind our tent. None of us knew anything about it!

"Those rotten thieves must have just abandoned it there!"

"Oh well, the Navy should be more careful with their equipment. What were they doing here anyway?"

At that point, our new lieutenant decided he'd better get control of us before we got into some real trouble. Maybe a little exercise might blunt our enthusiasm. He lined us up and away we went running around the block. The block was a mile on each side. By the time we reached three miles, the lieutenant was white as a sheet and gasping for air. He was new in-country and most of us had been here for months. When we turned down the path leading back to our tent, he peeled off and disappeared into his officer's quarters. It was the last time he made us run around the block for any reason. He must have been wondering what he had gotten himself into.

It turned out, he was a man after my own heart. His goal was for everyone to get back home in one piece. Since there were only twenty-five of us, and we were doing the same things a company did, he wanted to hide at night, and move quickly during daylight. He fulfilled his promise while I was there; we never lost a man to enemy fire. A man of his word, we moved quickly through the jungle and at night we set up "fairly close" to the trails we were supposed to ambush. It turned out that fifty yards was just a little too far for us to catch those "sneaky VC." Fortunately, it was equally difficult for them to find us.

Despite the care we took, we still ran into trouble. During one of our first outings, we were walking through a rubber plantation and ran right smack into an entire company of VC. They were walking in a column just like we were, and they were going to cross right in front of us. Fortunately, our Cambodian scout saw them first, and we were down on the ground when their point man slowly crept out from behind the trees. His boonie hat with rubber tree leaves for camouflage was the first thing that appeared over the grass in front of me. His shoulders, web gear, and black pajamas were next. He carried his AK in both hands and swung it slowly from side to side as he moved forward in a slight crouch. It was eerie, like looking into a mirror at myself. He didn't look like me, but I recognized his mannerisms and his controlled fear. I wanted to let him walk by and ambush the main body coming up behind him. We could get a higher body count, and the point man might live another day.

He got about thirty feet from me and was starting to walk past our position, when someone got too nervous and opened up. He dropped out of sight in the same tall grass where we were hiding. I knew exactly where he was, but my M-16 couldn't hit him shooting through the grass. He cracked a couple of shots in our direction. His AK fired a heavier bullet than our M-16s, and the two-foot-high grass wouldn't deflect them as much. It wasn't time to hold back; he might get lucky and kill one of us. I asked for the M-79 grenade launcher, and elevated the barrel to where the shell would come down on his head. Pop . . . bam! Right where he disappeared! Apparently, he had started moving back to the main body, because he jumped up about ten feet away and ran behind a rubber tree in a low crouch. I grabbed my rifle and had him in my sights, then hesitated to pull the trigger for a second. I shot up the rubber tree he was hiding behind and probably scared the crap out of him, but to my embarrassment, and relief, he got away.

We shot up so much ammo, they had to fly out a resupply chopper so we could go on with our mission. Our scout got wounded with shrapnel because he was standing in the open firing at the VC with his M-16. The rest of us were untouched. We were elated that our new platoon had come through this first test. All of us had fought, and no one held back. We frightened the heck out of a much bigger force and we were still in one piece.

This was no way to win a war, but it felt OK just seeing them run from us. I was starting to act out my unconscious beliefs about the war. I didn't *have* to kill that VC point man to survive. If this had been the Second World War, the point man would have been an evil "Jap" or "Nazi" soldier, and I wouldn't have hesitated to put a bullet in him. The VC were very different from us, but they didn't seem necessarily evil or a threat to our country. We weren't winning the war of ideologies. The imperialist perception of the U.S. helped fan the flames of communism's half-truths. And the image of the "ugly American" didn't help.

Brute force wasn't winning the physical war either. It was unrealistic for us to expect to eliminate an ideology by trying to shoot everyone who thought that way.

I wondered, "What would Jesus think about this war?" It seemed to me that He just wanted to change men's hearts, and even this war couldn't stop Him from doing that.

Recon had been reformed after nearly being wiped out before I arrived in country. We were a motley mix of misfits “volunteered” from the different companies of the regiment. We were small enough that everyone looked out for each other – we couldn’t afford to have any slackers.

- 13 -

RED RAIN

We were proud of our new platoon and thought we had it together pretty well before we were challenged to try and catch the "Swamp Fox." This particular VC had earned a reputation by sneaking his supply-laden sampan up and down one of the rivers at night near our firebase. A couple of companies had already tried to ambush him, but he outsmarted them both. We took the challenge with all the confidence that comes with youthful ignorance. How hard could it be to catch someone floating on a river? We added a night vision scope and a bazooka to our normal gear. Late that afternoon, we walked down towards the river's edge. The adjacent rice paddies were full of water, but they were untilled. That meant there was a little less danger in walking the levees. At least we'd go to bed dry that night. There was one last dike parallel to the river, between the rice paddies and the willows, at the water's edge. This would be a good place to set up for the night. We would have the protection of the dike to hide behind if the sampan had armament, plus there was a good view all the way across the river at this point.

We set the bazooka on the sand just above the water and aimed it so the round would fly all the way across the river about a foot above the water surface. When the sampan floated by, we just had to wait for the moment he crossed the line of fire and pull the trigger. It would be a piece of cake. I set up my bedroll on a little rise with the bazooka just below me. The rest of the platoon spread out along the dike for a hundred yards upstream. In our arrogance, we felt sure we had him in the bag. All we had to do was wait.

Darkness fell and the stars came out along with a half moon. It was light enough to see the dark outline of the opposite bank. We watched until 10:00 P.M. There was a large flat with hundreds of rice paddies on the other side of the river. As we lazily watched, a shower of red tracers began falling out of the night sky. They started from a thousand feet in the air and arced gracefully toward the ground like red water drops flowing out the end of a sprinkler hose. Four or five seconds later we heard the buzz of a Gatling gun. Someone said, "Spooky's out tonight."

Spooky was an old C-47 transport plane from World War II that had been converted to carry Gatling guns in the side door openings. The pilots flew around until they spotted targets through their night vision goggles, then the door gunner would pour out thousands of rounds in a few seconds on the unsuspecting enemy below. I watched in awe. Who could survive under that kind of fire? Someone had! A line of green tracers started from the ground and arced back towards the point where the red tracers came from. Another shower of red tracers and a returning line of green tracers. They must have some cover.

I'd hate to be there on the ground, even with cover. We'd walked through the jungle where Gatling guns had been used, and the trees were butchered with slashes and bullet holes every six inches or so. One more waterfall of red tracers and no answer from the green. It was over. Either they were out of ammunition or they were dead. I drifted off to sleep.

I woke up when someone whispered, "There he is."

"Where?"

I couldn't see. Everything looked different. I couldn't get oriented.

"Where's the bazooka?"

Why was there water everywhere? I saw something that looked like a log float through the reflection of moonlight on the middle of the river. No one fired a shot. We were all waiting for the bazooka, but no one could find it. After a few seconds trying to collect my thoughts, it dawned on me that the tide must have come in and raised the river level about three feet. The bazooka and most of our equipment was now underwater. Someone waded out and pulled up the bazooka. Water drained out the end as we watched. About seventy-five yards down the river, and now safely in the dark, a boat motor revved and the Swamp Fox made another clean escape. I imagine he laughed as he thought how stupid the GIs were.

It *was* hard to be serious. Our egos were a little bruised, but what a comedy! No one had bothered to inform us of the rising tide. Most of us had been asleep and woke up to find our rifles and gear under water. We got soaking wet retrieving everything, so we decided to walk back to our firebase instead of spending the rest of the night in the middle of what now was a swamp. Getting the sampan or not getting it wouldn't have made a great deal of difference. No one got hurt. He was brave and we *were* pretty dumb. I hope he lived to tell his grandchildren this story.

A few nights later we were sent out to ambush a trail at the far edge of our battalion's area of control. We found the trail all right. It was wide and a little muddy from heavy use. Darkness was quickly approaching, so our lieutenant, bless his heart, pulled us off the trail about forty yards to set up for the night. It couldn't have been more than five minutes when we heard what sounded like a freight train flying over our heads. Whoosh . . . wham!! The biggest explosion I ever heard was followed by the whizzing sounds of huge pieces of shrapnel just over our heads. It hit the trees and zipped through the brush all around. Another flying boxcar and another explosion with more shrapnel! Where was this stuff coming from? The VC didn't have anything like this! It had to be friendly fire! Another round came roaring in. We bounced off the ground every time one of these monsters hit!

Our lieutenant was on the radio trying to find out who was firing at us to get them to quit! It wasn't coming from anyone in *our* battalion. That meant another battalion was shooting at us, and we didn't have direct contact with them. The lieutenant was pleading for someone to find out who was firing on us and to let them know we were friendly. A half dozen more explosions and the firing stopped. They told us we'd walked by a listening device planted near the trail by our neighboring battalion. They could hear us walking and assumed we were VC, since none of *their* units were out in this direction. They had opened up with eight-inch guns. The shells were ten times bigger than the 105s we were used to.

The only thing that saved us was the fact that our lieutenant didn't set up beside the trail like he should have. The neighboring artillery knew exactly where the sound sensor was and where the trail was. They blasted the trail and anyone who may have been on it or next to it. Fortunately, they couldn't tell we were forty yards away hiding in the jungle.

We were joined by a guest the next time we went out. His name was Ruddy. He was a short-timer from another platoon and only had a couple weeks left. He was likable and talkative and went on about his R&R to Sidney, Australia. He was invited to stay with a family on a farm outside the city. It sounded like the whole country took a liking to GIs, maybe because they had troops here, too. Ruddy wanted to walk point!

"Sure, be my guest!"

He walked a trail out onto a little peninsula surrounded by rice fields. I was in the back of the formation taking it easy. I heard a single shot from up front. No one hit the ground, so I ran up to see what was going on. Ruddy was excited. He had just shot a VC who was trying to escape by running out into the middle of the rice paddies. He was explaining how he saw the guy running away and aimed at the neck, dropping him with one shot. The bragging was a little much, but he liked to talk. When we stopped for lunch I asked, "You like this stuff, don't you?"

"Yeah, I don't know what I'm going to do when I get home. That's why I'm out here; I want to stay out in the field to the last minute." I didn't say any more. God was protecting me and may have continued to protect me even with that kind of attitude. But it seemed disrespectful to take a person's life and enjoy the thrill.

We walked across the peninsula to the other side. Someone caught a glimpse of another VC just before he disappeared from sight. He must have jumped into a tunnel or something. We all went down into a lush green meadow where palm trees provided shade at the edge of another series of rice paddies. It was picturesque. We sat down and had lunch. The lieutenant radioed in what we had seen, and they decided to send out a dog and his handler to try to find the tunnel.

A slick flew in, and a big German shepherd jumped out pulling his handler by the leash. I guess we were supposed to get serious about finding a tunnel, so I got up and joined the rest of the platoon walking through the grass and bushes under the palm trees. There were trails everywhere. I started getting that feeling of danger and slowed down to really look at things. I walked one of the trails to see where it went. It branched several times within fifty feet then seemed to head back to the main part of the peninsula we'd just come from.

No one was finding anything, not even the dog. I decided to go back and follow one of the branches. Backtracking, I followed a small trail that turned to the left. It meandered around some bushes and stopped about twenty feet from where I'd picked it up. It didn't look right. Something wasn't making sense, and the hair started standing up on the back of my neck. Something was obviously out of place, but I hadn't figured it out yet. I just stood there staring at the ground for maybe thirty seconds.

How could a trail that was packed down hard from heavy foot traffic, just end and go nowhere? Were people walking down this trail and then turning around and walking back?

That didn't make any sense. I knelt down and brushed away the grass that overhung the end of the hard-packed trail and saw the faint edge of a thin board making a straight line across the end of the pathway. My fingers followed it to a corner. That was it! I had figured it out. The bush and grass were planted in a box that covered the entrance to a tunnel at the end of the trail!

Everyone was wandering around the palm trees and shrubbery. The dog and handler were already heading back to the helicopter landing site.

"Come on," yelled the Lieutenant. "They're going to fly us all out of here."

I heard the choppers coming over the treetops a quarter mile away. Did I want to open up that hole or get on the choppers? It would be dark before we could make a thorough inspection of the area. There would be more than just this one tunnel, and it might take hours to find a majority of the rest. Besides, I didn't have a need to see any more bloodshed that day. We killed one, that was enough for me. I ran for one of the three choppers that were starting to land next to the palm trees and took my usual seat in the open doorway with my feet on the skids. We lifted off and started to climb above the palms and a nearby hill.

There was a boom from below my feet, and a swoosh of sparks streaked by inches from my face, straight up through the main rotor blades! They had shot an RPG at us!

Those ungrateful SOBs! Didn't they understand I let them go? They could have blown us to bits! The image of a three-hundred-foot-freefall and consuming fireball flashed through my mind. They weren't playing by my rules! I knew where they were and how to get at them. My flush of anger made me wish we were back on the ground where I'd show them they weren't quite as invisible as they thought.

The chopper continued its slow ascent without hesitation. As the minutes passed and I realized we'd probably never go back there again, my anger quieted down. Sometimes I wonder how things would have turned out if I'd opened up that tunnel. What would we have found down there? How many might have died? Did I really do the right thing? In the end, no one was hurt. Maybe that was good enough.

- 14 -

THE WATER WHEEL

The monsoons had begun. Rain came down in buckets and turned muddy roads into bogs. Firebases became quagmires created by foot traffic alone. The mortar and 105 howitzer companies had to live in the sticky muck twenty-four hours a day. High traffic areas like the mess hall became swamps that stunk from the constant churning of mud and food scraps that putrefied and never dried out. Tents had to be elevated. We put in floors made of wooded pallets so we could walk and sleep above the mire. In some ways, it was easier being out in the jungle, where everything was wet but there wasn't as much mud, and the temperature was mild enough so it didn't get unbearably cold.

One afternoon while waiting for the rain to let up, a couple of guys from our new Recon platoon and I decided we needed a shower. There was no way to heat water; we hadn't seen the sun for days.

"Heck, why even go to the shower stalls," said Terry, to Dray and me. "Why not just step outside in the rain and shower right here next to the bunker."

We looked at each other and grinned, grabbed some soap, took off our clothes, and ran outside laughing like little kids. We had all the water we wanted. It felt good to lather up and just let the rain rinse us off. It wasn't a hot shower, but we stayed out until a breeze chilled us then scampered back into the bunker for our clothes.

Unfortunately, our normal routine of going into the jungle wasn't suspended because of rain. Visibility was limited, so we didn't ride the choppers. Instead, we walked out to the jungle from our firebase. Sometimes we'd walk a main road. This time of year they were usually impassable from the slippery, slimy mess left by truck wheels stirring up the gooey clay. There was no way to stay dry, but getting muddy meant dealing with the goop for the rest of the day. Inevitably it ended up on our hands, and eating with the muck mixed with our food was even less appetizing than usual. When night came, we picked our sleeping spots carefully. Thunderstorms could dump so much rain during the night that your bed might be flooded by morning.

It was one of those days as we set up late in the afternoon. I tried to heat C-rats under my poncho. The pork slices got hot, but the crackers were wet and soggy. There was no way to keep anything dry. We set claymores around our defensive position and prepared for a miserable night. I took the first guard then rolled up in my blanket and arranged my poncho to stay as dry as possible. The rain pounded down and splashed back into my face when it hit the ground. I wiggled over like an inchworm to get next to a rubber tree and found a comfortable spot that provided some shelter, then fell into a deep sleep. I didn't wake up until the next morning after the rain had stopped. My legs stretched out to get the circulation going when I felt water sloshing around all me. Somehow, I was lying in a six-inch-deep puddle with my head and feet out on dry ground. Moving in any direction would expose a seam to the depths of the puddle. There was no way to avoid it, so I jumped up quickly and brushed out the water that soaked my backside.

Well, at least the rain had stopped for a while. It was still cloudy and nasty looking, but we could eat without fighting the rain. After a quick breakfast, it was time to pack up for our morning hike. Several others joined in the morning routine to pick up our claymores. A bright flash and a sharp crack of thunder greeted us from a lightning strike about fifty feet away, then . . . WHAM! The explosion happened right in the middle of our defensive position. We all hit the ground and strained to see where the VC were hiding.

A couple of guys nearer to the explosion realized it wasn't the VC at all. One of our own claymores had exploded while its owner was carrying it back to the rest of his gear. We all rushed to see if we could help. He was on the ground, no hand on the end of his right arm and the bottom part of his body gone from the waist down. Lord, he was still alive! He looked back at us for a few seconds and calmly asked for a cigarette. He didn't smoke but probably didn't want to just stare back at us until he died. Someone lit a cigarette and put it in his left hand. He drew in the smoke as we were standing there watching. There was nothing we could do. I didn't want to see this. I glanced around, looking for the rest of his body but couldn't see anything. The claymore had shredded it into too many pieces.

I noticed our Cambodian scout was on the ground about thirty yards away. The claymore must have been pointing in that direction. I turned from the unbearable and ran over to the scout. He was in agony, holding a wound in his chest. Opening his shirt revealed bubbles of blood coming from a single small hole. The bubbles meant an iron pellet from the claymore had penetrated his lung. Each time he breathed, air came painfully from the hole in his chest. We had been taught to put a piece of plastic over the hole then bandage the wound tightly to stop the lung from collapsing. I wrapped him up the best I could and stayed with him until the medevac arrived. He seemed grateful that an American would spend the time with him. He didn't realize that a part of me was hiding from a more gruesome reality.

We figured the lightning strike must have been close enough to send an electrical charge through the ground and into the open end of the claymore's connecting wire where it laid on the ground. It was a tragic accident. When you play with these kinds of toys, even small events can be disastrous. We all felt the loss and waste of a life. There was no enemy to blame it on and no way to take out our frustration. That was our only death in Recon while I was there, and it turned out to be just an accident of timing and nature.

There were few days during the monsoon when it didn't rain. One of our next outings started in that unusual way. Big clouds were sailing overhead. The air was fresh. The countryside was lush with every shade of green set under the bright blue and white sky. Our platoon was walking along a river that now had clear, cold water running in a narrow channel lined with mahogany trees, tall grass, and blackberries. There were well-kept rice paddies in the open plain to the south. It felt like we were Boy Scouts going for a hike in the country. There was a village about a mile away, so we didn't concern ourselves when a farmer turned and started walking away as we drew near. He had a hoe over his shoulder, a white shirt, and a coolie hat. Everything seemed perfect.

We walked a trail between the river and the rice paddies. At one point, the river veered away from the fields and the trail dropped onto a flat to follow the river. At the water's edge was a twenty-foot diameter water wheel, made of small rubber-tree poles lashed together with grass ropes, and large pieces of bamboo lashed to the outside of the wheel. They had one open end, and were positioned to pick up water from a small pool at the base of the wheel. The water was then lifted and dumped into a trough feeding a small canal. With my engineering background, I was intrigued by this crudely made structure, placed and balanced so precisely that it operated using only the small force of water pushing the paddles just below the pieces of bamboo. It appeared delicate compared to the steel or timbered structures we would have made back home, but it looked like it incorporated the knowledge of the ages.

I hated to leave. It would have been nice to study the ancient machine for the rest of the morning, maybe throw out some blankets and have a picnic lunch. Someone else was walking point that day, so I stayed until everybody walked by and then I fell in at the rear. We continued along the trail another half hour, then stopped. There were some radio conversations, and it was decided we should turn around and head back the way we came. Off we went back down the same trail we just walked up a few minutes before. I didn't mind since we would be passing by that amazing water wheel again.

It was late morning and a nervous uneasy feeling suggested that something was going to happen. Ever since the ambush when half our company was lost, God had let me "sense" when we were walking into trouble. Things began looking different now. That's why the farmer left his field when we came into view. He knew the VC were here and didn't want to hang around. Or maybe he was one of them. Where were they now? What was going to happen? Walking in the rear, I'd be safe from ambush so I planned to maneuver behind the VC or hit them from the flank, depending on where they were. Each clump of brush and grove of trees became a possible hiding place where an ambush would definitely be to their advantage.

We started back down to the river toward the water wheel. Up on the small hill in front of us, the trail cut through a large blackberry patch. Blackberries weren't common in Vietnam, but that's what they looked like. The point man wouldn't go around. It wasn't logical. We'd just come down this trail an hour ago. It would be difficult to go around, and the trail was easy walking. What could change in an hour? The front of the column started up the hill and twisted with the trail towards the middle of the berry patch. My nerves became more tense, like watching a horror movie when you know the monster is going to jump out and grab someone but not knowing when. There was no time to stare at the marvel of ancient engineering as we passed by the water wheel.

My mind was occupied in looking for a path around the blackberries to cut VC down as they tried to escape, if they were there.

In the middle of the berry patch, my fears were realized by a sudden explosion. I ran to the left side of the berry bushes, away from the river, next to the rice paddies. No one was there. No gunfire, no more explosions. I stood for a moment, almost disappointed. One of the newer kids was screaming in pain. I ran back to see if I could help. Several people were dazed and still recovering from the blast. Fortunately, there were only two people down. The few guys remaining at the end of the column stepped over one of the bodies and pronounced him dead as they passed on to help the second kid who had both legs broken by the force of the explosion. He had stepped on a land mine. His steel-soled boots had kept him from losing his feet altogether, but one leg had a compound fracture with the bone sticking out through his pants, and the other foot was turned nearly backwards. He was screaming at the top of his lungs. Someone told him to get control of himself. He tried to quiet down but gave up in another surge of pain. The lieutenant was on the radio calling for a medevac.

I walked up the trail and stopped at the first casualty. It was Terry. He was face down in the soft mud of the trail. I could see from the back of his neck and from his hands that his skin had already turned the awful ash gray color of a dead man. There were four to five people around the kid with broken legs, so I decided to stay with Terry's body. I lifted his face out of the mud and was going to clean it off, when a voice inside me said, "He's alive. He'll be OK if you just talk to him."

I turned him over and put his boonie hat under his head. I saw no wounds so I said softly, "Terry, you're going to be OK. You just got the wind knocked out of you. You don't have any wounds. I know you can hear me. Just start to breathe slowly. Don't try to talk.

Stay calm. You'll be all right." Ten seconds went by and his skin color started to change back to normal as his heart started pumping again. His chest moved slightly as he took shallow breaths. Within a couple of minutes, he was trying to move and talk. I told him to be still until the choppers arrived.

When the medevac came, several people carried the kid with the broken legs to a stretcher and then to the chopper. Two medics ran over to Terry and me. They loaded him up on a second stretcher and asked what happened.

"It looks like he just got the wind knocked out of him from the explosion."

It was no use telling them about the voice I heard after everyone else had given him up for dead. From the hospital, he sent back a word of thanks to someone else. It made me happy to not be recognized for something I knew God had done.

Terry had sent thanks to a Christian named Marshall, who carried the machine gun and was the only one in our platoon who was strong enough to not drink or smoke dope.

Everyone else I knew in Vietnam was either a drinker or a druggie. He didn't hang out with me or the other dopers much. Wolfman carried ammo for him, and no one messed with Wolfman! Marshall was the kind of Christian you might expect God to use for miracles. He was a good influence on Wolfman and kept him out of a lot of trouble. He was the perfect example of living life without giving in to the crutches this world offers. I wanted to be like that, but I was too far into listening to myself. I wanted to be angry at the world, and somehow that made it easy for me to do drugs.

Even in my schizophrenic world, I got to play a small part in this miracle. I felt thankful that something was still connected in the right place.

- 15 -

THE THIRD MAN

I was never told why people would sometimes come into our platoon and leave after a brief stay. I was too far down the chain of command and too much of a loner to need that kind of information. Unless a new face was obviously a replacement, hardly anyone asked questions and treated newcomers as temporary guests. One such guest was a kid fresh from sniper school, and he seemed pretty green. There was no hardness in his eyes. Sniper school took about six weeks. It was a good sham for some. I'd talked one of my own friends into going to sniper school so he could get off line for a while. There were a few times when a sniper would have been handy, but our lieutenant would have told us to expect an addition if he was going to be with us permanently. He was probably here on a trial basis, and the lieutenant would decide if we really needed that kind of expertise. It was time to head out to the jungle again after a brief rest back at our new firebase.

The weather was clear enough to ride the choppers. It only took three "slicks" to carry our whole platoon. We came in low over a rubber plantation getting into position to land. As we passed the tree line our chopper rocked, and I heard the pilot say, "We're taking hits!" Our new sniper was sitting in the middle of the floor between the pilots where it was safe.

He looked down at a small hole in the floor between his legs and turned white as a sheet. A bullet had come up through the floor of the chopper and missed him by an inch or so. He looked around at us in horror, expecting us to react similarly. From my usual position in the open door I glanced at the hole in the floor and then looked at the ceiling. It concerned me more that the engine might have been damaged than the fact that the new kid had a close call. We all had seen too much to worry about the bullets that missed. Now, if the chopper was going down that would be cause for concern. The pilot quickly picked an alternate landing spot and dropped us off, then left as quickly as he could!

We walked back into the same rubber plantation we had just flown over. The VC were here, but even that didn't seem as ominous as it used to. It was difficult to see very far into this five-hundred-acre plantation. The ground hadn't been maintained for years and grass had grown up four to five feet tall under the trees. Visibility was about twenty feet which would be OK if the VC would just cooperate and stand up. After a few minutes of wading through the grass, we found a road that cut through the middle of the old plantation. At least we could see down the road a reasonable distance in both directions.

We decided to stay a while and watch the road which was the only clear trail for quite a ways. I climbed up into a nearby rubber tree where I could see maybe seventy-five yards in all directions. This might be a real turnaround to surprise the VC like they had done to us so many times. Life as a sniper wasn't as easy as it appeared. I found myself wondering if the VC could see me from the road. I was lying pretty low on a branch, and there were no other branches or limbs nearby to break up my silhouette. Ants were using the same limb to transport food to their nest on the ground. They weren't the big fire ants, but they were pesky and wouldn't reroute themselves. The squirming movements trying to avoid the ants were making it easy for anyone to spot this slightly clumsy green blob twitching on the low-hanging limb. In frustration I decided to give up my short career as the great American sniper and dropped back to the ground.

It was time to move on anyway. We walked down the road to the edge of the trees, where the road turned and headed west. We turned east and walked along a trail parallel to the tree line. It was getting hot again and it was close to noon. The trail turned and went between two big clumps of wait-a-minute bamboo. This would be a good spot to take a break. We split into two groups and set up in the shade of the bamboo. If any VC came up or down the trail, we would be in a good position to ambush them.

It hadn't been more than five minutes when someone whispered, "Hey, they're coming!"

"Where?" I asked.

He pointed back down the trail we just walked.

"How many?" He held up three fingers.

"How far?"

In silence he quickly held up his hand and dropped two fingers in a walking motion. He then pointed to the back edge of the bamboo where we were hiding.

We quietly dropped to the ground. The other half of our platoon had seen them also and was safely out of sight. We were closer, and they were going to walk within ten feet of us if they stayed on the trail. I saw the tops of their heads over the grass in front of me as they turned the corner beside us. Something was wrong! They came a few steps closer but there were only two heads. Where did the third one go?

Someone had to make a decision and quick! My adrenaline maxed out and time slowed to a crawl. I pushed myself up onto my knees to see better and get a clear field of fire. There were still only two VC. They were dressed in the typical black pajamas and coolie hats. AKs were slung over their shoulders, and their web gear had extra magazines of ammo hanging in front. They turned their heads and focused on my movement, then stopped in their tracks. Our eyes locked for an instant while my mind focused on the small plastic spoon wrapper I had put on the end of my rifle barrel to keep rain and moisture out. The bizarre thought flashed, "If I shoot these guys, this plastic will melt on the end of my barrel, and I'll have a heck of a time getting it off. Maybe I should take them prisoner." I had the drop on them, so there was no way they could swing the rifles off their shoulders in time to fire at me. "What happened to the third man? He'd been with these two. He must have seen us and dropped back. He'd probably start shooting or throw a grenade to cover their escape."

There was only one answer. I couldn't take the chance that the third man wasn't there. My rifle pointed at the belly of one VC, and three rounds snapped off. I turned to the next man as the first crumpled. His eyes widened and looked straight into mine. An explosion erupted in the bamboo behind me at the same moment I pulled the trigger. The second man dropped and so did I. All this happened in an eternity of about three seconds.

The third VC was there, and he was close! Everyone opened up for a few seconds.

Dray was beside me, and I could see his barrel was pointing too high in the air. "They're right in front of you. Shoot into the ground!" Visions of a wounded VC throwing a grenade or lying still until we walked up for a body check didn't sit well. It wasn't going to happen here if I could help it. They were only ten feet away, but I wanted to make sure they were dead.

We were the only ones shooting, so I yelled, "Cease fire!" We waited a minute, then started to get up.

"What was the explosion?"

"A grenade."

"Anyone hurt?"

"Lonny got cut on the heel."

We took a quick look at the two VC in front of us. Each one had a shot in the stomach, the chest, and the head, plus they had been cut up pretty badly from our close range fire.

"The other guy might still be around here." We slowly walked around the bamboo to see if anyone was running down the trail. No one was in sight. We walked a little farther to a spot where someone running off the trail had broken down the high grass. No one wanted to follow through grass high enough to hide a base camp! I took out a grenade and pitched it into the grass about eight feet away and dropped to the ground to wait for the explosion. BAM! "Ouch." There was a sting in my wrist and a small hole where a little blood trickled out.

Wouldn't you know it, hit by a piece of shrapnel from my own grenade. It stung like crazy. Maybe it would be good for a Purple Heart. Nah, I did it to myself, and it was too humiliating. We gave up on the third VC and went back to see how Lonny was doing. He sat under the bamboo in the shade. He turned his foot sideways so the blood ran out of the slice in the heel of his boot. It looked like a cut from a knife. He wouldn't take his boot off until he got to the hospital, so we never knew what the real story was. Even if it were a knife cut, everyone wanted off line. It was just another sham.

I picked up one of the AKs and slid the bolt open. The mechanism was filled with grease like it might have just come from the factory. If so, it had never been fired. The identification markings were Chinese. The workmanship wasn't the high quality of the Russian AKs. It had a grainy exterior unlike the polished and blued finish of Russian rifles. A long, narrow bayonet was folded back on the underside of the barrel. I folded it out and snapped it into place, imagining someone coming at me with the vicious looking spear. I never wanted to fight hand-to-hand and told myself to always save a few bullets so no one could get that close. I threw the AK over my shoulder and decided to keep it.

A few weeks later it was caught by a postal inspector before it reached my brother's house. The inspector turned up at his door with an empty attaché case and said there were about ninety David Wrights in Vietnam at the time, would he please identify where I was. My brother took the heat and didn't tell him! How bizarre it was to think that I was supposed to kill people carrying AKs, but it was illegal to keep the weapon they would have used to kill me.

A medevac was on the way. They were flying over the trees looking for smoke. The only clearing big enough to land in was between the two clumps of bamboo where we had been sitting. The chopper started coming down slowly. About five feet off the ground the pilot saw the two dead VC in the middle of the trail. He jerked the stick back and moved over a few feet so his skids weren't right on top of them. After he landed, the pilot got out and examined the bodies.

"You shot them up pretty bad."

"We wanted them dead."

I got a bandage for my wrist, but couldn't bring myself to ask about going into the hospital. Medevac pilots didn't get to see many dead VC. I guess we made his day. He flew off with a story to tell back at the officer's club in Lai Khe that evening.

We were still out in the jungle a few days later when we walked into a VC base camp. As usual, it had been evacuated before our arrival. We were checking things out and taking a break when someone heard Vietnamese voices outside the camp. We fell to the ground and crawled up behind a dead tree that was on the ground at the edge of the camp. Our new sniper was getting real jittery. He asked me what he was supposed to do.

I said, "Stay down; there's too many trees for you to shoot. We'll take care of it." We waited a few more seconds, and the same voice called from twenty feet away on the other side of the log.

The sniper couldn't stand it. He rose up and laid his M-14 over the top of our log, looked through the scope and fired. He dropped back down and announced he'd got him! The ambush was blown; we all jumped up and fired off a magazine. There was no return fire so we slowly stood and climbed over the log. Our sniper ran over to his kill like it was a four-point buck. He started going through a shoulder bag the VC was carrying. It turned out the guy must have been a pay clerk. There was over three thousand piasters, worth several hundred dollars in his bag. He must have been calling to the residents of the base camp to get their pay, not knowing they had left in a hurry. I walked down the trail a little and found another body. There were no visible wounds, so I swung the muzzle of my M16 toward his head and squeezed the trigger.

Back in the group surrounding the paymaster, our sniper was explaining in strained tones that since he had killed the pay clerk, he should get all the money. No one put up much of an argument. It was too disgusting to fight like mongrels over what amounted to a few hundred dollars. Maybe the kid really did have a killer's heart. He sure got greedy in a hurry. Fortunately, it was his first and last mission with our platoon.

We'd been standing around for ten to fifteen minutes now. The former residents would be back to see what happened pretty soon, and they weren't going to be real happy when they discovered we had killed their pay clerk and stolen their whole month's pay. We needed to get going and put some distance between us.

I took point and headed across the adjacent rice paddies. We were walking up to the edge of the paddies when I stopped. Just beyond the field was a road and a long line of pampas grass beside it. It looked like a long driveway going to one of those old French villas. The trail we were heading for crossed the road at a ten-foot opening in the pampas grass. It was a perfect place for an ambush. We sat down about seventy-five yards from the road to look the situation over for a few minutes. The road paralleled the rice paddies as far as we could see in either direction. We had to cross it somewhere, and we needed to move quickly. We were spending too much time in the open. It might give the VC time to set up an ambush if they hadn't already. I decided to go up by myself. No use exposing anyone else if it wasn't necessary. They could find out if the VC were there by watching what happened to me.

It was time to stand on what I believed. If I got shot, it would open the door to be with Jesus. If it happened instantaneously, there might only be a few seconds gap between the two realities, a couple of seconds of pain until my spirit left my body. Getting wounded would be worse and being taken prisoner would be the worst of all. The chances of getting my first wish were pretty good if this was going to be an ambush.

I stood up and told everybody to stay behind the small levee at the edge of the field. They would have good protection if the VC were waiting at the road.

"If something happens," I said, "don't leave my body up there."

I turned and began walking in a crouch towards the line of pampas grass, my heart pounding. About halfway, there came a rustle from behind, and I wheeled around to see the whole platoon catching up with me. It was hard to act angry. It felt a lot better not being out there alone. Turning back to the trail, I figured the two clumps of grass on either side would most likely have spider holes under the overhanging leaves. With my heart in my throat, I inched up to the closest one and lifted the long leaves with the barrel of my rifle. Nothing! I walked across the trail to the next clump of pampas grass and was relieved to discover nothing under it either. As the adrenaline started to drain, the stress and tension in my body reminded me, "You can't go through this too many more times."

My nerves were nearly shot. My body was thin and tired. I'd had been in-country for over eight months. I was close to becoming a two-digit midget (less than one hundred days left). When the new guys came in, I couldn't resist telling them that I was getting so short they could hardly see me. Somehow, it made us short-timers feel better to compare how little time we had left in-country to those who had just arrived. I was becoming more and more insensitive as time went on.

- 16 -

HONG KONG

It seemed ages ago that I'd flown into Vietnam. We talked less about what we were going to do when we got home now. We were not going back the same as we arrived. There would be a lot of baggage to carry back—all the physical and emotional wounds we'd accumulated during this year of hell. And we wouldn't fit neatly back into the lifestyles most of us had left. It wouldn't be like coming home from work to tell the little woman, "I blew away two more VC today honey, and last week Harry stepped on a landmine and lost one of his legs. Other than that, it was a pretty good trip out in the jungle."

Secretly, I did start to let myself think of actually going home. It was different from when we were bragging about doing this or that when we got back to the "world." It was more about the little things. I wasn't comfortable in a bed anymore. I liked sleeping outside on the hard ground and waking up to the sunrise. My body had adjusted to staying warm on cold nights with my thin poncho liner. How could I sleep in a heated bedroom with blankets and pillows? My back would kill me, and I'd roast!

What could I talk about when I got back home? Never very good at small talk, I always felt that discussing trivial things was a waste of time. This war had magnified the difference between what was important and what wasn't in my mind. Now, if it wasn't life threatening, it wasn't important. How was I going to muster up interest or concern about the "little things" that people back home felt were so critical? And what were big things to me here didn't have any relevance to those at home. I couldn't insert my stories into "normal" conversations; they were too gruesome. Even if someone did want to hear what it was like, I couldn't tell them without breaking down. Real men don't let themselves break down and sob! How was I going to fit into normal society again?

Another strange conflict started growing in my mind while thinking about going home.

I was the "Old Man." Like one of our Cambodian scouts, my eyes could see things from months of walking point that no one else could, and my mind could sense when we were walking into trouble. Nobody got killed when I was on point anymore. An obligation to protect the kids around me was growing. How could I just go home and abandon them? But at the same time, I *wanted* to go home. I *needed* to get away from this insanity. Extending my tour and staying longer would tempt me to start enjoying this stuff. It would be easy to live the reputation, and adrenaline *was* addicting. By now, I was very good at what I did. But it couldn't come home with me, and I couldn't live with myself by enjoying it.

Our platoon was sent back to Lai Khe for a short rest. Somewhere in the middle of getting drunk and loaded someone found out that our supply sergeant was making quite a bit of money on the black market. He had purchased a house in the Philippines and got frequent R&R's to visit his "housekeeper" and live the good life. Our envy quickly turned to anger when we found that he was selling our monthly rations of cigarettes, gum, candy, and liquor to help finance his fantasy. Wolfman got belligerent and intimidating when he was drunk, so we decided to let him vent his anger during a blanket party that evening. We hid beside the supply tent, away from the light hanging over the doorway. Someone asked the supply sergeant to come outside and talk. He obliged a few seconds later and opened the door. He was a fairly large man and didn't seem intimidated by the young GI standing in front of him. He took a few steps toward the inquirer, and the group rushed him and threw a blanket over his head. Two people held him while Wolfman beat him to the ground. We left him lying there with a stern warning that the next time any of our supplies disappeared he could expect a wake up from a grenade under his bed. Funny, our boxes of goodies started showing up just like clockwork.

While we were still in Lai Khe, one of the clerks tracked me down and asked if I wanted to go to Hong Kong on R&R. I assumed nobody else wanted it because I already had my R&R to Hawaii and then home. We were only supposed to get one. Maybe it was just God's way of showing me he cared. No matter what the reason, here was another chance to get out of

Vietnam for a few days. There'd be no flying home; it was too far and it would be too hard to come back this time. This would be different. It would be my chance to be a real tourist. I packed quickly and caught a transport flight to Bien Hoa.

A low-ranking clerk sat next to me on the flight to Hong Kong. He was nice, not much excitement going on where he was. There was nothing for me to say about what was going on in the jungle even to this fellow serviceman. My mind was full of fresh horrors, but I just grew silent and tried to hold down the emotions that accompanied each image. To be strong and ignore the emotions (if possible) would have sounded like bragging to a noncombatant, and I had zero interest in impressing others at the expense of the memories of friends who died. All together it was a pretty quiet trip.

There were maybe a half-dozen Aussies on the plane. I hadn't seen a group act that crazy since we were brought in to see the Christmas Show. They had one thing on their minds: have as much fun as possible. They were loud and obnoxious and funny. I loved their accents. Sometimes I couldn't understand what they were talking about because of their slang. It was pretty obvious they had been out in the jungle and had seen a lot of action together.

The U.S. Army, in its wisdom, wouldn't let us go anywhere in groups. They kept us pretty much isolated as individuals. We probably would have gotten too crazy if everyone on the plane had been from the same unit. The Army must have had too much trouble in the Second World War when units did everything together from basic to the end of the war. It was part of the Vietnam psychology that was frustrating. The Army wouldn't send over entire units from the States. Even our little group of three from AIT were separated and placed in different battalions after we arrived at our division headquarters. Everyone in my platoon had gotten to Vietnam at a different time. We only had to stay one year, so people were constantly moving in and out of the platoon. I suppose we never got as close to each other as they did in the Second World War. Maybe that was OK. Maybe it didn't hurt as much, only being together for a few months instead of for the duration of the war. Even so, we learned quickly to support one another just to stay alive. No one told us that at some point we'd have to learn it was OK to leave everyone and go home.

But at what point are you supposed to stop helping your friends and start thinking about surviving long enough to go home? Now the undesired owner of a great deal of knowledge gained through so many unwanted experiences, I felt obligated to those who died in some of those experiences to use that knowledge to help others stay alive. To do so meant placing myself in harm's way where I could see and "feel" things the best. That was the opposite of trying to stay alive and go home. There was no way to do both at the same time. But right now it was time for a vacation from this war, and there'd be no pushing myself out to the jungle for a whole week!

At the Hong Kong Airport, we were herded through customs and brought together in a room to be told the rules and to exchange our money for Hong Kong dollars. I kept a few U.S. twenties, hoping they'd be worth more as a souvenir than their actual value to some of the shopkeepers. It turned out that the shopkeepers loved to bargain and loved American money.

We broke up into buses that carried us to "approved" hotels. My clerk friend got a room with me at the Imperial Hotel. It looked to be straight out of the Fifties, but it was clean and not too expensive. We went upstairs to a restaurant at the top of the building for our first night's dinner. It was going to be great. No Cs or chow line. Anything we wanted! We were seated at a large table, European style. The waiter brought other guests over who spoke Chinese. The menu, of course, was in Chinese, but it had English subtitles. There were a few English groups at other tables. They all wore suits and ties and were obviously businessmen who could care less about two shaved heads in flowered shirts.

We stumbled through the menu and even asked the waiter what he recommended. We ordered a couple of drinks, and we tried to pass the time but felt out of place. Where did all the other GIs go? Silly us, they had all headed straight for the bars. Dinner finally arrived. Some chop suey, prawns, and other traditional Chinese food. It wasn't spiced like back home. I'm sure it was delicious if you had grown up there, but it wasn't the sumptuous meal I'd expected. A little disappointed, we headed back to our room.

Sitting on our beds, the age old question arose, "What do you want to do?"

"I don't know, what do you want to do?" The bar scene was never a high point for me, and picking up prostitutes was an adventure that never appealed either. By this time, my roommate thought I was gay. Without understanding it in words, it was enough to simply be out of the jungle, relaxing in a place where no one was shooting at me. My poor roommate had to go out by himself to look for a bar and some excitement. Leaving him stranded didn't bother me; excitement wasn't what I craved. Staying in the room and watching TV before falling asleep was good enough.

The next morning, we went back up to the restaurant for an English breakfast. There was no disappointment this time. The buffet was spread with everything imaginable, and a few oriental items that went beyond imagination. Meals for most of the last eight months had been eaten in haste from a can while looking over my shoulder for intruders. Large meals were also a rarity since we carried everything we ate. The opportunity didn't get away. A fifteen-minute feeding frenzy stuffed my 145 pound body with as much real eggs, bacon, and biscuits as my now distended stomach could possibly carry. No matter, it was time for a safe adventure.

Our hotel was in one of the main commercial districts in the huge city. The elevator took me down to the street level. Stepping out onto the sidewalk brought a little anxiety about being alone in a foreign country. It wasn't the isolation, which was becoming normal, but the language barrier was a bit frightening and getting around without embarrassing myself seemed important. It was a beautiful day; my short-sleeved shirt would be fine. My eyes swept the surrounding streetscape. To my right the street rose to the top of the hill above our hotel. I could make out the edge of the bay maybe a mile downhill in the opposite direction. This wasn't Chinatown back in San Francisco. The entire culture was Chinese, but the buildings and architecture were mostly European. There were several large hotels and a mix of multistory office buildings, banks, and apartments. The bottom floors of all the buildings were filled with restaurants, bars, clothing and furniture stores, jewelry and curio shops. Everything looked fairly high-class, but I slipped my wallet into my front pants pocket just in case. Looking like a dumb tourist didn't mean I had to be an easy target for some pickpocket.

My brother wanted me to shop for a particular kind of camera, and souvenirs would be necessary for everyone else. The camera was first. I'd start at the top of the hill and work my way down looking for the best deal. There must have been a dozen camera shops. My fear of poor communication was unfounded. Every shop owner spoke a little English or had an employee who did. Bargaining had to be a part of any sale. The marked price was only the high starting point and beginning of a friendly argument. Moving down the hill, every shop would beat the price of the previous competitor. At the fourth or fifth shop, we were approaching 50 percent of the marked value and it was time to get serious. The owner brought out a small table, sat me down, and gave me a Coke to drink while he explained that the fellow up the street was an unscrupulous crook, and I would undoubtedly get cheated by him. Besides, he had many children and if he reduced the price any more, his children would go hungry. I explained that I was just a poor GI, and this camera was for my brother. He would be real upset by spending too much of his money.

I don't like shopping in general, but the exchange was necessary to obtain the best price. Both of us knew the other was full of B.S. but it was part of the ritual. The price had leveled out and didn't look like it was going to come down further, so I purchased the camera.

Souvenirs were next. Janet was my first priority; something from a jewelry store would please her. Bargaining was more difficult without having a specific item like the camera to compare between stores. After looking through several shops, a jade ring seemed to be the best choice. I settled on large oval stone set in white gold. The owner told me the stone was high quality, but there was no way to know if he was telling the truth or not. It was pretty and Janet would like it.

Ivory seemed appropriate for Mom, Grandma, and my sister. The selection was huge. There were full-sized, intricately carved ivory tusks, spheres within spheres within spheres, all kinds of oriental figurines, bowls, and boxes and a hundred other ornamental pieces. There wasn't time to examine all of it, so the limiting factor became what I could carry back to Vietnam then mail home from there. I made my choices and took my booty back to the hotel room.

My roommate brought in a call girl while I had everything laid out on the bed to admire. He explained she was with him for the day, so there was no pressure to vacate the room.

She noticed the ring and asked if it was real jade. Of course I didn't know. She explained that real jade would keep a human hair from burning if it were held on the jade and a lit match was touched to the hair. We decided to try it. She donated a hair, and my roommate lit a match. We held the hair on the ring, turned it upside down, and put the flame underneath. The hair didn't burn! It wasn't a real test, but it made me feel better anyway.

The next two days were spent doing typical tourist things. Several bus tours ran from the hotel daily. One, including a stop at the main Chinese market, looked interesting. We could walk the streets for an hour or so and eat lunch at one of the many curbside cafes. It would be more intriguing to walk among the thousands of shoppers and see real Chinese culture than waste time trying to determine what might be good to eat. And I wouldn't have to stumble through the language barrier.

Incessant chatter engulfed us as we huddled close to the bus listening to our guide explain some of the history and facts about the market. My eyes surveyed the surroundings. Red flags were everywhere. Every street lamp, every building, shop and cubicle displayed a red flag. Our tour guide mentioned it was the twentieth anniversary of the Communist revolution in China, and tourists might choose to be a little cautious. Great!

Here I am, an American GI sent on vacation from fighting the "Red Scourge," in Vietnam to a country whose residents were supporting the twentieth anniversary of Communism in Asia. This was not one of the brighter decisions the U.S. Army had made, and its probably why no one wanted to go to Hong Kong on R&R.

It might have been my imagination, but from that moment on there seemed to be a little tension surrounding me, already conspicuous with my short hair, flowered shirt, jeans, and loafers. Shoot, why not just put a sign around my neck saying, "Here's one of the guys your Vietnamese comrades are trying to kill." Some of the fun of being a tourist drained away with political reality.

I began my walk a little disheartened and apprehensive, but my interest soon peaked at a shop that was the Chinese equivalent of a meat market, except the groceries were live. There were fish tanks with all kinds of fresh fish, clams, mussels, and lobster. There were cages with live chickens, a couple of baby pigs, and a glass aquarium filled with snakes. Transfixed by the undulating mass, I stared as a customer was chattering with the elderly owner and had apparently just ordered one of the slithering, crawling things. The owner lifted the lid, reached down, grabbed the selected meal, and pulled it out in a single motion. He let the tail dangle to the floor and stepped on it with one foot, then took out a small knife and cut the skin around the snake's neck, and peeled the skin down to the tail. He cut the head off, wrapped up the still wriggling body, and put it in a bag for the customer. Ah, lunch suddenly seemed less appealing than it had before.

The next day I signed up for a boat tour of the harbor. There were thousands of boats of all shapes and sizes. Small sampans glided by as skillful hands pushed and pulled a single oar swishing back and forth. All the necessities of life were here on the water carried by boats ranging from large ornately painted Chinese junks to individual sampans full of everything from fruits and vegetables to construction materials. Our guide said that the "boat people" created their own city here and most set foot on land only on special occasions. They had all they needed for life on these boats. There was no rent, and they could move whenever they wanted. There was an attraction to this lifestyle, but there were limitations also. There was the constant smell of rotting seaweed and other discarded material. Everything was damp, and what would happen during a storm or the not infrequent typhoon?

We landed in another tourist area at the base of a small mountain rising out of the sea that provided a spectacular view for several miles around. A cable car delivered me at the top where placards surrounded an observation platform describing what could be seen from each point. There was the bay and the boat people we had just visited. Over to the right a little was the main part of the city where my hotel was. Behind us was the mainland of China.

The afternoon was sparkling, and hundreds of Chinese were enjoying the warmth of the sun and the cool breeze at the top of the mountain. There, seated at one of the small granite tables in the park surrounding the lookout were a couple of men about my age playing a game. Their laughter and banter intrigued me. The game was unfamiliar. It looked something like dominos, but the moves were foreign. My curiosity made me move closer, then I thought of Janet. Why not get a picture so she could enjoy this? I pulled out my camera and walked a few steps closer, hoping the men might pose for me. One looked up, scowled and hissed to warn me I was being offensive. I snapped the picture anyway but was reminded again of the difference between our cultures.

Back at the hotel there were flashing lights from a couple of police cars parked outside the entrance. Not seeing any current disturbance, I stepped inside and took the elevator up to my room. Before I walked through the door, my roommate asked if I'd seen it.

"Seen what? There were some police cars at the front door. What happened?"

"Some of those Aussies were in a room way above ours. They had a girl in and apparently didn't like something she said. One of them hung her out the window by her ankles and threatened to drop her. There was such a ruckus, the cops finally showed up and pulled her back in."

We were six stories up. They must have been ten. How could anyone do that to another person? Then it hit me. How could I do some of the things I had done?

This was our last night in Hong Kong. I lay on my bed while my roommate left for a final night of excitement. I should go out and see what the bar scene was like. One of my tour guides had mentioned a famous bar down along the waterfront. Apparently, a movie had been made about one of the girls who worked there, or maybe she owned the place—*The World of Susie Wong.* I'd never seen it, but that would be as good as any other place. Located on the waterfront, sailors must frequent the bar on shore leave. How would they react to me?

I put on my best flowered shirt, and took a short taxi ride to a dingy street paralleling the bay. It wasn't anything special; a single neon sign identified the entrance in the middle of a block of tired brick buildings. I walked in and picked a booth where my back was against the wall and I could see the bar. There weren't any sailors, at least none in uniform. My drink came and I nursed it for half an hour. Something was eating at me. Why just sit here and become more and more sullen? Thoughts swirled of what sailors might brag about from their participation in the war. I wanted to tell them what it was like to fight and die in the place where they only sent planes out to bomb the faceless countryside. They didn't see the death or know the frustration or how painful it was. I ordered another drink and sat for an hour.

Fortunately, no one came in who needed to be enlightened. The barkeep could tell by the look on my face that I wanted to pick a fight, so my next order was cut with something that stopped the drunk I was headed for. That upset me too, but I knew inside that I shouldn't have come.

The waitress wanted to ask me to leave but was afraid. Instead she asked if I wanted a girl?

"No!"

I just wanted to be angry and let someone know about it. The manager sent over a young girl who started to explain all of her problems. The strategy was to get me to focus on her problems and forget my own for a while. The logic wasn't bad, but it was a distraction and I didn't want to be distracted. There was no bragging, obnoxious sailor to straighten out, so I decided it was time to leave before they called the police.

A taxi took me back to the hotel where I passed out in a sick sleep. All the way back to the airport the next morning between beats of a pounding headache, I thought about how stupid I'd been the night before. It was more than just trying to let off steam. I wanted to force someone to understand the hell I was going through. Not that they could do anything about it, but it seemed important that someone who might brag about lobbing a few shells into Vietnam should have to deal with some amount of pain those on the ground were experiencing. Violence to another person wouldn't have been revenge; it would have been taking out my anger on someone who had nothing to do with my personal situation.

I didn't want to pay duty on the souvenirs I was going to mail home from Vietnam, so they were carefully hidden in my luggage. That turned out to be a bad decision. Everything went through customs OK, but I had to go back into the field immediately after arriving in Lai Khe. I put everything in my foot locker in our platoon area for safe keeping. A few weeks later, when I made it back to Lai Khe almost everything had been stolen. All that was left to send home were a couple pieces of carved ivory. Janet's jade ring was gone along with her high school ring and a silver dollar her Grandfather had given her that she entrusted to me so I'd have something that meant a lot to her while we were far apart. No telling who the thief was. It could have been anyone in this place where nothing was sacred and no one was respected. It started sinking in that there were no limits to the depths to which men can fall.

- 17 -

A DIFFERENT KIND OF WAR

Lonny was short, dark haired, and looked as if he were forty. He was released from the hospital after my return from Hong Kong; he had been cut on his heel following a grenade explosion. It looked like a knife cut instead of a shrapnel wound, but what could I say after my sham a few months earlier. Lonny had that lucky aura. When Terry was knocked unconscious at the water wheel, Lonny was walking in front of the kid who stepped on the mine. After Terry was dusted- off, Lonny showed me his uniform. There were a half dozen cuts on the inside and outsides of his pant legs, in his shirt sleeves, even a slice through the brim of his hat. Shrapnel from the booby trap had silhouetted his body. That was too close. He didn't relish taking chances, and he was no cowboy.

Being sociable wasn't one of his strong points either. Usually it was just he and another friend, and rumors had it they were using hard drugs. None of us really knew what kind of trouble he'd gotten into—Recon inherited eight balls from the whole battalion. It could easily have been drugs, but he carried his weight in a fight, and that's all we needed from him.

While saddling up to go into the jungle again, Lonny came over and asked if I'd carry an extra medic's pack.

"Why?"

"Well, you're a nice guy and you care about everyone in our platoon. We're a pretty small group, and another medic's bag would come in handy if we get into trouble."

He held out the bag, and I took it not knowing what else to do. There was something not right about it, but there wasn't time to figure it out. The compliment was true, I did care for these guys and had helped Terry and our Cambodian scout. During my absence in Hong Kong, someone else took over the point position. Maybe hauling an extra medic bag would be an easier way to help the platoon than walking point. Lonny's compliment covered his deception until I found out he'd stolen the morphine and "left me holding the bag."

At the helipad we heaved our weight onto the choppers and were off for another "adventure." They deposited us into a small, fallow clearing between major rice paddies and a large patch of jungle. I took up a spot halfway back in the formation, right behind Lonny. It was hot and humid that morning, and clouds floated by while scenes from Hong Kong replayed in my mind. We turned into the jungle on a hard-packed trail leading through a lot of dry grass, clumps of bamboo, and tall mahogany. In silence, the line of bodies in front of me meandered around several large stands of bamboo, and only the plodding of our muffled footsteps disturbed the tranquility.

The front of our small column disappeared behind a big clump of wait-a-minute bamboo at the edge of a bomb crater. Rifle fire erupted and we fell to the ground. What had they run into? I needed to get up there. Lonny was lying about two feet to my left. The grass thinned a little at that point where he could see under the bamboo. While my mind focused fifty feet to our front, Lonny saw something under the bamboo and started blazing away. My eyes darted from the line of his rifle barrel to a VC under the bamboo so close we could have spit at each other. The small dark-haired figure was lying on his stomach, rifle stock to his cheek, firing back at Lonny. My mind could scarcely take in the scene. Both of them were shooting straight at each other on full automatic. Why wasn't one or both of them torn to shreds? They were less than ten feet apart, aiming right at each other!

Time screeched to a standstill as my thoughts accelerated with adrenalin. In a second or two Lonny would run out of ammo; our clips had only twenty rounds. The VC had thirty round magazines, and their AKs fired slower than our M-16s. That meant when Lonny stopped firing to change clips or got blown away, the young VC would turn on me as the next closest threat. Well, for the moment, he was preoccupied with Lonny. There was just a second to shoot him first. I swung over, took quick aim and fired on full automatic! One shot fired and nothing else happened. My rifle jammed! I hit the plunger with the heel of my hand. Still nothing!

With both of them firing, I snatched a moment to look through the dust cover of my rifle and saw a bullet hopelessly bent and jammed in the chamber. I would have to open my rifle and pull out the bolt along with the damaged cartridge. That would take an eternity! How could I do it with a VC lying right in front of us shooting everything he had!

Fear was redlining!! Lonny stopped firing to change clips. The only thing that flashed through my mind during that split second was to turn over and put my back to the VC while trying to un-jam my stupid rifle. There might be a chance he wouldn't see me as a threat with my back to him. There was no choice but to play the odds. Everything else was out of my control. It was extremely hard to turn my back, not seeing what was going on. The bent round wouldn't come loose. It would take more precious seconds to find my knife and pry it out. All the while my mind raced. Why did this have to happen? This is not good! What's happening? Was the VC dead? Was Lonny dead? The firing stopped for a couple seconds. Was the VC looking for another target? Were there more than one? Aw, shit! Come on fingers, move!!!

There was so much adrenalin flowing through my body I could barely function. Finally, the bolt slid back into position and my rifle slammed shut. I chambered a new round and rolled over. Lonny began firing again! The VC lay on the ground with his head down. Thank God, Lonny must have killed him. I took a couple of deep breaths and tried to calm down while yelling at Lonny that my damned rifle had jammed. He turned and stared for a second, not comprehending what I was saying. He didn't catch the movement under the bamboo.

The body both of us assumed was dead sprang up and started to run with about three others who had been hidden on the other side of the bamboo. Thump . . . wham! An explosion erupted in the branches of the bamboo two feet in front of his face. Like watching a movie switched into reverse, he fell back to the ground as quickly as he'd gotten up. I glanced to my right and saw Wolfman holding his still smoking M-79. We fired wildly as the others ran out of sight. We weren't trying to kill them as much as making sure they kept on running.

My thoughts returned to the front of our small column. They would need help. I grabbed my new medic bag and ran up to find the point man at the bottom of the bomb crater. I jumped into the hole trying not to push dirt down onto him. He had a nasty wound in his shoulder but was semi-conscious.

"Did I get him?"

"Get who?"

"I walked right up on 'um taking a nap under the bamboo. The closest one got a couple of shots off. I think I hit him though."

"Where was he?"

"Just over the edge of the bomb crater."

The point man would live, but someone needed to check out his story. We didn't need another wounded VC just a few feet away. Crawling up the wall of the crater, I peeked over to see a body in black pajamas lying on top of his rifle, which was pointed straight at me. I ducked back into the crater, my blood turning to ice. Was he dead or just waiting for a better shot? I had to finish him off in case he was faking it. I moved a couple feet to the left and slowly rose, took careful aim, and fired a single round. His body jumped in reflex, but the rifle didn't move. That was strange, so I fired a couple more rounds with the same results. Why was the body moving? He may have been immobile, but he wasn't dead! I dropped back into the bomb crater to figure out what was going on.

His head should have exploded from the rounds I'd been firing. How could I miss at six feet? It took a moment to realize that my rifle sights were nearly two inches higher than the barrel. Using the sights at this close range meant that bullets were hitting two inches lower than expected. I popped back up, aligned my barrel with the middle of his head and fired a single shot. He didn't move anymore.

My attention turned back to the new point man lying at the bottom of the crater. Ants were smelling blood and beginning to crawl up his bloody fatigues. It was too painful to move him. I brushed the ants away as best I could, then opened his shirt to see the torn flesh and shattered bone inside his shoulder. It took two of the biggest bandages from my pack to cover the bleeding. Dust and dirt from his shirt started sifting into the wounds but cleaning them caused screams of agony. This was out of my league. My limited training hadn't prepared me for this. I gave up further efforts and just tried to make him comfortable until others jumped into the crater and helped carry him down the trail where a medevac could land.

A bit shaken, I returned to the site of my previous terror where my rifle had jammed to find Lonny and Wolfman looking over the body of the VC he'd killed.

"Hey, Wright, look at this. Were we lucky or what?"

The body was lying face up with a five-pound grenade clutched in the right hand and the pull-ring on his finger. If Wolfman had delayed a second more, the grenade would have been tossed into the middle of our position to cover their retreat. Most grenades (ours and theirs) weighed about a pound. One this size would have wounded or killed many of us.

Numbed curiosity made me start looking for the fifty to seventy AK and M-16 rounds that had been fired. What could have happened? There had to be an explanation. I walked back to where we had been lying. There was a slight rise maybe four inches high between our positions. It must have been just high enough to catch the bullets but low enough to see over through our rifle sights. It was similar to my experience at the bomb crater. Lonny responded to my theory with unrelated mumbling and indifference.

The medevac arrived and left while we were still jabbering about the firefight and coming down from the rush. It had gone well considering everything. We had one wounded, but he would live. They lost two dead and maybe more wounded. If everyone hadn't engaged, it could have gone badly. They left an RPG behind in their hasty retreat. While admiring it, someone suggested we ought to shoot the thing. The mood changed to kids with a new toy. It looked simple enough, but what if it had been damaged? The kid who found it decided he would take the risk, and we all stepped back to watch. This was better than shooting off homemade fireworks. He aimed in the direction the VC had run and pulled the trigger. Boom! bam! An explosion threw up dust and bits of brush at the base of a mahogany tree fifty yards away. We yelled in excitement and gratitude that it hadn't been used on us.

It was time to move back up the trail, but one of the guys was leaning over Wolfman's dead VC and staring at something. I went over to see. Sheepishly, he pointed to a gold tooth in the open mouth of the dead man.

"Why leave it here?"

"Go ahead, take it. He's not going to miss it."

"How do you get it out?"

He was new and looked a little squeamish, so I stepped over, put my foot on the jaw and pulled back the cheek with the cleats of my boot. I smacked my rifle butt down twice, breaking the jaw bone and ripping the cheek apart to reveal the prize. I pulled the dangling tooth out of the gaping mouth, trying not to think of how grotesque this was. The kid recoiled a little as I thrust the gold crown towards him. He found a small piece of plastic to put it in then delicately dropped it into his shirt pocket. This was a new low for me.

A full company was being flown out to join our platoon in a chase after the VC who got away. While waiting, we broke out lunch in at the edge of the jungle where the choppers would be coming in. A Loach buzzed overhead. It was a small chopper compared to the slicks we rode in. Fast and maneuverable, it was used as a spotter or observation plane. When accompanied by a Cobra, the two became a lethal combination. The Loach would flit around the top of the tree canopy looking for enemy soldiers or occasionally drawing fire. The Cobra would stay high and out of sight until the Loach had a target, then it would pounce with all its heavy armament.

We sat eating lunch and watching the Loach hum around the treetops like a dragonfly.

As if on cue, someone on the ground couldn't pass up the tantalizing target and took a shot. Within thirty seconds, a Cobra swooped in firing its Gatling gun.

Two thousand rounds a minute blanketed the trees and everything underneath. On the second pass, we heard the thump, thump, thump of his automatic grenade launcher. M-79 rounds hit the ground at one-second intervals. The Cobra pulled off and the Loach came back with its own Gatling gun spitting fire. It sounded like a deep, powerful buzz. The Cobra returned, spewing out more fire from its Gatling gun and then shook the jungle with ten to fifteen rockets. It was an awesome display. The show went on for about ten minutes until they ran out of ammunition and fluttered away to rearm.

The beat of a familiar far off rhythm signaled the slicks were on their way. We popped smoke and they glided into the same spot where we had landed in just hours earlier. We escorted the company back to where we caught the VC napping. A conversation arose about the dead VC with the broken jaw. Someone whispered to me, "See that guy over there? He's got a necklace of ears." I glanced over and saw shriveled up chunks of dried skin under his collar. Was this a picture of me in the future? "God, don't let me become like that." I vowed to never show that kind of disrespect or callousness again.

We headed off in a gaggle toward the point where the surviving VC had vanished. They had to be around somewhere. When we flew in earlier that morning, this patch of jungle appeared to be a four- or five-hundred-acre island in the middle of a lake of rice paddies. Anyone trying to leave would be easily spotted. Whoever we shot up and whoever took a potshot at the choppers was still here. They were probably a little upset about getting caught napping, and the few we saw may have only been part of a larger force. Anyhow, we were supposed to find them and finish the job. It occurred to me that we might be stirring up a hornet's nest.

The battalion commander flew in to join us. He probably thought this would be an easy kill and wanted to be there for the action which gave the company C.O. an opportunity to impress him by having his people walk point. That was fine with me. Sometimes petty politics work out OK.

We saw nothing after following the company formation for nearly the entire length of our jungle island. Close to the far end, we found ourselves standing on top of a six- to eight-foot ledge that ran in a quarter-circle for several hundred yards to our left and right. Everyone jumped down to the next level, right onto a heavily compacted trail at the base of the vertical face. It paralleled the ledge in both directions. Lush green vines were growing at the top of the ledge and hung down its face to the bottom like a long green curtain. That feeling of danger rose up along with hair on the back of my neck. Our platoon was last to dismount the ledge. The rest of the column was already disappearing into the palms and banana trees ahead.

My stomach had been upset for the last fifteen minutes, and now extreme cramps were saying, go now or embarrass yourself. I got as far away from the ledge as possible before turning around to squat and then exploding at the base of a palm tree. My rifle remained in my hands and pointed towards the VC I felt watching from somewhere behind those vines along the ledge. Their tunnels were cut into the face, and the vines had been cultivated to hang down and cover their entrances. An entire complex could be dug into that bank; it was a nearly perfect place to hide and had obviously avoided detection up to now. Entrances were just one step off the trail through the vines, and we were too dumb to recognize it. It would be tough to fight the VC here. They had the protection of the hidden tunnels, and we would be on the open flat ground lying in front of the ledge. They could hold us off with a single machine gun by moving from entrance to entrance for hours. It would be a disaster. My ego didn't need this tunnel complex, and no one else knew it was there. I decided to let them go. Or maybe I decided to let us go.

My stomach was still cramping even as I scrambled to catch up. One of the guys toward the tail of the column yelled for the medic and let him know I couldn't keep up. Everyone stopped and suddenly my bowels became the center of attention. Even the battalion commander came over to ask how I was feeling. After discovering I could only walk about fifty paces between bouts of diarrhea, he radioed his helicopter to take me back to our firebase. There was no more excitement that day, and we avoided a lopsided battle where we would have been pinned down taking most of the casualties. I could have been a hero for finding those tunnels, but I chose instead to let us separate without firing another shot. My responsibility to destroy the enemy that day lost to my responsibility for those around me.

Unconsciously, I'd resolved part of the crisis that was beginning to rage in my mind by learning how to fulfill at least some of my deepest desire for this ugly war—keep people alive. The rest of my conflict revolved around the mechanics of keeping those around me alive, which by necessity included my continuing presence in the middle of situations that directly threatened my own chances of going home. There was a deep responsibility in my heart, even a compulsion to use the abilities God had given to help protect my platoon. Finally, I learned how to protect them by sensing and avoiding one-sided firefights.

Looking back from thirty years in the future, this was a turning point. Somewhere in my mind was the suspicion we weren't going to win this war the way we were fighting it.

It wasn't bad military leadership as much as having the wrong objective. We didn't want to take over the country; we just wanted them to be able to live like us! The trouble was that the Vietnamese version of democracy and capitalism was riddled with centuries of ruthless control and a different value of life from what Westerners could understand. Their government was more corrupt, ruthless, and uninspiring than our political and military leaders imagined.

And there was real passion on the Communist side. They were able to play the card of "freedom fighters" trying to stand up against the evil imperialists. Their country had seen invaders for a thousand years and had survived them all. Military might wasn't enough to change people's minds or convert them to seeing the world the way we did.

Even then, in the middle of 1969, it felt like our politicians were trying to buy time for one of two solutions. They either wanted to keep us here until the Communists got so bloodied and demoralized they might pack up and leave, or as time went on, maybe we could at least negotiate an honorable way to extricate ourselves from this mess.

This kind of war was very different from fighting for all-out victory like we had done in World War II. Here we were just trying to keep a failing government from collapsing, while hoping the other side would get too discouraged and tired to fight anymore.

- 18 -

WALKING HEADS

Recon had all the "characters," and that was OK as long as everyone did their part. Even though we were all eight balls, each of us had value, and we didn't pry into each other's lives. Fast Horse was a full-blooded Navajo, but he didn't quite fit the image. Instead of personifying one of John Wayne's strong, silent adversaries, he acted a little effeminate at times. Some guys said he was gay, but he would always walk second or third in the column. He wasn't a coward so he wasn't treated differently than anyone else. He bought a duckling from a Mama-san while we were in one of the firebases. It was really cute, and all of us took a liking to it immediately. Ten to fifteen of us hard-hearted killers were running across the compound, throwing our hats at the ground trying to catch grasshoppers for the little ball of feathers to eat. When it couldn't possibly eat another mouth full, we placed it, and more food and water into a bunker just before our next trip into the jungle.

The monsoons were nearly over and it was warming up again. By early afternoon it had already been a long hot day as we approached the edge of a beautiful, clear river. We were to spend the night somewhere on the other side, so we gathered on the bank to gauge the difficulty of crossing and bundle everything we wanted to keep dry. River crossings were always a problem. They were slow, with no place to hide, we couldn't swim with all the extra weight, and the shorter guys had additional trouble depending on how deep the water was. On the other hand, it was hot and a few minutes in the cool water would be refreshing, plus it might help dissipate the week-old lingering cloud of BO that followed us. It didn't look too deep from where we stood, so our new point man waded in. We held back so no more than five of us were in the water at a time. Fast Horse and a few others followed and safely reached the other side, then it was my turn. I walked down the short bank and eased into the river, my toes almost sizzling as the cold water rushed into my boots. It slowly rose to my chest and I raised my rifle and a few belongings over my head until I was able to crawl up the opposite bank and begin draining the water from my gear.

There was a well-traveled trail along this side of the river. Fast Horse was standing in the group drying off. He had his shirt unbuttoned and gasped that there were leeches in the river. We all started checking under our clothes. I didn't have any and was anxious to get moving. Standing around this trail seemed like an open invitation to any VC who might be in the area. It would take a few minutes to get everyone organized again, so

I asked a couple of guys to set up on the hillside above the trail about twenty-five yards in either direction.

Fast Horse turned to me. There were two big leeches, one on his belly and the other on his chest.

"How do I get these things off?"

"Well, I heard that if you pull them off, you might leave something behind that could get infected. Or maybe that was for ticks. You might try to burn them off, or maybe pouring salt on them would work like it does for slugs." "Would you help me?" he pleaded.

"Have someone else do it."

"No, I really don't want anyone else to take them off," he begged.

It was a little strange but since he asked . . . why not? It made him happy, and would get us moving again. "Anyone got a match?" Everything was wet, but someone came up with a couple packets of salt from his C-rations. I applied it to the body of one of the leeches which squirmed and dropped its grip. I treated the second one with similar results. I was so naïve to what was happening that it went completely over my head. The rest of the platoon wasn't as dumb and decided to set me up the next time we were back at the firebase.

Our gear had drained enough, and we were about ready to move on. A look at the trail revealed there was no other place to walk on this side of the river. Anyone traveling through here would have to be on this trail. It was a perfect place for a booby trap. There was an old tree stump next to the trail to hold the explosives about waist high. I pulled the time-delayed blasting cap from one of my grenades and filled up the hole with gunpowder then replaced the cap with a firing mechanism from a smoke grenade (they didn't have a time delay). Tape secured it to the stump and loose grass made it invisible. I wrapped a long strand of grass with a tripwire and fastened one end to a half-pulled grenade pin, the other to a small tree across the trail. A little more grass made it look natural. Everyone jumped the trail, and we brushed the rest of our footprints away.

We continued up the hill out of the river basin and started out onto a big flat of tall grass and brush. We'd gotten about a quarter of a mile away from the river when we heard the explosion, so we stopped a minute.

"That must have been the booby trap." The lieutenant called in the explosion and the approximate location. Ten minutes later, a Loach called and said he saw a body at the edge of the river. I felt bad thinking about the brief second after the VC realized he'd hit the tripwire. There must have been a moment of horror in his mind before the explosion killed him. Was he alone or had we wounded others who managed to crawl or be carried away?

It didn't seem to be a fair way to fight. It was close to terrorism, something the Communists used pretty effectively, but left me feeling uneasy. I'd been in-country long enough and had been through enough to start writing my own rules—no more booby traps.

We continued walking a trail through a flat sea of four-foot-high brush. It looked like it had burned once and had all grown back at the same time. We popped out into a two- or three-acre clearing. Our trail continued across its western edge, and another trail ran in the same direction about a hundred feet away on the eastern side. Sunset was an hour and a half away. We might not get out of this brush before dark, so we decided to set up an ambush on both trails. Half the platoon set up behind some brush on the western trail at the north edge of the clearing. My half set up on the eastern trail, at the south edge of the clearing. In daylight, the backs of both groups were exposed to each other's trail, so we had to be alert until the sun went down

My eyes followed our trail to where it disappeared into the neck-high brush about thirty yards behind the other half of our platoon. The scene became perceptibly darker as I stared, but the sun was still shining. Transparent heads appeared, bobbing above the brush like people walking down the trail towards us, then they evaporated. What was going on? Sunset was still forty-five minutes away. Was this a vision of something about to happen? I wasn't sure, but by this time I knew that God could do anything He wanted.

"If anything happens tonight, it's going to be just after sunset and they're going to come down the trail right over there," I said to the machine gunner and pointed to the opposite side of the clearing. "You'll be able to see their heads just above the brush before they reach the edge of the clearing."

The gunner looked at me trying to figure out if I was serious or joking. There was no smile as I repeated the warning. He picked up his machine gun and set it down in the direction I'd pointed. We finished our dinner and watched the sun go down. The other half of our platoon was relaxed and in a jovial mood, completely unaware of any reason for concern. I wanted to warn them, but that meant I'd have to explain everything over the radio. How could this be explained? This had never happened to me before. It was different from when God let me see through some bamboo when a VC was sneaking up on us. This was something that hadn't happened yet. I sat staring over the top of the brush, hoping I was wrong.

The sun melted behind a low layer of clouds then dipped below the horizon. Evening sped towards us as the clouds lit up in a final golden reflection. Right on cue, four or five heads appeared just at the top of the brush forty yards back from the clearing. I slapped the gunner's leg and announced, "Here they come!" He dropped into position, triggering the same reaction from everyone else except the other half of our platoon who was still unaware of the danger. The heads became bigger and closer. One man appeared at the edge of the clearing. Others joined him. They stayed for a few seconds and then started walking out into the open. Our radioman was whispering into his handset, but no one was paying attention in the other group.

Their point man jerked to a stop as he spotted fifteen guys sitting in the open, leisurely finishing their evening meal. He crouched and backed up to the edge of the brush. They were a hundred yards away from us, but it was time to act. I unlocked my claymore safety, pressed the plunger, and pulled the trigger of my M-16 at the same time. The machine gun opened up, and the other half of our platoon finally hit the dirt. I began yelling for the gunner to work back down the trail so they wouldn't try to stop and fire on the other guys." Thirty seconds of heavy fire elapsed before we stopped shooting. There was no return fire. Thank God we surprised them, though we were too far away to be very effective. Their point man went down with my first shot, and I congratulated the machine gunner for his good work. He needed the praise, and I needed to live with myself.

We carefully walked over to where the body dropped. There was no body, but his AK was there, and a heavy blood trail led off into the brush to our right. He didn't have his rifle, but he had enough strength to crawl away. We'd have to find him, but no one wanted to follow a blood trail. Most VC were terrified of being tortured at the hands of the evil Americans. If he had the strength, he would be waiting somewhere out of sight for the first man who came looking for him.

I couldn't ask anyone else to do it. I had wounded him and it was my job to finish him if I could. There were no volunteers anyway, and the "Old Man" was supposed to be used to this stuff. How can anyone get used to following the blood trail of an enemy soldier?

Everyone lined up along the trail to throw one grenade apiece, hoping to get lucky before I had to walk in after him.

"Fire in the hole!"

We all ducked until the explosions went off. It was time. The bright red stains on the grass and leaves of the low bushes were easy to follow.

My heart raced. I had followed blood trails of deer, but not a human, and not one who might still have a pistol or a grenade to defend himself. He was bleeding enough to see ahead where he crawled around some brush and went between two small bushes about fifteen feet away. I couldn't see any blood beyond that. I stopped and waited for movement, then crept forward a little to see what might be a foot lying in the grass. A couple more steps with my M-16 raised and there he was. He didn't move, but I had seen that before. I fired half a dozen rounds and walked closer. He was dead. Part of his skull was missing. It could have been from a bullet or one of the grenades. It didn't matter; he was no longer a threat to anyone.

In the little daylight that was left, we decided to switch locations since the VC we hadn't killed knew where we were. This time we set up in the brush at the other end of the trail, not out in the open where we might be seen in the moonlight. It was hard to find a place large enough to lie down in the thick brush, but we all managed to acquire a semi-comfortable spot as darkness covered our hiding place.

My watch was early, so I quickly fell asleep curled up between several bushes. Adrenaline bolted me upright at the boom of a claymore and crackle of M-16 fire. I came up with my rifle at the shoulder and swung it towards a shadow running down the trail. There was a split second to squeeze off a short burst then quickly look for other movement. Seeing none, I relaxed a little and allowed myself to start waking up. I mumbled to the guy on the other side of a bush.

"That was a heck of an alarm clock. What happened?"

"There were three or four of them. I blew my claymore but I think I missed 'em." We searched a short distance from our position but didn't venture out very far. Flashlights were not an option; they were an easy target. The next morning we found blood on the trail and searched a larger area, but the wounded or dead had already been carried off. For once we may have outsmarted the VC, or maybe it was a totally different group that just stumbled into our field of fire. It didn't matter. We made it through, and our only loss was a few hours of sleep. We ate a quick breakfast and walked back to our firebase.

Instead of heading for the showers, we went straight to the bunker where we left Fast Horse's duckling about a week before. There were no peeping sounds as we made our duck calls. Maybe one of the artillery guys was taking care of it. Fast Horse went down into the bunker and came out holding a little ball of motionless yellow feathers. We had been gone too long, and no one else cared enough to feed it. This was a crappy place to be.

Next door there was a bunker we called the "cave." It wasn't on the defensive perimeter and had no open holes or fighting ports, just a single entrance and a bench made of sandbags around all four walls. Someone had hooked up an extension cord and hung Christmas tree lights on the walls. I think the artillery guys made it as a hideout and a place where they could smoke dope in privacy. Of course, when we were in camp, we took over just about anything we wanted. No one would argue with us. We were the crazy guys who shot people, and we didn't bother to downplay the reputation.

After dinner Dray said, "Why don't we go down to the cave?" He was a pothead even before he got to this dope capital of the world.

"It's a little early, isn't it?"

"Nah, let's go!"

I followed him down the steps that had been carved out of the dirt. He pulled back the blanket covering the doorway. There was an unusually large crowd already there. I walked in looking for a seat; the benches were packed. Only one place left, right beside Fast Horse, who was smiling from ear to ear. Oh well, I didn't have anything against him.

A string hung from the middle of the ceiling. At the bottom was a loop that hung about a foot off the floor, and in the loop was a joint. Smoking became a group sport. After taking a hit, the joint went swinging across the bunker on its way to someone on the other side. At the time, it was hilarious to watch. Our reactions were a little too relaxed to grab the streak of fire without getting burned. A bungled catch cost a penalty two hits before you could pass it on.

Between burst of laughter, the conversation got pretty stupid as might be expected from a bunch of screw-offs who had nothing better to do than watch a joint fly through the air. The subject of gays was brought up, and someone asked, “Hey, Wright, what would you do if you were approached by a gay person?” I reacted by making a cross with my fingers and instinctively held it up to Fast Horse as if he were a vampire. This brought howls of laughter.

Then Fast Horse put his hand on my knee and said, “Well, you know how I am, don’t you?”

I looked at him in amazement, realizing for the first time that the rumors were true. He really was gay, and I’d been had. My mouth dropped open in surprise. Of course, this brought even more howls of laughter. Nobody was being mean. It was just a joke they pulled on me because I was so naive and had treated Fast Horse like he wasn’t gay. I was embarrassed but not angry. I didn’t have to prove anything to these guys.

- 19 -

THE SPIDER HOLE

Dray was a good friend even though he helped set me up at the "cave." He was easygoing, never got ruffled, and was funny, especially when we got loaded. Because of our friendship, I talked him into his first sham. We heard they were looking for volunteers to go to sniper school.

"Dray, why don't you try it? The school is six weeks long. If you don't like it, you can always flunk out. Think about it. You'll be off line for six weeks!" He saw the light and volunteered.

It was just after a medal awards ceremony when Dray came back to the platoon from sniper school. They gave me a Silver Star for being the only one left alive from my squad that day in January when my old company got ambushed. I never did feel right about that medal. God had saved me, but the citation read like I had done something important. Dray had purposely flunked out of sniper school. It was easy to understand why. If he had succeeded, he would have to pull the trigger on individuals that were no threat to us because they were so far away. I couldn't do it either. There was no problem shooting someone who was close enough to shoot me, but the long-range stuff was a little harder to justify. I added that one to my growing list of rules for my version of the proper war. Anyway, it was good to have Dray back with us.

He was not only a friend, but he was also willing to walk point. My compulsion to protect these guys had me following him down a trail that led from a cool morning walk through heavy jungle into the stagnant heat of tall elephant grass interspersed with clusters of large brush and a few trees. The grass was so thick that there was no place to walk except on the trail. Dray hesitated a moment, then started down the trail. We couldn't see a thing except the walls of the thick grass that constrained us. It wasn't a good situation. A hundred yards down the trail, Dray spun around and said, "There's a chicken!"

"Huh? Where?"

Chickens were not uncommon around VC base camps, but a camp in such a tangle of elephant grass and brush would be unusual. He moved forward a couple steps. POW, POW, POW! We dropped to the ground, and the rest of the platoon did the same. Dray was wounded, but still very much alive, judging from the pain he was in. My eyes frantically looked for movement or dust from a muzzle blast, anything to locate where the shots had come from. The heavy grass concealed everything. POW, POW, POW! A green tracer streaked up from the ground just a few feet to my left. He had to be in a spider hole not more than an arm's length from the end of my barrel!

All he had to do was lower his rifle to ground level and pull the trigger. He could easily shoot everyone within fifteen feet. He had to be stopped! I held my M-16 up over my head, aimed the barrel down at the point where the tracer came from, and held the trigger on full automatic. He fired again, his tracers cutting the air just over my head.

He had to be crouched in the spider hole with his AK resting on the edge pointing upward. He was probably too afraid to lift his hands or body enough to lower the rifle down to where he could shoot me. Without crawling into his hole, I'd have to try to hit his rifle so it wouldn't shoot anymore or get real lucky and shoot his hands, anything to make him stop firing!

My twenty-round clip was gone in less than two seconds, and it was time to reload. Will he realize I'm out of ammo and take the opportunity to rise up and shoot me? More shots cracked through the air just inches over my head! I jammed in another clip and started firing again, desperately trying to hit something! My best chance might be to shoot while he was up in his hole shooting at me! Another magazine sprayed from my rifle into the grass beside the trail. He stopped firing. Maybe he had to change magazines. I slammed in a fresh clip and squeezed off another burst. My mind raced. How about a grenade? He was so close, but the thick grass between us made him invisible. If it missed by even a little I'd be covered with shrapnel. If he was still alive, he might be able to toss the grenade back. At three feet, this wasn't the place for a grenade.

Three of my six extra clips were gone in less than thirty seconds. Number four was seated, but I started firing on semi-automatic. My goal now shifted to keep him down in his hole where he couldn't lay his AK down and kill me or someone else. Another clip gone! At least he had stopped shooting. I kept firing slowly, still hoping to catch his hand if he raised it up to shoot again. Only one clip left! As hard as it was, I stopped shooting. He might jump out of his hole to run or worse, charge me with his bayonet. If there was a next move, it was his. Seconds ticked by in silence. My mind took the opportunity to refocus. There had to be others. Cases of ammo were stacked fifteen feet down the trail where it split, probably to access the bunkers along the perimeter of a base camp—and there I was down to my last clip. Stew came running up from the rear. He wanted to be a cowboy. "Hey, there's ammo cases stacked over there! Let's go in and take the whole camp!"

"Got any extra ammo?"

He just looked and didn't respond.

"I need more ammo or I'm not going anyplace. Dray, do you have any ammo left?" He tossed over a single clip.

"Stew, Dray is wounded, and I don't have any ammo. You can go but I'm staying here."

Stew had extended his tour so he could stay longer in this violent insanity. That made me not trust him. While I shifted into survival mode, Stew wanted to go for the gusto! The rest of the platoon decided not to follow him either.

He didn't fit in well with the rest of us eight balls. He told us he had extended his tour and quit the LRRPs (pronounced "Lerps"). I'd heard about the LRRPs.

Recon was a little crazy, but as far as I was concerned, the LRRPs (Long Range Reconnaissance Patrols) had gone off the deep end. They worked in teams of five to seven. They would be flown miles out into the jungle to locate VC base camps and other targets, then they would run back to their own base of operations. They had to run because, according to Stew, they were usually being chased by the VC. Their groups were small enough that the VC felt they could kill or capture them. Stew told us stories about running for days to keep ahead of the VC.

He told us that his LRRP patrol had captured a VC base camp single-handedly. They all carried "LAWS" (Light Antitank Weapons), which was our equivalent of the RPG or rocket propelled grenade. They lined up outside an enemy camp and fired their LAWS into the middle. The VC thought they were being bombed and most of them ran away. The LRRPs went in to take over the camp, but a few VC had stayed behind. The LRRPs managed to take the camp, but nearly all of them were wounded in the process. Stew was one of two men left standing after it was all over. He never did tell us why he transferred out of a unit he seemed to like so much. His story may or may not have been true; I was way past caring whether people lied about their war experiences. It seemed that those who needed to brag had not been touched by the horror or the helplessness that kept the rest of us knowingly silent.

Charging a surprised base camp may have worked for the LRRPs, but we had lost the advantage of surprise. Taking this camp wasn't worth any more casualties to me. The VC wouldn't pick up and run because we shot up a few magazines of M-16 ammo. They'd dive for their bunkers, and I wasn't about to walk up on them to see who was home. Stew was frustrated, and a little twinge of guilt swept me for not encouraging him to go ahead and take the camp. Sure I was afraid, but I'd already crossed the bridge of being willing to die if it was necessary. Taking over this camp for a couple of hours and capturing some ammunition didn't seem to balance with the high probability of additional dead or wounded. It didn't meet my definition of being "necessary" to die for. Another note had just been added to the growing list of rules for Dave's war.

Everyone had stopped shooting now. Stew stood beside Dray, who was dealing with his pain and trying to reload his M-16 at the same time. I pointed at the spider hole just off the trail to his left. Stew glanced and dropped to the ground. I asked if he'd seen anything in the spider hole.

"There's blood all over the place," he said.

"I guess we got lucky."

It crossed my mind to toss a phosphorus grenade into the stack of ammo cases and the dry grass. The whole place would go up in flames and exploding ammo! It would be cool, but we had to get far enough away to bring in a medevac. How big would the fire get in this elephant grass, and how far would the bullets travel?

It was time to do the responsible thing first, get Dray out to a safe spot where he could be evacuated.

"Dray that was some chicken! How are you doing?" He was lying on his stomach.

"I can't turn over. He shot me in the upper thigh!"

"We need to carry you out. The medevac is on the way."

"Try to get me up, maybe I can walk."

We lifted him to his feet. He couldn't put weight on his legs so we tried to carry him with his arms around our necks. We got out of range of VC retaliation, but it was hard for the three of us to walk side by side down the narrow trail. With our stumbling and jerking, Dray needed to lie down and be still for a while before we got him back to the nearest clearing. In spite of his pain, he laughed and joked. "When people want to see my war wound, I'll have to pull my pants down."

The medevac was coming in about seventy-five yards up the trail, and someone ran to bring the medics back to where we'd stopped. We loaded Dray face down on the stretcher and followed as the medics carried him back to the chopper. I tried to console him.

"Man, you got the million dollar wound! No broken bones, and you'll be in the hospital for a couple of months with nurses from home! They might even send you back to the World!"

He grinned through the pain and waved as a cloud of dust was kicked up by the accelerating rotor blades. We turned our backs to the wind blast as the chopper leaned forward and rose from the ground. I'd miss him, but he would be out of the jungle now. He would probably be making some nurse laugh in a few days while he was recovering. That was better than being out here.

Back at the firebase, I reflected on the latest near miss. My nerves were raw. How could I go on without embracing it and living for the adrenalin, the danger, and the killing?

I couldn't let my life stand for that, to become like Stew, who didn't want to go home. But there were still three months to go. Three months can last forever here. Life can change in three minutes. You could die in less than three seconds. How could I manage another three months? There were no odds left for me, and I couldn't rest in the fleeting peace that was beyond my understanding and control— God had brought me this far and He'd get me home. The time came all too quickly to put reasoning aside and get ready to go out again.

Our next mission took us into unfamiliar country. There were no wide river valleys. Instead, small rice paddies were sandwiched between triple canopy jungle and heavily traveled trails everywhere. Several days were filled with foreboding, but nothing unusual happened until the day we got lost. The entire morning was spent moving as quickly as we could. The tactic worked well. If the VC didn't have time to run ahead and set up an ambush, then we only had to worry about running into them, and the surprise usually worked to our advantage. We had been hiking so quickly that before he realized it, we apparently crossed into an area that was not on the lieutenant's map.

Stew was convinced that because of his LRRP background he could lead us back to safety. I didn't know where we were and was always happy to let someone else walk point, so the lieutenant let him take over. I picked up the rear to provide cover while we moved through this uncharted territory.

Stew kept up the pace, but he didn't try to retrace where we'd come from. That could have easily been a mistake. Lunch came and went, and we were still moving through an area where nothing was recognizable on our map. The large trees thinned, and the soil changed from red clay to a dark gray volcanic ash. I'd never seen this type of country before. There were no rice paddies, rivers, or streams and the largest trees weren't more than twenty feet tall. It was hot, dry, and dusty and there was no shade from the dense but short trees surrounding us. It felt eerie and foreign compared to the areas where we normally operated.

From the rear it took a few minutes to realize that Stew was walking a well-used trail. My nerves tensed, and I kept looking over my shoulder to make sure the trail remained clear. Stew took the right fork of a "Y" that veered off the main trail. About fifty feet beyond the "Y" my instincts prodded me to check the rear once again. My rifle raised automatically as a half-dozen VC trotted passed the opening on the main trail we'd just left. The last three would have been easy targets, but none of them had weapons, shirts, or shoes. They just wore their black pajama bottoms and looked like they were out on a conditioning run like back in basic.

We had to be at the edge of a base camp. These guys were no immediate threat to us, and my firing could bring the whole camp down on us. Word was passed forward that unarmed VC were behind us, and we'd better get moving. A couple of miles of quick-time brought us to the middle of a rolling plain of lava beds. Big blocks of lava, boulders, deep holes, and crevices made progress difficult but also gave some protection if the VC were following. Our lieutenant abandoned his pride and called for artillery to spot our location. We could barely hear the first half dozen explosions. We were out of range of our own artillery, but they finally got a few rounds close enough so we could get a bearing and estimate the distance. They were going to send slicks to pick us up, since we were out too far to walk back.

During the wait of nearly an hour, Stew and the lieutenant had a few words about being more lost now than when we'd started, and it was pretty dumb to be out here where the VC might catch us without direct artillery support. It wasn't a good situation but to his credit, the lieutenant never let it happen again. Finally, we heard that sweet sound of incoming choppers. It took about fifteen minutes for the lieutenant to talk them into our position. We didn't want to pop smoke too early and give the VC time to ambush them and us.

Stew didn't stay with us after that. Maybe we weren't gutsy enough for him, or maybe we weren't impressed enough by him. His leaving wasn't much of a loss. I wonder if he found what he was looking for.

Back in the safety of the firebase my private war began to rage again. I'd been in country nearly nine months. God had been so good to me. What if I screwed up and made Him mad? Would He stop protecting me? And it wasn't just me, it was all those around me. How could I think of going home? How could I not think of going home?

- 20 -

TRIPWIRE

When not fighting the inner battle, thirty other guys and I would look for something to fill the few days of downtime between excursions into the jungle. Our range of entertainment was a little more restricted than back in the World. We could listen to the radio, play cards, write letters, eat whatever we could scrounge, and get loaded. We couldn't go into town to whoop it up, but there was usually a mama-san outside the gate who would sell about anything we wanted.

Vietnamese women were very resourceful when it came to supplementing their income by selling just about anything GIs had an appetite for. Most firebases were built next to some sort of road and had a main entrance and gate. Women and children would hang around the gate with anything we wanted for the American money we'd pay. Their normal lifestyles were hopelessly disrupted; their men were often dead or away somewhere fighting us. We would pay five dollars just to get our clothes washed. That might provide enough food for a week or two (or buy Daddy a new AK). Some ladies carried baskets of goodies ranging from watches to dope packed in cigarette cartons that looked like the cellophane had never been touched. If they didn't have a requested item, they would trot to the village and bring it back within twenty minutes! The black market thrived with a flare of capitalistic greed seldom exhibited in the States.

One Mexican kid thought he would take advantage of these third-world, back-country neophytes in the system of free enterprise. He had a twenty-peso note (worth less than twenty cents) and figured he could convince Mama-san that it was roughly equal to twenty dollars, American. He spent about fifteen minutes haggling for a Timex watch. A worried expression indicated she suspected a scam but didn't quite know for sure. Reluctantly, she handed over the watch in exchange for the twenty pesos. He walked away beaming and bragging to everyone how he'd gotten to Mama-san. Fifteen minutes later his watch stopped. Opening up the back of his new fourteen-jewel Timex, he found no jewels were left. We had a great laugh about Mama-san's revenge.

The moon in Southeast Asia was bright enough to read and write letters by. Evenings within the protective perimeter of a firebase were sometimes the most peaceful and best times to write home. Conveying fear, pain, and helplessness wasn't acceptable in our "good time" culture, so writing about things that were happening became impossible. It would cause too much anxiety at home. There was nothing they could do about any of this, so why burden them with the details. It definitely limited the subjects to write about, and it set up a huge gap between everyone at home and myself.

Radio Vietnam was OK. They played all the latest tunes from home, which fit well with our desire to keep the daydreams alive about what we would do when we got back to the World. Fortunately and unfortunately, it wasn't like World War II where we'd be stuck for the duration. Going home after three hundred and sixty-five days was guaranteed, *if* we survived! That was the trick—surviving! Daydreaming helped. As the radio played the Top Ten, we spent "peaceful" hours remembering people we loved, places we'd been, and things we had done just months before.

Card games were serious business. There were kids who could make the dealers in Vegas look like losers. They always seemed to be from one of the artillery or mortar companies who had lots of time to practice. I was way out of their league. Some poor kids gambled away their entire paychecks in one sitting. I was too conservative to risk losing much money, so I'd watch for a while and leave when it stopped being a "fun" game. It wasn't cool to play Hearts or Pinochle in this place where kids had to become "killers of other men."

That left eating and getting loaded as recreational outlets for me. Sometimes they went hand in hand. "Smoking and joking" often led to ravenous binges that set us on the prowl for food. There wasn't much variety to choose from.

We staggered over to the mess tent one night trying to hold back our snickers with hands over our mouths. The cook slept inside, and officers slept next door where the cases of food were stacked. It was basic training with the eight balls all over again. No one wanted to take the chance of getting caught. What could they do, put me in jail? That would be safer than walking point! I sort of crept over to the stack of cases. Everything was canned. I flipped back the flap of an open case and lifted out a large one. It was too dark to read, so I tossed whatever it was to one of the guys standing a safe distance away. One more large can from a different box and a case of Cs should do it. The footsteps of my partners in crime faded away when a lone figure emerged from the darkness. Rats, caught red-handed! I hefted the Cs onto my shoulder and started walking, hoping against hope that the man coming towards me wasn't an officer. We passed without a word. That night we feasted on chicken, ham, and our pick from a case of Cs. It could have been a lot more fun in a different place.

Once in a while we would get a show from the tanks or PCs that parked outside our perimeter. They were nervous people, which was understandable knowing a VC could kill an entire track crew with a single RPG. One particularly dark night they spotted movement by the tree line a quarter mile away. Their machine guns started belching red tracers from four or five different positions. A hundred streaks of red phosphorous hit the ground then ricocheted in all directions, straight up in the air, sideways, even spiraling and somersaulting through the blackness. A few cannon rounds flashed, followed by fan shaped explosions a split-second later. It was quite a sight for grunts carrying M-16s and a few grenades for protection.

It was a couple of days after the tanks left that the VC took their revenge. I'd pick up my wash from the front gate and was heading back to my bunker that evening. There was quite a competition for our laundry between one small boy and several girls from the nearby village. He spoke broken English, wore a GI shirt, ball cap, and dog tags just like one of those little orphan kids in the old war movies. We paid three bucks for the luxury of having our fatigues washed, starched, and pressed. Of course it didn't make any difference out in the jungle, but back in the firebase, or at the big base camps, it was a sign that you really had your stuff together. Most of us favored the little guy. The girls would pout, and someone would give them laundry or buy something to make them smile again. It became quite a game. We paid more money than most of the villagers could make in a week, so it became serious business between the children.

I started down the road to my bunker and caught sight of someone sitting on the crapper, which was only twenty-five yards from the front gate. Why did they build it so close to the gate, and why they didn't build the usual "house" was beyond me? It was just a square box with one hole and a toilet seat on the top. We learned not to be modest, but here everything was exposed to everyone, even the kids at the gate. As my mind started wandering off to something else, an explosion behind the crapper lifted the guy who had just seated himself and sent him flying through the air in somersaults. He landed face down about 50 yards from me. He didn't seem to be hurt too badly, just in shock mostly. He began to move slowly then started mumbling something about not even being able to take a crap around here. He was right, no place was safe or sacred.

Time came to go back out into the jungle. We had a new guest join us, a Ranger, fresh from the world and just out of training. Henderson was a little cocky and overconfident.

He'd been well trained, but I suspected no amount of training in the States could prepare him for this reality. We got acquainted the evening before we went out. He didn't ask many questions but held back a little to not appear like the typical new guy or "cherry." If he would have let himself be a little more human, I wouldn't have done it, but he needed to discover his limitations out here before he got himself or someone else into trouble.

"If you really want to know what's going on over here, you need to walk point for a while."

"Well, I guess I could do that."

My conscience got me. "I'll follow you and try to point things out if you miss anything."

He stayed cool and shrugged his shoulders as though, "I could follow him if I wanted to."

The next day we walked into an open area that had been settled years before. There was an old graveyard with headstones and a fence still guarding it from intruders. The direction we were going led diagonally through an old tree-lined field, and we were headed towards one corner where the trees met. A trail crossed our path and headed roughly in the same direction. The back of my neck began to tingle, so I stopped to check things out. The Ranger kept moving another forty feet up the trail before I whispered to him, "Hey, it looks like there might be spider holes under those trees." He stopped and stared. "We'd better check them out. It would be a great place for an ambush."

He waited for me to catch up so we could walk together. If there was an ambush, they would have already blown it on the Ranger, so at this point I wasn't too worried. We walked over the tree-line on our right. Sure enough, there were spider holes dug under every other tree. Thank God nobody was in them. We found the same thing under the trees to our left.

"How did you see those?" asked the Ranger.

"I didn't at first. I felt them." He gave me one of those "you're weird" looks. By now, weird was OK as long as it kept us alive. He left after that mission, hopefully a little more humble.

We had another guest a few weeks later. He was a rather hefty, grimy-looking cook who wanted to go home with a "CIB" (Combat Infantry Badge) on his shirt. CIBs weren't handed out like candy; you actually had to work with a combat unit for a period of time before you could get one. It was one of the few distinctions between the grunts and all the support troops. A CIB meant recognition; you were one of the few who knew what it was like to be shot at or to shoot at someone else. If you made it home, you had a story to tell. Ironically, most of us with stories can't tell them.

Anyway, this cook decided he wanted his tour in Vietnam to stand for something more than heartburn and bad food. He wanted to show people back home he was a real man, like John Wayne. He asked to join our platoon then next time we went out. Unfortunately, he'd been in the kitchen too long to feel any real danger of being a target out in the jungle. Without thinking, he lit up a cigarette one night while we were on ambush. Before I had a chance to do anything, two other guys grabbed his cigarette and told him the VC could see the match and lit cigarette a hundred yards away. He tried to pooh-pooh the idea but they said if he ever did that again, they'd shoot him. That ended the whispered conversation. I couldn't have done it better myself.

The next day I walked point up a trail that led right down the middle of a clearing with heavy jungle on both sides. It wasn't a good place to be so I moved quickly. Just past an area that had been torn up by PC tracks, something hit my foot. The instant it happened I knew I'd hit a tripwire. My foot was still in mid-stride, and I couldn't stop the momentum. My heart sank, realizing I had just triggered a booby trap. My body fell to the ground before completing the last step, and the whole platoon was so in tune that they followed in a single motion. Everyone except Cooky. As soon as we hit the ground, a flare popped at the edge of the jungle. Cooky just stood there. He laughed and asked why we were all on the ground just because of a flare.

"If it'd been a Chinese claymore, you'd be dead!"

He tried to laugh it off as we got up. The flare must have been left by the PCs to illuminate anyone walking the trail at night. Cooky transferred without getting his CIB. It was for the best. He was dangerous.

- 21 -

WOOD TRUCKS

With less than one hundred days to go, I became a "two-digit midget," but the countdown still wouldn't go any faster than one day at a time. How many more days would I be lucky? Going out into the field was getting more difficult as time went on. The prospect of being killed in my last few months was real. It had happened to others. What a waste to go through so much pain, get so close, and not go home alive.

The platoon walked southeast out of the firebase and began to make a big arc to the west. On our second day we broke out of the jungle on the edge of several rice paddies. As usual, we stopped at the tree line. Exposing ourselves in the clearing without checking it out first would have been a mistake. The jungle continued unbroken again three hundred yards across the rice paddies. We stood waiting for everyone to emerge from the trees when someone dropped to his knees and motioned for everyone to get down. A half dozen VC were trotting up the trail between the paddies and the tree line directly across from us.

We got down and watched. It was a little too far for our M-16's. They probably knew that and felt safe enough to just keep moving quickly along the trail. They were carrying something. Two groups of two had cylindrical objects on their shoulders that were too fat to be carrying-poles. They were 122 mm rockets, the kind they'd shoot into our big base camps once in a while. They didn't waste them on us, but it usually made the news back home, and it made the REMF's (Rear Echelon Mother . . . . . .) pretty nervous.

Our lieutenant radioed for artillery. By the time the 105s cranked up, the VC were out of sight down the trail. We tried to start the cannon fire a few hundred yards ahead of where we guessed they were, and then walk the explosions back down the trail forcing the VC to run back to us. It didn't work, but the 105s made a heck of a racket. Trees went down and brush was hurled up in the air as we watched from five hundred yards.

The next two days were uneventful. We were still heading in an arc back towards our firebase. The heat of the afternoon was softened by the shade of the trees we were walking through, but it looked like the jungle was thinning and we'd be back in the heat with a clearing up ahead. Without a shot being fired, everyone crouched and stared through the trees. I crawled forward from my position in the rear. There, moving through the clearing, maybe four hundred yards in front of us, was an entire column of VC. They were walking single file through the clearing, so we could only see maybe twenty-five at a time. There was no way to tell how many had already walked through or how many were still coming.

I wanted to get close enough to take advantage of this golden opportunity. They'd caught us in the open so many times, maybe we could return the favor. We got within two hundred yards when the last of their column entered the clearing. There were those two rockets again! We didn't get close enough to fire before they disappeared into the foliage on the far side of the clearing. We sat transfixed while the lieutenant called in what we'd seen. It was too big a prize to pass up. The battalion commander decided to go after them.

Armor units were driven out ahead to intercept them. We would be the blocking force if they were driven back in our direction. As soon as we stepped into the clearing, I recognized it as the same place I'd hit the tripwire a week before. We spread out across the clearing in a defensive line. It felt uncomfortable to be in the open with no cover and one protecting our rear.

The blistering sun beat on us all afternoon. Fortunately, nothing happened and we were released to head back to the firebase which was only a half-mile away. We saddled up and started through the jungle where the VC column had disappeared. In minutes we broke out the other side. The firebase was a quarter-mile to the northeast, but there were four or five flatbed trucks parked between us and the tree line. A couple of men sitting on stumps looked surprised as we walked out of the jungle fifty yards from them. They grabbed their chainsaws and started cutting fallen trees into firewood. We paid little attention. Our focus was on a shower, hot food, and sleeping inside the perimeter that night.

The next morning we were told to head out and walk through the village next to our firebase. Something was up. We hadn't done this since pacification ceased a couple of months earlier. Oh well, "Ours is not to reason why . . ." We picked up our rifles and some ammo. No need to take anything else; we would be back in a few hours.

A rain shower from the night before made the ground soft and gave a fresh smell to everything as we walked into the village. A lot of people were out milling around. Was it some Buddhist holiday? There was no parade or gathering point, just people wandering around. They seemed to be generally heading for the road that ran along the downhill side of their village next to a stream. I headed down to the road to take a look myself. Around the bend at the far end of the village came the whine of motors revving and gears grinding as the wood trucks we'd seen the previous day came swaying into view. They came up a little grade in front of me where they might have had trouble on the muddy road.

The first truck passed, and the second started up the hill. He'd just reached the top and had to stop behind the first, which was waiting for a villager to get his water buffalo out of the road. The driver's eyes followed me as I stared at him and then at the truck.

There was that feeling of looking at something that wasn't right but not knowing what it was. The driver was getting more nervous. I looked at the wheels and the two-inch deep ruts they made in the mud. A fully loaded truck should make deeper ruts than those. The wood was neatly stacked at least eight feet high and completely filled the bed from front to back. There had to be tons of wood on these trucks. How could they move through the mud so easily?

Why were all these villagers milling around? What about the water buffalo? Why couldn't Papa-san get him out of the way before the trucks got here? My suspicions were rising, and I glared at the driver, who turned white as a sheet. He reached for something between the seats without taking his eyes off me. My rifle barrel moved towards him. What if these wood trucks were being used as transports? What if the wood was just stacked around the outside, and the inside was left hollow to carry troops? The VC didn't have deuce-and-a-halves or regular military vehicles. These wood trucks were a perfect cover.

From fifteen feet away I could only see darkness in the cracks between the pieces of wood. If the stack was hollow, I couldn't tell from the outside. If I stopped the trucks to search, how would the occupants inside react (if there were any)? If it were me in there, I wouldn't want to get caught inside a wooden box and just give up. I'd rather try to fight my way out and make a run for freedom. How would they get out of the truck? There was enough room underneath the trucks for a trap door, or maybe there was a door hidden in the tail end of the stack of wood, or maybe they simply undid the tarp covering the top.

My imagination saw fifteen to twenty troops pouring out of each of the four trucks. There were only about twenty-five of us, and half were still back in the village. We couldn't control what would happen if they tried to break out. I looked back at the terrified driver and thought, there are too many villagers. Which side would they be on in a firefight? Maybe they came out to wave goodbye to sons and husbands being shipped to a new location. There were too few of us, and nobody was in a good position or frame of mind for a sudden fight. There'd be too many casualties. I'm letting them go.

It was a decision I've questioned many times. It fulfilled my growing desire to protect myself and those around me. It did nothing to control the VC in our sector, and I felt guilty about that. Maybe we could have caught an entire enemy company hidden in those trucks. Somebody would probably have gotten a medal, but many of us would have died on that hillside with no cover. If my instincts were right, the driver had a story to tell his kids of how he almost got caught driving a troop transport through an enemy patrol. The GIs were too dumb to see what was happening. But one of those GIs had decided the risks weren't in his favor, so he survived along with the rest of his platoon that day. It was their kind of war—to pick only the best opportunities—and I had learned how to fight it.

Our next mission was really strange. They asked for volunteers to fly around in helicopters all day and land in LZs (Landing Zones) that were supposed to be hot! All we had to do was jump out of the helicopters and fire up a lot of ammo, throw a few grenades and see if we could get return fire. If the VC shot back, Cobras would move in and fire them up. It sounded like fun!

We loaded up and jumped onto the choppers. Within ten minutes we were flying into a "hot LZ." The door gunners opened up on the tree-line on both sides, and the choppers hovered for a moment as we jumped out and hit the ground. As the slicks were making a quick exit, we shot up as much ammo and threw as many grenades as we could. There was no response from the surrounding jungle, so we called the choppers to come back and take us to the next LZ. After nine or ten uneventful assaults, it was getting a little boring. We got to play with our toys, but now it seemed like work and it wasn't fun anymore.

After lunch we went out again. We flew into a narrow field of rice paddies with a ditch running through the middle. We went through our routine and again nothing happened. A kid named Spencer was carrying our radio. He was a tall, heavy kid, bigger than most. He and the lieutenant had called the choppers to let them know it was OK to come pick us up. We waited a long time. They must have had to refuel or maybe they just took a break. We sat around the ditch because it was the best protection in the middle of the open rice paddies. For some reason my eyes glanced at Spencer. He was calling the choppers again to see how long they would be.

He started to bend over at the waist the same instant an explosion boomed from the tree line to my left. Spencer stayed bent over and a whoosh of sparks passed inches over the radio strapped to his back. It was an RPG. They were aiming at the biggest target in our group. If they had hit the radio, shrapnel would have gone everywhere. The shooter was good; he would have hit his target squarely if Spencer hadn't picked that exact moment to tie his shoe.

We all hit the ground and returned fire on the tree line. A half-dozen shots came back and then everything went quiet. Two Cobras moved in as soon as they heard we were engaged. They put on a show, circling and bobbing up and down to get the best shot. The VC just ran away. We checked the edge of the jungle and found nothing. The slicks came back and took us to our firebase. We shot up so much ammo with so few results that the exercise was called off.

We still hadn't suffered a single death from enemy fire in Recon. But, as the days slowly turned into weeks, I was getting closer and closer to becoming a mental casualty.

I started having anxiety attacks just hours before it was time to go out into the jungle. Once through the gate, my nerves calmed down because I had to focus on staying alive.

In spite of the chest pains and a couple of previous episodes, I forced myself out the gate for one more uneventful mission. When we got back, I had to talk to someone. Maybe the chaplain could get me off line. He listened to my conflicting desires of wanting to stay with my platoon to protect them, and wanting to get off line so I could go home. I'd been there the longest, had the most experience, and could see things that they couldn't sometimes. I didn't get into all the times God had saved me. He seemed a little helpless and cut me off, suggesting a doctor might be able to do more.

Great! I didn't want a medical discharge. I needed someone to recognize that I had done all I could, for as long as I could. A medic was my next hope. The thing that tripped him was my reference to the platoon as "my people." It was my responsibility to keep them alive. He would talk to someone and see if they could get me into Lai Khe to talk to a shrink.

I didn't like where this was going, but I had to get off line or talk to someone who could resolve my conflict. Either solution would be OK, but I couldn't go on with these anxiety attacks. My body was forcing me to change my thinking or change my situation.

Word came back that I'd been reassigned to the support company. I didn't have to go out in the field again. Getting off line almost two months early was unheard of. Everyone had to stay in the jungle up to their last couple of weeks. It made me feel relieved and guilty at the same time.

God had worked another miracle. He got me off line without having to go through the embarrassment of a medical discharge. I didn't have to disobey any orders or go to the hospital. In one short day, my infantry career was over.

- 22 -

THE TOWER

The support company was home for the last two months of my tour. They should have sent me back to the battalion headquarters in Lai Khe, but no one ordered me out of the Recon tent so I just stayed there. An old top sergeant from the support company would come to find me once in a while to ask for help doing odd jobs. He was gruff, old army, but he treated me with respect. He'd been a paratrooper in the "Big War" and broken his back in a bad landing. They told him he'd never walk again, but by sheer willpower and guts, here he was helping build firebases in Vietnam.

One morning he asked for help to clear the brush and bamboo from the perimeter of a new firebase. We loaded into a Chinook and flew to a clearing already bustling with activity. Grudgingly, I joined a small work detail, expecting to spend the rest of the day flailing away at the jungle with axes and machetes. To my surprise, someone had brought out a dozen cases of Bangalore torpedoes. They were five-foot-long tubes, three-inch diameter, filled with explosives. During the Second World War, several of them would be connected end to end and shoved under barbed wire barriers and even through mine fields. When detonated, they would clear a pathway wide enough for men to run through.

We laid them in long strings through the bamboo and brush. They instantly cleared a strip ten to fifteen feet wide. We moved the jungle back in decimated increments as we blew up case after case of torpedoes. It was a little expensive, but we cleared fifty feet in a couple of hours.

The next thing to be done was lay out razor wire around the entire firebase. We strung two rolls on the ground and stacked a third roll on top. It was hard, sweaty work. Helicopters were constantly flying in and out delivering supplies. Their rotor blast caught the wire and rolled it over. We had to go back, untangle five hundred feet of coils and roll it upright again, but this time we drove stakes to hold it down. We even set up a wire protection for the helicopter landing area, something that hadn't been done before. We finished a little before sunset when the firebase commander came out to congratulate us and say how impressed he was with all the work we'd done. I thought to myself, "This was a piece of cake compared to being out in the jungle."

My last two months went well. Besides a few details and guard duty, they left me pretty much alone. Alone was good, since I had little in common with the men in the firebase. They were caught up in the trials of their day—as anyone would be—but a crisis to them might arise from whose turn it was to pull guard duty or who got to go back to Lai Khe with the supply truck that day. I was on another planet; no one was shooting at me, so it was time to kick back. Anything that wasn't life-threatening was trivial, which led to a slight lack of interest or motivation to participate in about 99% of the daily routine of our firebase.

There was still a close connection with my platoon, even while they were out in the jungle. One morning after waking up to the dampness and sounds of drizzling rain on our tent, I knew the guys must be cold and miserable but they would also be coming in that morning. I fired up the wood stove and went searching for all the packets of instant hot chocolate I could find. An hour later, right on cue, they came sloshing in through the wire. A couple of gallons of hot chocolate and a warm tent greeted them. Someone asked where the home baked cookies were.

"Didn't have time to make 'um!"

In spite of the joke, they were pleased that somebody cared in this forgotten place.

One of the oddest odd jobs was to build a "foo-gas" bomb to protect a portion of our perimeter. I had heard of the device but had never made one. It turned out that no one else had either. We were given a container with some sort of powder and a fifty-five gallon drum of gasoline. We mixed the two together, and the gasoline turned to a thin jelly, like napalm. The jelly would stick to anything it touched and burn furiously when ignited.

"OK, how do we explode it and not kill ourselves at the same time?"

My engineering background came galloping to the challenge. This was going to be another toy we could build.

"Let's dig a hole and lay it in at an angle so the end is sticking out of the ground pointing toward the perimeter. We'll put a shape charge behind it and hook up some det-cord to blow off the top at the same time the shape charge explodes. That should throw the gas out in front of us, onto the razor wire."

"Are you sure it will work?"

"It should! We'll sandbag the top and the back so it can't blow back on us."

"Ok, but I don't want to be here if we have to use it"

"Believe me, if we have to use it, you won't care."

We dug the hole about halfway between our bunkers and the razor wire, then laid the drum of napalm in and carefully placed the shape charge behind it so the explosion would go into the bottom of the barrel and push the napalm out the top. We wound det-cord around the top to cut it off when the shape charge detonated. A couple dozen sandbags over the shape charge and the bottom of the barrel completed our homemade firebomb.

A week later, some high-ranking mucky-muck came out to our firebase for part of his tour of the war. The commander wanted to impress him, but there were no real bullets flying so he set up a demonstration of our firepower. We nailed a big sheet of plywood to a tree outside the perimeter to simulate an attacking horde of VC. Of course, the simulation had them attacking in mid-morning, and they were kind enough to hold still just outside the wire while we prepared to shoot everything we had at them.

First, the mortars thumped and exploded around the target. Then they knocked out the blocks of one of the 105s so its barrel could be lowered down to the tree line and fired a canister of flashettes, thousands of little nails that spread out like shotgun pellets to rip apart anything at close range. Then we got to fire a hundred rounds from the M-60 machine gun. There wasn't much left of the plywood at that point. I was duly impressed.

Word came down that the grand finale would be blowing up the "foo-gas" we made last week. I broke into a cold sweat. We were actually going to fire this thing. Maybe it would make sense if we were getting overrun. Who would even have time to notice if it didn't work right. Everyone was standing around waiting to see the show. What if it just blew straight up and some of the napalm fell back on us. I grabbed the detonator and stretched the wire as far back from the bunker as it would go. At least I could run if something went wrong. The safety flipped off and my chest tightened while I squeezed the plunger.

Whoom! A huge ball of flame rose fifty feet in the air. The heat was intense and grew as the ball of fire expanded. Thank God the wind wasn't blowing. There wouldn't have been time enough to run anywhere. Napalm fell in blobs over a one-hundred-foot circle and burned with thick black smoke for the next five minutes. Everyone cheered. My tension eased with a long sigh of relief. This was not a toy. Thank God no one was hurt.

Guard duty consisted of sitting awake on one of the bunkers for a two-hour shift or spending the same amount of time in the guard tower in the middle of camp. The tower was about thirty feet tall and had a sandbag enclosure like you see in most war movies. Someone had put a fifty-caliber machine gun on the north-facing wall. All in all, it was pretty worthless as protection for the camp. It was a great target, and would be the first thing hit with an RPG if the VC were trying to overrun the camp. The gun was so big it couldn't be turned around if the VC decided to attack from any direction but north. The only thing the tower was good for was a 360-degree view of the perimeter.

Night vision scopes were in their infancy. The one in our tower was so big it had to be mounted on a tripod, and the view was in grainy shades of yellow/green and black dots. But if you could hold it steady enough, you could really, kind of, see what was going on even when it was totally black. My turn came in the tower one night. I felt pretty safe even though we were vulnerable to RPGs. No firebase in our battalion had gotten attacked during my tour in-country. In the tower we were above it all. The stars glowed on clear nights. The mosquitoes didn't seem to find us up there. Even the top sergeant couldn't surprise us. It became a regular hangout for a few of us potheads. We would smoke and joke and occasionally look at the perimeter.

The word got out quickly and before long there were a dozen smokers sitting around inside the protective walls of the tower. Most of them were just escaping boredom. I was still trying to let go of my platoon and not feel guilty. There were bowling tournaments to see who would be the last to pass out. No one else was haunted by the horror, so they dropped like flies. I'd make sure someone was awake and pulling guard when the rest of us stumbled back down the ladder to our tents.

It didn't take long for our old top sergeant to figure out what was going on. After a few weeks he could stand it no longer. He waited until we had all gathered just after dark and were well on our way to oblivion. Then he stood at the bottom of the tower and announced that he was coming up. We bolted upright and just stared at each other in shock. The tower started to shake as Top stomped up the steps.

"I'm coming up there to check who's on guard duty and there better not be any one else there!"

"Who's supposed to be on duty?"

"I don't know, what time is it?"

"It's about 9:30."

"Ah . . . ah, Mikey, you're supposed to be on guard from 8:00 to 10:00!"

All the time we were deciding who was going to be the victim, the tower was shaking with Top's footsteps and he's yelling, "There had better not be anyone else in that tower when I get there."

Panic ensued and kids started climbing over the sides and down the corner posts of the tower. The tower was rocking with a dozen kids scrambling down the outside while Top climbed the ladder.

He started yelling, "Hey, who are you? What were you doing in that tower? Come back here, you! Wait a minute, come back here soldier!"

Running away just wasn't in me, but I didn't want to face Top's wrath either, so I slid back under the plywood table made to hold the 50-caliber machine gun. It was pitch black in the shadow. To reassure myself, I passed my hand in front of my face. It was invisible.

The moonlight shined on Top's baldhead as it popped above the step at the level of the floor. I held my breath while he swept our hideout with his eyes. His body continued to rise, taking the last few steps, then his feet stomped onto the floor. He pretended to be angry, but his heart wasn't in it. He was probably trying to hold back his laughter at the sight of all those kids getting slivers climbing down the rough timbers of the tower. I was tempted to reach out and grab his leg, but I held back in case he might not think it was as funny as it appeared to me. A few more gruff words and back down the ladder he went.

I slid out from under the table and almost gave Mikey a heart attack. We had to hold our mouths and swallow our laughter until we knew he was out of earshot. Top didn't really want to catch us or he wouldn't have given the warning at the bottom of the ladder. He just wanted to scare us into not doing what we were doing. He accomplished part of his purpose. The guard tower was no longer a safe place for our social gatherings.

It didn't bother me much. There were only a couple of weeks left before I'd be on that big bird heading home. It wasn't even fun to tease the new kids anymore. A new worry invaded my bleary consciousness. How would I get loaded when I got home? Then the fear struck that I might not be able to stop smoking dope. It scared me so much I quit on the spot and remained straight for my last few days of my vacation in Vietnam. I completed my preparations to leave by giving away the last of my stash, my air mattress (which made me sweat anyway), and my extra camo blanket. I even purchased a couple of fifths for the boozers as a parting gift.

I was actually going home. Nothing else mattered.

- 23 -

HOME

After three hundred and sixty three days in-country, it was time to go back to Bien Hoa and get ready to fly home. I had anticipated this since the first day. I turned in my rifle and gear at our battalion base camp in Lai Khe. It felt strange to not need them anymore. A few of us got on a truck headed for Bien Hoa. They wanted us there a couple of days early to see if we were hooked on hard drugs or had some social disease that might keep us from going back to the World. We drove back through the same streets that had seemed so exotic a year earlier. All I saw now was a sea of foreign people we didn't understand. Some were offended by our arrogance in trying to direct their political future, and others didn't seem to care about politics at all. They just wanted to be left alone by both sides and live in peace. A small number tried to appreciate our good intentions, but our wavering resolve was painting a picture similar to their experience with the French, and we couldn't be trusted. Anyway, I was leaving and they would deal with their own problems. Those left behind would change little if anything. We were wearing out faster than the VC. They had a cause; we couldn't seem to rally behind anything worth dying for.

I got off the truck at the Bien Hoa staging area and wandered over to the Headquarters shack. I didn't realize the level of my apprehension until the relief flooded me when I found my name on the boarding roster. Up to this point there had been an unconscious fear that the Army might lose track of my paperwork and not let me go home. Even today, I have occasional nightmares about having to go back for a second tour because of some paperwork mix-up. That detail taken care of, I went looking for a bunk to use for the next couple of nights.

"Hey, Wright, is that you?"

I turned to see Rob and Thor walking towards me. They made it! It was hard to believe that all three of us had survived.

They were skinny and drawn and had the same haunted look in their eyes. We got bunks close together and tried to bridge the chasm of the past year. Thor explained in slow sentences that his firebase had been overrun. He and two others were outside the wire on an LP (Listening Post) when the VC charged through the jungle en masse. He and the others hid in a clump of bamboo during the attack. They had to kill one VC who tried to climb through the bamboo between them. There were unspoken volumes of fear, helplessness, and guilt for hiding and surviving between the spoken phrases. Rob stayed pretty quiet. Bits and pieces were all we managed before tears and anger threatened to overtake us. Each of us had survived the horror. There was no glory or pride in it and no way to return to the carefree innocence of a year ago.

New recruits were unloaded in a different area. The Army probably didn't want us mixing together. One group of new kids drove by in a deuce-and-a-half. They looked so young with their shinny scrubbed faces, their clean uniforms, new OD ball caps, and undershirts! We stood at the edge of the dusty road watching them rumble by. Some turned to stare back. They must have wondered if we were in the same Army with our long hair, boonie hats, and dirty wrinkled uniforms hanging from haggard bodies. I felt sorry for them. They had no idea of what was going to happen to them in the coming year. There was no way they could prepare for it or even prevent themselves from becoming the same grizzled images they were staring at. Each would have his own story and return home changed or dead.

The next day we took blood tests and listened to lectures about drugs and what souvenirs were illegal to take home. The following morning we got in line to get our tickets for the plane. This was really it. I had held a little back even to that point, thinking we might get hit by a rocket or have something weird happen to prevent us from going home. A clerk handed me a ticket and said to hold it up against my chest as the line continued. It seemed a little juvenile, but I would put up with just about anything at that point to go home. There was a little second lieutenant around the next corner looking at each man in the line as they passed.

I was just about to walk by when he snatched the ticket right out of my hand! I almost decked him! He had no idea what that ticket meant to me. In an arrogant little voice he recited some section of military code and told me that before going back to the States, the handlebars of my mustache would have to be trimmed even with the corners of my mouth. I glared at him and thought, "If you only knew what I've been through to get here, you'd realize how close you are to getting your throat ripped out right here in front of everyone."

Fortunately, I held back long enough to realize that losing a couple of inches of facial hair was nothing to get my ticket back. I walked to the nearby restroom, took out a razor, and removed the offending facial hair along with a lot of personal individuality. I returned in a controlled rage and grabbed my ticket from his hand. He started to say something but changed his mind when he saw the look on my face. Back in line and heading out the door, I uttered some obscenity just loud enough for him to hear.

Once out the door there would be no further interruptions. It would have been akin to standing in front of a cattle stampede. Thor and Rob saved a seat for me. The doors were closed, and we started to taxi out to the runway. Nobody said a word. We practically held our breaths as we waited on the tarmac for clearance to take off. At last the plane started rolling forward then quickly accelerated to take-off speed. When the wheels left the ground we breathed a collective sigh and relaxed for the first time in a year. Not long into the flight, a stewardess commented on how quiet everyone was. She had flown in with a load of new recruits and noticed that they were much more talkative. No one could explain to her our mixed feelings of relief at leaving this place and our anxiety about going back home. We had changed so much. Instead of partying all the way home, the mood was somber. We had lost something in Vietnam and were not going home as heroes. Instead, we had been reduced to unwilling participants in a war that had no cause worth cheering.

Rob, Thor, and I chose the same seats we had the year before. Our celebration was that we were alive, and our three hundred and sixty-five days were over. Little time was spent in conversation; most was used to catch up on our reading or staring out the window reflecting on past and future events. We had done our duty, but that carried precious little weight in offsetting the physical and emotional cost that had been extracted for it. Time disappeared as quickly as answers to our questions.

The pilot announced that we were flying over the California coast and would be landing in fifteen minutes. You could hear a pin drop. Once we were on the ground it would all be over. No helpless terror, nobody shooting at us, no more dying or screams of pain. The pilot turned on the "fasten seatbelt" sign and started his final approach. We held our breaths, as the plane descended. Just a few feet from the ground someone in the back yelled, "Is that all there is?" They were words from a dreary song by Peggy Lee that trivialized the major crises of life. It was the understatement of the year. We broke into groans and laughter. The wheels yelped as they thumped to the ground. A years worth of tension evaporated.

* * *

We were back in the World. We were home! It was finally over, and I had survived. The anxiety of wanting to come home lifted like a heavy weight, leaving only sorrow for those who remained. For the first time in months my responsibility to protect those around me was gone. There was nothing to do for them now. The agonizing anxiety over whether I could hang on until tomorrow or next week didn't mean anything here. I had made it. The thought almost overwhelmed me.

A mind-warping year was over, but its effects continued. Janet met me at Oakland with hugs and kisses. It was time to put away all those things that had been so important over the last year. But how? Could I just drop it into a hole somewhere in my mind and go on with life? I didn't know the answer, but I didn't know what else to do.

My few weeks of leave were spent with Janet, and visits to both our families. I felt uncomfortable, but it became easy to lose myself in the dreams and plans we had made. Life would move forward from this point. There was no reason to look back.

Dinner with my future in-laws uncovered one of the many changes that popped up unexpectedly. Janet's mother was an excellent cook, and eating a meal that hadn't come out of a can was going to be a real treat. Her custom was to serve guests and family first, then sit down and begin her meal. She set a plate before me filled with generous portions of all kinds of food I hadn't enjoyed for more than a year. It took her a couple of minutes to complete her serving ritual, then she looked over before she sat down to ask if I were enjoying the meal. Her expression turned to shock when she saw my empty plate.

Everyone looked at one another and began to laugh. "How could you eat so fast?" Embarrassed, I realized I had vacuumed my plate while everyone else was just starting. Due to proper Army training and most of a year in the jungle, I could wolf down meals so quickly that eating was only a limited distraction from any surrounding danger. Eating slowly and enjoying meals became an elusive goal.

Dad's job moved them to a small town in upstate New York while I was overseas. I grabbed a plane and they met me at JFK. Mom hugged my neck and cried. Dad, as usual, was a little more conservative. I got caught up on the family news during the trip to their new temporary home. Everything was unfamiliar and it seemed to spill over into our relationship. I couldn't fit back into the image they saw of me before I left for Vietnam.

Maybe I was just growing up and couldn't go back to being their "child." They seemed distant somehow. Were they reacting to something in me? Had I changed that much? I tried to hide everything about the war and be "normal," but it didn't seem to be working. I couldn't laugh anymore. Life was deadly serious. Perhaps it would just take time to get back into the old grove. Our visit was too short to think it through, and maybe that was for the best.

I was done with Vietnam but not the Army. My orders sent me to Fort Hood, Texas for the remaining six months of my two-year obligation. Dressed in a summer Class A uniform in California was marginally OK, but in Texas it was no match for the sleet and bone chilling cold of early January. Boredom and a yearlong craving for a hamburger and a chocolate milkshake drove me to walk to the PX the afternoon of my arrival. A curse passed my lips at the stupidity of military planning for issuing summer uniforms in the middle of winter. My body wasn't accustomed to the cold, and my thin cotton uniform left me quaking. But that hamburger was out there. I'd survived a year in Vietnam, and twenty minutes of freezing cold couldn't be worse than a firefight. Sleet was blowing horizontally and stung my eyes when a tall figure appeared on the frozen sidewalk in front of me. My head was down and my face half-turned away from the wind and the oncoming stranger. We nearly passed when he stopped and yelled at me for not saluting a superior officer, and a Canadian officer at that! He was surprised the U.S. Army would allow its soldiers to be so undisciplined. I hesitated long enough to give the required hand motion and mutter a complaint about the thin summer uniform that the same U.S. Army felt was good enough for this Texas winter.

I was in no mood to stop and have a long conversation while the sleet was biting through every inch of my clothes. It was wrong but I turned and walked away, forcing the Canadian to run after me if he wanted to berate me any further. He decided it wasn't worth the effort and continued on to his destination, where I'm sure he vented his feelings about the poorly trained soldier he had just encountered.

The meeting did nothing to improve my attitude either. Polished shoes and snapping salutes didn't mean anything out in the jungle. I knew what it took to survive in a real war and didn't want to play army anymore. Unfortunately, the Army didn't share my peculiar perspective. The gap in our logic was further confirmed when my assignment turned out to be with a communications section of a tank division. What were they thinking? All my training and a whole year's worth of survival was in the infantry. My closest encounter with a tank was walking beside one for a few minutes, and their communications equipment was completely foreign. Besides, I'd only be there for six months. It was clear that the Army and I had little use left for each other. That was fine with me; just six more months and I'd be a free man. What could go wrong in six months?

It turned out that the kid who had the job before me totally fried his brain on acid and anything else he could get a hold of. The Inspector General (IG) was coming to Fort Hood in about thirty days to see if the troops were up to snuff. It was apparently a big deal to everyone except me. My new company commander assigned me to his communication section in hopes of pulling it through the IG inspection.

A lieutenant in charge of battalion communications tried to go through the manual and a fifty-page list of things that needed to be in order before the IG showed up. He hadn't seen the war and was more frightened about the upcoming inspection than most men were about bullets flying over their heads. This had nothing to do with the reality I knew, and there was no way for me to take it seriously. No one was shooting at me and no adrenalin was flowing, so in my mind there was nothing to worry about. War games were meaningless. I'd already been there, and it was nothing like this.

My attitude resulted in the individual distinction of being the only member of my new battalion to flunk the IG inspection. It wasn't a proud accomplishment, but it was hard to feel too bad, knowing I had survived more combat than the rest of them combined. The IG inspected our company formation last. As General "so-and-so" and his entourage walked through our ranks he brought everything to a stop in front of me. We had met the day before when my radio equipment and maintenance logs hadn't passed inspection. He asked why I had an oak leaf on my Air Medal and three stars on my Vietnam Service Medal.

"The 1st Infantry Division allowed one air medal for every thirty air combat assaults. I had over sixty assaults in Vietnam and participated in three campaigns, sir!"

After looking at my Silver Star and Bronze Star, he flashed a smile that said to me, "You've done your job. You shouldn't have to be here."

The captain called me into his office the next day to say he was supposed to discipline me for flunking the IG inspection. He seemed to understand that this was an odd situation. For punishment he sent me out to the line company to be a gunner for his oldest tank commander. A gunner got to shoot the 105 cannon and the machine gun mounted in the turret. Within days, our company went out to the target range to practice our craft. With all of five minutes instruction, I was seated in the gunner's chair ready to shoot at targets the tank commander would call out. The periscope sight had a grid of calibrations to account for target distance and spin of the round, which caused an arc to the right. The farther the target was away, the higher and farther to the left you'd aim.

My crash course didn't include using the calibrations to zero in precisely. One thing Vietnam gave me was a natural instinct for being able to shoot quickly and accurately, but this was a tank. We started rumbling down the road and slowed to a stop at the sight of an old APC carcass that had been turned into Swiss cheese from previous hits. A quick aim and my first shot was on the way. A hit! We moved on to the next area and the tank lurched as thirty or forty infantry silhouettes popped up in rows as if they were charging our position. The machine gun spit out a continuous burst, as the turret swung back and forth from the first row to the last. Got them all! This was beginning to be fun. Throughout the course, I hit targets both near and far using instinct only. We rolled to a stop at the end of the course, and a young lieutenant jumped out of a jeep that had followed us to record our scores. He seemed excited as he threw open the flap of the tent where the course cadre were set up. He handed a piece of paper to someone standing next to a large chalkboard. They were keeping tally of the scores from all the companies who were participating in the exercise. There was some discussion, and the old tank commander and I were called into the tent. The lieutenant explained that this was quite an occasion. No one had scored this high in years. Somehow we had managed to make a perfect score. We were congratulated, and I was dismissed.

My tank commander came out a few minutes later and said that we had only completed half the course. We had to travel through it again at night, but before we could finish the course we had to change the cannon barrel since it had reached the limit of rounds it was supposed to shoot. Three hours later a new barrel had been installed, and we were off to get in line for the night run. Our second run was a disaster. Every target was the same, and my war-trained mind had each position locked in from the day run, but this time the barrel moved a little just before I pulled the trigger. The old tank commander had a sight at his location and could manipulate the barrel also. The last second movement had to be him trying to help. After several misses, I began to suspect he didn't want to hit the targets at all.

We rumbled up to the scoring tent, and the lieutenant came out to ask what had happened. It crossed my mind that someone probably decided it wouldn't look good for a grunt with an attitude to outscore the best of the tankers, so I told him the new barrel wasn't acting the same as the old one and left it at that. It was no skin off my nose. The Army had been crossed off my career track long ago. This exercise was just taking up time until my discharge. My damaged pride didn't require justification from these stateside warriors.

Back in the barracks one evening, our top sergeant opened my door and yelled that I was to meet him in his office ASAP. Crap! What had I done now? He sat behind his desk and continued typing as I entered.

"Wright, your fiancée called from Sacramento. She needs you to come home right away!"

"Ah . . . why?"

"She's contracted hepatitis and can't take care of herself alone."

"What about her mom?"

"She won't set foot in the apartment. She's afraid she'll catch it. Here are your orders and a voucher for a plane ticket. I've made arrangements for you to get a shot of hemoglobin at McClellan Air Base after you arrive tomorrow. I'm giving you two weeks hardship leave. If you need more, just call."

Wow, two weeks leave and a paid ticket home! Janet must have really laid it on. Top acted like he couldn't do enough. It was late March, just two months of active duty left. This was unusually kind. The Army does not like to give this kind of leave so close to discharge and especially for a non-family member.

"Thanks."

Janet was so weak when I got to her apartment she couldn't get out of bed to open the door. With two weeks of my nursing, she recovered enough strength to take care of herself, so I returned to complete my obligation to the Army.

Back in Texas, Top called me into his office one more time.

"You plan on going to college when you get out, don't you?"

"Yeah, I suppose so, but school won't start until September."

"Don't worry about that. I can get you an early out for college if you'll fill out this paperwork."

The thought of getting out of the Army early sat well with me. I could go to school.

That would be a snap compared to the last year and a half.

"I'll have these papers back on your desk this afternoon!"

"OK. I'll have your discharge orders ready."

There was no animosity in Top's voice, but there was no sadness either. He was just following through on a decision that had already been made. There was nothing I was going to contribute to their world, and it was pretty obvious that the stateside Army wasn't going to change for me.

A few more lines for medical exams and filling out forms that released the Army from responsibility for anything that might have happened to me, and suddenly I was out! The flight home was almost as exciting as coming home from Vietnam. Getting back into civilian life still made me nervous, but Janet and the familiar thought of going back to school should ease the transition. In July, 1970, Janet and I were married. We bought an old trailer and spent the summer remodeling and painting it before pulling it into a trailer park a few miles from school. We were ready to start our life together.

Janet, my fiancé, and I after coming home from Vietnam. The long handle bar mustache had to be trimmed at the corners of my mouth before a squeaky little second lieutenant would let me board the plane back to the States. I was going to grab him by the throat but that would have just caused further delay.

Janet, my beautiful wife, and I over forty years later. She insists that her hair is platinum blond instead of gray. She has stood by me all these years. I can't imagine being without her.

- 24 -

MY HELL/GOD'S GIFT

School started in September, and three years later I managed to graduate in the top 10 percent of my engineering class. Janet didn't know Jesus at the time, and I ventured into Yoga searching for some kind of anchor for my shattered beliefs. Smoking dope was another attempt to cope with the incongruities of life, but it produced contention and more stress in our marriage. Dray came home from Vietnam, and it was through his girlfriend that Janet was introduced to and accepted Jesus Christ. Watching her change drew me back to my pre-Vietnam relationship with Jesus, which filled the hole in my life enough to give up smoking dope, but not enough to give God full control of my life.

An excellent job offer came from a small coastal community three months before graduation. The job was great and it looked like I could forget about Vietnam. After three years the city administrator left for another job and the city council offered his position to me. Everything seemed to be going extremely well. With Janet's help, I had obtained a college degree, and started our marriage with a great job and a new home on the picturesque northern California coast. We had been blessed with all the things most people dream of.

Without knowing it, the seeds that had been planted so deeply in Vietnam would soon sprout and eventually choke out everything. My attitude and outlook on life had changed in ways that I didn't understand and even denied. It would take years to realize that the things I learned to stay alive in Vietnam did not and would not go away just because I came home.

I began feeling the city administrator position was over my head and didn't want to fake it. My lessons in the jungle taught me how to survive in a shooting war, but I had no skills for surviving in a political environment. To me, politics meant doing things the REMFs and lifers did in their dull, boring jobs in the rear support area. That wasn't me. Politics seemed to be corrupt and dishonest. I wanted to stand on the high moral ground and not stoop to political reality.

It was less than a year before the new mayor and I went sideways. He was from the old school and believed that if your employees weren't cussing you, you weren't doing your job right. God had given me an ability to stay in tune with everyone around me, which was absolutely critical to support one another to stay alive. I couldn't turn my back on this skill that had been so important. Over the next few months, the mayor collected enough votes on the council to force my resignation.

Janet was having difficulty with my lack of patience and inability to communicate feelings. Without my knowledge, the symptoms of Post Traumatic Stress Disorder (PTSD) were beginning to surface. In response to feeling inadequate and stressed, I hunkered down and prepared to survive. My emotions were numbed to stay in control, and adrenaline was pumped up through flaring anger at any perceived threat. These byproducts of Vietnam had never left and now jumped to my defense again. Even if I'd been aware of PTSD, the reactions came so "naturally" that they were unidentifiable.

Many vets, including me, failed to realize that skills to survive a year of hell in Vietnam might not be appropriate for the rest of life's issues. I felt inadequate, stressed, threatened and helpless again, and my survival mode kicked in to endure the mayor's attack without stooping to politics. I couldn't fight effectively; we were supposed to be on the same side, doing the best for our community. A majority of the council was understandably confused at my reactions and eventually sided with the mayor. In frustration, I gave up and hoped this might just be the wrong place for me. My ego was crushed. Why hadn't the good guys prevailed? This wasn't Vietnam, life back in the World was supposed to be fair!

Mercifully and quickly, we were blessed with another job in the Imperial Valley of southern California. The pay was excellent, and my boss was easy to work for. The torrid climate and cultural shock were enormous, but I could handle anything after Vietnam.

That attitude didn't allow me to understand why Janet couldn't share the same prospective and shrug off the desert heat and different way of life. We stayed active in our church and helped with the teen youth group. Janet was unable to get pregnant and subjected herself to some fairly severe medical procedures related to the problem.

Outward appearances only hid the difficulties continuing to grow between us. I couldn't explain my feelings in enough detail for Janet to understand why there was no tolerance for all of her "little" calamities. Identifying, much less explaining my feelings was impossible since my emotions were shut down to survive. No feelings only made it difficult to identify "normal" problems, but it gave me total control of my emotions, which was essential in Vietnam. The extreme stress of firefights allowed nothing but quick reflexes and automatic reactions. Walking point and sensing everything around me meant there could be no distractions from anything that wasn't life-threatening. Staying in control meant staying alive. I couldn't risk the emotions of losing more friends, so after the first few months, all relationships became superficial. Janet tried to be supportive, but how could she ever understand? All she knew was I had changed.

After four long years in the desert, she begged to move away from the smell of alkali, the heat, the bugs, the lack of trees and streams, and everything else that was familiar. Both our families were in northern California. Most of our vacation and recreational activities focused on the rambling streams and clear lakes embracing the Sierras. There was nothing remotely familiar in the Imperial Valley or for hundreds of miles in any direction. I had to admit it would be enjoyable to get back to the smell of pines along a small river with fish waiting to be caught just around the bend. My boss gave his full permission and an excellent recommendation to search for jobs back up north.

An interview came up in a small town in southern Oregon. It turned out to have the same characteristics we loved in the mountains of California. I accepted a job offer and caught a bus for Oregon while Janet stayed to sell our house in the desert. This might be the chance we needed. A new start in an area we could both relate to might be good medicine for our relationship, but my mind was still blind to the changes needed in me.

After all, I was coping with things that Janet couldn't begin to understand! All she needed to do was quit worrying about all those details that didn't put a blip on my radar screen. Of course, my radar was tuned to a far different frequency from hers. My solution was to pray for God to change her. Needless to say, our conflicts continued to build.

I rented a mobile home in a quiet valley not far from town. It had a seasonal creek, deer in the meadow, and even a few rattlesnakes to remind us of the Sierra foothills. Janet did a great job selling our house in southern California, and we drove two moving vans to haul our accumulated belongings to southern Oregon in 1981.

Through God's love for us, we were presented with an opportunity to adopt a newborn child. Our son was very active. It was difficult for either of us to keep pace with him, but life was good. We bought a piece of property along a beautiful river and built a log house. We were living our dream with our son, who was two, when the world crashed down on us. We found out that our beautiful little boy had been molested at his day care center.

Stunned was an understatement. My mind couldn't comprehend how anyone could be so evil. After a long walk along the river running behind our house, I decided to take the life of the creep who took our son's innocence away.

In Vietnam I had dispatched many with little animosity. This was different; the man was a perverted animal who preyed on defenseless children, and he needed to be eradicated from the face of the earth. It meant jail if caught, but something had to be done. Nothing would change what happened to my son, but there was a compulsion to acknowledge his loss with something of equal weight and put action to the cold fury and blinding helplessness that was beginning to consume me. Murder would be justified by the rationalization that it might keep something similar from happening to other helpless children. As details unfolded over the next few days, even that option was taken away. The perpetrators turned out to be two boys, ages eight and ten. If they had been men, I'd have killed them, but I wasn't prepared to murder two boys. Of course, we went to the police and the day care was shut down, but the offending children never did get help. Their mother quickly moved out of state and the authorities could do nothing more.

A deep depression overtook me. Life in the "world" was as unfair and brutal as it had been in Vietnam. But here at home, even the little control I had walking point was gone. I couldn't even protect my own son, and I couldn't fight back. Stress, despair and total helplessness overwhelmed me again and triggered *severe* PTSD. Increasing amounts of anger boiled up. To cope at work I detached even more from people to continue providing at least the minimal functions of my job.

In contrast, our home and family life was filled with years of anguish and pain that were beyond my control or ability to change. Not realizing how far I'd withdrawn, my heart broke when Janet told me of the time Jonathan sat in her lap and cried, "Why does Daddy hate me?" I tried as hard as I could but was unable to even show my son that I loved him.

Equally distant from others, it tortured me knowing that as a Christian we are to love people. How could I love people when most were deeply immersed in instant gratification and self-centeredness? Somewhere in the terror of the jungle my ability to see the base nature of humanity had expanded to see the depths we can all sink to. My awareness of the evil we can do to one another outweighed the little good I perceived. We went to church, but even that didn't balance the scales. Disappointment in mankind and myself grew to despair. My self-protective silence didn't help either. To avoid the pain, my logic said that people didn't want to hear my horrors. They couldn't understand, and most would probably be repulsed by the blood and gore and how could that help anything today? Even if they were willing to listen, and I could somehow tell my stories, there was nothing they could do. So why bother? Besides, like so many other vets, there were no close relationships to confide in. We learned to only depend on ourselves.

Despite withdrawal from everything besides work and church, I tried my best to change things for my family. Nothing worked. Janet interpreted my inability to respond with proper emotions and support as hatred for her. What else could she think? Confusion and resentment grew in me toward expectations of behavior that had to be "acted out" instead of relying on feelings that could no longer be identified. In mutual frustration, we ripped one another apart, pointing out each other's sins, accusing one another of destroying our marriage, and being too hard or too soft raising our son.

When Jonathan was a junior in high school, I could stand it no longer and decided it would be better to separate and maybe divorce rather than continue to make each other miserable. I saw no other way to stop screwing things up. Janet wasn't perfect and owned a few of our problems, but she didn't understand how to fix things, and I couldn't keep trying to do what I thought was right only to see things continually getting worse. I was ready to give up. I couldn't do it right and didn't know why. Maybe I just wasn't smart enough or didn't have enough insight or self-control to pull it off.

One Sunday Janet confided in a couple at church. They invited us to come over and talk that evening. Harry greeted me and whispered, "How are you doing?"

I almost broke down but managed to breathe out, "Not so good, Harry."

"You're in a good place."

His answer struck me as curious. I was totally miserable. Maybe he was talking about being in church.

When I walked through their doorway my pride didn't matter any more. I had failed as a husband and father and could deny it no longer. I was ready to listen to anything they had to say and could discount nothing, because the only answer for me was to walk away, broken inside. I couldn't depend on myself anymore.

Instead of pointing out our shortcomings, Harry and Kim told us some of their own story. They were going through difficulties and hard times, but they were trusting in God's understanding more than their own. It was true when Harry said Janet was God's gift to me, and Janet came close to believing Kim when she said David really doesn't hate you. From that meager beginning, God started healing us and continues today. We are not perfect by any means and we still have several areas to work out. God has put a key into my heart which has opened many doors I thought would stay closed forever. When He brought me to the point where I finally admitted I was unable to achieve the desire of my heart with my strength and my will that opened me to trusting Him for everything. There was nowhere else to turn but to that distant hope which said only Jesus could fix us.

On our son's eighteenth birthday and for several weeks afterward, God showed his love again by saving my life one more time. Janet convinced me to see our doctor for treatment of a continuing ache in my lower intestines (miracle number one—I never go to the doctor!). He was convinced it was appendicitis and insisted I go straight to the emergency room to have it taken out. After calling Janet, they prepped and wheeled me into the operating room where the surgeon found a fairly normal appendix. After further investigation, he discovered my colon was badly infected and had burst some hours earlier. I woke up in the recovery room with a plastic bag glued to my stomach and was told I might have to excrete into it for the rest of my life. That was not good news!

My third day in the hospital was highlighted by having to get up for the first time and walk down the hall. My nurse followed me about twenty feet before I passed out and fell into a wheelchair. He was convinced that my reaction was not just a normal "blackout" and rushed me to intensive care. Janet was advised that she might be alone by morning. An MRI later revealed dark stains throughout my lungs left by the massive blood clots that had passed through my heart. My doctor called it a pulmonary embolism. His stern face and tone said it was a miracle I was alive.

Everything after that was a blessing. Soon after my wheelchair disappeared into intensive care, Janet called everyone she could think of to pray. As a result, I had little to no pain through the entire episode. Two months later, my family went elk hunting and we carried four elk off the mountain. The following month I convinced my doctor to reverse the colostomy. By this time, even I was amazed at what God was doing.

Janet felt led to start a Bible study for Jonathan and his friends. Jonathan had always been curious about my experiences in Vietnam, but I could only verbalize small segments before feeling overwhelmed. Janet suggested I write them down, then she would read them to the boys before we started each study. My stories of Vietnam were part of Jonathan's legacy, but I couldn't share them if it just left the boys feeling my frustration.

God began to jog my memory of His mercy and grace in situations that many haven't seen. This might be good for the boys.

As I began to write, God released buried memories and revealed what He had done during that year of hell in Vietnam. The stories flooded out. As they flowed onto paper the amazing account of His love and miraculous protection was repeated over and over. The intervening thirty years prepared me to look back with different eyes. Now ready to let go of my understanding, my heart opened to His reality. All the questions without answers aren't as significant as they used to be. The pain is now a memory that tells others it doesn't have to last forever. The years spent immersed in anger and depression were regrettable, but God reminds me that's what it took to bring me to this place.

Now I can see some of the astounding things God did through those terrible times. He works in our lives even when we don't see it or believe we deserve it and He doesn't stop because of our bad moods or even because of our mistaken views of life. Nothing that happens is wasted. He uses all things for our good, even the hardest times.

After surviving Vietnam, I thought I could do anything. Like most people, I've always understood that sin was wrong. My pride (thinking I should be able to do things right), led me to punish myself for failings so as not to repeat them. Through the years, self-punishment became self-destruction when I saw myself continually fall short. All my mistakes and inabilities made me realize how far I was from doing things right.

And that's where God has stepped in and said it's OK. He knows me. I'm not hiding anything from Him and can't deceive Him. He's been with me all along, and the amazing thing is, He loves me anyway! In fact, He wants to have a relationship with me so badly that He made arrangements to pay for all my imperfections and sins, then He forgave me so we don't have to be separated any longer. It's what I deserve but now there's no need to destroy myself with guilt anymore. That's the way He is. He's full of grace (giving me what I don't deserve just because He loves me) and He will not deny His promises to me. He is capable and willing to do anything, even miracles to change people's hearts and He doesn't give up. He's here for the entire game. He won't walk out in the middle of the last inning. It was disappointing to discover that I couldn't change others, but I found out that God can be trusted to change me! Giving permission for Him to change my life is one of the few things I can give back for so many miracles that were given to me. In exchange, I'm becoming what my heart desires, and He gets the glory. It's a great deal! In God's economy, accepting more of his grace makes Him happy. What He wants to continue doing in my life is the best thing for me. How can I turn down a deal like that? It's still difficult to comprehend His grace.

For years my image of Jesus was the epitome of a mighty man who lived His way and bent to no temptation—which is true—but it led me to think that in order to be a good Christian I'd have to be the same. I had to stand up to sin and not bend from what was right for anyone or anything. The problem was I couldn't do it. Jesus was a lot bigger than my simple image. I had completely missed His compassion, grace, motivation, and where His strength really came from.

When writing about my first day in the field, a different picture was given to me. I was totally exhausted from breaking my own trail through the jungle and had no idea what was going on. The same can be true in life. I made it back to the column and just followed someone else. It was so much easier. "I can do this!" Jesus showed me that He had absolutely no desire to "do things His way." He was totally focused on following someone else. He didn't strike out on his own, cutting His own trail, doing what He thought was right. He did what His Father showed Him. He believed His Father knew what was best, and He obeyed to make it happen. Jesus did this from love for His Father and us, not from a self-absorbed desire for adoration or fear of looking bad.

Trusting someone else to the point of death was opposite from the lesson burned into my mind in Vietnam: "Don't depend on anyone. They will leave, they will die, or they will get wounded." In any case, all relationships are temporary at best and there's no one to rely on but myself. (You can imagine what damage this has done in my marriage.) It twists my brain to believe God wants to be with me for eternity and presents it as a gift through Jesus' complete trust and selfless obedience.

Following Jesus doesn't seem as grand as "doing it my way." I would love to take a little credit for doing something right. Anything! After all these years of trying, I can only say that rightness is the true desire of my heart. Jesus offered Himself on the cross to take my punishment so God can forgive me. Now, He fulfilled, my desire as my trust is placed in Him.

Our wise pastor has said, "The school of hard knocks is an excellent teacher, but the tuition is very high." I pray for those who are now just starting their lives, "Please believe that Jesus is real, and He came to give us life free from all the sins that are destroying this world." Jesus told his disciple Thomas in John 20:29, "Because thou hast seen me, thou hast believed; blessed are they that have not seen and yet have believed."

After these thirty years, I know God is faithful and his thoughts toward me are of peace, not of evil. A part of me knew this while going through the hard times, but another part focused on the situation around me, and I was torn between the physical and spiritual realities.

Experience now confirms that God truly is trustworthy in all that He has promised.

My pain was a result of my own misunderstandings and wrong decisions. Now it's a tool that allows me to see where "doing it my way" will lead. If I had chosen to really trust Him years ago, walking point might have been done without continual fear, and the death of close friends could have been accepted knowing He was in control and His ways were higher than mine. It would have been so much better to trust Him for every detail instead of deciding what was best on my own and then failing.

Jesus was the only one to do things perfectly. I could have chosen to believe instead of wading through thirty years of "I'm not sure that God knows best. I want to test things myself." Well, things tested me, and there's nothing left outside of God that works.

For those of us who decide we must find out what is true on our own, I offer the next two verses from John, Chapter 20: "And many other signs truly did Jesus in the presence of his disciples, which are not written in this book. But these are written that ye might believe that Jesus is the Christ, the Son of God; and that believing ye might have life through His name."

My stories are certainly not of biblical quality, but they are a true record of what Jesus has done in my life.

* * *

Let Him bless you.

By: Dave Wright
November 11, 2003
(Revised May 1, 2016)

I was the Point Man

Sitting on a log,
Head in my hands,
The ambush is over,
And emptiness stands,

Where moments before,
My squad and me,
Were bound in life,
And thought we'd be,

Forever friends,
But you see,
The only one left,
Now is me.

Alone with death,
In an empty world,
Devoid of life,
While smoke still swirled.

Was this real,
Or just a dream?
I sense they're here,
But now unseen.

I must move on,
Then I cussed,
"Can't sweep aside,
Men like dust."

The loss was huge,
My mind declared,
But no one knew,
So no one cared.

It wasn't right,
It should have been me,
They had more to give,
Than I'd ever be.

They died and left,
Me to cope, through
The rest of life,
With little hope.

Their part was easy,
Mine was hard,
Collecting my soul,
Shattered and charred.

It didn't make sense,
I wasn't raised,
To view life cheap,
And not be fazed.

Someone should grieve,
Give weight to their loss,
But no one was left,
Who felt the cost.

So the burden is mine,
Not to forget,
To carry the memory,
And pay the debt,

That America owes,
These young men,
Whose lives were torn,
Never to mend.

But there's no time,
To show respect,
I'll bury it deep,
To not reflect.

There'll be time,
When things are right,
To unlock my mind,
In hopes I might,

Reach back in time,
With new meaning found,
To explain their blood,
Here on the ground.

It's such a waste,
To walk away,
From sacred ground,
They bought today.

We'll stay tonight, but
Tomorrow we'll leave,
Giving them back,
Our place to grieve.

We've got to move on,
A small voice bade,
My body stood slowly,
The rest of me stayed.

(pause)

I've waited these years,
Trying hard as I can,
To do what's right,
But don't understand.

We should've done better,
Than Vietnam!
Was it all just greed,
And politics wrong?

Can anything good,
Come out of that hell,
A different perspective,
From which to tell?

Our children and theirs,
What Grandpa did,
During the war,
While just a kid.

Well it drove me to God,
Who gives to all,
Freedom that's real,
At a price not small,

It cost Him His son,
To set us free,
He understands,
You and me,

It is His gift,
That paid our price,
If only we accept,
His sacrifice.

Jesus walked point,
Straight to the cross,
Taking my offences,
And restoring my loss.

I've found help from:

1. Veteran's Service Office, find address and phone number of your local VSO. They have helped outline the process, submitted all my paperwork to the VA for free counseling and financial assistance for PTSD, diabetes, and tenitis.
2. Vietnam Veterans of America, find a local chapter online, or call 1-800-VVA-1316. A chance to meet other vets like yourself and discover you're not the only one feeling the way you do. It's surprising how many issues we have in common as veterans.
3. Point Man Ministries, find the location of your nearest outpost online, or call the national headquarters @ 1-800-877-VETS. This group deals with the spiritual side of our issues from Vietnam.
4. Vietnam Veteran reunions, I thought reunions were made up of old men telling their war stories. I found genuine support, understanding, a mutual fear of the War Story syndrome, and the "Welcome Home" I never received thirty years ago. There are reunions advertised in most veteran or military magazines, and web-sites related to veterans, veteran organizations, or military units.
5. God's Word and Holy Spirit. God wants us to live with Him forever, but all we've done wrong keeps us separated from Him. We know we're guilty. Most of us spend our lives trying

to fix the wrongs telling ourselves we can live life the way it's supposed to be when all that's wrong is out of the way. Logical, but God's word says we can't fix ourselves or the World. After 30 years of trying I had lost all hope and was ready to give up. That's when I could accept that I needed help. After years of failure I knew all I hated, now it was time to learn that I loved all that's good, right, just and true – all of which, plus restoration, is found in Jesus and God's word.

AFTERTHOUGHTS

Can Christians be good soldiers? Isn't there a huge gap between living for Christ and killing for peace? How could both live in the same man's heart?

In 1526, Martin Luther identified several parameters establishing characteristics of a just and moral war which Christians could/should support. For me, war was very personal, intimate and invasive. The right and wrong of it seemed bigger than my ability to judge. There appeared to be enough right and wrong on both sides to support nearly any argument in favor or against that particular conflict. The deciding factor for me came down to --- if my country called me to serve, I couldn't in all good conscience, run away or hide from my obligation.

Having accepted Christ at an early age, there always seemed to be a moral compass that at least told me when I was stepping way out of bounds. I knew God was with me from the start of basic and advanced infantry training, through heavy combat and an honorable discharge, but I didn't really "know" God. In spite of my immaturity, He proved His unconditional love with unquestionable miracles and divine intervention to the point I could take no credit for the physical safety that followed me.

Wish I could say my actions were such shining examples of God's glory that readers would fall to their knees and beg for salvation. The real story is an example all right, but it's about His mercy and grace to a young, naïve, self-centered Christian who hadn't a clue about the bigger picture of life (like many young people). That posed no problem for God of course. For me, it took many years learning to thank Him for all things.

Everything I learned growing up was challenged in a crucible of the worst men can do to one another. There was never a danger that God might abandon me (though I feared making Him angry enough to do that). My biggest torment came from not trusting Him totally. Leaning on my understanding, my perceptions of what was going on allowed guilt, anger, redlined fear and helpless disillusionment that nearly destroyed me.

God was faithful, full of mercy and grace the whole time. The problem was my lack of spiritual maturity and inexperience with the depths of evil in the hearts of men. Nothing prepared me for the shock of dropping into a world where life is not fair or just, and having to kill others just to survive. It was surprisingly easy to pull a trigger and throw grenades. The injustices bothered me more, and my own capacity for evil was an unwanted surprise.

I wish someone had warned me that I would change, and that no one can change back. The young man who returned from war was not the same as the one who had left home for the first time. It took another thirty years to realize I couldn't go back in time. I wanted to, my wife wanted me to, my family wanted it, so I tried as hard as I could. It seems so transparently self-deceptive now, but I really thought if I buried the memories deeply enough and denied they bothered me strongly enough that I could go back and pick up the plans I'd made before the war, like nothing had happened. I wanted the whole sorry episode to be obliterated from the time line of my life.

My heart aches for other veterans who might be blindsided or unaware of the damage denial can cause. Don't isolate, talk to someone about the things that make you angry or frustrated, or helpless to change. God is a good listener. He didn't come to condemn us. He has answers for the questions our understanding demands but we can't produce, for example:

"God, why did you let me survive when the rest of my squad was killed? I was walking point, why didn't I see something or hear something that might have saved them. They wouldn't have screwed up life as much as I have. One of them should have made it home instead of me." … His answer … "I SAVED YOU BECAUSE IT PLEASED ME."

(nothing else could have taken the guilt off my shoulders, He didn't ask for my opinion)

"God, why is humanity so fouled up? How can we do such terrible things to one another?" … He asked …"HOW MANY OF THOSE PARTICIPATING IN THE WAR FOLLOWED MY WAYS? … (Lord, you know there weren't many). … WELL, WHAT DID YOU EXPECT WOULD HAPPEN?"

(I lowered my expectations for unsaved mankind - they're all going to hell without Christ; then I lowered my expectations for Christians because of the capacity for evil I found in my own heart)

<u>"God, life just isn't fair!</u> … He said … "IF IT WERE FAIR BY YOUR DEFINITION, YOU

WOULD NEVER CHANGE!"

(Ok, you're God, I'm not. Thank you for **<u>all</u>** things)

ABOUT THE AUTHOR

Born in 1945, Dave Wright grew up in Northern California. He was drafted after dropping out of college in 1967. The Army taught him how to survive in our nation's undeclared war in Vietnam. Thus began Dave's transformation from innocence to hardened combat veteran. He received the Bronze and Silver Stars while walking point in the dense, steaming jungle.

He completed college in 1973 with a degree in civil engineering and is finishing his career as City Engineer in Southern Oregon.

Surviving Vietnam, and burying its effects with denial, anger, and isolation meant Dave and his family suffered with PTSD for the next thirty years. He now speaks at high schools about his experiences and the slow process of recovery.

CPSIA information can be obtained
at www.ICGtesting.com
Printed in the USA
FFOW05n1138310117

S0-ALJ-930

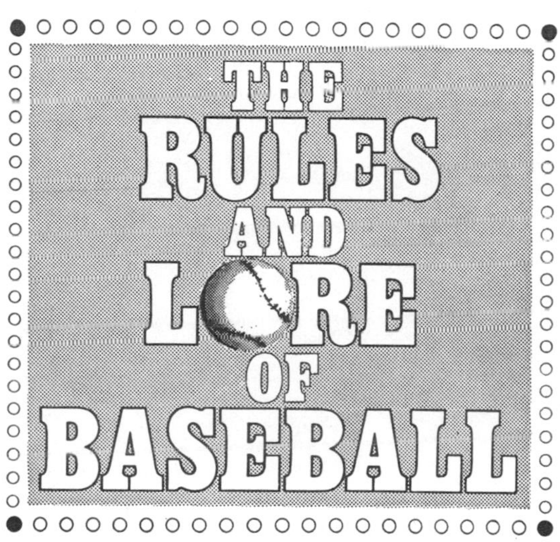
THE
RULES
AND
LORE
OF
BASEBALL

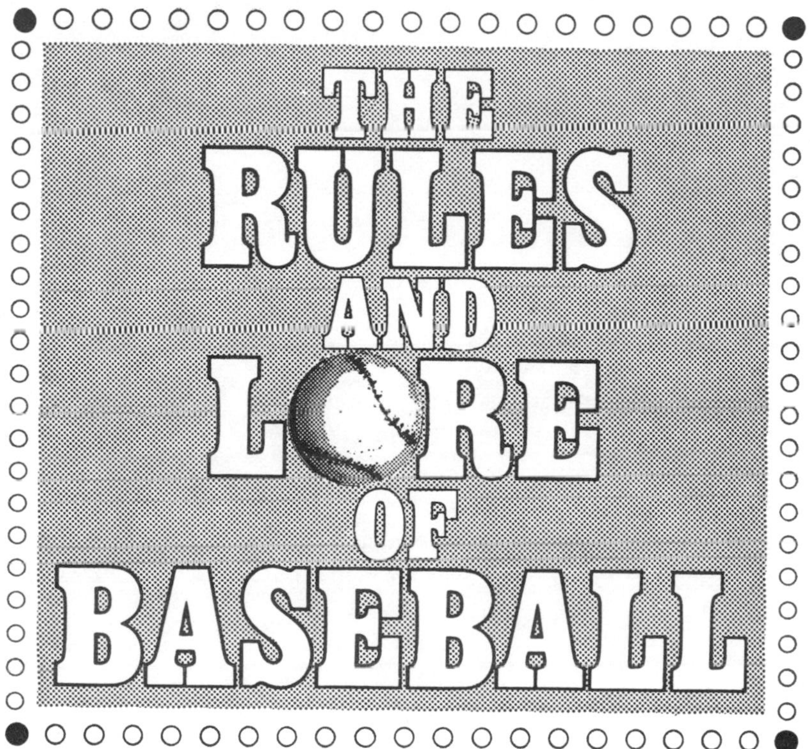

Richard Marazzi

SB

A SCARBOROUGH BOOK

STEIN AND DAY/*Publishers*/New York

First published in 1980

Designed by Louis A. Ditizio
Printed in the United States of America
Stein and Day/ *Publishers*/ Scarborough House
Briarcliff Manor, N.Y. 10510

Library of Congress Cataloging in Publication Data

Marazzi, Rich.
The rules and lore of baseball.

Includes index.
1. Baseball—Rules. 2. Baseball—Umpiring.
I. Title.
GV877.M35 796.357'02'022 79-3896
ISBN 0-8128-2715-5
ISBN 0-8128-6058-6 (pbk.)

To Lois,
an understanding and patient wife,
and to my Dad,
who would have been proud.

Contents

Foreword

NICK G. BREMIGAN, *American League Umpire*

Are you a baseball enthusiast? Have you ever wondered what is actually being said between players, managers, and umpires during an argument? Are you looking for a storehouse of interesting trivia information? If you answer "yes" to even one of these questions, you are really going to enjoy this book.

Rich Marazzi has authored a baseball masterpiece. It is unique in the field of sports publications, because it doesn't have a bad word to say about anybody. And it doesn't bore you with a lot of cold statistics, presented in uninteresting and tedious lists. Rather, this book is written in a fast moving, yet smooth style, spiced with interesting anecdotes and provocative situations concerning many of your favorite baseball stars.

This is Marazzi's first attempt at a major publication. I personally have read just about every book written about the world of professional baseball, and they are going to have to invent a new category for this one. It was obviously a labor of love for Marazzi. The book is very extensively and painstakingly researched, and being an American League umpire, I can personally testify as to its accuracy and authenticity in all respects.

This book is a must for all baseball fans. In it you will see your favorite stars from past and present involved in plays and situations, record-breaking feats, great plays, bonehead plays, humorous plays, controversial plays, as well as many weird situations which have occurred over the years and had to be ruled on by the men in blue. You will discover why protests are rarely upheld; what causes umpires to send players and managers to the showers early; why umpires rarely change their decisions; and why they think the advent of the television replay has helped enhance their credibility. You will be made privy to an impressive volume of inside information about what actually goes on behind the scenes in America's most popular spectator sport. You will find page after page of personal stories, anecdotes and situations—some hilarious, some emotional, some tragic. And all of it is presented in a lively, fluid style that will hold your interest as you read about the game we all love.

The book's intrinsic value for the baseball trivia buff is unparalleled. In these pages you will discover a plethora of useful trivia information that will make you the hit of your next trivia session. In addition, this book will become a valuable reference guide for years to come. You will refer to these pages again and again—every time an unusual play occurs in a baseball game; and every time you just want to impress somebody that you know the answers and where to find them. This is a book that can never go out of date as long as they are still playing the game of baseball.

This book will also make you the resident expert on rules and interpretations. It is not written in the boring format of a rule book or manual; but each play situation is meticulously documented with the relevant information on how it was ruled and why it was ruled that way. You will discover why the doubling up of a runner who left a base too soon is not a force play; how a batter can get hit with a pitch and not be awarded first base; why umpires have long been reluctant to enforce the rules against spitballs; how a batter can hit a fair ball out of the ball park and not get a home run; and much, much more. So, the next time you see or listen to a baseball game, you will know what is going on probably long before the announcers even figure it out.

Find yourself a nice, quiet, comfortable place and turn the page. You are about to embark on a most unique, imaginative and lively journey through the world of professional baseball.

Introduction

American League umpire Ron Luciano once said, "You gotta be dumb, a masochist, or a sadist or something to be an umpire." Although Luciano's statement might be somewhat exaggerated, it does contain a great deal of truth.

The umpire is expected to be a robotlike mechanical perfectionist, executing the proper decisions at all times. National League umpire Dick Stello philosophically declares, "Umpiring is the only profession where you're supposed to be perfect the first day on the job, and after that you must show constant improvement."

Baseball is not only "a game of inches," a thesis propounded by some mathematical phrase-maker, but is also a game governed by inflexible rules. The men in blue are expected to have a good understanding of baseball's statutes and properly enforce them. Since the rule book is at times inconsistent and ambiguous, the arbiter's job becomes a complex one.

Determining whether a runner is "out" or "safe" or if a pitched ball is a "ball" or "strike" entails most of the umpire's game duties. However, as former American League umpire Charlie Berry stated,

"Umpires must be ready for the one-in-a-thousand situation. That's why they must know every word of a rule and not have to reach for the rule book in the middle of a situation." The game has produced such knotty problems as a dead man scoring a run, three runners on the same base, two baseballs in play at the same time, runners circling the bases in reverse, and many more unusual situations.

For some unknown reason, the one-in-a-thousand situation has always fascinated me. Because of this, I became determined to research as much baseball as possible to find play situations and relate them to the proper rules.

When I began this nine years ago, I received some excellent advice from the late Arthur Daley, well known sportswriter for *The New York Times.* He advised me to read every baseball book ever written, a task almost impossible to carry out. However, I did read just about everything I could possibly get my hands on.

Aside from that, I distributed a form letter to many past and present major league players in search of situations relevant to my project. I will be forever grateful to the following men for their assistance: Fred Snodgrass, Johnny Vander Meer, Bobby Richardson, Johnny Klippstein, Bobby Bragan, Charlie Silvera, Dale Long, Tracy Stallard, Don Heffner, Charlie Maxwell, Danny Litwhiler, Virgil Trucks, Bobby Cox, Dick Cole, Hal Woodeschik, Ed McGhee, Ken Berry, Joe Garagiola, Billy Hitchcock, Henry Aaron, Solly Hemus, and the late Sid Gordon. Special thanks go to my friend Steve "Champ" Wynnick who allowed me to research countless editions of *The Sporting News* which he has collected over the years.

I would also like to thank Marty Appel of the Baseball Commissioner's Office for granting me permission to use the baseball rules in my text.

A special thank you is also in order to Mr. Fred Lieb, the legendary baseball writer, for giving me permission to use various anecdotes researched in some of his books.

I will be forever grateful to L. Robert Davids and the Society for American Baseball Research (SABR) for stimulating my thought and to retired Lieutenant Colonel Al Kermisch, a fellow member of the SABR, for allowing me to use a most unusual story he discovered concerning Walter Johnson.

To Tom Hammill and the staff at *Referee* magazine, thank you for the interest you have given my manuscript, and your encouragement.

To *The Sporting News* for its detailed and quality reporting of baseball situations, a most valuable aid in the completion of the text.

To Lauren Matthews, the former Director of Promotions for the New York Mets, for his help in my research.

To Cliff Kachline, Historian at the National Baseball Hall of Fame, for his prompt answers to the information I requested.

To Augie Guglielmo, former National League Umpire, for the colorful stories he provided.

To Art Ballant, my editor at Stein and Day, for his interest in my manuscript and his comprehensive review of the text.

To my wife Lois, who typed the revisions and who has been a supporting force throughout this project.

Baseball's playing code is covered in ten segments. Chronologically the rules begin with figure 1.00, "Objectives of the Game," and terminate with the "Official Scorer" contained in the 10.00 section. Because of the large number of rules, some of which are complicated by their interpretation, problems frequently occur among players, managers, and umpires. I have attempted to cover most of baseball's playing code with illustrated case studies.

Throughout the course of the book the term case book comment is used. For many years this was a section at the end of the rule book to explain various rules using practical examples. Following the 1975 World Series, in which American League Umpire Larry Barnett was involved in the famous controversial decision involving a possible interference call on Cincinnati batter Ed Armbrister, the case book was moved forward into the regular section of the rule book. The case book also includes special instructions given to the umpires.

It will appear in several instances that I am attempting to ridicule the men in blue by openly criticizing some of their decisions. However, it should be understood that the umpires listed in this book are my superiors by far and in most cases are shown to have properly interpreted the rule book. This publication suggests compassion for the men who make their living enforcing the rules that govern our national pastime.

A Special Acknowledgment to Nick Bremigan

When I completed this project, I felt the book needed a touch of major league class. Through the efforts of Tom Hammill, the Managing Editor of *Referee* magazine, I made contact with American League Umpire Nick Bremigan.

Upon reviewing my manuscript, Nick agreed to act as consultant for the book. His advice, corrections and lively additional anecdotes, provided the exact touch the text needed.

A graduate of the University of Rochester who has done graduate work at Syracuse University, Bremigan rates in the upper part of his class by his peers when it comes to knowledge of baseball's playing code.

Nick has been a member of the American League Umpiring staff since 1974. For the past several years he has been an instructor at the Bill Kinnamon Umpires' School in St. Petersburg, Florida. His ability to get his point across is easily seen in his writing.

Nick's presence is felt throughout the book. As a major league umpire his knowledge and expertise has been an invaluable aid.

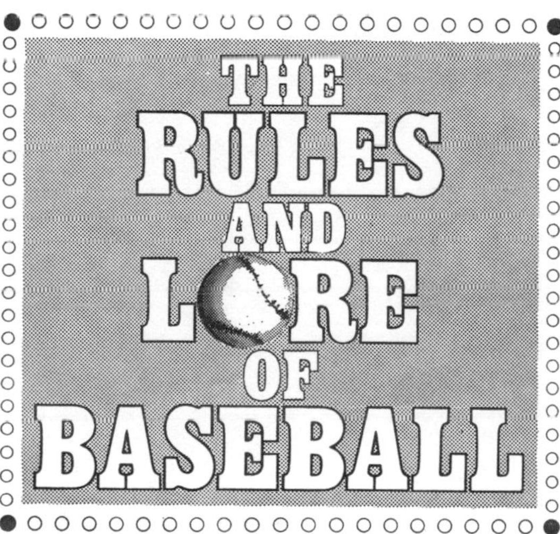
THE
RULES
AND
LORE
OF
BASEBALL

1.00

Objectives of the Game

In 1912 Casey Stengel played in the Southern League with the Montgomery, Alabama club. Playing a game one day at Pensacola, Florida, Casey noticed that in left field the groundskeeper had a sunken box containing the water pipe extension for sprinkling the field.

In the seventh inning, with his team several runs ahead, Casey removed the lid and crawled down in the box. The first two batters on the opposing team were put out. The next batter hit a fly to left field, the crowd began to howl when they could not see a left fielder. Mr. Stengel popped out of the box and caught the ball.

Rule 1.01 states *Baseball is a game between two teams of nine players each under direction of a manager, played on an enclosed field in accordance with these rules, under jurisdiction of one or more umpires.* I have to wonder if Casey's team had nine men on the field when he was below ground level. The rule states that both teams must have nine players. If a fielder forgets to take his position, and the umpire allows play to start with only eight players on the field, any subsequent action could be nullified. In 1955 in a semipro game played under the lights in Danbury, Connecticut, a player hit a home run with the defensive team fielding only eight players. The umpire had to nullify the four-bagger.

In 1874 the experiment of playing ten innings and using a tenth man was used without success. The tenth man was used as an extra shortstop between first and second, similar to the fifth infielder sometimes used in softball rather than the fourth outfielder or short fielder.

The rule that the defensive team must have nine players on a field caused Jeff Leonard of the Houston Astros to go one for three in only one at bat. It happened on the night of August 21, 1979, at Shea Stadium in a game against the Mets.

Leonard was batting with two outs in the ninth inning. At the time the Mets were leading 5-0. Leonard flied out to Lee Mazzilli in center field to apparently end the game. But before the pitch was delivered, Mets' shortstop Frank Taveras had called "time," forcing Leonard to bat again. Thinking the game had ended, Mets' first baseman Ed Kranepool left the game and entered the dugout.

Mets' chucker Pete Falcone pitched again. While the Mets had only eight players on the field, Leonard singled to left. As Jeff approached first base, Kranepool emerged from the dugout realizing he had made a mistake.

The umpires decided that since the Mets had only eight men on the field, Leonard would have to bat again. In his third try, Leonard flied out to left to end the game.

The Astros protested the ruling which was upheld the following morning by N.L. President Chub Feeney on the grounds that "time was in" when Leonard got his hit. So before the August 22 game started, the August 21 game resumed with two out in the top of the ninth with Leonard at first base.

Kevin Kobel replaced Falcone on August 22 and got Jose Cruz to ground out. The Mets' 5-0 victory was official, even though Jeff Leonard went one for three with one at-bat.

In my opinion, Chub "flubbed" this one as his decision is in direct conflict with the rule. According to Nick Bremigan, "All precedents in major league history indicate a team must have nine players to continue playing. There is no higher court to appeal to than the league president. Unfortunately there is no recourse even when the president is flagrantly wrong as was Mr. Feeney."

1.02—*The objective of each team is to win by scoring more runs than the opponent.*

During the 1979 season, Clemson demolished North Carolina State by an outrageous score of 41-9. That's a baseball score my friends, not a football score.

1.03—*The winner of the game shall be that team which shall have scored, in accordance with these rules, the greater number of runs at the conclusion of a regulation game.*

It would be safe to assume that if a team scores 23 runs in a game it should be sufficient to insure victory. However, on August 25, 1922, the Phillies scored 23 runs and lost to the Cubs, since the team from Chicago scored 26. In the game there was a combined total of 51 hits. There were 21 walks, a hit batsman, and 9 errors. The Cubs scored 14 runs in the fourth inning. Marty Callaghan batted three times in that high-scoring inning. The official scorer, a subject which I shall cover later in this book, had his work cut out for him that day.

Historically, the game almost paralleled itself with opposite results on May 17, 1979, when the Phillies defeated the Cubs, 23-22. A record of 97 total bases was established on this zany day at Wrigley Field.

The Cubs proved early in the 1976 season that an eleven-run lead is not necessarily safe until the game is over. Leading the Phillies by a score of 13-2, the Cubs became reckless and eventually lost the game, 16-14. Mike Schmidt of the Phillies hit four home runs to spark the great comeback.

Just to prove that the game is never over until the last out, the Red Sox scored nine runs in the ninth inning with two out against the Senators in 1961. Going into the bottom of the ninth at Fenway Park, Boston trailed Washington by a score of 12-4. The nine run ninth inning gave the Sox a well-earned 13-12 victory. Imagine how the fans felt who left in the eighth inning.

1.04—*The Playing Field*

The above rule is a long, detailed rule governing the dimensions of the field including the catcher's box, the batter's boxes, and the coaches' boxes. This section also specifies the use of wet lime, chalk, or other white material to be used to indicate the foul lines and all other playing lines.

Baseball historians credit Alexander Cartwright Jr. with formulating many of the basic rules in baseball. For instance, Cartwright has been credited with putting nine men on a side, playing nine innings, and is also noted for his rule that the distance between the bases should be 90 feet. At that time 90 feet was referred to as 42 paces.

When one thinks about numbers used in the game of baseball, it's uncanny how many rules and dimensions involve multiples of three. Let's take a look at a few.

1. Three outs to an inning.
2. Three strikes to a batter.
3. Nine innings to a ball game.
4. Nine players on the playing field.
5. 90-foot baselines.
6. The 45-foot line halfway between home plate and first base, which happens to be 3 feet wide.
7. Pitcher's slab or rubber to home plate is 60 feet 6 inches.
8. Three outfielders.
9. Six infielders (pitcher and catcher are considered a part of the infield).
10. Infield shall be a 90-foot square.
11. The base bags are 15-inch squares.
12. The pitcher's plate is a rectangular slab of whitened rubber 24 inches by 6 inches.
13. The ball cannot be less than nine inches in circumference.
14. The bat cannot be more than 42 inches in length.
15. Each fielder, other than the first baseman and catcher, may wear a leather glove not more than 12 inches long.
16. The pitching mound should be an 18-foot diameter circle.
17. The slope of the mound starts six inches from the front edge of the rubber.
18. The level area surrounding the rubber should be 6 inches in front of the rubber and 18 inches to each side.
19. There are 108 double stitches on a baseball.

Prior to 1950, pitching mounds were limited to 15 inches in height but could be less. In 1950, the height was made mandatory at 15 inches, and in 1969 it was reduced to 10 inches, no more, no less. You might think the layout of a pitching mound to be a thing that players and managers ignore and leave to the groundskeepers. However, pitching mounds have been known to vary from stadium to stadium. Major league umpires are required to inspect each park at least twice a year. This also includes the pitching mound in the bull pens. Certain teams in the major leagues have been accused of doctoring the mound on the playing field as well as the one in the visitors' bull pen.

With the 1976 season only two days old, Yankee manager Billy Martin protested a game against the Brewers because of the slope of the mound. Catfish Hunter thought the mound was too steep and used this as his reason for his control problems in a 5-0 opening-day defeat by the Brewers.

Umpiring supervisor John Stevens made a fifteen-hundred-mile round trip to measure the mound. Stevens found the mound was acceptable in meeting playing standards, and Martin lost the protest.

The procedure for measuring the slope of the mound is quite interesting. Two stakes are pounded in the ground—one at the center of the back edge of the rubber, the other at the back corner of home plate where the foul lines converge. A string is then connected to both stakes; the string is placed at ground level on the stake at the mound, and is elevated ten inches above the ground on the other stake. The string is then pulled tight so that there is no slack. A level is then run along the entire length of the string. If the level is even the entire length of the string, then the mound is all right. A similar procedure is performed at one inch intervals to ascertain the correctness of the slope. If any irregularities are found, the groundskeeper is called in to correct them.

Such irregularities are most commonly found toward the end of the baseball season at fields where both professional baseball and football are played. Most such parks construct the entire mound on a portable platform which can be completely removed intact to prepare the field for a football game, and then be replaced intact for baseball. Sometimes irregular adjustments can occur from frequent removal and replacement of this portable apparatus.

We will now take some time to explore the rule which states that the infield shall be a 90-foot square.

Prior to 1887, all three base bags were centered on the intersecting points of the 90-foot baselines. This caused a problem because it meant that half of the 15-inch square bags at first and third extended into foul territory. Umpires found this to be a problem in several fair and foul decisions. Because of this, first and third base were moved completely inside fair territory. However, second base was not moved, and part of the bag remains outside the 90-foot perimeter today.

Let's devote a little space now to the 4-foot by 6-foot rectangular area known as the batter's box. The batter must be standing in the box when he makes contact with the ball. If any contact is made while the batter is outside the box, the batter is out. Hank Aaron lost a home run because of this rule, which I shall cover in another part of the book.

On July 15, 1973, the Kansas City Royals met the New York Yankees at Yankee Stadium. Royals' slugger John Mayberry was standing so deep in the batter's box that Yankee catcher Jerry Moses complained to umpire John Rice that Mayberry was actually out of the box. Rice promptly pulled out a tape measure and measured the proper outline of the batter's box. He ruled that Mayberry's position was all right, and the game proceeded without incident.

Before 1869 the foul lines were made by digging a furrow with a plow. William Wing was the groundskeeper for the Cincinnati Red Stockings in 1869. Mr. Wing has been credited by baseball historian Lee Allen with the idea of marking the foul lines with a chalky substance.

1.05—*Home base shall be marked by a five-sided slab of whitened rubber.*

The rule also goes on to mention other dimensions that are not necessary to go into. It should be noted that before 1900 home plate was round and then evolved into a square. Baseball authorities believe it then evolved into a five-sided object because it made it easier for the umpire to call balls and strikes. When a batted ball hits the plate, the ball is alive and in play.

Rules 1.06 and 1.07 deal with the measurements of the bases and the pitcher's plate, which have already been mentioned.

1.08—*The home club shall furnish players' benches, one each for the home and visiting teams. Such benches shall be not less than twenty-five feet from the base lines. They shall be roofed and shall be enclosed at the back and ends.*

When ball parks began to be constructed out of steel and cement at the turn of the twentieth century, enclosed dugouts became popular. If a player catches a fly ball and falls into a dugout, the ball is dead and all runners advance one base. However, if he remains on his feet, the ball is alive and in play. By the way, the first team to have a dugout that wasn't "dug out" was the San Francisco Giants at Candlestick Park.

1.09—*The ball shall be a sphere formed by yarn wound around a small core of cork, rubber or similar material, covered with two strips of white horsehide, or cowhide tightly stitched together. It shall weigh not less than five nor more than 5¼ ounces avoirdupois and measure not less than nine nor more than 9¼ inches in circumference.*

A white baseball is as American as hamburgers and french fries. Larry MacPhail, general manager of the Brooklyn Dodgers in 1938, suggested using a dandelion-yellow baseball. The ball was used on August 2, 1938, as the Dodgers defeated the St. Louis Cardinals by a score of 6-2 in a game played at Ebbets Field.

In 1939 the yellow ball was used in three games. The Cardinals beat the Dodgers in two of the games, 12-0 and 5-2. The Dodgers defeated the Cubs 10-4, in the other game when the dandelion ball was used. After that game it was never used again.

In 1973, the Oakland Athletics under the direction of their owner

Charlie Finley experimented with an orange baseball during spring training. He claimed that the hitters could see the orange ball better than the conventional white baseball.

The orange ball was used at the Astrodome in Houston when the covered stadium first opened. The ball was supposed to help reduce the glare of the lights.

During the war the major leagues experimented with an ersatz balata ball with a synthetic-rubber center. The ball sounded like a rock when it was hit. It made the dead balls of the distant past seem lively. The synthetic ball didn't last too long, either.

As an economy measure, cowhide is used in place of horsehide today in many leagues. It is estimated that club owners save about two thousand dollars a year using the inferior cowhide covering.

1.10—(a) *The bat shall be a smooth, rounded stick not more than two and three-fourths inches in diameter at the thickest point and not more than 42 inches in length. The bat shall be* (1) *one piece of solid wood or* (2) *formed from a block of wood consisting of two or more pieces of wood bonded together with an adhesive in such a way that the grain direction of all pieces is essentially parallel to the length of the bat. Any such laminated bat shall contain only wood or adhesive, except for a clear finish.*

Cardinal catcher Ted Simmons had a fourth-inning home run nullified on the night of July 21, 1975, as the Cards hosted the San Diego Padres. Simmons's bat was ruled illegal because of grooves in the bat. The Cardinals played the rest of the game under protest but won the game anyway by a score of 4-0. Simmons was called out because he hit an illegally batted ball.

The New York Yankees were in first place by only a half-game margin when they played the Detroit Tigers in the second game of a double-header on September 7, 1974.

In the fifth inning of the nightcap, Graig Nettles lofted a soft opposite-field single to left and hesitated for a second before running to first base. He didn't stay there long, since plate umpire Lou DiMuro called him out for using an illegal bat.

DiMuro said, "About a two-inch piece was sawed off the end of the bat." The umpire further explained, "A hole had been drilled in the barrel of the bat, and what appeared to be cork had been placed in the hole. The piece was then glued back onto the bat, but when Nettles hit the ball it flew off. When I saw it fly off, I thought it was mud or something, but Freehan (Tigers' catcher Bill Freehan) called it to my attention, and I called Nettles out for tampering with the bat. That's illegal."

Although illegal, loading a bat with cork is fairly common among baseball players. Usually, a hole is drilled directly in the thick end of the bat rather than sawing off a segment of the barrel. The cork makes the bat feel lighter, and, for some reason, the ball jumps off the bat.

Earlier in the game, Nettles had hit a home run that was the winning run as the Yankees won the nightcap, 1-0. The question is, did Nettles use that bat when he hit the home run?

"It was the first time I used that bat," Nettles insisted. "A Yankee fan in Chicago gave it to me the last time we were there and said it would bring me luck. There's no brand name on it or anything. Maybe the guy made it himself. It's been in the bat rack, and I picked it up by mistake because it looks like the bat I've been using the last few days." How could anyone question a guy with an honest face like Graig Nettles?

1.10—(b) *The bat handle, for not more than 18 inches from the end, may be covered or treated with any material to improve the grip. No such material shall improve the reaction or distance factor of the bat.*

Yankee catcher Thurman Munson was the culprit in this episode. The Yankees and Twins met on the night of July 19, 1975 at Minnesota when umpire Art Frantz enforced this rule against Munson in the top of the first inning.

After Munson knocked in Sandy Alomar with a single, Minnesota manager Frank Quilici complained that the pine tar on Munson's bat exceeded 18 inches, which is in violation of the rule. The bat was checked by Frantz, and Munson was ruled out with the run being nullified. Minnesota catcher Glenn Borgmann was credited with a putout on the play.

Nick Bremigan recalls the incident vividly. "I was the ump at first that night. Munson always had a very wry sense of humor. When he returned after rounding first base, he kiddingly said to me, 'Better check the ball for blood.' He was referring to the fact that his single had been a bleeder, which indeed, it was. Munson was unaware of the situation at home plate where Quilici and Borgmann had prevailed upon Frantz, the plate umpire, to measure the pine tar on the bat. When Frantz found the bat to be illegal, he ruled Munson out.

I was aware of what was going on and casually said to Munson, 'Checking the ball would probably be irrelevant, because I think you've just been called out.'

Still unaware of the situation, Thurman retorted, 'Why? Did I hit the ball too softly?' He quickly became aware of the situation, and became very volatile. One of his major objectives each season was to get 100 RBI's.

Never being able to accept adversity calmly, Munson proceeded to vent his wrath for being deprived of an RBI—not so much at Frantz, but at Quilici and Borgmann for catching him."

1.11—(a-1) *All players on a team shall wear uniforms identical in color, trim and style, etc.*

Umpire Bill Haller laid rule 1.11(a) on Vida Blue on April 16, 1977. Haller forced Blue to remove the old, discolored cap that he had worn for some time. Blue superstitiously looked at his hat as his "lucky" cap. Vida said, "I'm going to wear it next time or I won't pitch." The Oakland pitcher had a change of heart the next day and proceeded to burn his cap in front of his teammates.

The 1.11 rule continues to deal with the uniform regulations. *1.11—(c-1) (1) Sleeve lengths may vary for individual players, but the sleeves of each individual player shall be approximately the same length. (2) No player shall wear ragged, frayed or slit sleeves.*

The basic reason for the rule is that it is a distraction to the batter to have to face a pitcher with ragged sleeves.

On the night of May 5, 1972, the Athletics hosted the Yankees at Oakland. Going into the bottom of the third inning with Oakland batting and the Yankees leading 1-0, umpire Bill Kunkel went out to the mound to check pitcher Fritz Peterson's shirt. It appeared that the shirt Peterson wore under his uniform shirt was slightly slit or frayed. Umpire Kunkel ordered Fritz to the clubhouse to change his shirt. The Yankee southpaw followed the umpire's order, and the game went on.

Frayed sleeves have been a baseball no-no for a long time. On June 7, 1938, the Indians and Red Sox played at Fenway Park. Umpire Bill McGowan ordered Cleveland chucker Johnny Allen to cut off part of his sweat shirt sleeve which dangled when he pitched. McGowan viewed this as a distraction to the batters.

Allen emphatically refused to cut his sleeve. The stubborn hurler refused to pitch and angrily walked off the mound. He was fined $250.00 for his obstinate actions. Allen's ragged shirt was eventually sent to the Hall of Fame at Cooperstown, N.Y.

1.11—(e) *No part of the uniform shall include a pattern that imitates or suggests the shape of a baseball.*

Joe Adcock protested the 1967 season opener when he managed the Indians in a game against the Athletics. The Athletics were not wearing a baseball shaped pattern on any part of their uniform, but they were wearing white shoes, which Adcock thought were deceptive and tended to confuse the hitter.

Adcock protested the game as soon as A's pitcher Jim Nash threw the first pitch to Vic Davalillo. The protest was rejected by A.L. President Joe Cronin.

Billy Martin was involved in a protest concerning the uniform when the White Sox made their first visit to the new Yankee Stadium early in the 1976 season. The White Sox invaded the stadium wearing their new uniforms, navy blue pants and blouses, clamdiggers, white hats, white lettering, and white undershirts.

Martin thought there must be something in the rules against white undershirts, especially if worn by a pitcher. Umpire Marty Springstead agreed but wasn't sure. Since it was too late to check with the league office, the umpire ordered Sox pitcher Bart Johnson to remove the white-sleeve shirt. The shirt was snipped with a scissors, and Johnson conducted his pitching chores. Relief pitcher Clay Carroll replaced his white shirt with a blue one. White Sox manager Paul

Richards protested the game, which the Yankees won, 5-4. American League president Lee MacPhail ruled the white shirts were acceptable but disallowed the protest lodged by the White Sox.

1.11—(f) *Glass buttons and polished metal shall not be used on a uniform.*

Umpire Ed Runge ordered Indian pitcher Dean Chance to remove a tiny flag pin from his cap on July 3, 1970, when the Indians met the Red Sox at Boston. Glass buttons and metal objects can cause a glare for the batter and therefore are illegal.

1.11—(g) *No player shall attach anything to the heel or toe of his shoe other than the ordinary shoe plate or toe plate.*

Most footwear protests in baseball involve the type of spikes used by players. During the 1976 season, Rangers' manager Frank Lucchesi protested when he observed Dan Ford of the Twins and Matt Alexander of the Athletics wearing illegal spikes. Instead of wearing the conventional baseball metal spikes, they wore spikes similar to those on golf shoes. In both instances the umpires ordered the players to change to shoes with spikes that conform to the rules.

Aloha Stadium in Honolulu was the site for a problem involving footwear in a Pacific Coast League game that was scheduled to be played between the Tacoma Twins and Hawaii Islanders on the night of May 7, 1976.

The wearing of metal cleats was prohibited at Aloha Stadium to protect the Astroturf surface.

Before the game, Tacoma manager Cal Ermer announced that starting pitcher Bill Butler would wear metal cleats. When Butler walked to the mound in the first inning to warm up, stadium officials switched off the outfield lights. After thirty minutes, plate umpire Bill Lawson ruled a forfeit in favor of Tacoma since the home team is responsible for playing conditions, which I will explore in rule 4.16.

Roy Jackson, Pacific Coast League president, supported Lawson's decision but was overruled a few weeks later by Bobby Bragan, Minor Leagues president. Bragan ordered the game replayed, saying that neither team was actually at fault.

1.12—*The catcher may wear a leather mitt not more than thirty eight inches in circumference, nor more than fifteen and one half inches from top to bottom, etc.*

Some fans might remember Orioles' catcher Gus Triandos wearing the oversized mitt to handle Knuckerballer Hoyt Wilhelm in the early sixties. Because Oriole receivers were having a difficult time holding Wilhelm, Orioles' manager Paul Richards requested the Wilson Sporting Goods Company to make a new glove. At the time the rule book stated, "the catcher may wear a leather glove or mitt of any size, shape or weight." Richards' pillow type mitt measured as much as 45 inches in circumference.

Storms of protest came in from all corners. Finally a restriction was placed on the size of the glove. The current wording of the rule went into effect in 1965. Other sections of the rule are concerned with the spacing between thumb section and the finger section including the webbing.

It should be understood that a catcher can only wear a mitt, while a first baseman can wear a mitt or glove. Since the measurements pertaining to a first baseman's mitt are less than those specified for a catcher, a catcher should be allowed to wear a first baseman's mitt, but not a first baseman's or any other fielder's glove.

On September 21, 1958, the Cubs hosted the Dodgers at Wrigley Field in Chicago. Dale Long, who usually played first base, became the Cub catcher in the ninth inning. He had done the same thing about a month earlier that season in a game against the Pirates as a fill-in.

A few things were strange about Long going behind the dish. To begin with, it is very rare to see a left-handed catcher. And secondly, Long caught with a first baseman's glove in the Pirates' game, which although not common is legal. In the game against the Dodgers, he caught with a left-handed catcher's mitt. How many people in this world have ever seen a left-handed catcher's mitt?

Long became baseball's first left-handed catcher since 1906. Before the turn of the century, Fergy Malone, Jack Clements, and Pop Tate, among others, caught left-handed. Tom Doran was the last previous left-handed catcher in the majors, playing for Boston and Detroit from 1904 to 1906.

Oriole catcher Clay Dalrymple tested this rule on the night of July

17, 1969, when the White Sox and Orioles met in Baltimore. In the first inning, Dalrymple came out with his regular catcher's mitt on his left hand and a fielder's glove in his back pocket. The fielder's glove would be used if there was a play at the plate since it might be easier to catch the ball with the more flexible fielder's glove.

The situation confused umpire John Rice since he had never been faced with this kind of problem before. Rice got Dalrymple to promise he wouldn't use the glove in the first inning or until he could get the other umpires and managers together.

Rice said, "About the only thing we could figure that covered it in the rules was the rule stating there cannot be any extra gloves on the field." He was referring to rule 3.14 which I will cover later.

1.13—*The first baseman may wear a leather glove or mitt not more than twelve inches long from top to bottom and not more than eight inches wide across the palm, measured from the base of the thumb crotch to the outer edge of the mitt,* etc.

This rule similar to the previous one regarding the catcher's mitt also goes into the spacing and the webbing of the glove.

1.14—*Each fielder, other than the first baseman and the catcher may wear a leather glove not more than twelve inches long nor more than eight inches wide, measured from the base of the thumb crotch to the outer edge of the glove,* etc.

The remainder of the rule also deals with the spacing between the thumb and the forefinger and the webbing.

In the case of an illegal use of a glove, the umpire directs the fielder to remove it and use one of regulation size. If the player refuses, he is subject to ejection.

1.15—(a) *The pitcher's glove shall be uniform in color and shall not be white or gray.* (b) *No pitcher shall attach to his glove any foreign material of a color different from the glove.*

The reason for this rule is to protect the batter. A white or gray glove could be a distraction to a batter since it would make it difficult for him to follow the white baseball. The rule is sometimes violated on the amateur level, but I know of no instance where it was abused in the major leagues.

2.00

Definitions of Terms

Rule 2.00 defines the various terms covered in the game of baseball. For purposes of this writing, it is not necessary to list each one since many will be discussed in other sections of the publication. I will, however, attempt to explain some of the terms that are frequently used, such as fair or foul ball, the strike zone, and the infield fly rule, which is so often misinterpreted.

The first item is the fair ball. According to the rules, *A fair ball is a batted ball that settles on fair ground between home and first base, or between home and third base, or that is on or over fair territory when bounding to the outfield past first or third base, or that touches first, second or third base, or that first falls on fair territory on or beyond first base or third base, or that, while on or over fair territory, touches the person of an umpire or player, or that, while over fair territory, passes out of the playing field in flight.* It should also be noted here, that it is not the position of the player's feet, but the position of the ball (fair or foul) that determines if a ball is fair or foul. This is unlike football or basketball, where the opposite holds true.

Also, *A foul ball is a batted ball that settles on foul territory between home and first base, or between home and third base, or that bounds past first or third on or over foul territory, or that first falls on foul territory beyond first or third base, or that, while on or over foul territory, touches the person of an umpire or player, or any object foreign to natural ground.*

During Casey Stengel's days as a Brooklyn Dodger player, he was involved in a tricky "fair ball." Stengel topped a roller down the first base line. The umpire yelled, "Foul!", but it rolled back into fair territory. The first baseman picked up the ball and tagged Casey. The umpire then changed his call from "Foul!" to "You're Out!" If this happened today, Casey would have been given another life since the foul call would have killed the play. This is the reason umpires never make a call on a slow trickler down the first or third base line until either a fielder touches the ball or the ball stops rolling.

As far back as 1885 a protest developed in a game between the Chicago White Stockings and the St. Louis Club. The White Stockings were enjoying a three run rally in the sixth inning when Ed Williamson sent a slow spinning roller "foul" up the first base line. The ball hit a clump of grass, bounced against the base, and was ruled a fair ball. The St. Louis Club protested that it was not a fair ball. Getting nowhere with the argument, St. Louis left the playing field, and the game was forfeited to Chicago.

Mickey Rivers of the Yankees was credited with an infield hit on that exact type of play on the night of June 9, 1976, when the Yankees played the Angels in New York. Rivers' slow roller went foul up along the third base line, hit a clump of dirt, and then the third base bag.

The Tigers met the Pirates in the 1909 World Series. This was the first Series to which four umpires were assigned, although only two worked at a time. The first game was umpired by Jim Johnstone and Silk O'Loughlin. The second game was handled by Bill Klem and Billy Evans. It was in this game, played in Pittsburgh, that Dots Miller of the Pirates hit a Bill Donovan pitch, leading to a controversial decision.

In the bottom half of the first inning the Pirates were batting with Tommy Leach on third with one run already in and two outs. Miller then hit a low line drive along the foul line in the direction of a temporary bleacher deep in right field.

Part of the bleacher was in fair territory, and part of it was in foul territory. As the ball sailed for the stands, the crowd stood up and obstructed the vision of the two umpires. Neither Evans nor Klem saw the ball land. They both proceeded to march to the outfield to investigate the play. Evans raised his hands and asked the bleacherites where the ball had landed.

Several Pirate fans sitting in the front row pointed to a spot inside fair territory. Evans then decided that the ball must have hit in fair territory and bounced into the crowd. The play was ruled a ground-rule double. Miller, having rounded all the bases, had to go back to second because of the fans' honesty. Leach was allowed to score on the play, but the Pirates still lost, 7-2.

Today screens are attached to the foul poles, and always on the fair side extending over fair ground. This is done to alleviate indecision as to whether a ball is "fair" or "foul." If a batted ball hits the foul pole or attached screen, it is a fair ball. A baseball misnomer deals with foul lines and foul poles. Since they are both in fair territory, shouldn't they be called fair lines and fair poles?

As a member of the Valley Umpires Association, in Connecticut, I am often involved in sessions after meetings where we discuss strange plays and situations. One night one of the members related a strange foul ball situation he had witnessed in a local Little League game. The batter hit a line drive off the pitcher's plate on the mound. The ball caromed off the plate and landed near the first base dugout in foul territory. Since the ball did not make contact with the pitcher, the ball was ruled foul in accordance with the rule. If the same play had occurred in the 1860s, it would have been ruled fair because of the so called "fair-foul" hit. If a bunt struck fair and then rolled foul it was ruled a fair ball because the ball originally landed in fair territory.

The strike zone is that space over home plate which is between the batter's armpits and the top of his knees when he assumes his natural stance. The umpire shall determine the strike zone according to the batter's usual stance when he swings at a pitch.

Some credit Hall of Fame umpire Bill Klem for originating the practice of getting down on the ball by going into a crouch behind the catcher's shoulder to judge "balls" and "strikes." Others believe that John H. Gaffney, called "The King of the Umpires," began the practice of working behind the plate in the nineteenth century. Regardless of who began the practice, it is from this position that the strike zone is best seen by the umpire. If the pitch is out of the strike zone, the umpire will simply say "ball!" If the pitch is a strike, the ump will raise his right hand or make some gesture with that hand and yell "strike."

Klem is credited with "inventing" the inside chest protector for umpires. Until that time, all umpires behind the plate wore the outside-type chest protector, commonly called the "balloon" since they were made with an inflatable bladder which would be deflated for packing and travel purposes. Klem believed that an umpire could get a better look at the pitch if he could work over the catcher's shoulder, looking at the pitches between the catcher and the batter.

The Hall of Fame arbiter took a catcher's protector, added shoulder pads and began wearing it under his shirt instead of outside. Thus the inside umpire's chest protector was born. According to Nick Bremigan, "Since Klem was the dean of the National League umpires, the league made it mandatory that all its umpires wear this type of protector. The only exception to this was Jocko Conlon, who wore a sawed-off version of an outside protector in the National League during the last years of his career. The reason for this was that Jocko's doctor told him if he was ever hit in the throat again, it could lead to very serious complications."

For years the umpires of both leagues rivaled each other. The N.L. followed the practices of Klem, their patron saint, while it is generally believed that A.L. arbiters followed the lead of Tom Connolly who worked in both circuits during a career that spanned 33 seasons.

In 1975, A.L. President Lee MacPhail made it optional for American League umpires to wear either type of chest protector. But in 1977 the inside protector was made mandatory for any umpire who came into the league after the 1976 season.

The outside protector will eventually become as extinct as the dinosaur as years go on. Today only a small number of umpires wear the outside protector which is now made with a hard foam type of material. Among the more popular ones include Bill Haller and Ron Luciano.

Because the new outside protectors couldn't be deflated and packed, the A.L. bought two for each ball park, and they are left in the umpires' dressing room.

Dummy Hoy, a deaf mute, who played for the White Sox in 1901 and Cincinnati in 1902, has been credited with initiating the practice of umpires raising their right hand on a called strike. He asked the umpire to raise his right arm to signify a strike, since he had no way of knowing what the count was. The idea soon became a standard procedure.

Cy Rigler, who umpired in the major leagues from 1905-1922 and from 1924-1935, is credited with being the first big league arbiter to raise his right hand to indicate a strike.

Baseball trivia experts inevitably ask the question, "Who was the midget that batted for the St. Louis Browns in 1951 in a game against the Detroit Tigers?" Eddie Gaedel, the 3′ 7″ midget sent up to bat by Bill Veeck, has become a legend among baseball triviots through the country. Since this was Gaedel's first (and last) major league at bat, he could determine his own natural stance. He was told to crouch to even further decrease his strike zone. In his crouched stance his strike zone measured one and a half inches.

Tiger pitcher Bob Cain walked Gaedel on four straight pitches. The Tiger catcher was Bob Swift, and the umpire making the calls was Ed Hurley.

When Gaedel, who wore uniform number 1/8 and also wore elves shoes, reached first base via his walk, he was replaced by Jim Delsing. What a trivia question! Who ran for Eddie Gaedel on first?

Stan Coveleski was the mound ace for the Cleveland Indians from 1916-24. In one game, Coveleski pitched seven innings without throwing a single errant pitch to the batter. Every pitch that wasn't hit was called a strike by the umpire. That is what you call control.

It is commonly known that it is a strike if the batter swings and misses. It becomes confusing to the umpire and fans when the batter takes only a half swing or less. If the umpire thinks the batter "broke his wrists," he will call a strike. With a left-handed batter the umpire will often check with the third base umpire on a checked swing. He will check with the first base umpire with a right-handed batter at the plate.

When Jocko Conlan was umpiring, he made it a rule that every batter be entitled to a full swing. Conlan never believed in "a half-swing strike" with an argument over whether or not the wrists were broken. Jocko used to inform each manager before any game he worked behind the plate of his ideas concerning a swing.

Plate umpires have been involved in some peculiar scenes, but nothing compares to the stunt pulled by N.L. umpire Augie Guglielmo while working an International League game between Buffalo and Toledo.

In his first at bat that night, Buffalo first sacker Fred Hopke took a pitch that was called a "strike" by Guglielmo. The game was to be Hopke's last professional game as he was going to call it quits after a long minor league career. Hopke turned to Augie and said, "I always thought you were a great umpire, but I really think you missed the pitch."

Realizing that this was Hopke's swan song, Guglielmo in an unprecedented shocking move, turned to the press box and yelled, "Change that 'strike' to a 'ball'."

When Toledo skipper Frank Verdi came out to argue, Gugie said, "Did you ever hail a cab and decide you didn't want it? Well this is the same thing."

Who said that umpires never change their decisions?

It is also a strike if *a legal pitch touches the batter in flight in the strike zone.* Minnie Minoso in his playing days with the White Sox had a major bearing on this rule. Minoso was frequently struck because he crowded the plate so much. Minnie was hit in the strike zone several times and was not awarded first base because of this rule.

In 1895 the infield fly rule was instituted. *An infield fly is a fair fly ball (not including a line drive nor an attempted bunt) which can be caught by an infielder with ordinary effort, when first and second, or first, second and third bases are occupied, before two are out. The pitcher, catcher and any outfielder who stations himself in the infield on the play shall be considered infielders for the purpose of this rule.*

When it seems apparent that a batted ball will be an infield fly, the umpire shall immediately declare "Infield Fly" for the benefit of the runners. If the ball is near the baselines, the umpire shall declare "Infield Fly, If Fair."

The ball is alive and runners may advance at the risk of the ball being caught, or retouch and advance after the ball is touched, the same as on any fly ball. If the hit becomes a foul ball, it is treated the same as any foul.

The next time you're at a game or talking baseball with your friends ask them to define the infield fly rule. Chances are the answers you will receive will vary from amusing to absurd. Allan Funt could have a great deal of fun asking this question as one of his Candid Camera stunts.

The purpose of the rule is to protect runners from being caught in a double play because an infielder intentionally allows the ball to drop. This rule, which has been in baseball for more than eighty years, is often times misunderstood, as you will see in the next few anecdotes.

In a game played between the Chicago White Sox and Kansas City Athletics on April 27, 1956, fast thinking by Jim Finigan enabled the A's to turn a double play against the White Sox. With Luis Aparicio on second base and Billy Pierce on first in the second inning, the K.C. keystoner let Jim Rivera's pop fly hit the ground. Rivera was automatically out under the infield fly rule, and Aparicio was nailed sliding into third base on Finigan's toss to pitcher Art Ditmar, who covered. Aparicio did not have to run, as the infield fly rule states, the batter is automatically out, but runners may advance at their own risk.

It should be understood that if a runner advances at his own risk, the fielders are required to tag the runner. Gene Freese, Ron Santo, and Ken Boyer each had to learn this rule the hard way.

Confusion over this aspect of the infield fly caused a problem in the Cub-Cardinal game played on July 25, 1961.

Ron Santo was on second and Jerry Kindall on first for the Cubs, in the second inning, when Ed Bouchee popped to second baseman Julian Javier. As there were less than two out, the infield fly rule was in effect, and Bouchee was out according to the rule.

Javier dropped the ball, and, as the rule states, Santo was free to advance at his own peril. Javier recovered the ball and threw to Ken Boyer, who stepped on third base. The force play was not in order, but Santo, believing he had been retired, started toward the dugout; Cardinal pitcher Ray Sadecki yelled to Boyer, who tagged Santo when the Cub runner attempted to return to the bag.

This next situation was created in the first game of a double-header between the Braves and Pirates at Milwaukee on June 3, 1956.

With none out in the Milwaukee half of the ninth inning and Braves on first and second, Frank Torre hit a fly to short center field. Either shortstop Dick Groat or center fielder Bill Virdon could have caught the ball. But when Groat got under it, umpire Augie Donatelli signaled that Torre was automatically out under the infield fly rule. Groat, however, dropped the ball, and the confusion began. Former Dodger slayer Bobby Thomson, who was on second base, forgot that Torre was automatically out and headed for third, thinking a force play was in effect. The throw beat Thomson to third, but Gene Freese, the Pirate third sacker, also committed a mental error, stepping on the bag instead of tagging Thomson, who was then safe at third. Bill Bruton, the runner on first, advanced to second in the confusion. During the Pirates' argument that ensued, catcher Hank Foiles was banished.

Among other things, the odd play created an official scoring problem. The error originally was charged to Freese because of his failure to tag Thomson. It was transferred to Groat, however, since his failure (deliberate or otherwise) to catch the ball had induced the base runners to try to advance, and since Freese's mistake had been one of omission rather than commission. The Braves failed to capitalize on the play, and the Bucs won, 3-1.

In defense of Santo, Freese, and Boyer, the rule book should specifically state that a tag is necessary in situations of that type.

On Monday, August 7, 1972, the following fiasco took place. The Minnesota Twins were playing the Texas Rangers. With the Rangers batting, Dick Billings and Ted Ford began the inning with singles. Bill Fahey followed with a looper back to the mound with plate umpire Bill Haller calling the infield fly rule. That meant that Fahey was automatically out. Pitcher Gaylord Perry, not hearing Haller's call, let the ball drop, then grabbed it and raced to third for an attempted force play. And when, in the confusion, Billings assumed he was out on the force and wandered toward the dugout, Perry tagged him for the second out. I wonder if Perry really didn't hear Haller's call.

Frankie Frisch, while managing the Cardinals in 1934, won a protest concerning the infield fly rule in a game against the Cubs.

The Cubs had the bases loaded with one out when Chuck Klein hit a towering fly in foul ground behind the catcher. The ball was buffeted about in the wind and then proceeded to land in fair territory, about twenty feet from home plate on the first base side. Umpire Bill Klem refused to enforce the infield fly rule, since no Cardinal infielder would have been able to catch the ball with ordinary effort. Klein ran to first base and pitcher Lon Warneke scored on an errant throw to first baseman Rip Collins.

The Cardinals' protest was upheld by League president John A. Heydler, who said, "Klein's fly should automatically have been called an infield fly as soon as the umpire was able to determine it was fair." I think most umpires would disagree with Heydler's decision, although his thinking does protect the runners very well.

If a batter bunts the ball and the ball goes high into the air, it is not considered an infield fly as defined in the rule. Confusion over this aspect of the rule caused a triple play in an International League game played between Syracuse and Charleston on July 28, 1972.

Charleston had runners on first and second with nobody out in the second inning. Charlie pitcher Frank Frontino's sacrifice bunt attempt looped toward first baseman Frank Tepedino. The Syracuse first baseman thought quickly and allowed the ball to drop, then threw to third baseman Rich McKinney for a force at third. McKinney then relayed the ball to shortstop Frank Baker for the second out, and Baker's throw to second baseman Tom Grayson, covering first, was in time to nip Frontino.

I once umpired an American Legion game when a knotty problem developed concerning the infield fly rule. The team at bat had the bases loaded with one out when the batter hit a high fly ball between home plate and first base. I yelled, "Infield fly if fair!" The ball came down in foul territory without any infielder touching the ball. It landed on a pebble about three feet from the first base bag and rolled into fair territory. The pitcher picked up the ball and the batter was out, since the ball had trickled into fair territory.

3.00

Game Preliminaries

This chapter of the rules deals with game preliminaries, the doctoring of the ball, player substitutions, player and fan fraternization, weather conditions affecting the start of a game, spectator interference, authorized personnel on the playing field, and the home team's responsibility to preserve order.

3.01—*Before the game begins the umpire shall* (a) *Require strict observance of all rules governing implements of play and equipment of players;* (b) *Be sure that all playing lines are marked with lime, chalk or other white material easily distinguishable from the ground or grass.*

Often the base coaches will try to erase the chalk lines so that they can wander and get a better look at the catcher's sign. Players have been instructed by certain managers to drag their spikes when they cross the coaching box so that the chalk lines will disappear.

Al Barlick enforced this rule umpiring a Met game at Shea Stadium a few years ago. Barlick stopped the game and ordered the groundskeepers to rechalk the lines.

When the Dodgers played in the Los Angeles Coliseum they were caught tampering with the infield to give base stealing Maury Wills an edge on the bases. One of the umpires working the game that day arrived at the Coliseum early to watch batting practice. He noticed a bulldozer coming on to the playing field and was surprised by the whole thing. He soon realized that the heavy machine was being used to harden the base paths for the purpose of giving Wills more traction. The groundcrew was ordered to come out and put the field in a more normal playing condition.

3.01—(c) *Before the game begins the umpire shall receive from the home club a supply of regulation baseballs, the number and make to be certified to the home club by the league president. Each ball shall be enclosed in a sealed package bearing the signature of the league president, and the seal shall not be broken until just prior to game time when the umpire shall open each package to inspect the ball and remove its gloss. The umpire shall be the sole judge of the fitness of the balls to be used in the game.*

Lena Blackburne, a former player for the St. Louis Browns, discovered a special type of mud along the banks of the Delaware River. Baseballs used in major league games are rubbed up by the umpires with this so called "super mud." The mud dulls the gloss of a new baseball without significantly changing its color.

Before the start of the game, umpires are given sixty baseballs to be rubbed this way. Eight dozen baseballs are prepared for a double-header.

There has been much talk about Eddie Stanky being responsible for storing baseballs in a cool, damp place when he managed the White Sox. An ex-Sox catcher said, "You had to wipe the mildew off the balls before the game. First you'd take them out of the boxes, which were all rotted away anyway, wipe the mildew off, and put them in new boxes. Then you gave them to the umpires, and they never suspected a thing."

It would not be fair to credit Stanky with the idea. This was done many years ago by the "Grand Old Man" himself, Connie Mack.

Frederick Lieb describes the freezing practice in his book, *The Pittsburg Pirates.*

"There used to be an icebox in the Pittsburgh Club's offices, and Connie conceived the idea of stuffing boxes of baseballs into the icebox, and freezing them overnight. The practice supposedly froze the life out of baseballs."

301—(d) *Before the game begins the umpire shall be assured by the home club that at least one dozen regulation reserve balls are immediately available for use if required.*

The St. Louis Browns played their last game at Sportsman's Park at the end of the 1953 season. The Browns lost their one-hundredth game of the season, a 2-1 defeat at the hands of the White Sox that lasted 12 innings.

Plate umpire Art Passarella called for a fresh supply of baseballs when the game went into extra innings but was told that the supply was exhausted. It looked as though the game might have to be called because of a lack of baseballs, but Passarella saved the day for the Browns by picking the least damaged balls that were thrown out during the game. The Browns found many ways to lose games that season, but I don't think they expected to lose because of a shortage of baseballs.

3.01—(e) *Before the game begins the umpire shall have in his possession at least two alternate balls and shall require replenishment of such supply of alternate balls as needed throughout the game. Such alternate balls shall be put into play when* (1) *a ball has been batted out of the playing field or into the spectator area;* (2) *a ball has become discolored or unfit for further use;* (3) *the pitcher requests such alternate balls.*

National League umpires had to be alert when they worked at Wrigley Field in Chicago. It seemed that Pat Peiper, the ex-Cub field announcer would sit alongside the ball bag near the dugout. Peiper was suspected of throwing out the best balls to the ball boy to be used when the Cubs were at bat. According to umpire Harry Wendelstedt, "It got so bad that the umpires had to mark each ball that was thrown out of the game with a ballpoint pen so that Peiper couldn't slip them back in when the opposition was at bat." The rule prohibiting the use of a soiled baseball was enacted in 1908.

3.02—*No player shall intentionally discolor or damage the ball by rubbing it with soil, rosin, paraffin, licorice, sand-paper, emery-paper or other foreign substance. PENALTY—the umpire shall demand the ball and remove the offender, and if the pitcher delivers such discolored or damaged ball to the batter, the pitcher shall be removed from the game at once and shall be suspended automatically for ten days.*

Supposedly there is something about the slippery-elm bark that sets off the salivary glands. Ed Walsh, who pitched for the Chicago team in the American League from 1904 to 1916 and Boston of the National League in 1917, is known to have used the slippery-elm bark.

Walsh used to carry a supply of tablets made from the bark of the slippery-elm tree. Before a game he would put a couple of sticks of gum and one of these tablets in his mouth. He would chew real hard, and the combination made the ball do some fancy things. Believe it or not, certain pitchers use the slippery-elm tablets today, although it is illegal.

Dodger chucker Don Sutton and ump Doug Harvey were the main characters in a scenario that developed on July 14, 1978. Harvey collected three baseballs that were scuffed, then shocked the Dodger hurler by ejecting him in the seventh inning of the game at St. Louis. Harvey said in his defense, "I represent the integrity of the game and I'm going to continue to do it if necessary."

3.03—*A player, or players, may be substituted during a game at any time the ball is dead. A substitute player shall bat in the replaced player's position in the team's batting order. A player once removed from a game shall not re-enter the game. If a substitute enters the game in place of a player-manager, the manager may thereafter go to the coaching lines at his discretion. When two or more substitute players of the defensive team enter the game at the same time the manager shall, immediately* *before they take their positions as fielders, designate to the umpire-in-chief such players' positions in the team's batting order and the umpire-in-chief shall so notify the official scorer. If this information is not immediately given to the umpire-in-chief, he shall have authority to designate the substitutes' places in the batting order.*

It was probably due to the antics of Mike Kelly known as "King Kelly" that prompted rules-makers to insert the first sentence of this rule.

Kelly played for the Boston Braves before the turn of the century and was also the team's captain. Once he put himself into a game so that he could catch a foul fly even while the ball was in the air.

Here is what took place. Charlie Ganzel was catching, and Kelly was sitting on the bench when the batter hit a high foul fly. Ganzel was having trouble locating the ball. Kelly noticed that Ganzel was having trouble. Immediately Kelly shouted to thc umpire, "Kelly now catching for Boston." The King jumped off the bench and caught the ball. At that time lineup changes did not have to be announced to the spectators by the umpire. Today substitutions can be made only when the ball is dead.

As the rule states a player cannot reenter the game once he has been removed. Pinch-hitting for a pinch hitter would be an example. Once a pinch hitter is announced, he is considered to have entered the game.

In 1908 the Phillies sent in a pinch hitter against the Pirates. The Pirates then retaliated by sending in a relief pitcher. The Phillies then re-retaliated by putting in a pinch hitter for the pinch hitter.

During that game an argument developed as to whether the first pinch hitter could be used since he never did pinch-hit. The argument was won by the Pirates. The umpire decided that the pinch hitter in question was put officially in the game and thereby was not eligible to return. The rule still stands today because of this weird incident.

On May 1, 1967, Cedar Rapids of the Midwest League protested a 4-3 loss to Quincy because a Quincy player who had been removed from the game was allowed to coach first base later on.

League president, Jim Doster, ruled that the incident had no bearing on the game's outcome, and the protest was disallowed. Doster did say the umpire should not have allowed the player to go to the coaching lines, which is a violation of rule 3.03. If the Quincy player had been a player-manager, he would have legally been allowed to go to the coaching lines.

The maneuverings of Spokane manager Bobby Bragan led to a dispute in a Pacific Coast League game played on June 17, 1959, between Spokane and San Diego.

In the seventh inning, Bragan sent up three successive pinch hitters, Ernie Rodriguez, Wilson Parsons, and Dick Young. When the Spokane Indians took the field in the eighth, Rodriguez was in left field and Young at third with Parsons on the bench and Phil Paine the new Spokane pitcher.

Following Paine's first pitch to Bill Moran, leading off the eighth for San Diego, Bragan ordered Parsons to go to left field in place of Rodriguez. Bragan claimed he told plate umpire Tom Dunn before the inning started that Parsons was going to left field and that Dunn had written the change on his lineup card. San Diego skipper George Metkovich challenged the shift. His stand was that since one pitch had been thrown with Rodriguez in the lineup, Parsons could not legally reenter the game. When the umpires ruled that Parsons could take the field, Metkovich announced he was finishing the game under protest. However, he evidently changed his mind later, since no official protest was filed with league headquarters as the rules require.

Ironically, Parsons figured in the winning rally in the ninth. He opened the frame with a walk and scored the tying run on a double by Tom Davis, who later scored the winning run on Steve Bilko's single. Spokane won, 11-10.

It would have been interesting to see how P.C.L. officials would have ruled on that unusual situation.

Mr. Bragan flirted with the substitution rule when he managed Hollywood during the 1955 season. Upset with the umpiring as his team was losing to Los Angeles, Bragan sent in eight consecutive pinch hitters in the last inning. They kept replacing each other after one pitch.

It isn't often that you see a pinch runner for a pinch runner, but it happened in the 1960 Cub-Cardinal Labor Day double-header. In the tenth inning of the first game Cardinals' manager Solly Hemus sent Curt Simmons in to run for George Crowe. However, before the next pitch was delivered, Hemus withdrew Simmons and this time sent Alex Grammas in to run for him.

3.04—*A player whose name is on his team's batting order may not become a substitute runner for another member of his team.*

The idea of this rule is to eliminate the practice of using courtesy runners. I have not found this rule violated on the major league level. However, courtesy runners are allowed in some sandlot games.

3.05—(a) *The pitcher named in the batting order handed the umpire-in-chief, as provided in rules 4.01(a) and 4.01(b), shall pitch to the first batter or any substitute batter until such batter is put out or reaches first base, unless the pitcher sustains injury or illness which, in the judgment of the umpire-in-chief, incapacitates him from pitching.*

In a Southern Association League game played on August 13, 1957, Manager Peanuts Lowrey of New Orleans listed the wrong pitcher on his official lineup cards, which led to an unusual situation and a protested game.

Lowrey wrote down the name of Jerry Buchanan, although intending to start Walt Kellner. When Kellner took the mound for Birmingham's half of the first inning, plate umpire Frank Girard would not allow him to start. Instead, he ordered Buchanan to the hill. Allowed no extra time for warm-up, Buchanan walked the Baron leadoff batter, and then Kellner replaced him.

Later in the inning, Baron manager Johnny Pesky filed an official protest, contending Girard shouldn't have notified the Pels of the mistake. New Orleans went on to win, 7-5. League President Charley Hurth nixed the Baron protest the next day, ruling that Pesky had not entered his protest immediately after the disputed point, as required by league rules.

3.05—(b) *If the pitcher is replaced, the substitute pitcher shall pitch to the batter then at bat, or any substitute batter, until such* *batter is put out, or reaches first base, or until the offensive team is put out, unless the substitute pitcher sustains injury or illness which, in the umpire-in-chief's judgment, incapacitates him for further play as a pitcher.*

As long as a pitcher stays in the game after he is relieved a pitcher can technically relieve himself. Such was the case with White Sox pitcher Harry Dorish when manager Paul Richards sent Dorish to third base and brought in left hander Billy Pierce to pitch to Red Sox slugger Ted Williams. After Pierce retired Williams, Dorish returned to the mound and was the winning pitcher when the White Sox beat the Red Sox 9-7 in 11 innings. The clever substitution took place on May 15, 1957 at Fenway Park in Boston.

Pittsburgh manager Chuck Tanner took a page from Richards' book on Sept. 1, 1979, when the Pirates beat the Giants 5-3 at Candlestick Park.

With two outs in the ninth inning, Bucs' chucker Kent Tekulve was relieved by southpaw Grant Jackson so Jackson could pitch to Darrell Evans, a lefty swatter. Tanner apparently had plans to use Tekulve again as he sent the lanky Pirate to left field replacing John Milner. Ironically the game ended when Evans flied to Tekulve in left field.

Johnny Antonelli lodged a successful protest under this rule when he managed Memphis of the Texas League in 1972 in a game against Amarillo.

In the bottom of the ninth with Amarillo leading, 9-7, pitcher Frank Riccelli was removed with two outs. Amarillo manager Denny Sommers brought in Less White to relieve Riccelli.

After White completed his warm-up tosses, Sommers decided to use Hal Jeffcoat as his pitcher. Antonelli protested, saying that under the rules White was obliged to pitch to at least one batter or retire one man.

League President Bobby Bragan upheld the protest and fined the two umpires twenty-five dollars each for negligence of rule 3.05(b).

"The game was resumed at a later date with Amarillo winning 11-9 in 11 innings." Memphis skipper Johnny Antonelli should not be confused with the former N.L. hurler. It might be hard to believe, but there were two players in big league history named Johnny Antonelli. This one was an infielder for the Cardinals and the Phillies during

1944 and 1945. Most fans only remember the Giants' pitcher of the 1950s.

It is rare to see a pitcher become incapacitated on the mound, but it happened to baseball-pitcher-turned-author Jim Brosnan as he went to the mound to pitch for the Cubs in the tenth inning in a game played against the Giants on July 21, 1957, at Wrigley Field. Brosnan fell while warming up and suffered an injury to his Achilles tendon forcing him to leave the game without throwing a pitch to a batter.

Umpires must be keenly alert concerning the enforcement of 3.05(b). It can get confusing during a long inning, and particularly if there has been a rain delay during such inning. In this one particular game, Nestor Chylak was the plate umpire in Chicago. After a rain delay, the White Sox manager inserted a new relief pitcher, Rich Gossage. The previous relief pitcher, Clay Carroll, was still pitching to his first batter when the rains came forcing the delay.

Just as Gossage finished his warm-up tosses and action was about to resume, it clicked in Chylak's mind that Carroll should still be pitching. He directed Carroll to return to finish pitching to the batter, which he did. Then Gossage was allowed to come in, and the game continued. Incidentally, Gossage was not considered as having entered the game the first time he appeared on the mound and warmed up, because he never threw a pitch. He was not considered an unannounced substitute because he was an illegal substitute. He was, therefore allowed to come in when Carroll was finally removed legally.

3.05—(c) *If an improper substitution is made for the pitcher, the umpire shall direct the proper pitcher to return to the game until the provisions of this rule are fulfilled. If the improper pitcher is permitted to pitch, any play that results is legal. The improper pitcher becomes the proper pitcher as soon as he makes his first pitch to the batter, or as soon as any runner is put out.*

On August 27, 1972, the Kansas City Royals played the New York Yankees at Yankee Stadium in a double-header. In the bottom of the ninth inning of the second game the Yankees scored two runs to tie up the game, 8-8. In that inning Thurman Munson batted for relief pitcher Ron Klimkowski.

In the top of the tenth, Klimkowski strolled out to the mound forgetting that Munson had pinch-hit for him. When he saw Lindy McDaniel come in, he promptly left for the dugout.

I do not see how Klimkowski would have been allowed to remain in the game, but any pitch that he had made would have been considered legal according to this rule. It would have been most interesting if Klimkowski had thrown a pitch.

Ex-Phillies' manager Gene Mauch protested a game against the Cardinals during the 1968 season. The protest involved rules 3.06, 3.07, and 3.08.

3.06—*The manager shall immediately notify the umpire-in-chief of any substitution and shall state to the umpire-in-chief the substitute's place in his batting order.*

3.07—*The umpire-in-chief, after having been notified, shall immediately announce, or cause to be announced, each substitution.*

3.08—(a) *If no announcement of a substitution is made, the substitute shall be considered as having entered the game when* (1) *If a pitcher, he takes his place on the pitcher's plate;* (2) *If a batter, he takes his place in the batter's box;* (3) *If a fielder, he reaches the position usually occupied by the fielder he has replaced;* (4) *If a runner, he takes the place of the runner he has replaced.* (b) *Any play made by, or on any of the above mentioned unannounced substitutes shall be legal.*

As reported by Allen Lewis to *The Sporting News,* "The Phillies scored three runs in the fifth inning to take a 6-3 lead, and Mauch wanted to move Richie Allen from third base to left field, switch Tony Gonzalez from left to center, switch Tony Taylor from second to third, and send Gary Sutherland into the game at second."

"I was thinking Sutherland, but I said Lock," Mauch commented later. "We got a three run lead, and I came all undone. I told Lock to go in.,"

Mauch then walked up to plate umpire Ed Sudol and told him Sutherland was playing second and would bat in place of center fielder Johnny Briggs, but while he was doing this, Lock was taking his place in center field, and the other players were switching.

When Mauch then motioned Lock out of the game, Sudol informed him that since he had taken his defensive position, Lock was in the game.

Mauch argued the point, then filed his protest, which he later dropped, and left Lock in the game, also reluctantly removing Gonzalez.

Rule 3.06 states that the manager shall notify the umpire-in-chief of any subs and their place in the batting order. Rule 3.07 says the umpire-in-chief shall have subs announced, and Rule 3.08 states that if the umpire is not notified and no announcement is made, then a fielder shall be considered as having entered the game when he reaches the position "usually occupied by the fielder he has replaced."

"Since I was informing the umpire of the (Sutherland) change at the time Lock took his position, I think that rule (3.06) should take precedence over the other (3.08)," Mauch said later. "I think I had a good chance to win the protest."

In another substitution problem Oriole manager Earl Weaver protested a game played against the Yankees during the 1974 season after the umpire-in-chief did not force Yankee Manager Bill Virdon to name an immediate replacement for Bill Sudakis when Sudakis was ejected for disputing a called third strike. The protest was not upheld.

Weaver was also involved in a similar situation in Cleveland the same year. As told by Nick Bremigan, "Dave Duncan was catching this day and John Ellis, also a catcher, was the D.H. Both were ejected for arguing the same play in the bottom of the eighth inning, in Cleveland. With both Cleveland catchers gone, Weaver demanded that Indians' skipper Ken Aspromonte name replacements for both players immediately. Weaver lost this argument. According to the rules, when players of the offensive team are ejected, the manager doesn't have to replace them until his team goes on defense. The only exception would be if the ejected players's position in the batting order came due to bat again in the same half-inning, in which case the manager would have to announce a pinch-hitter. But this did not happen.

When the Indians took the field in the top of the ninth, Aspromonte announced a new catcher, but not a new D.H. Well, Weaver was ready. The D.H. rule came into being in the A.L. in 1973. The rule is well written and has been relatively free of abuse and knotty problems, but this situation brought one problem to light which had not been anticipated by the authors of the rule. Weaver protested, claiming that if a manager must name all replacements when his team goes on defense, then he should also have to name a new D.H. Aspromonte claimed he shouldn't have to, pointing out that the D.H. is an offensive player only and does not play defense. Therefore, according to Aspromonte's thinking, a new D.H. shouldn't have to be named until the D.H. comes to bat again. Chylak, McCoy, Brinkman and I got our heads together and decided that Aspromonte was right. The Orioles went on to win the game, so Weaver never actually filed his protest. But the situation still forced MacPhail to make a ruling. His ruling supported Aspromonte's position."

If you take a close look at rule 3.07 you will notice that the umpire-in-chief is expected to announce, or cause to be announced, each substitution. Before loudspeaker systems were used in major league baseball, the umpires or club employees made announcements through cupped hands or megaphones. The Giants were the first team to use a public address announcer at the Polo Grounds in New York on August 25, 1929.

Umpire Tom Gorman invoked section (a-3) of rule 3.08 on Braves' manager Chuck Dressen on May 5, 1960. When the Dodgers went to bat in the eighth inning, Al Spangler went to left field. Dressen called Spangler back and told Lee Maye, who had pinch-hit, to go to left. Gorman ordered Spangler to return, pointing out the rule to Dressen.

An incident that took place in September, 1979 during a game between the Tigers and the Yankees prompted an amendment to 3.08(a-3).

Yankee first baseman Chris Chambliss went to the clubhouse between innings for an "equipment adjustment." When the Yankees took the field to warm up before the start of the inning, Chambliss was still in the clubhouse so Lou Piniella did his deed for the day by going out to first base to take infield practice.

Chambliss returned to the playing field without undue delay, but Detroit skipper Sparky Anderson protested, claiming Piniella had technically replaced Chambliss in the Yankees' lineup because of his between-innings appearance.

The protest was disallowed. Rule 3.08(a-3) now reads: *If no announcement of a substitution is made, the substitute shall be considered as having entered the game when as a fielder, he reaches the position usually occupied by the fielder he has replaced and play commences.*

At this writing the amendment is subject to approval by the Major League Players Association.

Umpire Hank Soar invoked the nonfraternization rule on Billy Hoeft of the Tigers in a game played at Griffith Stadium against the Washington Senators on May 8, 1958.

Hoeft took a seat in the bleachers so he could get a better view of the game. Soar ordered him to rejoin the relief pitchers or return to the dugout utilizing rule 3.09 which states, *"Players in uniform shall not address or mingle with spectators, nor sit in the stands before, during, or after a game. No manager, coach or player shall address any spectator before or during a game. Players of opposing teams shall not fraternize at any time while in uniform."*

In the National League the third base umpire usually has the responsibility of monitoring the field before each contest. It is the job of this umpire to sit in the stands before the game, observe batting and infield practice, and enforce the nonfraternization section referring to players from opposing teams.

One of the reasons for the nonfraternization rule is that fans might get the wrong idea if they see the pitcher for the day's game mingling with one of the opposing team's hitters.

The last sentence of rule 3.09 has been referred to by several players and writers as the "Stargell rule," because Willie is a very friendly and outgoing person who enjoys playing the game and talking to anyone, including the runners he holds at first base.

3.10—(a) *The manager of the home team shall be the sole judge as to whether a game shall be started because of unsuitable weather conditions or the unfit condition of the playing field except for the second game of a double-header.*

The most common adverse weather condition causing the postponement of games is too much rain. But would you believe a minor league game between Memphis and Chattanooga was postponed because of too much sun? It happened on July 31, 1960, in a Southern Association League game played at roofless Tobey Field in Memphis. The temperature at game time was 94 degrees, and there was no overhead protection for the spectators.

The sun can be a severe problem. Nick Bremigan relates a story about the star that is the central body of our solar system.

"The playing field in Pittsfield, Massachusetts, is laid out so that a line running from home plate through the mound and second base runs almost due west. This means that the sun sets almost directly behind the centerfield fence in mid-summer. According to rule 1.14, such a line should run north-northeast. This would cause the sun to set behind the third base dugout, where, theoretically, it can do the least harm. Thus right field becomes the "sun" field, on the theory that fewer balls are hit to right field than to left or center field.

On a sunny evening in Pittsfield in June or July, it was customary for the umpires to suspend play during the last half hour before sunset, because the batter, catcher, and the plate umpire would be blinded.

The only playing field in the A.L. that doesn't conform to this rule is Toronto, where the sun sets directly behind the left field foul pole. Exhibition Stadium was constructed solely for football, and the baseball field just couldn't be laid out to strictly conform to this rule. This causes a minor distraction for the batter, catcher, plate umpire and first baseman, but certainly not as extreme as in Pittsfield."

You might think it an impossibility to have a game postponed in the Houston Astrodome, but a long period of heavy rains forced the Astros to postpone a game on July 15, 1976, because the visiting team's bus and the umpires had a difficult time getting to the Astrodome in flooded streets leading to the stadium.

The date was April 19, 1959. The place was cold Comiskey Park in Chicago. Bill Veeck, general manager of the White Sox at that time, had planned a promotion day for the fans. Between innings of the White Sox game with the Tigers, numbers were to be drawn to determine winners of such prizes as 1,000 hot dogs, 1,000 cans of beer, a year's supply of bread, 150 quarts of motor oil, 1,000 cigars, and season passes.

But with a sparse crowd in Comiskey Park twenty minutes before game time, and with the temperature in the 30s, Veeck discussed the problem with Chuck Comiskey and then requested umpire Bill Summers to walk on the field and judge for himself whether the game should be played.

This was unusual, since the decision on calling a game rests with club officials until game time. Umpires are authorized to call a game only when it is slated to begin or when it is under way. Summers agreed with Veeck and the game was postponed. Later, Veeck said he wanted the game to be called because he didn't want the players to risk injury in the cold weather. Then, referring to Summer's role in the decision, he winked and added, "But it's always nice to have someone take the heat off you."

These conditions are rather mild compared to weather conditions often experienced in Montreal in early April. The Expos postponed a game early in the 1976 season because the thermometer was hovering around the zero mark.

The only exception to this rule can come about toward the end of a season when the league president can assume the authority usually granted to the home team manager. The purpose of this is to insure that league championships are decided on merit rather than the biased judgment of the home team.

In the case of a double-header the umpire-in-chief of the first game makes the decision as to whether the second game should be postponed because of *unsuitable weather conditions or the unfit condition of the playing field.* This is covered in section (b) of this rule.

The next section of the rule gives the umpire-in-chief the sole authority to allow a game to be played or to call a game. The National League has a rule which states that umpires must wait one hour and fifteen minutes before calling a game because of rain. Since six of the twelve N.L. parks are covered with Astro-turf, it is the thinking of N.L. authorities that the field can usually be made playable if it stops raining. In the American League, only three of the fourteen fields are covered by Astro-turf, so it goes by the book rule of thirty minutes. (3.10=c)

Rain stopped the Braves-Expos game in the fourth inning at Montreal on May 15, 1975 with Atlanta ahead 4-1. The umpires eventually called the game off. However, Atlanta protested, contending the umpires did not wait the required 1¼ hours before calling the game off. N.L. President Chub Feeney upheld the protest. The game was completed July 20th with Atlanta winning 6-5 in 11 innings.

During a rain delay the umpires are in constant communication with the local weather bureau. Both managers are kept informed of the circumstances and the intention of the umpires.

The umpires waited in vain an hour and twenty-six minutes for the fog to leave Ebbets Field on the night of June 6, 1957. In the second inning the Dodgers were leading the Cubs by a score of 1-0, when Cub left fielder Bob Speake lost Charley Neal's fly ball in the fog. The ball fell for a double. The Ebbets Field public address announcer, Tex Rickards, known for his witticisms, announced, "Ladies and gentlemen, time will be called pending results of the fog."

3.11—*Between games of a doubleheader, or whenever a game is suspended because of the unfitness of the playing field, the umpire-in-chief shall have control of the groundskeepers and assistants for the purpose of making the playing field fit for play.*

As mentioned earlier, a popular ruse used by teams is to doctor the infield for the advantage of the home team. Several years ago the Giants met Maury Wills and the Dodgers at Candlestick Park in San Francisco. Veteran arbiter Tom Gorman caught the Giants' ground crew soaking down the first and second base paths. Gorman held up the game for an hour and a half until the base paths were completely dry. Walter Alston, Dodger manager, wanted the game forfeited but was not granted his request. If the umpires feel that the field is not playable, the game could be forfeited to the visiting team.

The next rule to be discussed caused tremendous rhubarbs during the 1960 and 1976 seasons. The main victims of this rule were Ted

Kluszewski and Don Money. Rule 3.12 reads as follows: *When the umpire suspends play he shall call "Time." At the umpire's call of "Play," the suspension is lifted and play resumes. Between the call of "Time" and the call of "Play" the ball is dead.*

Memorial Stadium in Baltimore was the scene of a donnybrook on August 28, 1960, as the Orioles entertained the White Sox. In the eighth inning of that game, Ted Kluszewski hit a three-run pinch homer that put the White Sox ahead 4-3. But third base umpire Ed Hurley had called "time" as Milt Pappas was in his pitching motion. Pappas, ignoring the "time" call by Hurley, pitched to big "Klu." After "Klu" connected, Hurley nullified the four-bagger claiming that he had called "time."

The White Sox protested on the grounds that Pappas already was in his pitching motion when Hurley called "time," and rule 6.02(b) states: *The batter shall not leave his position in the batter's box after the pitcher comes to a set position or starts his windup.* The White Sox argued that it was impossible to call time when the pitcher had started his delivery.

"Time" was called by Hurley because he claimed Earl Torgeson and Floyd Robinson, who were warming up to enter the game for "The Hose," weren't exactly in the bull pen area. Kluszewski eventually flied out, and the Orioles won the game 3-1.

Manager Al Lopez and White Sox president Bill Veeck staged a long and detailed protest to American League president Joe Cronin. In disallowing the protest, Cronin cited rules 3.12 and 9.04(b-2). The latter rule gives a field umpire *concurrent jurisdiction with the umpire-in-chief in calling "Time," balks, illegal pitches, or defacement or discoloration of the ball by any player.*

Hurley, umpiring first base, had gotten himself involved in a jam the previous season in a related incident in a game between the Red Sox and Tigers at Detroit.

Hurley called "time" at the start of the fifth inning as a result of becoming involved in a discussion with players in the Boston bull pen.

However, none of the players on the field or umpire Joe Paparella, who was working behind the plate, were aware that Hurley had called "time."

Paul Foytack, who was holding a 4-0 lead over the Red Sox, was pitching to Frank Malzone, and Paparella had called two strikes on Malzone before Hurley notified him that "time" had been called.

Paparella then cancelled the two strikes and Malzone, starting off from scratch, belted a homer into the left field seats.

Don Money of the Milwaukee Brewers was victimized by this rule on April 10, 1976. Umpire Nick Bremigan, who worked second base that day, recalls the bizarre incident:

> Trailing 9-6, the Brewers proceeded to load the bases in the bottom of the ninth inning. There was a full house at County Stadium that day, and they were making enough noise for ten times as many people. You couldn't hear a thing on the field except the roar of the crowd.
>
> Yankee manager Billy Martin was making gestures to his defense to make certain shifts which led to some confusion on the part of the Yankee infielders. Relief pitcher Dave Pagan was oblivious to all of this, and proceeded to wind-up and pitch after receiving his sign from Thurman Munson.
>
> Meanwhile, Yankee first baseman Chris Chambliss was asking for "time" from first base umpire Jim McKean. Suddenly, McKean came running in to call "time," but all attention was focused on Money and Pagan, who continued to pitch, totally unaware of McKean's call of "time." Money then unloaded the ball into the left field bleachers, and County Stadium went completely nuts.
>
> The grand slam of course was nullified. Amazingly enough, no Braves were ejected from the game during the argument which ensued. Money, in fact, never said a word.
>
> Brewers' pilot Alex Grammas had to be sent for, as he was already in the clubhouse along with half the Brewer bench.
>
> Money came back to hit a sacrifice fly to make the score 9-7 which became the final score. The game was protested, but to no avail.

Bremigan goes on, "The only other situation in which "time" can be called during action where the ball isn't dead is when the lights fail during a play. I was the plate umpire in an Eastern League game played in 1971 when the following one in a million incident took place.

John Wockenfuss was batting for the Pittsfield Senators when he took the pitch down the middle for an apparent third strike. However, the lights on six of the eight poles went off while the pitch was in flight. As the plate umpire, I had to nullify the pitch and let Wockenfuss continue batting with an 0-2 count when the lights came back on. He struck out anyway on the 'fourth' strike."

Conversely, Al Zarilla received an extra life at bat and benefitted from the rule because of a "time" call made by an umpire.

The year was 1944, and Zarilla was the St. Louis Browns' batter with two outs in a game against the Yankees at Yankee Stadium. Gene Moore was on first. The Browns' slugger hit a line drive that was caught by Yankee right fielder Bud Metheny. However, first base umpire Bill McGowan had called "time" because Moore was tying his shoe at first base.

Because "time" was called, the catch was nullified, and Zarilla was given another life. Zarilla demonstrated his gratitude by swatting a two-run homer.

Prior to the start of the game, the managers meet with the umpires in the area around home plate to discuss the ground rules. Their conferences often times are centered around small talk or something interesting that might have recently taken place. According to rule 3.13, *The manager of the home team shall present to the umpire-in-chief and the opposing manager any ground rules he thinks necessary covering the overflow of spectators upon the playing field, batted or thrown balls into such overflow, or any other contingencies. If these rules are acceptable to the opposing manager they shall be legal. If these rules are unacceptable to the opposing manager, the umpire-in-chief shall make and enforce any special ground rules he thinks are made necessary by ground conditions, which shall not conflict with the official playing rules.*

In 1903, the first World Series, between the Red Sox and Pirates, was played in Exposition Park in Pittsburgh. Due to the overflowing crowd that extended onto the field, a ground-rule triple was established by the managers and umpires. It is common today to see a ground-rule double, but a ground-rule triple is unheard of in the modern enclosed stadiums. The four games played at Exposition Park produced seventeen triples, twelve by Boston.

The Polo Grounds in New York was the site of this unusual ground rule several years ago. There was a dirigible that was flying about 200 feet over the playing field. A ground rule was made that if a ball hit the dirigible it would be a ground-rule double.

According to Wrigley Field ground rules, the rain gutter at the base of the left field wall is in play. This ground rule plus some good acting by the Cub relief pitchers allowed Tony Taylor of the Cubs to hit an inside-the-park home run on July 1, 1958.

Taylor hit a ball inside the third base line that went into the gutter. Leon Wagner, who was a rookie San Francisco outfielder at the time, chased the ball.

The Cub hurlers sitting in the bull pen looked intently under the bench to decoy Wagner. The ball actually was in the rain gutter forty to fifty feet farther down the line. Wagner was duped, and Taylor had himself an inside the park clout.

The advent of domed stadia has made it necessary to devise special ground rules. In both Houston and Seattle, there are speaker gondolas, guy wires, and other overhead obstructions, as well as the roof itself, that can cause complications if hit by a batted ball. In both parks, if a batted ball strikes any overhead obstruction, while over fair territory, the ball is kept in play and treated as if it never hit the object. The ball can be caught for an out and becomes fair or foul just like any other batted ball. For example, it is not necessarily fair because it hit an object in fair territory. It's possible that the ball could carom over the fence for a home run. If however, a batted ball strikes an overhead object over foul territory, it's a foul ball no matter where it comes down, but it can be caught for an out. Willie Horton of the Seattle Mariners was deprived of a home run during the 1979 season when his clout hit a speaker at the Kingdome in Seattle.

The Phillies' Mike Schmidt might have hit the longest single in major league history on the night of June 10, 1974, in a game played at the Astrodome in Houston. Schmidt hit a ball that hit the bottom left side of a speaker that was suspended 117 feet in the air out in center field, 329 feet from home plate. Dave Cash and Larry Bowa were on base for the Phils at the time of the blast. But since the Astrodome ground rules call for the ball to be in play under such circumstances, Schmidt was credited with a long single rather than a tape measure home run. Cash said, "I took one look and knew it was gone. Then I took another look, and there it was coming down in front of Cesar Cedeno."

3.14—*Members of the offensive team shall carry all gloves and other equipment off the field and to the dugout while their team is at bat. No equipment shall be left lying on the field, either in fair or foul territory.*

It wasn't long ago that players left their gloves in the area of their positions when they changed from defense to offense. This practice was outlawed after the 1953 season. It was also common practice that pitchers warming up in the bullpen would shed their jackets on the ground. Because these practices led to some confusing plays, rule 3.14 was established. The following story is a good example of what you might see today if 3.14 had never been written into the rule book.

In a game played between the Cubs and Reds at Wrigley Field in 1929, Norm McMillan of the Cubs hit a ball that disappeared. Going into the eighth inning, the score was tied at 5-5. The Reds failed to score, and then in their half of the eighth, the Cubs loaded the bases. Out in the Cub bull pen, alongside the left field foul line, Kenneth Penner began warming up.

McMillan came to bat and smashed a line drive inside third base. After passing the bag the the ball headed into foul territory. Left fielder Evar Swanson had been playing McMillan over toward center, but now he came racing toward the foul line. He caught sight of the ball as it hit into an open gutter running along the base of the stands. Arriving on the spot, he looked in all directions but saw no ball. Meanwhile runners were rounding the bases and scoring. The confused outfielder now saw Ken Penner's Windbreaker lying on the ground in the bull pen. He grabbed it and shook it. Nothing came out. He glanced toward home plate and saw that the fourth run had scored, and so he gave up.

A short time later, however, Penner finished his warm-up, walked over and picked up the jacket, started to put his right hand through the sleeve, and the hand encountered an object—the missing ball.

3.15—*No person shall be allowed on the playing field during a game except players and coaches in uniform, managers, news photographers authorized by the home team, umpires, officers of the law in uniform and watchmen or other employees of the home club. In case of unintentional interference with play by any person herein authorized to be on the playing field, except umpires, the ball is alive and in play. If the interference is intentional, the ball shall be dead at the moment of the interference and the umpire shall impose such penalties as in his opinion will nullify the act of interference.*

Using one baseball in a game often causes some hilarious and absurd situations. But allowing two baseballs to be used could create problems beyond the thinking of baseball's most imaginable minds.

The Cubs entertained the Cardinals on June 30, 1959. Jerry Holtzman describes one of the most remarkable plays ever seen: "Stan Musial was at bat with one out in the top of the fourth inning. The count was 3 and 1. Bob Anderson's next pitch was called a ball by umpire Vic Delmore, entitling Musial to a base on balls.

"But then the confusion began. Cub catcher Sammy Taylor claimed the ball had hit Musial's bat and therefore was foul. Taylor was so convinced of this that he didn't even chase the ball as it rolled back to the screen. Instead, he argued with Delmore.

"Cub manager Bob Scheffing and Anderson joined Taylor in the argument, contending that the ball had either grazed Musial's arm or hit his bat. 'It hit something,' Scheffing said.

"'That's right,' Delmore agreed. 'The ball hit Taylor's glove and then bounced off my arm.'

"Musial, in the meantime, was strolling down to first. When he had almost reached the bag, he heard his Cardinal teammates shout from the dugout and point toward the ball, which had now reached the screen behind home plate.

"'Run, Stan, run!' they yelled.

"At the same time, Alvin Dark, playing third for the Cubs, realized that if it were ball four as umpire Delmore ruled, then the ball was still in play, and Musial would be entitled to as many bases as he could get.

"So Dark ran in, full speed, toward the screen. By this time, however, the batboy for visiting clubs, Bob Schoenfeldt, a high school freshman, had picked up the ball and had tossed it to field announcer Pat Peiper.

"Now the storys begin to vary. Peiper said he never actually touched the ball and instead let it drop to the ground. Schoenfeldt said first that Peiper caught his toss, but later added: 'Maybe he didn't. I'm not sure.'

"Solly Hemus, Cardinal manager, said later: 'I know damn well Peiper caught the ball. But he dropped it like a hot potato as soon as he saw Dark charging in!'

"Peiper, relating what happened, said Dark yelled, 'Gimme the ball.'

"'"There it is," I told him,' Peiper explained.

"Dark reached down, grabbed the ball, and threw to shortstop Ernie Banks. But at this very same moment another ball flew out toward second base.

"Where did this ball come from? Well, while umpire Delmore was listening to the beefs registered by catcher Taylor and pitcher Anderson, he automatically reached into his pocket and gave Taylor a new ball.

"Anderson, seeing Musial run for second, grabbed the new ball out of Taylor's hand and threw it toward second. Anderson's ball—hereafter referred to as Ball No. 2—and the one thrown by Dark were in the air at precisely the same moment.

"Dark's throw was low. Banks came in and fielded it on one hop. Anderson's throw, however, was high and sailed over second baseman Tony Taylor's head into center field. While all this was happening, Musial had slid safely into second.

"But Musial didn't know two balls had been thrown. He said later he saw only the ball that went into center field. (That was Anderson's ball—Ball No. 2.) He picked himself up and started for third.

"Stan hadn't taken more than two or three steps off the bag when Banks tagged him with the original ball. Ball No. 2 had been retrieved in center field by Bobby Thomson, who then lobbed it toward the Cub dugout.

"One can imagine the confusion which resulted. The umpires

appeared to be just as confused as everyone else. They huddled once and ordered Musial back to first. Scheffing continued squawking and they huddled again and this time ruled that Musial was out, the play going from Dark to Banks.

"Hemus protested immediately, claiming (1) that two balls were simultaneously in play, and (2) that there had been interference on the part of the batboy, who admitted on the spot that he had picked up the ball when it had rolled back to the screen.

"The protest, though, was never filed because the Cardinals won, 4-1."

The umpires—Delmore, Shag Crawford, Bill Jackowski, and crew chief Al Barlick—were not very eager to talk about the play after the game.

However, they relented after a few minutes. Crawford said that Hemus's protest about the batboy interfering with the ball would not stand up because of rule 3.15, which states that when a qualified person (such as a batboy) unintentionally interferes with a ball on the field, then the ball is in play.

"If there had been intentional interference that would have been different," Crawford said.

Umpire Jackowski, who was working at second base, said there was never any question in his mind that Musial was out after he started for third, "because I kept my eye on the original ball all the time. I saw Dark pick it up and throw it, and I didn't look away even when I realized another ball had sailed into center field."

There is no doubt in my mind that the men in blue missed this one. I do not see how a play could be allowed to continue when there are two balls in play at the same time. As Al Barlick said, "That's something I never want to see happen again."

In analyzing this mess, Nick Bremigan claims, "The batboy's action in this case would be considered intentional interference on the theory that he wouldn't have picked it up unless he intended to, although he may not have intended to interfere with the play itself. Such interference would only be considered unintentional if the ball had inadvertantly struck or ricocheted off the batboy, and he had not actually secured possession of it."

Umpire Vic Delmore was involved in another controversial play that developed on the night of July 23, 1958, in a game between the Dodgers and Pirates at Forbes Field.

Norm Larker of the Dodgers hit a ball just inside the first base line that rolled into the Pirate bull pen in right field. Roberto Clemente, playing right field, and the Pirates in the bull pen thought it was a foul ball, but Delmore, umpiring first base, signaled fair. Bob Porterfield, who was in the bull pen, picked up the ball in anger. Larker continued to third, but plate umpire Jocko Conlan waved Larker back to second base and ejected Porterfield from the game for intentionally interfering with a ball in play. The umpires ruled that under ordinary circumstances Larker could have gone no farther than second.

The next rule in this chapter concerns the spectators at the park. Every fan who attends a game would like to bring home a baseball that he caught at the park. Frequently, spectators interfere with the field of play in their eagerness to grab the round sphere.

Rule 3.16 reads as follows: *When there is spectator interference with any thrown or batted ball, the ball shall be dead at the moment of interference and the umpire shall impose such penalties as in his opinion will nullify the act of interference. If spectator interference clearly prevents a fielder from catching a fly ball, the umpire shall declare the batter out.*

The Reds opened the 1958 season against the Phillies at Crosley Field in Cincinnati. In the top of the seventh inning, the Phillies, down by one run, had Richie Ashburn on first base with two outs. Granny Hamner then hit a ball off Don Hoak's shins, the ball caroming into foul territory against the fence off the field boxes in left field.

Ashburn, running hard on the play, scored the tying run. Hamner ended up on second with a double.

Redlegs' manager Birdie Tebbetts argued that Ashburn should have been restricted to third since a fan reached out and interfered with shortstop Roy McMillan.

However the rule clearly gives the umpire the authority to impose such penalties that nullify the interference. In the judgment of the umpire, Ashburn would have scored whether or not a fan had interfered.

The Phillies eventually won the game 5-4, and Tebbetts's protest went for nought.

The thing that umpires watch for on fly balls that are close to the stands on the field is whether the fielder had to reach into the stands or not. If the fielder reaches into the stands and a fan interferes with the fielder, the act of interference is not enforced. If a spectator leans over and onto the field and interferes with a fielder, the umpire will utilize 3.16.

Catcher Del Rice of the Braves and a box seat spectator traded a few punches after the fan knocked a ball from Rice's mitt. Umpire Babe Pinelli allowed the putout since Rice did not have to reach into the stands for the catch and was interfered with on the playing field. The brief boxing match took place on June 27, 1956, at Philadelphia where the Phils and Braves collided.

In reaction to fan interference Bremigan said, "Many fans, announcers, and even players think that spectator interference results in an automatic award of two bases such as a ground rule double. This is not the case at all. It often does result in a two base award, but it doesn't have to.

Many instances of spectator interference occur at Fenway Park and Yankee Stadium because the stands just beyond first and third bases are so close to fair territory. Many balls hit just inside first or third base are touched on the playing field by spectators reaching over for a souvenir. On such plays, the batter often is awarded second base, but it is because the umpires feel he could have gotten a double had the interference not occurred, not because it is an automatic award of two bases."

3.17—*Players and substitutes of both teams shall confine themselves to their team's benches unless actually participating in the play or preparing to enter the game, or coaching at first or third base. No one except players, substitutes, managers, coaches, trainers and bat boys shall occupy a bench during a game.*

The late Tony Venzon, ex-National League umpire, was very alert and had some guts as he enforced rule 3.17 against former Phoenix mayor Sam Mardian Jr. in an exhibition game played between the Giants and Dodgers in 1961.

Venzon spied Mardian in the Giants' dugout talking with manager Alvin Dark and requested his "Honor" to leave the dugout. Dark was very critical of Venzon's hospitality and became quite verbal with the ump. In a few short moments, Dark was asked to join the executive officer.

This section terminates with a rule that has caused several teams to forfeit their games because they could not control the crowd.

3.18—*The home team shall provide police protection sufficient to preserve order. If a person, or persons, enter the playing field during a game and interfere in any way with the play, the visiting team may refuse to play until the field is cleared. If the field is not cleared in a reasonable length of time, which shall in no case be less than fifteen minutes after the visiting team's refusal to play, the umpire may forfeit the game to the visiting team.*

Bill Klem who umpired 36 years from 1905-1940, and who was considered to be the greatest umpire in the history of the game, enforced this rule on opening day of the 1907 season at the Polo Grounds with the Phillies leading the Giants in the eighth inning 3-0. The New Yorkers had only one hit, a single by Cy Seymour, and the fans were getting frustrated and bored.

Due to an unusual heavy April snowstorm, the field was surrounded with piles of snow. The white stuff became ammunition for the fans, and a tremendous snowball fight developed among the spectators. Eventually, the fans pummeled the players and the umpires. It was at this point that Klem forfeited the game to Philadelphia, 9-0.

The Braves finished seventh in 1942 for the fourth year in a row. They won 58 games, and had one given to them on the next to the last day of the season in the same Polo Grounds in New York. The Giants were winning 5-2 in the eighth inning when nine thousand juvenile guests of the Polo Grounds management swarmed onto the field so the game could not be finished. Umpire Ziggy Sears forfeited the game to the Braves, 9-0.

The Giants finally got a forfeit to go their way in August 1949 at Philadelphia's Connie Mack Stadium. The Giants were leading the Phillies 4-2 in the ninth inning, when the umpires ruled that Richie

Ashburn had trapped, not caught, a ball hit by the Giants' Joe Lafata.

Philly fans threw various objects on the field. When umpire Al Barlick was hit by a tomato and umpire Lee Ballanfant was hit on the shoulder with a bottle, the game was awarded to the Giants.

The Washington Senators played their last home game in Washington D.C. on September 30, 1971. The Texas-bound team, a fixture in the American League's basement for many of its 71 years, seemed headed for a certain victory. In the top of the ninth the Senators led 7-5, and the Yankees were batting with two out and no one on base.

At this point hundreds of fans poured out all over the field, jamming the base paths, pulling up the bases, running off with the pitcher's rubber, and roaming the outfield. Since the home team could not keep order the game was forfeited to the Yankees. The final score was 9-0 Yankees.

On Tuesday night June 4, 1974, the Texas Rangers met the Cleveland Indians at Cleveland. It was Beer Night, and fans could buy all the brew they wanted for ten cents a cup.

With the score tied 5-5 in the bottom of the ninth, the Indians had runners on first and third with two out.

Before Jack Brohamer could step up to the plate, two youths jumped out of the right field stands and raced toward Texas right fielder Jeff Burroughs intent upon stealing his cap. As Burroughs fought them off, other youths leaped onto the playing field, and in a matter of seconds all hell broke loose with both the Rangers and Indians galloping to the aid of Burroughs.

With the players from both teams fighting probably 50 or so spectators, a metal folding chair was hurled onto the field, landing on the head and shoulder of Indian pitcher Tom Hilgendorf. Fortunately, he suffered only bruises.

Umpire Nestor Chylak was cut on the right wrist, Burroughs jammed a thumb, and Texas pitching coach Art Fowler and Texas pitcher Steve Foucault were struck in the eye by blows.

After about ten minutes, order seemed to be restored, and, apparently, the game was going to continue.

However, as the Rangers walked across the infield toward their dugout, another fight broke out near the pitching mound, and that was all Chylak needed.

As soon as it was broken up and he was sure all the players and other umpires had reached the dugout, Chylak declared the game forfeited and awarded Texas a 9-0 victory

All individual performances, except the crediting of a victory and defeat to pitchers, were entered into the record book.

Bill Veeck, the promotion czar of baseball, outdid himself on the night of July 12, 1979, when he staged what was called Disco Demolition Night at Comiskey Park in Chicago. A crowd of more than 50,000 spectators, many of whom were teenage rock fans, packed the old park in Chicago to witness a double-header between the Tigers and White Sox.

The ill-advised promotion was devised by a Chicago disc jockey. Fans gained entrance to the park for 98 cents. Part of the idea was for each rock fan to bring a disco record, thousands of which would go up in flames in a between-games show.

Following the first game, an avalanche of young fans, estimated between 5,000 to 7,000, stormed onto the field and ran about in merriment for several minutes delaying the start of the nightcap.

A.L. Prexy Lee MacPhail stated, "It was the judgment of the umpire (Phillips) that it was not possible to start the second game because of inadequate crowd control and damage to the home team." Therefore, the game was forfeited to Detroit.

4.00

Starting and Ending a Game

The beginning and ending of games have caused some very interesting problems for umpires and official scorers. When the elements intervene, many other questions arise. This chapter deals with these areas plus how a team scores, suspended games, rules governing double-headers, and rules involved in forfeitures and protested games.

The umpires take the field five minutes before the hour set for the game to begin and walk to home plate where they are met by the rival managers.

4.01—(a) *First, the home manager shall give his batting order to the umpire-in-chief, in duplicate.* (b) *Next, the visiting manager shall give his batting order to the umpire-in-chief, in duplicate;*

Lineup card chicanery has caused fans to look twice at the scoreboard prior to the start of the game. Paul Richards and Gene Mauch have masterminded some lineup stunts worth mentioning.

Managing the Orioles on September 11, 1958, Richards listed three pitchers in his starting lineup against the Athletics. Starting hurler Billy O'Dell was scheduled ninth in the order as is customary. In addition to O'Dell, Richards had Jack Harshman as his center fielder, hitting fifth, and Milt Pappas as the second baseman batting in the number seven slot.

Richards's strategy was to remove Harshman and Pappas if the Orioles had a scoring chance in the first inning.

The chance came in the first frame as the Orioles had two runners on base with two out when Harshman was scheduled to bat. Gene Woodling batted for Harshman and flied out. Richards then inserted Jim Busby in center and Billy Gardner at second.

Billy O'Dell was involved a second time in a similar thing on June 29, 1961. Philadelphia Phillies manager Gene Mauch engineered this one in the first game of a twi-night double-header between the Phillies and Giants at Connie Mack Stadium.

Mauch and Giant manager Al Dark each had a right-hander and left-hander warming up before the game.

Since the home team manager must turn in his lineup card first, Mauch listed pitcher Don Ferrarese as the leadoff man playing center field. Next were Tony Taylor, 2b; pitcher Jim Owens, rf; Pancho Herrera, 1b; Don Demeter, lf; Charles Smith, 3b; pitcher Chris Short, c; Ruben Amaro, ss; and Ken Lehman, p. When Mauch saw that the Giants had O'Dell scheduled to start, he immediately replaced three of the pitchers with right-handed hitting regulars—Bobby DelGreco for Ferrarese, Bobby Gene Smith for Owens, and Jim Coker for Short.

Although they were included in the box score, the three pitchers never entered the game.

Not to be outdone, Giant skipper Al Dark allowed O'Dell to pitch to DelGreco, since O'Dell had to pitch to at least one batter as provided by rule 3.05(a). Right-hander Sam Jones then replaced O'Dell.

The Giants won the game 8-7 with a tenth inning home run by a regular named Willie Mays.

A lineup card oddity occurred on September 6, 1971, at Yankee Stadium where the Yankees hosted the Red Sox in a Sunday double-header. In the second game of the twin bill, Boston manager Eddie Kasko started a team in which not one man had played in the first game.

You can expect anything to happen in a pre-game meeting around home plate between the managers and umpires. The following anecdote was reported in *Referee* magazine:

> Alex Grammas, manager of the Milwaukee Brewers, went to home plate and handed his line-up card to the umpire for the final time in 1976. He then turned and started to chat with Ralph Houk of the Tigers.
>
> The umpire interrupted, "Have a good winter, Alex." Grammas responded, "Thanks." Then he turned to the umpire and did a double take. What he saw was Jim Colborn, one of his pitchers.
>
> Colborn had borrowed a uniform from the umpiring crew for his stunt. He didn't begin the game behind the plate, but he did manage to eject two of his teammates before heading to the clubhouse himself.

4.01—(c) *The lineup in the plate umpire's possession is the official batting order regardless what is listed on the manager's cards.*

This rule was applied on August 23, 1959, as the Cubs played the Braves. Manager Bob Scheffing of the Cubs listed catcher Cal Neeman twice and omitted first baseman Dale Long on the card he gave to Braves' manager Fred Haney.

When Neeman doubled in the seventh inning, Haney protested. Since the lineup given to the umpires by Scheffing was correct, Haney had no grounds for protest.

4.02—*The players of the home team shall take their defensive positions, the first batter of the visiting team shall take his position in the batter's box, the umpire shall call "Play" and the game shall start.*

Prior to 1950, the home team had the choice of batting first or last. Did it ever happen? Yes it certainly did.

The New York Highlanders (forerunners of the Yankees) played the Senators in Washington on April 22, 1903, to open their first major league season. For some mysterious reason the Senators elected to bat first against pitcher Jack Chesbro. Washington won the game 3-1. Would it be correct in saying the New York Yankees played their first away game ever as the home team?

4.03—*When the ball is put in play at the start of, or during a game, all fielders other than the catchers shall be on fair territory.*

In 1895 Sam Thompson played the outfield for the Detroit Tigers. As previously mentioned, it was a common practice for a fielder to leave his glove in the area of his position when he left the field to go on the offense. In a game against the New York Highlanders, Mr. Thompson did something that might give umpires fits today.

Dan Hoffman led off for New York and hit a George Mullin pitch to right field where Thompson with his back turned was hitching his belt and fixing his cap before picking up his glove near the foul line. When Thompson heard the people in the grandstand and Mullin shouting, he turned around and made the catch about 40 feet from where he normally would have been playing. The catch was made in fair territory in a spot that a hitter would usually get an extra base hit.

If Thompson had been in foul territory at the time of the pitch, all subsequent action would have been nullified and Hoffman would have been allowed to bat again.

Although the rule states that all fielders other than the catcher shall be on fair territory, it's common to observe right handed first basemen with one or both feet in foul territory while holding a runner on first. This is one area where umpires are lenient in the enforcement of this rule, and allow first sackers to do this.

Rule 4.03 also prevents the defensive team from stationing another fielder behind the catcher during an intentional base on balls, which was customary before this rule was inserted many years ago.

The next rule covers the most famous substitution in major league history. Rule 4.04 states: *The batting order shall be followed throughout the game unless a player is substituted for another. In that case the substitute shall take the place of the replaced player in the batting order.*

Lou Gehrig began his long consecutive game playing streak of 2,130 games on June 1, 1925, when he pinch hit for Pee Wee Wanninger. The following day Lou replaced Wally Pipp at first base. On that same day, Benny Bengough became the Yankees' catcher replacing Wally Schang. Gehrig completed his consecutive game streak on May 2, 1939, at Detroit. Attending the game that day as a spectator was Wally Pipp, the only Yankee on hand at both the beginning and the end of the streak.

The rule book now unpredictably jumps from substitutions to base coaches. Base coaches usually go unnoticed by the fans. Ask someone to name five base coaches in the major leagues today, and you might be lucky if they could give you three. Some coaches are more proficient than others and are greatly respected by the manager and the players. Rule 4.05 deals with the men who make their living in the 10-foot by 20-foot rectangular box along the baselines.

The coach is not considered out of the box unless the opposing manager complains. If this should happen, the coaches from both teams are to remain in the boxes. Coaches Del Baker of the Red Sox and George Myatt of the White Sox were in the spotlight on July 13, 1956, as the Red Sox entertained the White Sox at Fenway Park. In the eighth inning of that game, Ted Williams came to bat with the Red Sox down by a run. Baker, coaching first base, went about three feet in back of the coaching lines. The White Sox didn't like it.

First base umpire Bill Summers told Baker to stay put behind the coaching lines after plate umpire John Rice tried to get Baker back into the box. Summers was concerned about Baker's safety with the "Splendid Splinter" at bat.

White Sox manager Marty Marion questioned Summers about Baker. Summers explained to Marion why he was allowing Baker to stand in back of the box. The umpire also declared that if Marion wanted Baker to stay in the box, he would enforce the rule. Marion didn't want Baker to get hurt either, so he consented to having Baker behind the box.

Now it was White Sox third base coach George Myatt's turn. In the top of the ninth Dick Donovan was at bat with one out. Myatt stepped out of his third base coaching lanes and moved within a foot of third base. The third base coach was caught trying to pick up Boston catcher Sammy White's signals. The umpires then forced Myatt to get back in the coaching box for obvious reasons.

Umpire Dusty Boggess once forced Braves' coach Johnny Riddle to remove a University of Pittsburgh football jacket he was wearing to keep warm. The Braves-Pirates game at Pittsburgh, May 3, 1957, was held up for five minutes because of Riddle's attire. Boggess ruled that Riddle was out of uniform and ordered him either to vacate the coaching lines or doff the jacket. Riddle removed the jacket with the temperature in the low forties.

Base coaches, particularly at third, will leave the confines of the coaching box to give instructions to runners approaching and rounding the base. This is permitted unless the coach actually interferes with play.

The next set of baseball statutes, (4.06, 4.07, and 4.08) deal basically with the behavior of the players and managers. It is these rules that umpires must be constantly aware of to maintain discipline on the field.

4.06—(a) *No manager, player, substitute, coach, trainer or batboy shall at any time, whether from the bench, the coach's box or on the playing field, or elsewhere—*(1) *Incite, or try to incite, by word or sign a demonstration by spectators;* (2) *Use language which will in any manner refer or reflect upon opposing players, an umpire, or any spectator;* (3) *Call "Time" or employ any other word or phrase or commit any act while the ball is alive and in play for the obvious purpose of trying to make the pitcher commit a balk;* (4) *Make intentional contact with the umpire in any manner.*

Virtually all ejections in the game of baseball reflect on sections (2) and (4) of this rule. If I were to list some case studies here this text might change from a general reading audience to adults only.

Part (3) of this rule has caused several rhubarbs over the years since players will often times intentionally do something to deceive the pitcher into committing a balk.

In the first story Al Lopez was the "Hunter" and Hugh Casey was the "Hunted" during a game between the Dodgers and Pirates near the end of the 1941 season. In the bottom of the eighth inning, the

Pirates had Vince DiMaggio at third base with two outs. Lopez was at bat with a count of no balls and two strikes. When Casey started to throw his next pitch, Lopez made a motion to step out of the batter's box, causing Casey to stop his delivery. Umpire George Magerkurth ruled the pitch a balk, which set off an explosion by Dodger manager Leo Durocher. Magerkurth waved DiMaggio in on the balk. Lopez eventually got on base and was tripled home for the winning run.

The Twins' Jerry Terrell copied Lopez's style on the night of May 29, 1974, when Minnesota hooked up with the Red Sox at Boston.

The score was tied 4-4 in the top of the 13th inning. The Twins had runners at the corners and one out with Terrell at the plate. Sox pitcher Diego Segui became confused and balked when he noticed Terrell reaching down in the batter's box for some dirt. Terrell had learned the trick when he played amateur baseball and admitted so. Because of the balk, both runners advanced one base, and the Twins won the game, 5-4.

According to statements made by Terrell this was an intentional act, therefore the balk should have been nullified and Terrell ejected from the game since the penalty for violation of this rule calls for ejection. The problem here is that it is the judgment of the umpire that determines if the act is intentional or not. The umpire has to make the quick decision and is not expected to be a mind reader, or is he?

Major league umpires would rather use rule 6.02(b) to handle such gimmicks on the part of the batter. According to 6.02(b), *The batter shall not leave his position in the batter's box after the pitcher comes to Set Position, or starts his windup. PENALTY: If the pitcher pitches, the umpire shall call "Ball" or "Strike," as the case may be.* Under this rule, if the pitcher stops his windup it is not a balk. "Time" is called and no balk is charged. It also negates the necessity of ejecting the offender (if a batter) as specified in rule 4.06(a-3).

Why does one rule, (4.06=a-3) give the umpire the opportunity to eject a player while the other (6.02=b) spares the umpire from having to eject a violator? If the intent is not to remove a player from the game, then why not delete the word "eject" from rule 4.06(a-3)?

An opposite twist of this rule occurred in a college game played in Connecticut a few years back. Dr. Jim Moore, who coached baseball at Southern Connecticut State College for several years, was offended when one of his players once pulled this ruse in a game.

SCSC had a runner on first. When the pitcher went into his set position and turned to check the runner, the SCSC batter knelt down in the box. Startled by the actions of the batter, the pitcher stopped his motion to the plate and balked.

Dr. Moore was so angry over what had happened that he went out on the field and ordered his runner to return to first.

Now with time out the runner returned to first base. The question I have to ask is this: "What is the legality of returning the runner back to first base?" The rules state the runner is entitled to a base that is legally touched. The opposition did not contest the runner returning, and the game went on.

According to rule 7.01, *a runner acquires the right to an unoccupied base when he touches it before he is out. He is then entitled to it until he is put out or forced to vacate it for another runner legally entitled to that base.* Therefore, it would be illegal on the part of the offensive team to return a runner. But then again, chances of the defensive team complaining are about as good as the elimination of taxes in the future.

Eddie Stanky was richly deserving of his nickname, "The Brat." The next case finds "The Brat" violating rule 4.06(b) which says, *No fielder shall take a position in the batter's line of vision, and with deliberate unsportsmanlike intent, act in a manner to distract the batter.*

When Stanky was playing for the Giants, he discovered one day in Boston that if he moved around at second base just as the pitcher was getting ready to throw, it distracted the batter. The Braves argued and the umpire told "The Brat" to stop. There was an argument, and later Ford Frick, then the league president, after reading the umpire's report, warned that Stanky would be thrown out of the game if he did it again.

Warnings were never enough for Stanky. He always required proof. With Durocher's approval, he pulled the same stunt in Philadelphia a few days later. Andy Seminick, the Phillies' catcher, came to the plate in a critical situation halfway through the game. Just as the pitcher came down from his stretch, Stanky began moving back and forth, waving his arms over his head at the same time. Umpire Lon Warneke gave him the thumb for his actions.

Umpire Ed Hurley ejected the Indians' Jimmy Piersall during the 1960 season for doing what appeared to be a war dance when Ted Williams of the Red Sox batted in the sixth and eighth innings. According to the umpire, Piersall appeared to be trying to distract the batter and was ordered to the showers.

Ejection of players and managers in a baseball game is a common occurrence. Rule 4.07 states *When a manager, player, coach or trainer is ejected from a game, he shall leave the field immediately and take no further part in that game. He shall remain in the clubhouse or change to street clothes and either leave the park or take a seat in the grandstand, well-removed from the vicinity of his team's bench or bullpen.*

A rather amusing ejection came in 1969 prior to a game played between the Baltimore Orioles and Minnesota Twins at Minnesota. Earl Weaver, manager of the Orioles, got thrown out of the game before it started by umpire Frank Umont for smoking in the dugout. In the major leagues, smoking is allowed in the alleyway, but not in the dugout.

The next day, before the start of a nationally televised game, the umpires and Billy Martin (Minnesota manager at the time) waited at home plate for Weaver to go over the lineup and ground rules. After keeping them waiting just a bit, Weaver came out of the dugout, lineup card in hand and a candy cigarette hanging from his lips.

As Weaver approached home plate, he casually ate the cigarette and handed Umont the lineup card.

A few years later, Billy Martin was ejected from a game before it began because of a dispute with umpire Joe Brinkman. The removal took place early in the 1974 season at Shea Stadium when Martin was managing the Texas Rangers in a game against the Yankees.

In 1955 in the American Association, Omaha defeated Minneapolis by a score of 3-1, but it was nullified when league president Ed Doherty upheld a Minneapolis protest that Stu Miller, Omaha pitcher, had been removed from the game and then permitted to remain in the game.

Doherty made a similar ruling a year later in a game played on June 17, 1956, between Indianapolis and St. Paul.

St. Paul manager Max Macon returned to the playing field during a fight after having been ejected from the game two innings earlier. Doherty ruled that the game had to be replayed from the third inning with Indianapolis leading 3-2.

In a game between the Reds and Dodgers in 1952, Dodger second baseman Jackie Robinson was sent to the showers by umpire Augie Guglielmo after "Robbie" "kicked" about a call. The Reds' Eddie Pellagrini barreled into Robinson at second on a steal attempt and was called safe by Guglielmo. In violent protest Robinson used his college football talents by drop-kicking his glove a mile high into the air. Guglielmo at a loss for words said to Robinson, "If that glove comes down, you're out of the game."

Digger Phelps, the colorful Notre Dame basketball coach, was ejected from an Irish baseball game a few years ago. Phelps, who was seated in the Notre Dame dugout during the game, was getting on the plate umpire concerning his calling of balls and strikes. The umpire walked over to the dugout and ordered Digger to leave the field. In ejecting Phelps, the umpire said, "I don't question your four corners, so don't you question mine."

Clearing the entire bench isn't a common occurrence, but rule 4.08 gives the umpire the authority to do so if the situation warrants this action. *When the occupants of a player's bench show violent disapproval of an umpire's decision, the umpire shall first give warning that such disapproval shall cease. If such action continues, the umpire shall order the offenders from the bench to the clubhouse. If he is unable to detect the offender, or offenders, he may clear the bench of all substitute players. The manager of the offending team shall have the privilege of recalling to the playing field only those players needed for substitution in the game.*

The rule produced a baseball oddity concerning Bill Sharman, ex-Boston Celtic great. Sharman, who had never played in a major league game, was a member of the Dodgers on September 27, 1951, when they were visiting the Braves in Boston. After a violent argument precipitated by a play at the plate involving the Braves' Bob Addis, umpire Frank Dascoli eventually ejected the entire Dodger bench. Sharman was later shipped back to the minors and never appeared in a big league game. The bench ejection made Sharman the only player to ever have been thrown out of a major league game although having never played in one.

Plate umpire Bill Jackowski enforced this rule in a game between the Phillies and Reds on May 15, 1960. After Reds' pitcher Raul Sanchez had hit Gene Conley, the last of three Phillies' batters hit by pitches in the inning, Phillies' skipper Gene Mauch went after Sanchez.

The Reds' Frank Robinson and Robin Roberts of the Phillies tangled near first base a short while later. It was after this that Jackowski cleared both team's benches of players not participating in the game.

The Pirate bench was cleared a few years earlier by umpire Stan Landes. The Pirate bench rode Landes all during the game as they battled the Phillies on the night of May 24, 1957.

In the fifth inning, Pirate chucker Vern Law was dismissed by Landes. An inning later, he couldn't stand the heckling and cleared the Pirates' bench, including trainer Doc Jorgensen, coach Clyde Sukeforth, and eleven players.

When Red Jones was umpiring in the American League, the White Sox bench was giving him a tough time one day. Since Red couldn't identify the chief jockey on the bench, he cleared the dugout. When one of the lesser agitators protested, Jones replied, "You know how it is. When the cops raid a gambling joint, the innocent are pinched along with the guilty."

The rule book now takes an unusual course and jumps from the behavior of the participants to how a team scores.

As mentioned in rule 4.09(a), *One run shall be scored each time a runner legally advances to and touches first, second, third and home base before three men are put out to end the inning. Exception: A run is not scored if the runner advances to home base during a play in which the third out is made (1) by the batter-runner before he touches first base; (2) by any runner being forced out or (3) by a preceding runner who is declared out because he failed to touch one of the bases.*

The second part of this rule refers to a force out. As defined in the rule book, *A force play is a play in which a runner legally loses his right to occupy a base by reason of the batter becoming a runner.* (2.00)

The most famous force play in the history of baseball took place on September 23, 1908, at the Polo Grounds in New York. The Chicago Cubs were the Giants' opponents on that day.

In the bottom of the ninth inning with the scored tied, 1-1, Fred Merkle was on first base and Moose McCormick was on third base with two outs. Al Bridwell singled to center. That's where the fun began.

As soon as Merkle, who had not reached second base saw McCormick touch home plate, he sprinted for the clubhouse in center field. The Cubs were alert to the rule and called for the ball with spectators swarming all over the field. Floyd Kroh, a Cub pitcher, grabbed the ball from a spectator and gave it to Joe Tinker, who flipped it to Johnny Evers standing on second base.

Umpire Hank O'Day was aware of what had happened and called Merkle, the nineteen-year-old rookie, out on a force play.

The crowd now was all over the field, and the Polo Grounds was in a state of utter chaos. Cub manager Frank Chance claimed a forfeit because the home team could not clear the field, and giant manager John McGraw protested that the Giants won the game on the field.

National League president Harry Pulliam ruled the contest a 1-1 tie and ordered the Giants and Cubs to play off the game on October 8, the day after the regular season ended.

The season ended with the two teams tied. Mordecai Brown defeated Christy Mathewson, 4-2, giving the Cubs the National League pennant. The play has been known as the boner that cost a pennant. [Pulliam, who endured a tremendous amount of public criticism, later committed suicide in Atlantic City, N.J.]

National League umpire Andy Olsen was on the short end of ruling 4.09(b) when he worked a minor league game between Fargo-Moorehead and Minot on June 30, 1960.

The two Northern League teams were tied in the ninth inning, 11-11. Fargo had the bases loaded in the home half of the ninth with two out. Fargo batter Tut Thublin walked to force in Jim Horsford from third base with the apparent winning run.

Players from both teams, as well as plate umpire Olsen and base umpire Tony Favano, began to leave the field. The umpires then gathered near first base with several Minot players. After a short discussion the Fargo team was ordered back on the field since Ken Slater, who was on first base when Thublin walked, failed to touch second. The umpires ruled that Slater was forced at second, retiring the side and nullifying the run.

Minot went on to score a 12-11 victory. The game was protested by Fargo manager John Fitzpatrick.

The protest was upheld by League president Herman White. Fargo-Moorehead was declared the winner in nine innings, 12-11. White's decision was based on section 4.09(b), which states, *When the winning run is scored in the last half-inning of a regulation game, or in the last half of an extra inning, as the result of a base on balls, hit batter or any other play with the bases full which forces the runner on third to advance, the umpire shall not declare the game ended until the runner forced to advance from third has touched home base and the batter-runner has touched first base.*

The rule does not mention anything about a runner going from first to second or from second to third. Therefore, Slater did not do anything wrong by leaving the field. Since Thublin touched first and Horsford touched home, the run should have been allowed to count.

4.10—(a) *A regulation game consists of nine innings, unless extended because of a tie score, or shortened (1) because the home team needs none of its half of the ninth inning or only a fraction of it, or (2) because the umpire calls the game.*

On May 1, 1920, the Dodgers and Braves played a 1-1 tie game that extended for 26 innings. An oddity of this game was that both pitchers went the distance. Leon Cadore hurled for the Dodgers, and Joe Oeschger pitched for the Braves. The game lasted 3 hours and 50 minutes and was finally called because of darkness.

The New York Mets and St. Louis Cardinals went at it for 25 innings on September 11, 1974, with the Cards winning 4-3. On May 31, 1964, the Mets lost to the Giants 8-6 in a deformed 23-inning contest that lasted 7 hours and 23 minutes, the longest game in major league history. Early in the 1976 season, the Mets defeated the Cardinals by one run in a 17 inning game on Del Unser's home run. The strange thing about the above three marathons is that umpire Ed Sudol was the plate umpire in all three games. On April 15, 1968, Houston defeated the Mets 1-0, but Sudol didn't work the dish that game, which lasted 24 innings. The Yankee-Tiger game on June 24, 1962, lasted exactly 7 hours, an A.L. record. The 22 inning contest was won by the Yankees, 9-7, on Jack Reed's only home run of his major league career.

Thanks to the efforts of the Official Playing Rules Committee, the rainout rule has been amended to alleviate tactics that are unworthy of the professional label which have plagued our national pastime for many years. Effective as of the 1980 season, rule 4.11(d) was amended to read: *(d) A called game ends at the moment the umpire terminates play. EXCEPTION: If a game is called while an inning is in progress and before it is completed, the game becomes a SUSPENDED GAME in each of the following situations: (1) The visiting team has scored one or more runs to tie the score and the home team has not scored. (2) The visiting team has scored one or more runs to take the lead and the home team has not tied the score or taken the lead.*

Under the old rule if the visiting team either tied the score or took the lead during an uncompleted inning, the score would revert to the last completed inning. The following anecdote illustrates how ridiculous the rule was.

The Astros met the Cardinals at Busch Stadium in St. Louis on the night of August 25, 1975. In the top of the eleventh inning, Cliff Johnson of the Astros hit his sixth home run in six consecutive games which put the Astros ahead 4-3. However, in the bottom half of the inning with two outs and the Cardinals at bat, a sudden cloudburst turned the field into a quagmire. After waiting 134 minutes, trying to get that last batter to the plate, umpire Ed Sudol called the game and made the rainout rule official. Thus Johnson's home run was erased as the score reverted back to the last completed inning. The four bagger, if credited, would have made Johnson only the second man in National League history and the sixth overall to hit home runs in six consecutive games. Dale Long, who hit homers in eight straight games for the 1956 Pirates, was the only other National Leaguer to do it.

The game entered the records as a 3-3 ten-inning tie and was replayed from the start the following night as part of a double-header. All performances in the ten innings went into the record books. Imagine a game with 65 putouts having to be replayed!

A couple of more situations come to mind that further illustrate the senility of the former rule.

On August 13, 1978, the Yankees-Orioles game was called because of rain. Trailing 3-0, the Yankees exploded for five runs in the top of the seventh inning to take a 5-3 lead.

In the bottom of the seventh, the Orioles were at bat trailing 5-3 when a heavy downpour forced umpire crew chief Don Denkinger to call the game. The decision proved fatal to the Yanks since the score reverted to the last completed inning giving the "Birds" a 3-0 victory.

Tiger manager Ralph Houk was fuming on the night of June 17, 1976, when his Bengals became victims of this rule in a game against the Twins. Detroit trailing 4-0 after five innings scored four runs in the top of the sixth to knot the score 4-4. In the bottom of the sixth inning, Minnesota had two runners aboard and one out when the rains came. The umpires' decision to call the game after two delays totaling 94 minutes sent Houk into a justifiable rage. The score reverted to the last completed inning and the Tigers lost 4-0.

Pitching a no-hitter is a rare achievement, but hurling a no-hit game while giving up a hit in baseball is an oddity that was born out of the defunct rule. Mike McCormick pulled off the bewildering feat pitching for San Francisco against the Phillies in Philadelphia on June 12, 1959.

Entering the bottom half of the sixth-frame, the Giants were leading by a score of 4-0 and the southpaw chucker had not as yet yielded a hit although he did give up a walk. The first two Philly batters walked and Richie Ashburn beat out an infield hit to load the bases with nobody out. At this point the rains came and the game was eventually called. Since the Phillies had not completed the sixth inning, the entire frame was wiped out including Ashburn's hit and the Giants' fourth run which they recorded in the top of the sixth inning.

Thus credit McCormick, the lucky Giant with a no-hitter, and reflect for a moment to consider all those ill-fated pitchers who threw 8 2/3 innings of no-hit baseball only to come up short. Under today's rules, McCormick would be credited with a one-hitter.

Under the old rule, if the home team either tied the score or took the lead during a regulation game, the score would not revert back to the last completed inning. If the home team didn't tie the score during an uncompleted inning the score would revert back to the last completed frame. Do you realize that this rule could actually punish the home team for tying the score?

Let's say the White Sox lead the Tigers 1-0 going into the top of the sixth inning at Comiskey Park in Chicago. Detroit scores five runs and goes ahead 5-1. In the bottom of the sixth, Chet Lemon ties the score with a bases loaded home run. Suddenly the skies become angry and the game is a washout. Because Lemon tied the score with his grand slam, the game ends in a tie. If Chet did not hit the big blast, the score would have reverted back to the last completed inning which was the fifth, giving the White Sox a 1-0 win.

The amendment to rule 4.11(d) certainly appears to help the visiting team, but what about the home team?

Baseball maxim 4.10(c) says, *If a game is called, it is a regulation game (1) if five innings have been completed; (2) if the home team has scored more runs in four or four and a fraction half innings than the visiting team has scored in five completed half innings; (3) if the home team scores one or more runs in its half of the fifth inning to score.*

The way the above rule is currently written, the visiting team as well as the home team can use stalling tactics to prevent requirements for a regulation game. The following story brings out my point.

Red Faber is one of the few pitchers in the history of baseball to steal second, third, and home in one inning. Playing for the White Sox in a game against the Athletics on July 14, 1915, Faber intentionally tried to get picked off in a rain threatened game, but the Athletics, trying to delay the game, didn't make much of an effort to retire him. To the dismay of the Connie Mack nine, the rain never materialized, and Faber was credited with a base-stealing sweep. Ironically, his "steal" of home was Chicago's fifth run of the game which proved to be the winning run as the White Sox defeated Philadelphia 6-4.

A rainout problem presented itself in Detroit where the Tigers met the Milwaukee Brewers on August 1, 1972. In the following scenario the home team (Tigers) did everything it could to prevent a regulation game.

Trailing by several runs, Detroit made several attempts to prevent completion of five innings. For example, outfielder Jim Northrup refused to catch a fly ball and pitcher John Hiller repeatedly threw to first base, though the runner was practically standing on the bag.

Milwaukee speedup maneuvers were equally farcical. Base runner Mike Ferrara walked idly toward second, inviting the Tigers to tag him out. Ellie Rodriguez left his base too, but the Tigers refused to tag him. The comedy lasted six innings with the Brewers winning 9-0.

Umpire-in-chief Frank Umont was so appalled with tactics utilized by Brewers' manager Del Crandall and Tigers' pilot Billy Martin that he recommended a $1,000 fine for each.

The Lords of Baseball might consider all rained-out games in the future to be suspended, not just those under the amended provisions of 4.11(d).

To enforce my argument, I list the case of Earl Williams. Playing for the Atlanta Braves he was deprived of two home runs in June of the 1976 season since he hit both of his roundtrippers in a contest that was declared "No Game" when it was postponed in the third inning. According to the last part of the 4.10 rule, *If a game is called before it is a regulation game, the umpire shall declare it "No Game."*

Lou Gehrig might have been on his way to a triples record, but became a victim of rule 4.10. Gehrig smacked 3 triples in 4½ innings at

Washington on June 30, 1934. However, they all went down the drain when rain prevented the Senators from completing the home half of the fifth inning. Case Closed!

Al Kaline once had a home run washed out and finished his career with 399 home runs. One more would have given him the distinction of being the first man in A.L. history to collect 400 home runs and 3,000 base hits.

If each team has the same number of runs when the game ends, the umpire shall declare it a "*Tie Game.*" (4.10=d)

The 26 inning Dodgers-Braves game has to rank high when referring to tie games, but in my opinion, the most amazing tie game took place on August 13, 1910, when Brooklyn met the Pirates. The game ended in an 8-8 tie in which each team had 38 at-bats, 13 hits, 12 assists, 2 errors, 5 strikeouts, 3 walks, a hit batsman, and a passed ball. I don't think you will ever find a game more evenly matched than that.

The next baseball statute that will be covered is rule 4.11(c), which has been referred to in a couple of situations not too frequently encountered.

If the home team scores the winning run in its half of the ninth inning, (or its half of an extra inning after a tie) the game ends immediately when the winning run is scored.

Exception: If the last batter in a game hits a home run out of the playing field, the batter-runner and all runners on base are permitted to score, in accordance with the base-running rules, and the game ends when the batter-runner touches home plate. Approved Ruling: Play (1) the batter hits a home run out of the playing field to win the game in the last half of the ninth or an extra inning, but is called out for passing a preceding runner. The game ends immediately when the winning run is scored.

Harvey Haddix will long be remembered as the man who pitched twelve perfect innings for the Pirates against the Braves on the night of May 26, 1959, but lost the game in the 13th inning. The game, which ended on a bizarre note, will be discussed here in relation to 4.11(c).

After retiring thirty-six consecutive batters, Felix Mantilla reached first in the Braves' home half of the 13th on a throwing error by Don Hoak, the Bucs' third baseman. Eddie Mathews then bunted Mantilla to second. Hank Aaron was given an intentional pass. Joe Adcock then hit a shot over the right-center field fence. Everyone in Milwaukee's County Stadium thought it was a home run except Aaron. Hank, who had touched second base, figured the ball had dropped at the bottom of the fence instead of over it, and figuring that Mantilla had already scored the winning run, headed toward the Braves' dugout. Adcock, running with his head down, ran toward third base and technically passed Aaron, even though Aaron returned to the field and preceded Adcock around the bases after players and coaches urged him to return to the base paths. The umpires declared Adcock out, but allowed two runs to score.

The next day, National League president Warren Giles nullified Aaron's run, since he left the base paths, and also disallowed Adcock's home run, since he passed a runner. Giles declared the final score to be 1-0. Adcock was credited with a double on the peculiar play.

I asked Aaron about this play. He answered, "There were some low chicken-wire fences in Milwaukee, and I thought the ball had hit the base of the fence rather than go in between the fence. Joe Adcock took it very well. It was just one of those things that happened."

Ed McAuley was the official scorer in Cleveland on June 25, 1961, when the "Injuns" hosted the Tigers. Because of an unusual base-running blunder by Vic Power, McAuley developed a pretty good case regarding an unfinished aspect of 4.11(c). In my opinion McAuley also proved that the rule book is not only confusing at times, but tends to be ambiguous.

Here is what happened as described by McAuley to *The Sporting News.*

The bases were loaded and there was one out when Chuck Essegian produced the pinch-hit that sent the fans home happy. To some observers, it looked like a home run. Power says he thought it was beyond the fence and was waiting near first base to congratulate the timely slugger, then precede him in the jog around the bases. Al Kaline, playing right field for Detroit, returned the ball to Jake Wood, who forced Power at second . . .

Well—Rule 10.06(a) says a base hit shall not be scored when a runner is forced out by a batted ball, and 10.06(b) says when a batter apparently hits safely and a runner who is forced to advance fails to touch the first base to which he is advancing and is called out on appeal, said batter similarly goes hitless.

But rule 4.11(c) says when it is necessary for the home team to use its half of the ninth inning both the inning and the game end immediately when the winning run is scored before three men are out. The only exception listed covers the case of a home run with the bases filled.

Now, obviously, this rule calls for a footnote. Unless the word "scored" implies that certain conditions besides stepping on home plate must be met, or unless the word "winning" here is given special meaning, this rule ignores a variety of circumstances in which the game is not over as soon as that runner touches the plate. At the very least, the batter who knocks in that run has to reach first base.

In case you've never heard of Chuck Essegian, he is one of two men who have hit two pinch hit home runs in a World Series. Essegian accomplished the feat in the 1959 fall classic as a member of the Dodgers when they met the "Go-Go" White Sox. Bernie Carbo duplicated the feat in the 1975 series playing for the Red Sox against the Reds, his former teammates.

Our next problem deals with suspended games under rule 4.12. The rule is a very extensive one and extremely detailed. The book devotes 47 lines to this long but easily understood rule.

4.12—(a) *A league shall adopt the following rules providing for completion at a future date of games terminated for any of the following reasons:* (1) *A curfew imposed by law;* (2) *A time limit permissible under league rules;* (3) *Light failure or malfunction of a mechanical field device under control of the home club; (mechanical field device shall include automatic tarpaulin or water removal equipment)* (4) Darkness, when a law prevents *the lights from being turned on.* (The amendments listed in Rule 4.11(d), effective in 1980, can be added to this rule also.)

For several years it was the thinking of the American League that there would be no suspended games. This idea was abandoned on April 21, 1957, when a Senators-Oriole game was suspended because of a power failure at the end of five innings. A.L. president Will Harridge said, "In a situation, unprecedented in American League history, the league office decision was made in the spirit of fair play to both clubs."

Prior to the 1954 season, lights could not be turned on in Philadelphia to complete a Sunday game that began later than 6:00 P.M. But the Sunday restriction had been lifted before the season, and all the teams were notified.

The most violent donnybrook of the 1954 season was related to the rule under discussion at Philadelphia. Phillies' manager Terry Moore, Cards' pitcher Cot Deal, St. Louis catcher Sal Yvars, Phils' first baseman Earl Torgeson, umpire Babe Pinelli, and Card manager Eddie Stanky were the main cast of characters on the eighteenth of July.

The Cardinals were under the impression that the lights could not be turned on to complete a Sunday game in Philadelphia. In the second game of a rain-delayed double-header, which had commenced at 6:48, trailing 8-1 with two outs in the fifth, the Cards began to use stalling tactics.

Deal began throwing pitches out of the strike zone. Yvars and Torgeson then engaged in fisticuffs which precipitated a free-for-all.

After the free-for-all, Stanky went to the mound to remove Deal, and bring in Tom Poholsky. It appeared that Pinelli also thought that the lights could not be turned on when he awarded a forfeit to the Phils because of the Cardinal antics. It is doubtful that Pinelli and Stanky were aware of the lifting of the ban. National League President Warren Giles said later, "If the Cardinals had protested a misinterpretation of the rules, the protest would have been upheld."

4.12—(a) *Any game called for the reasons in 4.12(a) shall be known as suspended games. No game called because of a curfew or a time limit shall be suspended game unless it has progressed far enough to have been a regulation game under the provisions of Rule 4.10.* The aforementioned Cardinal story might have been the result of a misinterpretation on the part of the Cardinals concerning the latter rule. *A game called under the provisions of 4.12(a-3 or 4) shall be a suspended game at any time after it starts.*

During the 1956 season the Cubs met the Pirates at Pittsburgh. After three innings the Cubs were leading 2-0 when there was a power failure at Forbes Field. It was ruled then that because the power failure came before five innings had been completed, the entire game had to be replayed.

The Braves visited the Dodgers at Ebbets Field in Brooklyn during the 1954 season when this knotty problem came about. At the time, Brooklyn had a curfew that no inning could start after a certain time. The night game was stopped by rain and couldn't be resumed when the curfew was reached. The umpires couldn't decide whether it should be an official game stopped by rain or a suspended contest halted by curfew. It was declared an official game terminated by rain as covered by a part of 4.12(b) which says, *Weather and similar conditions shall take precedence in determining whether a called game shall be a suspended game.*

The umpires were all wet in the following rain-out situation as they almost failed to properly interpret the above rules regarding weather precedence.

On May 22, 1955, the Giants met the Pirates in a Sunday doubleheader at Pittsburgh.

In the nightcap the Giants went ahead 5-3 with three eighth-inning runs, and the Pirates did not score in the home half of the frame.

Before Willie Mays, first Giant up in the ninth, completed his time at bat, a downpour halted play. It was 6:32 P.M. with the Pennsylvania Sunday curfew only 28 minutes away.

A call was put through to the umpires' room, and they offered the opinion it would go into the books as a suspended game. They felt they had to wait at least 30 minutes before calling the game, and that would have placed the time at 7:02, 2 minutes past the curfew hour.

Chub Feeney, the vice-president of the Giants, was in the stands. When he heard of the umpires' decision, he got the rule book and went searching for the umpires. Feeney showed the umpires the rule, and the Giants went away with an eight-inning victory, as the game became a called game.

If the Pirates couldn't have finished their half of the eighth inning, the score would have reverted back to the end of the previous inning. That would have made the final score 3-2 in favor of the Pirates.

For several years rule 4.12(a-3) stated that light failure would be cause for a suspended game. Because of a situation that occurred in

Philadelphia a few years ago, the rule was expanded to read as follows: *Light failure or malfunction of a mechanical field device under control of the home club; (mechanical field device shall include automatic tarpaulin or water removal equipment).*

The Phillies were losing by several runs when the rains came and the umpires suspended play in the fourth inning. The rain eventually stopped, but as the groundskeepers were readying the field for play, a strange event took place. One of the "zambonis" used to suck up the water from the Astro-turf sprung a leak and wound up flooding the field to the point where play could not be continued and the umpires had to call the game. Under the existing rules at the time, it was "No Game" and had to be played over in its entirety. The visiting team protested, claiming the Phillies could have purposely done this, since it was certainly to their advantage to have the game rained out at that point. I guess we'll never know, but the rule was changed the following year to put an end to such suspected chicanery.

Most suspended games are resumed preceding the next scheduled single game or double-header on the same grounds unless the game is suspended on the last scheduled date between the two teams in that city. If this should happen, the teams will meet on the field of the opposing club if possible. If the game cannot be resumed or completed, it shall be a called game as dictated by 4.12(c).

The Florida State League had a ticklish situation concerning a player's eligibility in relation to rule 4.12. The West Palm Beach Expos were the opponents for Fort Lauderdale on June 19, 1972. The Expos' Dale Harrington threw only one pitch before the elements forced suspension of the game. The game was continued two days later, since a well-conceived league rule allowed games postponed before they became official to be resumed. Expos' manager Lance Nichols listed Jim Horsch as his pitcher instead of Harrington. Horsch, who had joined the team the night before the game, became the subject of controversy among the umpires. After a few minutes of deliberation, the umpires ruled Horsch ineligible since he was not on the Expos' roster when the game began. Nichols then appointed Al Collazo as his pitcher for the evening. In a sense, West Palm Beach required three pitchers to throw the first two pitches of the game.

I have to question the reasoning used by the umpires in not allowing Horsch to play. A section of 4.12(d) supports my argument that the pitcher in question should have been allowed to participate.

A player who was not with the club when the game was suspended may be used as a substitute, even if he has taken the place of a player no longer with the club who would not have been eligible because he had been removed from the lineup before the game was suspended.

The next section in this chapter deals with double-headers under rule 4.13. Most of the information contained in the rule involves umpire control over the time interval between games, which is 20 minutes and in some cases 30 minutes, plus umpire control over the start of the second game. It is the job of the umpire to start the second game if at all possible even though the game might be started 30 minutes before curfew.

According to rule 4.13(d), *The umpires shall start the second game of a doubleheader, if at all possible, and play shall continue as long as ground conditions, local time restrictions, or weather permit.*

On August 7, 1972, a massive invasion of millions of grasshoppers appeared between games of a twin bill at Midland, Texas, and forced the umpires to postpone the second game as the grasshoppers made field conditions unplayable.

Nick Bremigan was involved in a situation in 1973 that resulted in an International League rule change. He explained, "A double-header was scheduled between Syracuse and Toledo in Toledo. We didn't even begin the first game until 9:30 P.M. because of the weather, and finished the game right at midnight. That meant the second game which was scheduled to begin at 12:20 A.M. would have given us only thirty minutes to play before we would have to enforce the league curfew of 12:50 A.M.

"The players of both teams knew this and also realized that none of the records would count if we didn't get four and a half innings in before 12:50 A.M. Of course that was impossible, but under the rules we had to start the game. The resulting half hour of baseball was a complete farce, as players on both teams clowned around and committed intentional errors because they knew none of it would count.

"The next day, league President George Sisler made a special league rule which stated no game would start unless it could start at least an hour and a half before curfew. A good rule, but so far, the major leagues have not adopted it."

Before the start of the second game, the managers meet again at home plate to exchange lineup cards. On May 30, 1922, the Cardinals and Cubs played a morning-afternoon double-header. Between games outfielder Cliff Heathcote of the Cubs was traded to St. Louis for outfielder Max Flack. Both players appeared on the lineup cards in both games, but for two different teams.

The Braves played nine consecutive double-headers from September 4 to 15, 1928. They lost five of the double-headers in succession, one at Philadelphia and four straight to the Giants at Boston.

Rule 4.13(b) says, *After the start of the first game of a double-header, that game shall be completed before the second game of the double-header shall begin.* The rule reads clear and precise. However, there is no mention of triple-headers in the rules. On October 2, 1920, the Pirates and Reds played the only triple-header of the century. The Reds won two of the three tilts that day.

Whenever darkness makes further play in daylight hazardous, in the opinion of the umpire-in-chief, he has the authority to order the playing lights turned on. Those are the details of 4.14. This rule is enforced by umpires frequently in the tail ends of double-headers or when a field such as Yankee Stadium casts shadows that make visibility difficult.

Forfeits to visiting teams were covered in the preceding chapter. However, there are other ways that a team can win by forfeit as dictated in 4.15.

4.15—(a) *A game may be forfeited to the opposing team when a* *team fails to appear upon the field, or being upon the field, refuses to start play within five minutes after the umpire has called "Play" at the appointed hour for beginning the game, unless such delayed appearance is, in the umpire's judgment, unavoidable.*

This is a very obscure and seldom used rule, but it was invoked on June 22, 1958, in a minor league game between Olean and Erie. Olean had originally announced a 7:00 P.M. starting time for its Sunday games, but later changed the time to 4:00 P.M. in an official league release to all clubs.

Manager Steve Gromek's Erie Sailors arrived 50 minutes after the game was supposed to start. Gromek claimed that the game was originally set for 7 P.M. but his words were wasted when umpires Bob Brooks and Francis Powers forfeited the game to Olean.

New York-Penn. League president Vince McNamara upheld the forfeiture.

4.15—(b) *A game may be forfeited to the opposing team when a team employs tactics palpably designed to delay or shorten the game.*

On June 6, 1937, Philadelphia's Baker Bowl was the site of this forfeit, in which Joe Medwick lost a home run that compelled him to share the league title with Mel Ott, who also hit 31 homers that season.

Philadelphia had the previously mentioned blue law in effect at the time that permitted no inning to begin past 6:59 P.M. on a Sunday. In the second game of a double-header, which began at 5:36 P.M., Medwick had homered for St. Louis as the Cardinals built a 3-0 lead in the third inning.

Then the Phillies' manager, Jimmy Wilson, began to stall in an effort to prevent the contest from reaching the legal limit of five innings. Wilson began by changing pitchers, finally bringing in Sylvester Johnson.

As Johnson, known for his control, threw one pitch after another far off the plate, Bill Klem, umpiring at second base, began to creep in behind the pitcher. Suddenly, he bellowed, "This game is forfeited to St. Louis!"

Games may also be forfeited for the following reason.

4.15—(c) *A team refuses to continue play during a game unless the game has been suspended or terminated by the umpire. (d) A team fails to resume play, after a suspension within one minute after the umpire has called "Play."*

Umpire Vic New gave Missoula of the Pioneer League five minutes to return to their positions after Rocky Tedesco, Missoula skipper, pulled his team off the field after being ejected from the game on the night of August 10, 1960.

New forfeited the game to Idaho Falls, 9-0, when the Missoula team refused to go back onto the field. Tedesco was fined $250 by league president Claude Engberg.

Who can forget Earl Weaver's Toronto caper on the night of September 15, 1977, when the Orioles forfeited a game to the Blue Jays at Toronto when umpire Marty Springstead and his umpiring crew refused to remove a tarpaulin in the Toronto bull pen at the request of Weaver. The volatile Baltimore manager claimed the tarp could create a hazard for his fielders. The "Earl of Baltimore" removed his team from the field and refused to resume play until the tarp was removed.

Springstead, invoking rule 4.15(c) and (a), gave Weaver five minutes to return his team on the field. The Orioles' skipper refused, and the game was forfeited to Toronto with the Blue Jays leading 4-0 after four and a half innings.

Other stipulations of this rule include forfeiture in instances *when a team after warning by the umpire, willfully and persistantly, violates any rules of the game;* (4.15=e) or *when a team fails to obey within a reasonable time the umpire's order for removal of a player from the game.* (4.15=f)

In a California League contest played on June 23, 1968, between the Visalia Mets and the Lodi Crushers, plate umpire Carl Harder gave the Mets an automatic forfeited 9-0 victory after Lodi manager Jim Marshall refused to leave the field when he was ejected.

The last section of 4.15 was violated in a Mexican League game played between the Coahulia Miners and the Saltillo Saraperos during the 1976 season.

Coahulia refused to play the second game of a double-header after a severe argument ended the first game with Saltillo winning 10-9. Coahulia manager Willie Calvino protested a close call at the plate that won the game for the Saraperos. When umpire Antonio Calderon refused to change his decision, Calvino ordered his players to leave the field and board the bus. The Miners were fined 8,000 U.S. dollars for refusing to play.

The rule states, *A game can be forfeited if a team fails to appear for the second game of a double-header within twenty minutes after the close of the first game unless the umpire-in-chief of the first game shall have extended the time of the intermission.* (4.15=g)

4.16—*A game shall be forfeited to the visiting team if, after it has been suspended, the orders of the umpire to groundkeepers respecting the preparation of the field for resumption of play are not complied with.*

The Senators hosted the Red Sox on August 15, 1941. With Washington leading, 6-3, the game was stopped in the eighth inning because of rain and was eventually called after a 40-minute wait. Boston Manager Joe Cronin protested because of the Washington club's failure to cover the field. League President Will Harridge upheld the protest and ordered the game forfeited to Boston.

In a sense Rocky Tedesco, manager in the case noted above under rules 4.15(c) and (d), violated 4.17 which says, *A game shall be forfeited to the opposing team when a team is unable or refuses to place nine players on the field.* In local sandlot games, teams do not always have nine players, and the rule is put into use. However, on the major league or minor league level, this is not likely to occur. When Tedesco refused to allow his team to take the field, the latter part of 4.17 was violated.

In 1913, the Giants met the Phillies at Philadelphia in a late season Saturday afternoon headliner. The Giants claimed that some of the people sitting in the bleachers flashed mirrors into their faces when they were at bat. Umpire Bill Brennan instructed Phillies' pilot Charley Dooin to go out to the bleachers and take care of the problem.

The fans continued flashing mirrors, and Brennan awarded the Giants with an 9-0 forfeit win.

National League president Tom Lynch supported his umpire, but the National League's Board of Directors overruled the forfeiture, and the game was ordered completed from the point where Brennan declared the forfeit the next time New York visited Philadelphia. The Giants won the interrupted game.

The above story relates to rule 4.18. *If the umpire declares a game forfeited he shall transmit a written report to the league president within twenty-four hours thereafter, but failure of such transmittal shall not affect the forfeiture.* Brennan reported the forfeit to Lynch but was overruled. Reversal of an umpire's decision to forfeit a game is an unheard-of thing on just about any level of the game.

This chapter concludes with a brief discussion of protested games. *Each league shall adopt rules governing procedure for protesting a game, when a manager claims that an umpire's decision is in violation of these rules. No protest shall ever be permitted on judgment decisions by the umpire. In all protested games, the decision of the League President shall be final.* (4.19)

It is rare that a protest is upheld, but it has happened, as we have seen. It is important for the reader to understand that a team cannot protest a game because of a judgment call on the part of the umpire such as an out or safe call, a ball or strike decision, or declaring a hit to be fair or foul.

A slight revision of rule 4.19 was made at the 1979 winter meetings in Toronto. The following is revised rule 4.19: *Even if it is held that the protested decision violated the rules, no replay of the game will be ordered unless, in the opinion of the league president, the violation adversely affected the protesting team's chances of winning the game.*

The revision, which becomes effective in 1980, was obviously made to protect a team that has won a game convincingly from being penalized on a technicality.

I would like to throw you an amusing little story related to this rule before you close the book on chapter four.

On September 15, 1959, Minneapolis of the American Association used an ineligible player, and the game was protested by Omaha. Ed

Doherty, league president, ordered the game replayed after upholding the protest. The player in question was a guy named Carl Yastrzemski, who scored the winning run in that game. "Yaz" was not eligible until September 18, the day outfielder Lee Howell was to leave the team for military duty.

Putting the Ball in Play—Live Ball

What happens when a runner continues to circle the bases while a fight is in progress on the field with several players from both teams participating? What happens if a runner keeps going around the bases after he has been put out? What happens if an umpire gets hit with a batted ball? What happens if an umpire is holding the ball while a play is in progress? What happens if a ball gets lodged in the catcher's chest protector?

The above questions will be answered in the next few pages. The 5.00 rules are concerned mainly with putting the ball in play. Confusion as to whether time is in or not has caused several zany things to take place on a baseball field.

The umpire calls "Play" when the game begins. *After the umpire calls "Play" the ball is alive and in play and remains alive and in play until for legal cause, or at the umpire's call of "time" suspending play the ball becomes dead. While the ball is dead no player may be put out, no bases may be run and no runs may be scored, except that runners may advance one or more bases as the result of acts which occurred while the ball was alive (such as, but not limited to a balk, an overthrow, interference, or a home run or other fair hit out of the playing field).* (5.02)

National League President Chub Feeney, disallowed the Cubs' May 6, 1973, protest against the Giants on the grounds that no time was taken on the play and the players who entered the field did not interfere with the play. Here is what transpired.

Cub hurler Milt Pappas threw a pitch behind the back of San Francisco right-hander Jim Barr, and the ball sailed to the backstop. Dave Rader, who was on first at the time, was running with the pitch. Cub catcher Randy Hundley ran to the backstop to retrieve the ball. Noticing Rader heading for third, he threw the ball, but the sphere sailed into left field and Rader scored easily. As this action was taking place, Barr went after Pappas accusing the Cub right-hander of throwing at him. Players from both benches also poured out on the field, and a brawl ensued. The Cubs claimed that the run should not count since players from both teams were on the field. The Giants won the game, 11-9.

Knowing when time is out is very important, as it could save moments of embarrassment for the men playing the game.

In a game played between the Cardinals and Cubs during the 1916 season, Cub third sacker Heinie Zimmerman committed the following mistake. Albert Betzel was the Cards' hitter with John Smith on second base. Betzel took a swipe at the ball, and the bat flew out of his hands. Heinie went to pick up the bat, which had gone past third base. As soon as Zimmerman started toward the bat, Smith alertly broke for third and was safe. "Time" was never called on the play, and the ball was alive.

Pee Wee Reese was also involved in a similar blunder when he played for the Dodgers in a game against the Cubs in 1947. Pee Wee was on first, and Dixie Walker was the hitter. "The People's Cherce" swung hard, and the bat flew out toward the spot where Reese was taking his lead. Pee Wee went over to pick up the bat and throw it toward his teammate. As he was bending over to pick up the bat, Cubs' catcher Clyde McCullough threw to Eddie Waitkus at first, and

Eddie tagged the Dodger shortstop. I guess you can say the Cubs learned their lesson 31 years earlier.

When ex-Met Rod Kanehl played with Nashville in the Southern Association in 1960, he stole home while the catcher was visiting the pitcher on the mound. Catcher Don Williams of Little Rock went out to the mound to settle down pitcher Frank Mankovitch, but never called "time." The bases were loaded at the time, and Kanehl, who was on third base, broke for home and scored the winning run.

5.03—*The pitcher shall deliver the pitch to the batter who may elect to strike the ball, or who may not offer at it, as he chooses.* This rule almost makes the batter appear to have full control while at the plate. In 1876 a booklet entitled *Dime Baseball Player* contained some interesting pitching rules. "The batsman, on taking his position, must call for either a 'high ball,' (above the waist but not higher than the shoulders) a 'low ball' (not lower than within one foot off the ground but not higher than his waist) or a 'fair ball' (between shoulder high and one foot from the ground)."

Can you imagine sluggers like Hank Aaron, Babe Ruth, Willie Mays, Mickey Mantle, Jimmie Foxx, and Ted Williams calling their own pitch?

5.04—*The offensive team's objective is to have its batter become a runner, and its runners advance.*

On May 21, 1952, the Brooklyn Dodgers had 19 men reach base consecutively, scoring 15 runs in the first inning in a game against the Cincinnati Reds. The Boston Red Sox had 20 batters reach base in the seventh inning in a game against the Detroit Tigers on June 18, 1953. The Bosox scored 17 runs during the marathon inning.

5.05—*The defensive team's objective is to prevent offensive players from becoming runners, and to prevent their advance around the bases.*

The 1930 Phillies allowed 1,199 enemy runners to cross the plate. The 1936 St. Louis Browns were bombed for 1,064 runs. I wonder if these teams knew about rule 5.05?

As was mentioned earlier, the Cubs defeated the Phillies 26-23 in 1922. The Red Sox and Philadelphia Athletics had a football score of 22-14 in favor of the beantowners on June 29, 1950.

Five years later, Philadelphia was playing their games in Kansas City. It is questionable how much their defense improved. The White Sox defeated the hapless A's by a score of 29-6. The debacle took place on April 23, 1955.

5.06—*When a batter becomes a runner and touches all bases legally he shall score one run for this team.*

In that high scoring Red Sox seventh inning in 1953 against the Tigers, Sox catcher Sammy White scored three runs. In 24 years in the major leagues, Ty Cobb touched all the bases and scored 2,244 times. Tim McGinley of Boston is credited with scoring the first run in major league history on April 22, 1876. Since that time many runs have been scored. On Sunday May 4, 1975, the one millionth run was scored by Bob Watson of the Houston Astros in a game against the Giants. After the game, Watson's shoes and the home plate that he scored on were sent to Cooperstown's Baseball Hall of Fame.

In an article to *Referee* magazine, Nick Bremigan related an amusing story relating to the one millionth run:

> This play happened to N.L. umpire John McSherry. It was a Sunday afternoon, and the commissioner's office had set up a system on that day to determine who would score the millionth run. That was quite a feat, considering the exact time of every run scored that day by all 24 major league teams playing games in three different time zones had to be computed. Houston was playing in San Francisco; the Astros had Watson on second, and Cruz on first with two outs, when Milt May hit the next pitch off Montefusco out of the ball park. Watson raced home knowing he had a chance to be the millionth run, but Cruz held up between first and second watching the ball sail out of the ball park. May broke into his home run trot and rounded first, also watching the ball as he ran. May was almost on top of Cruz before he stopped. The "Count" who doesn't like home runs being hit off him anyway, began yelling and pointing that May passed Cruz, but McSherry was right there and

ruled that he hadn't. Cruz and May corrected themselves and ran the rest of the way properly. This would have been a time play concerning Watson's run, and the timing was such that Watson would not have scored baseball's millionth run if May had passed Cruz. All of the players and umpires on the field that day received a watch from the commissioner's office commemorating the scoring of that run.

Had Watson's run been nullified, baseball's millionth run would have been scored seven seconds later in a game in Milwaukee which I was working.

5.07—*When three offensive players are legally put out, that team takes the field and the opposing team becomes the offensive team.*

Ebbets Field in Brooklyn has been the scene for some of the zaniest baseball ever seen. On the day the park opened in 1913, a peculiar incident developed which forced Brooklyn to put out four enemy batters instead of the customary three.

Milton J. Shapiro describes the "four out" inning in *Laughs From the Dugout*. "No sooner had the Brooklyn pitcher struck out the first batter, however, than it was remembered that the guest of honor, the Mayor, had neglected to throw out the first ball in the traditional ceremony. So they disregarded that first out. The Mayor threw a ball, and the game began all over again." Unofficially, the Dodgers had 28 putouts in a nine-inning game.

It's bad enough Brooklyn had to give four outs to the opposition. But to add insult to injury, the Dodgers were allowed only two outs in an inning at Ebbets Field about four decades later.

The rival Giants were the opponents for Brooklyn. Dolph Camilli singled for the Dodgers with one out. Joe Medwick then hit a double play ball to Giants' shortstop Bill Rigney, who flipped the ball to Mickey Witek at second. Witek straddled the bag but did not touch it, and umpire Al Barlick signaled safe. Witek then threw to first to get Medwick.

Camilli, not realizing he was safe, dusted himself off and departed from the field. The Giants left the field also, thinking they had executed an inning-ending double play. Since it is the coaches' job to instruct the runners whether they are out or safe, the umpires held tight. The Giants actually earned their at bats with a two-out inning. Actually, Camilli was recorded as an out.

There might have been other two-out innings in major league history, but we will probably never know about them because of the umpires' silence. Unless appealed to, umpires remain silent in plays such as a runner missing a base, or a runner leaving the base too soon. The umpires remain inactive so as not to help one team to the detriment of the other.

The following rule has no relationship with the previous one. Rule 5.08 states, *If a thrown ball accidently touches a base coach, or a pitched or thrown ball touches an umpire, the ball is alive and in play. However, if the coach interferes with a thrown ball, the runner is out.*

The Houston Astros and Atlanta Braves clashed on May 15, 1973, at Houston. The play started with Atlanta runners on first and second and one out in the ninth. Dave Johnson grounded to third baseman Doug Rader, who tossed it to Tommy Helms at second to start a double play.

Helms relayed to first baseman Lee May to apparently end the inning, but umpire Bruce Froemming ruled Helms did not touch second, and Atlanta's Mike Lum was safe. May didn't see Froemming's signal and routinely tossed the ball to first base umpire Paul Pryor, as Dusty Baker of the Braves went from second to third.

Pryor said he dropped the ball when he saw Froemming's signal, and Baker raced home before May could retrieve the ball. Helms cussed Froemming and was ejected.

Manager Leo Durocher protested the run scoring after Pryor had caught the ball.

"He had the ball in his hand two or three seconds," Durocher said of Pryor. "If he throws the ball back to May, May throws the ball to the plate and gets the guy."

General manager Spec Richardson was openly critical of the umpires. In poor taste he ordered the publicity department to post the following notice on the scoreboard for everyone to see: "Manager Leo Durocher has announced the game is being played under protest and that umpires Froemming and Donatelli have blown decisions in two of the last three games.'

Donatelli was mentioned because of a call he made regarding a fair home run ball a couple of games earlier.

Plate umpire Ed Vargo said that the message was inciting the fans to riot.

National League president Chub Feeney fined Richardson $300 for his tactics and disallowed the protest, referring to rule 5.08.

The National League had a hot pennant race during the 1940 season between the Cards and Dodgers. During the last month of the season, the Dodgers went into St. Louis one game ahead of the Cards in a big series.

In the bottom of the first inning of the opening game of the series, base umpire Lee Ballanfant got in the way of the throw to first on a double play ball and got hit on the back. The Dodgers were upset by the play, but there was nothing that could have been done about it. The Dodgers eventually won the game in the eleventh inning with Freddie Fitzsimmons on the mound.

The rule book recognizes only two types of umpire interference: (1) When he hampers a catcher's throw; and (2) when a fair ball touches an umpire on fair ground before passing a fielder. This aspect of interference is covered in rule 5.09.

5.09—(b) *The ball becomes dead and runners advance one base, or return to their bases, without liability to be put out; when the plate umpire interferes with the catcher's throw, runners may not advance. Note: the interference shall be disregarded if the catcher's throw retires the runner.*

Rookie N.L. umpire Eric Gregg made a rare interference call on April 30, 1978, in a game which saw the Cardinals beat the Dodgers, 4-0.

Gregg called interference on himself for bumping St. Louis catcher Ted Simmons as he attempted to throw the ball in the third inning. The seldom seen umpire interference call nullified a double steal by the Dodgers' Dave Lopes and Bill Russell. Gregg had to feel relieved when the Dodger pair executed the double theft later in the inning.

A plate umpire who interferes with a catcher's throw on a pick-off attempt is also guilty of interference. On the Thursday following the All-Star Game in 1976, the Tigers had runners on first and second with one out in a game at Tiger Stadium against Oakland. Following the pitch to the next batter, A's catcher Jeff Newman attempted to pick the runner off first, but the ball went sailing into the right field corner, allowing the lead runner to score, and the runner from first to wind up at third. The Tigers and their fans were elated, but when the dust cleared, plate umpire Nick Bremigan was noticed standing near the mound frantically waving his arms and directing the runners to return to their bases. While the play was in progress, nobody noticed Bremigan; but he had very little trouble being noticed when it finally dawned on Tiger manager Ralph Houk what he was doing. Houk charged out to find out what was going on, and was informed by Bremigan that he had interfered with Newman's throw, causing it to go wild. Houk was victim of rule 5.09(b) that night, and proceeded to demonstrate his displeasure, which promptly led to his ejection.

Houk was quoted in the *Detroit Free Press* the next day as saying, "I've never heard of that play before and that's why I was upset. But I guess it must have happened; otherwise, he wouldn't have called it."

The next evening, Houk was his usual smiling, joking self at home plate before the game. Bremigan mentioned, "One thing about Houk—he'd go nuts on you one day, but the next day was always a new day. He never carried a grudge. Umpires respect that in managers and players, and they respect that in umpires."

5.09—(f) *The ball becomes dead and runners advance one base, or return to their bases, without liability to be put out, when a fair ball touches a runner or an umpire on fair territory before it touches an infielder including the pitcher, or touches an umpire before it has passed an infielder other than the pitcher.*

On April 18, 1956, the Giants and Pirates met in the Polo Grounds. In the bottom of the first inning with one out, the Giants had Don Mueller on first with Al Dark at the plate. Dark hit a shot that struck the left heel of umpire Stan Landes, who was on the infield grass just right of second base.

Pirate second baseman Johnny O'Brien fielded the ball and made what seemed a force play at second. But Landes declared the ball dead and awarded Mueller second base and Dark first base. Dark was also credited with a hit.

Shea Stadium was the scene on the night of May 20, 1967, in a game between the Mets and Cardinals.

In the fifth inning with the score tied, 4-4, the Mets were batting with two outs and Jerry Buchek on second. Ron Swoboda hit a sharp grounder up the middle. Julian Javier, the Cards' second sacker, started to move toward the ball, but before he could get near it, the ball struck second base umpire Frank Secory on the leg.

The ball blooped into the air and Javier caught it, but too late for a play on Swoboda. However, Buchek, who had rounded third and headed for home, was trapped and tagged out.

That seemed to have ended the inning, the Cards leaving the field and the Mets going on. Arguments then developed from all directions. The umpires met and invoked rule 5.09(f). Buchek was sent back to second and Swoboda was given first.

A note is attached to rule 5.09(f). *If a fair ball goes through, or by, an infielder, and touches a runner immediately back of him or touches a runner after being deflected by an infielder, the ball is in play and the umpire shall not declare the runners out. In making such decision the umpire must be convinced that the ball passed through, or by, the infielder and that no other infielder had the chance to make a play on the ball: runners advance, if forced.*

Let's assume the Reds have Johnny Bench on third, George Foster on second, and Dave Concepcion on first with one out in the last half of the seventh inning with the score tied 3-3 in a game against Pittsburgh. With the infield in on the grass, Ray Knight hits a shot to the left and out of reach of Bucs' shortstop Tim Foli. The ball strikes Foster on the foot as he is going from second to third.

If the ump is convinced that no other fielder had a chance to make a play after it went by Foli, Foster would not be out. The ball would be alive and in play.

As you can see, it is not true that a runner is automatically out when he gets hit by a batted ball.

The home plate umpire and the catcher perform their jobs wearing a great deal of paraphernalia for protective reasons. *If a pitched ball passes the catcher and lodges in the umpire's mask or paraphernalia runners are allowed to advance one base and the ball is dead.* (5.09=g) Can you imagine a play of this type deciding the seventh game of a World Series? However, *if the ball lodges in the catcher's mask, protector or uniform, it is a live ball and in play.*

I have to question umpire Rich Garcia's decision in relation to this rule in a game between the Milwaukee Brewers and the Oakland Athletics on June 11, 1976.

The Brewers, leading 3-2, had runners on first and third base in the eighth inning. A Paul Lindblad pitch to Bernie Carbo struck the dirt in front of home plate, bounced up, and hit A's catcher Tim Hosley in the throat. The ball then fell between Hosley's chest protector and uniform jersey.

When the ball disappeared from view, first base umpire Rich Garcia ruled that Sixto Lezcano should be allowed to score from third base and waved the other runner, Robin Yount, from first base to second.

A's manager Chuck Tanner complained after the game that Lezcano's run, the difference between a one- and two-run deficit for the A's, had forced him to alter his strategy in the ninth inning. He said it probably had affected the pitching strategy of winner Jim Colborn.

Garcia said, "As soon as the ball went out of sight, we did what we felt we had to do on the basis of common sense, and that was to declare the play dead and award each runner an extra base."

A close check on rule 5.09(g) reveals that the umpires ignored the rule book in favor of common sense. The rule says, *If a pitched ball passes the catcher and lodges in the umpire's mask or paraphernalia, on the third strike or fourth ball, then the batter is entitled to first base and all runners advance one base. A ball lodging in the catcher's mask, protector or uniform is a live ball and in play.*

Official scorer Edgar Munzel brought rule 5.09(g) to the attention of the umpires the following day. The umpires consulted with Dick Butler, the supervisor of American League umpires, and he told them that under the circumstances it was a proper decision. The decision handed down by Butler satisfied Tanner, and he therefore withdrew his protest.

This chapter comes down the home stretch with a brief study of the 5.10 rule.

5.10—(c-1) *If an accident to a runner is such as to prevent him from proceeding to a base to which he is entitled, as on a home run hit out of the playing field, or an award of one or more bases, a substitute runner shall be permitted to complete the play.*

Nick Bremigan tells a story about an incident that took place in a minor league game in the mid-1960s.

> The batter hit a long shot down the left field line that would easily clear the fence, but there was some doubt whether it would be fair or foul. As the batter was trotting to first, intensely watching the ball to be certain that it remained in fair territory, he tripped over first base while jumping for joy, and turned his ankle. The fair ball was signaled a home run by the umpire, but it was physically impossible for the batter to circle the bases because of his injured ankle.
>
> The manager then asked the umpire if he could insert a pinch-runner to complete the circuit around the bases. Following a brief conference among the umpires it was decided that, while this was highly unusual, it was legal.
>
> According to the rule book, a stustitute may enter the game any time the ball is dead. (3.03) A home run is technically a dead ball situation in which the batter is awarded four bases.

5.10—(e) *When an umpire wishes to examine the ball, to consult* *with either manager, or for any similar cause, the umpire-in-chief shall call "Time."*

This rule came to focus on the night of June 11, 1957, in a game played between the Yankees and White Sox.

In the contest, Minnie Monoso swiftly ran from first to third on a wild pitch. There was a close play at third base, but umpire John Stevens called Minnie safe. Yankee third baseman Andy Carey disputed the call with Stevens, but the third base umpire repeated that Minnie was safe and asked to look at the ball, which had caromed past batter Sherm Lollar to the backstop. The umpire asked for it again, but each time Carey jerked his hand back and wouldn't give him the ball.

Minoso, seeing that the plate was unguarded, headed for home. Carey then threw the ball to Bobby Shantz, who had come over to cover the plate, and Bobby gave Minnie a pushing tag that knocked him down as he went by.

As Minnie leaped to his feet and bellowed belligerently at Shantz, manager Al Lopez of the White Sox rushed to third base and reminded Stevens that he had asked to look at the ball and, therefore, "time" automatically was called.

Stevens realized that Lopez was right and ruled it no play. The play was the third out of the inning, and the Yankees had left the field. Stevens called Minoso back to third and ordered the Yankees to return to the field.

Yankee manager Casey Stengel protested, but, since the Yankees won 3-2, his protest was voided.

American League president William Harridge revealed that Stengel had no grounds for protest, but that if Stevens hadn't ruled that "time" was called, Lopez definitely would have had grounds for a protest, and that it would have had to be allowed.

5.11—*After the ball is dead, play shall be resumed when the pitcher takes his place on the pitcher's plate with a new ball or the same ball in his possession and the plate umpire calls "Play." The plate umpire shall call "Play" as soon as the pitcher takes his place on his plate with the ball in his possession.*

A play is not necessarily "killed" when a player becomes injured. In the tenth inning of the fourth and final game of the 1939 World Series played between the Reds and the Yankees, the Yanks poured three runs over the plate with Reds' catcher Ernie Lombardi lying stunned and out of action a few feet from home plate. Charley "King Kong" Keller of the Yankees hit "Botcho" at the plate and knocked him over. Yankee third base coach Art Fletcher waved the other runners in for the big three-run play.

6.00

The Batter

The pitcher and the batter are the two players on the field on whom television cameras and fans alike focus their attention. The batter has many rights, but also has several restrictions.

The first case relates to Rule 6.02(c). *If the batter refuses to take his position in the batter's box during his time at bat, the umpire shall order the pitcher to pitch, and shall call "Strike" on each such pitch. The batter may take his proper position after any such pitch and the regular ball and strike count shall continue, but if he does not take his proper position before three strikes are called, he shall be declared out.*

Umpires Larry Goetz, Charlie Berry, and Billy Evans enforced this rule at different times.

Frank Robinson was the culprit in the first case in a game played between the Reds and Giants on June 1, 1956. Robinson protested a called second strike in the eighth inning of that game. Goetz warned Robinson to resume his batting position, or he would order Giant pitcher Steve Ridzik to pitch. Goetz called strike three while Robinson was still arguing.

Dave Philley discovered this rule the hard way on June 14, 1959, at Yankee Stadium. Philley, playing for the White Sox, stepped out of the batter's box and did not return soon enough, as far as umpire Charlie Berry was concerned. Berry told Yankee right-hander Bob Grim to pitch. On the pitch, Philley was called out on strikes.

There have been other reasons why a batter refused to take his proper position in the batter's box. In 1920 Ray Chapman of the Cleveland Indians was killed by a fastball thrown by Carl Mays of the Yankees. That same season umpire Billy Evans had to invoke rule 6.02(c) when Chapman walked to the dugout after the great Walter Johnson had thrown two strikes by him. When Chapman started to walk away from the plate, Evans yelled, "You got another strike coming." Chapman looked over his shoulder and said to Evans, "You can have it. It wouldn't do me any good."

Although Hank Aaron holds the all-time home run record, his home run total is one short of what it should have been because of a violation by Aaron of rule 6.03 which says, *The batter's legal position shall be with both feet within the batter's box.* If a batter hits the ball and one of his feet is outside the box, he is considered to have hit an illegally batted ball and is out for this illegal action. The lines defining the box are considered within the batter's box.

Aaron violated the rule and was called out by Chris Pelekoudas when he walked up to a blooper pitch thrown by Curt Simmons of the Cardinals and hit it out of Sportsman Park in St. Louis on August 18, 1965. Pelekoudas ruled the home run illegal because Hank was out of the batter's box when he hit the pitch. For clarification of this rule, it should be understood that the batter is not out unless he makes contact with the ball. If Aaron missed the pitch, he would not have been called out.

6.04—*A batter has legally completed his time at bat when he is put out or becomes a runner.*

St. Louis Browns' pitcher Bobo Newsom once hit a ball back to the pitcher's mound but refused to run to first base. The White Sox, the team on defense, refused to make a play on Newsom when Sox skipper Jimmy Dykes shouted, "Don't throw the ball." Dykes insisted there was nothing in the book to make a fielder complete a play within a certain time limit. Newsom was called out by the umpire after a short wait. Here was a case where a batter completed his time at bat before he was put out or became a runner.

The next two rules, 6.05 and 6.06, cover the many ways a batter can be put out.

Rule 6.05(a) says, *A batter is out when his fair or foul ball (other than a foul tip) is legally caught by a fielder.*

Frequently it becomes a question as to what is a legal catch. It is necessary that an explanation of the rule be given. *A catch is the act of a fielder in getting secure possession in his hand or glove of a ball in flight and firmly holding it; providing he does not use his cap, protector, pocket or any other part of his uniform in getting possession. It is not a catch, however, if simultaneously or immediately following his contact with the ball, he collides with a player, or with a wall, or if he falls down, and as a result of such collision or falling, drops the ball. It is not a catch if a fielder touches a fly ball which then hits a member of the offensive team. If the fielder has made the catch and drops the ball while in the act of making a throw following the catch, the ball shall be adjudged to have been caught. In establishing the validity of the catch, the fielder shall hold the ball long enough to prove that he has complete control of the ball and that his release of the ball is voluntary and intentional.*

If a batted ball strikes a fielder and is then caught by another fielder before it hits the ground, it is considered to be a legal catch.

The Washington Senators played the Yankees in New York on July 26, 1935. The Yankees had runners on first and second with one out in the bottom of the second inning when Jesse Hill hit a liner that hit the head of Senators' pitcher Ed Linke and rebounded back in the air to catcher Jack Redmond. The Senators' catcher then threw to Red Kress at second base, retiring base runner Ben Chapman, who was several feet from the base.

Yankee Stadium was the site once again several years later when another rare legal catch was witnessed by several thousand fans in a game between the Yankees and Orioles. The Oriole batter hit a shot to right center. The ball bounced off the glove of Hank Bauer into the outstretched hands of Mickey Mantle.

It should be understood that a runner may legally tag up and advance as soon as the ball is touched by the fielder. He doesn't have to wait until it is securely held by a fielder for an out. If it were the other way, a team could never score on a sacrifice fly. All a fielder would have to do to hold a runner at third, would be to juggle the ball all the way into the infield, instead of actually catching it. This was an old ruse pulled by outfielders during baseball's so-called pre-historic days.

The same type of play happened to Jim Busby and Ed McGhee in 1948 when they played for Waterloo, Iowa in the Three-I League in a game against Evansville, Indiana. A line drive was hit to Busby in center field. The ball hit Busby in the shin and then glanced over to McGhee in right field for the put out.

In the bottom of the first inning in a game played between the Dodgers and Pirates on June 8, 1961, at Los Angeles, the following freak double play occurred.

With Maury Wills on first base, Jim Gilliam hit a liner that caromed off pitcher Bob Friend's shoulder into the glove of second baseman Bill Mazeroski, who fired to Dick Stuart, doubling up Maury Wills.

The rule is officially worded in the Case Book Comment Section of the rule book. *Catch is legal if ball is finally held by any fielder, even though juggled, or held by another fielder before it touches the ground.* Credit Jack Redmond, Mickey Mantle, Bill Mazeroski, and Ed McGhee with putouts.

In 1956 Harry "The Hat" Walker managed Houston in the Texas League. Houston pitcher Bill Greason hit a fly ball to left field in a game with Tulsa. As outfielder Frank Ernaga waited to make the catch, the ball struck a bird flying overhead. Ernaga caught the ball while center fielder Bob Will grabbed the bird. Walker protested that the ball could not be legally caught since the ball hit the bird which is a foreign object on a baseball field. The umpire disagreed and ruled that Ernaga's catch was legal, and that foreign objects as described in the rules were limited to such things as the ground, fences, walls, or utility guy wires.

According to *Knotty Problems of Baseball* published by *The Sporting News,* the batter should not have been out since the ball was no longer legally "in flight" and therefore was not legally caught. The ball remains in play and the batter can advance at his own risk.

Al Smith, the Indians' outfielder in the mid-fifties, leaped so high on a ball hit by the Yankees' Billy Martin that he catapulted over a 5′ 6″ barrier one night in Cleveland. As he fell over the fence, he had possession of the ball, but on landing dropped it. The drive was ruled a homer. The umpires said if Smith had held the ball they would have called it a catch since Smith was still legally on the playing field. Had Smith caught the ball after having landed on the other side of the fence, it would have been ruled a homer. If the Indians' outfielder had held the ball and assuming Mickey Mantle was on second base, Martin would have been out, but Mantle would have been allowed to advance one base.

In the third game of the 1925 World Series played between the Pirates and Senators, the umpires had to rule on a controversial catch concerning Sam Rice.

In the eighth inning, Fred Marberry went in to pitch for the Senators. Marberry proceeded to strike out the first two Pirates. Then Earl Smith stepped to the plate and drove a long fly to right-center field. The Senators' flychaser backpeddled as far as he could against the wall, and then suddenly the player, the ball, and the crowd all merged into one confusing picture. Sam Rice had fallen into the bleachers. The question was, did he catch it? There was a delay by Rice in getting out of the stands, and manager Bill McKechnie of the Pirates charged out of the dugout, protesting that Rice had dropped the ball and that it had been recovered for him by a spectator.

After a long debate, the four umpires (McCormick, Moriarty, Owens, and Rigler) decided that Rice had caught the ball before he fell into the bleachers.

A batter is also out when *a third strike is legally caught by the catcher.* (6.05=b)

The term *"legally caught" means in the catcher's glove before the ball touches the ground. It is not legal if the ball lodges in his clothing or paraphernalia;* (a la Tim Hosley) *or if it touches the umpires and is caught by the catcher on the rebound.*

If a foul tip first strikes the catcher's glove and then goes on through and is caught by both hands against the body or protector, before the ball touches the ground, it is a strike, and if a third strike, batter is out. If smothered against his body or protector, it is a catch provided the ball struck the catcher's glove or hand first.

The following case deals with a ball that was not legally caught because it hit the ground first. However, the umpire erred on the play when he called the batter out. The arbiter's mistake led to an Eastern League protest.

The West Haven Yankees and Three Rivers Eagles met on July 25, 1973, at West Haven. It was the top of the fourth inning and Eagle right fielder Toro DeFreitas was at bat. Yank pitcher Ron Klimkowski bounced a good curve in the dirt a foot outside of home plate. DeFreitas, a free-swinging power hitter, lunged at the ball and missed.

Umpire Hal Vann signaled him out. Yankee catcher Bill Stearns bounced into fair territory to make the throw to first base and clinch the out. Suddenly, Stearns relaxed and flipped the ball to third baseman Doug Stodgel throwing the ball around the horn. DeFreitas alertly went to first. Eagle manager Jim Snyder ran out of the dugout to Vann and, after a consultation with base umpire Fred Brocklander, Vann awarded DeFreitas first base.

Ignorance of the rule by yours truly allowed Dan Zipkin to set a strikeout record for the State University at New Paltz, New York, in 1965. On a third strike that was in the dirt, I threw the ball to our third baseman. The batter realizing he was not out ran to first. The third sacker then threw the ball over the first baseman's head, and the runner landed on second.

The miscue on my part forced Zipkin to still retire three batters as there were none out at the time. "Zippy" struck out the next three batters and was credited with a four strikeout inning. He eventually struck out 18 batters that day, breaking the old school record of 17.

I shouldn't have felt too bad because the same thing happened in a World Series game. This time the goat was Jimmy Wilson.

In the 1931 World Series played between the St. Louis Cardinals and Philadelphia Athletics this boner took place in the second game.

The Cardinals were leading 2-0 when Jimmie Foxx opened the top of the ninth inning with a base on balls. The next batter, Bing Miller, flied out, but Jimmy Dykes drew a walk. So now there were runners on first and second. Dib Williams then struck out. Jimmy Moore, who was at bat with the count 2-and-2, swung at a low pitch and missed it. But the ball hit in the dirt and Jimmy Wilson, the catcher, instead of tagging Moore or throwing to the first baseman fired the ball to Jake Flowers, the third baseman. Many of the Cardinals thought that Wilson made a clean catch of the third strike and started running off the field, assuming that the game had ended. However, Eddie Collins, coaching for Connie Mack, knew what had happened and yelled for Moore, who was standing at the plate, to run down to first base. Moore made it to first safely as did Dykes to second and Foxx to third.

Mike Lamey reported the following play to *The Sporting News* during the 1970 season.

> Tiger pitcher Earl Wilson almost circled the bases when he struck out in a game against the Twins at Minnesota on April 25, 1970.
>
> In the seventh inning of that game, Wilson struck out for what appeared to be the final out of the inning. However, Tiger third base coach, Grover Resinger, saw that Twin catcher Paul Ratliff had trapped the ball in the dirt on the third strike. Ratliff, according to the rules, was compelled to tag Wilson or throw to first base. Instead, Ratliff rolled the ball back toward the mound.
>
> Most of the Twins were in the dugout when Resinger told Wilson to start running. Wilson ran and was already rounding third and beginning for home when the Twins decided to play defense. Twins outfielder Brant Alyea got the ball and threw to Leo Cardenas who was waiting at home plate along with Ratliff who decided to return. Wilson tried to get back to third, but was tagged out by Alyea who took Cardenas's return throw.

So you can score that a 7-6-7 out.

Another play involving a catcher holding a third strike happened to Nick Bremigan when umpiring a Florida State League game in 1969. The bases were loaded, with two outs and a 3-2 count on the batter. The next pitch was swung at and missed, but muffed by the catcher and wound up laying on the ground beside home plate. In this situation, the batter is allowed to try for first base, since there are two outs. The catcher retrieved the ball and as he was making his throw to first, he inadvertantly stepped on home plate with his front foot while he still had possession of the ball. Although the ball wound up in right field, I had to nullify all "runs," since the catcher legally recorded the third out by stepping on home plate and forcing the runner from third, even though he had no idea what he was doing. But there is no rule that says he has to know what he's doing to execute a force play—and he didn't! The offensive team didn't buy it right away, but the ruling stood.

In the cases just covered, the batter would have been out if first base was occupied and there were less than two out.

A batter is also out if he should bunt foul on a third strike (6.05=d) a play commonly seen, or if an infield fly is declared (6.05=e) as we saw with Bill Fahey, Frank Torre, Ed Bouchee, and Jim Rivera.

If a batter attempts to hit a third strike and the ball touches him, he is also declared out. In this kind of situation the ball would be dead and runners would not be allowed to advance. Let's say that Minnie Minoso, who was known for crowding the plate, was struck by the pitch as he swung on the third strike. Minnie would be out according to rule 6.05(f).

The 6.05 rule also punishes a batter and declares the batter out if the ball touches him before touching a fielder. (6.05=g) Fans have seen the play occur when a batter bunts the ball and the ball rebounds back and hits him just as he leaves the batter's box.

Rule 6.05(h) says, *A batter is out when after hitting or bunting a fair ball, his bat hits the ball a second time in fair territory. The ball is dead and no runners may advance. If the batter-runner drops his bat and the ball rolls against the bat in fair territory and, in the umpire's judgment, there was no intention to interfere with the course of the ball, the ball is alive and in play.*

In the third inning of the third game of the 1942 World Series between the Yankees and Cardinals, Yankee manager Joe McCarthy claimed that the rule under study was not called by the umpires.

Marty Marion laid a bunt down the third base line and was thrown out by Yankee pitcher Spud Chandler. The bunt advanced Whitey Kurowski to second base. But the Cardinals argued that Chandler fielded the ball in foul territory, and the umpires agreed. Marion bunted again down the third base line, but this time beat Chandler's throw to first. Ernie White then bunted both runners (Kurowski and Marion) to second and third. Kurowski then scored on Jimmy Brown's infield grounder.

The Cardinals eventually won the game, 2-0, scoring again in the ninth, then won the next two games to win the Series. McCarthy argued that Marion's second bunt hit the bat twice and should have been called out. If "Marse Joe" was correct, the play could have had a serious effect on the series.

The Mets and Padres tangled on August 10, 1976, at Shea Stadium. Batting in the sixth inning with the score tied 4-4, the Mets had Roy Staiger on first with Leon Brown at the plate. Brown attempted a sacrifice bunt that umpire John McSherry voided because the ball hit Brown's bat twice.

Mets' Manager Joe Frazier protested the game, but it was never carried out as the Mets defeated Randy Jones and the Padres, 5-4.

Concerning a batted ball hitting the bat twice, the following should be noted. The foul lines intersect each batter's box in such a way that approximately 5/6 of each box is in foul territory, and approximately 1/6 is in fair territory. The rules say that if a batter is hit by his own fair ball or a fair ball hits his bat a second time in fair territory, he is out. But since it is often very difficult to ascertain a fair ball from a foul ball in these situations, it is commonly accepted that umpires rule "foul ball" on these plays. This includes a batter who bats a ball directly into his foot or leg; and a batter who beats the ball into the ground, which then immediately shoots up and strikes the bat or the batter, while the batter is still holding the bat. As a rule of thumb, if a batter is hit with his own batted ball, or such batted ball hits his bat while he is still in the batter's box, it is generally ruled a foul ball. This concept is only meant to refer to plays where the action is immediate, and not plays where the ball has left the immediate vicinity of home plate, and some subsequent action occurs.

Umpire Bill Kinnamon called Minneapolis's Red Robbins out when the ball hit his bat a second time while he apparently was still in the batter's box. Fort Worth appealed to Kinnamon who was umpiring at first base, and the ump ruled Robbins out.

Minneapolis manager Gene Mauch protested, but his protest was not upheld. If Robbins' bat hit the ball a second time while still in the batter's box, he would most likely not have been in fair territory, which is a prerequisite to carry out the rule. If Kinnamon believed that Robbins was in fair territory, his call was justified. Fort Worth won the game, 5-3.

A broken bat, related to this rule, was the cause of interference during a Texas League game at Houston in 1952. Houston's Bud Hardin broke his bat into two pieces on a high hopper down the third base line. Frank Shofner, Oklahoma City third baseman, was waiting to field the ball when the big part of the bat came spinning toward him and hit the ball again, sending it into the stands. Hardin was declared out for the unintentional interference of his bat since the ball hit the bat a second time. The question is—should Hardin have been called out? If the same thing were to happen today, Hardin would not be called out as provided by the case book statement pertinent to rule 6.05(b) which states, *If a bat breaks and part of it is in fair territory and is hit by a batted ball or part of it hits a runner or fielder, play shall continue and no interference called. If a batted ball hits part of a broken bat in foul territory, it is a foul ball. If a whole bat is thrown into fair territory and interferes with a defensive player attempting to make a play, interference shall be called, whether intentional or not.*

It shall be noted that a broken bat is considered an "act of God," and the batter is not responsible in such circumstances. The batter is responsible for control of his bat. If part of the bat remains in his hands, there is nothing that can be done there. However, if he loses his entire bat, he would be guilty of interference if it hindered a fielder from making a play.

Harry Simmons has published many articles in *Baseball Digest* concerning knotty problems that occur. Simmons had this puzzler set in a hypothetical situation. I will describe the play and then give you the answer to the problem using rule 6.05(i).

The Los Angeles Dodgers lead San Francisco, 3-2, in the fifth at Candlestick Park, with the Giants at bat. The first batter up, Bobby

Murcer, swings at a curve, but barely nicks the ball. It hits the ground and proceeds to trickle down the first base line in foul territory. Murcer breaks for first with Dodger catcher Steve Yeager right behind him.

As they race, the ball begins to swerve toward fair ground. It is only an inch inside foul territory when Murcer, sensing there will be plenty of time to get a fair ball to first base for the out, kicks the ball toward the stands.

The Dodgers claim the batter should be declared out for interference, but the Giants contend, "You can't call him out for interference on a foul ball."

How would you rule this play if you were the ump? If you called Murcer out, you're doing the job. Rule 6.05(i) would support your call. *A batter is out when after hitting or bunting a foul ball, he intentionally deflects the course of the ball in any manner while running to first base. The ball is dead and runner or runners shall return to their original base or bases.*

Most baseball arguments involve the judgment of the umpire as to whether or not a runner reached a base before the base or the runner is tagged. *A batter is out when after a third strike or after he hits a fair ball, he or first base is tagged before he touches first base.* (6.05=j) I guess you could say that this rule is used on almost every play. It would be difficult for me to pick out any one play for special attention.

The Mets' J. C. Martin made rule 6.05(k) come alive in the fourth game of the 1969 World Series between the Orioles and the Mets. The Mets were batting in the bottom of the tenth with the score tied, 1-1. Jerry Grote was on second, and Al Weis was on first. Martin bunted the ball toward the first base line. Oriole pitcher Pete Richert fielded the ball and threw to first. The ball struck Martin on the wrist, as he was running the entire distance from home to first base illegally inside the baseline, according to Oriole manager Earl Weaver. The ball bounded into foul territory, and Grote raced across home with the winning run.

Martin's path was not ruled illegal, and the Mets won the game, 2-1. Observing a play on the instant replay is often very deceiving. However from my standpoint, Earl Weaver had a legitimate gripe according to rule 6.05(k), which states, *A batter is out when in running the last half of the distance from home base to first base, while the ball is being fielded to first base, he runs outside (to the right of) the three foot line, or inside (to the left of) the foul line, and in the umpire's judgment in so doing interferes with the fielder taking the throw at first base; except that he may run outside (to the right of) the three-foot line or inside (to the left of) the foul line to avoid a fielder attempting to field a batted ball.*

It is quite possible that the umpire adjudged that Martin's position on the baseline did not interfere with the fielder at first base taking the throw. In most instances a runner would be called out on a play of this type.

There is an interesting sidelight to the story. Weaver could only have seen the play on replay, as he was not around to see it in the flesh. N.L. umpire Shag Crawford sent Earl packing earlier in the game—a rare World Series ejection. The last manager to be "chased" in a World Series game was Billy Martin, whom N.L. umpire Lee Weyer ejected in the fourth game of the 1976 fall classic.

Rule 6.05(l) declares, *A batter is out when a fielder intentionally drops a fair fly ball or line drive, with first, first and second, first and third, or first, second and third base occupied before two are out. The ball is dead and runner or runners shall return to their original base or bases. Approved Ruling: In this situation, the batter is not out if the fielder permits the ball to drop untouched to the ground, except when the Infield Fly rule applies.*

Prior to 1975 the ball remained alive and the rule began with the words "Any Fielder." Because of an alert umpire student, rule 6.05(l) was amended. Nick Bremigan discusses what happened.

> When they changed it in 1975 to kill the ball in this situation, the new rule still began with the words "Any Fielder," and was going to be sent to the printer that way. Bill Kinnamon, John McSherry, and I were instructing a class at Kinnamon's Umpires' School that February. A student asked a question concerning the new rule change. He asked, 'If the rule pertains to *any* fielder, and the ball is dead if the fielder does intentionally drop the ball, and all the runners remain at their original bases, what happens if a center fielder pulls it on a long fly to center field with runners at first and third and less than two outs?' Kinnamon, McSherry, and I looked at each other in complete astonishment. As so often happens when

a rule is changed, the authors try to anticipate any new problems that might result from the change, but in this case, they missed completely. The way the new rule was going to be worded, it would have taken the sacrifice fly right out of the game of baseball. We immediately notified Fred Fleig and Dick Butler of this, as they were both members of the Rules Committee. We managed to get to them in time, and the rule was re-amended to begin "An infielder"—but only because of the alertness of a student at the umpires school.

If rule 6.05(l) and the Infield Fly Rule overlap, the Infield Fly Rule takes precedence. Play: Bases loaded, one out, the batter hits a pop up to third. The third baseman intentionally drops the ball. Ruling: Since the batter is ruled out because of the Infield Fly Rule before the ball ever gets down to the fielder, the ball remains in play and 6.05(l) is not invoked. The thinking is that the runners should be aware that the batter is out before the fielder ever gets a chance to intentionally drop the ball.

Note: Rule 6.05(l) includes bunted balls and line drives, which the Infield Fly Rule does not.

Fielders have been known to intentionally drop a fly ball or allow a fly ball to fall to the ground untouched when they feel the batter is not as much of a running threat as the runner or runners on base.

The Tigers were defeated by the White Sox on September 2, 1960. In the seventh inning of that game, Detroit began to rally. Al Kaline led off with a single, then Sox second baseman Nellie Fox dropped Rocky Colavito's pop fly and tossed to shortstop Luis Aparicio, forcing Kaline at second. Tiger Manager Joe Gordon argued that Fox deliberately dropped the ball to retire Kaline, a faster runner than Colavito, but the umpires ruled Fox's misplay unintentional.

A play of this type is strictly judgment on the part of the umpire. Gordon protested the game, but it did not do him any good.

Umpire Ed Vargo enforced the rule three months earlier on May 20. Stan Musial hit a bases-loaded liner to Joe Nuxhall, Cincinnati pitcher. Vargo claimed that Nuxhall dropped the ball purposely and signaled "no play."

Apparently Vargo used common sense and killed the whole play even though the ball would have been alive and in play because of the way the rule was worded in 1960. At the time, only the batter would be out, but the play remained alive. Today the batter would be out and the play would be dead. The current wording came about in 1975.

In the last two stories the fielder touched the ball and dropped it. The next case involves a fielder allowing a ball to drop in front of him, which is perfectly legal according to the rule.

Boog Powell, Oriole first baseman, duped the Yankees on September 17, 1974. The Yankees were batting in the bottom of the sixth with the score tied, 0-0. Jim Mason was on first base, and Sandy Alomar was the hitter with nobody out. Alomar hit a pop fly bunt to Powell. The big first baseman intentionally allowed the ball to drop, seeing that Alomar did not make much of an attempt going down the first base line. Mason left first base and attempted to go to second. Powell threw to first base to get Alomar. Mason attempted to return to first and was tagged out. The Yankees played the game under protest, but had no cause since "Boog" was playing by the rules.

There are times in baseball when a batter is called out because of the actions of a runner. Rule 6.05(m) covers this the following way: *A batter is out when a preceding runner shall, in the umpire's judgment, intentionally interfere with a fielder who is attempting to catch a thrown ball or to throw a ball in an attempt to complete any play.*

In 1926 the Yankees were hosting the Tigers at Yankee Stadium. The "Iron Horse" himself, Lou Gehrig, was on first base with nobody out. Tony Lazzeri then hit a ground ball to short. Tiger second baseman Frank O'Rourke went over to the bag to receive the ball to start a double play. As O'Rourke pivoted on the play, Gehrig hit him so hard as he was about to throw the ball that umpire Billy Evans called Lazzeri out for Gehrig's interference.

Umpire Stan Landes exercised the rule during the 1972 season against Doug Rader. Landes ruled an automatic double play when Rader ran over catcher Fred Kendall of the San Diego Padres. Rader, the Houston Astros third baseman, was eventually ejected from the game.

Prior to the 1978 season, major league umpires were instructed to enforce the "automatic double play" to discourage base running cannibalism which frequently occurs when a runner leaves his base path going from first to second to break up a potential double play. The dangerous area around second base is frequently referred to as baseball's "combat zone" when a base runner tries to "take out" the second baseman or shortstop with the ferocity of a roaring lion.

The Yankees' Chris Chambliss was a victim of the "automatic double play" in the 1978 season opener at Texas when he slid wide of second in an attempt to destroy Rangers' shortstop Bert Campaneris as "Campy" was in the process of completing a double play. Because of Chambliss's base path piracy, the batter was also called out.

I would venture to say that most people who have played the game of baseball have never seen rule 6.05(n) invoked in a game and probably never will. The rule covers a very obscure but possible situation. Rule 6.05(n) states, *A batter is out when with two out, a runner on third base, and two strikes on the batter, the runner attempts to steal home base on a legal pitch and the ball touches the runner in the batter's strike zone. The umpire shall call "Strike Three," the batter is out and the run shall not count; before two are out, the umpire shall call "Strike Three," the ball is dead, and the run counts.*

Let's say the Atlanta Braves are batting in the bottom of the ninth with the score tied, 2-2, in a game against the Chicago Cubs. Rowland Office is on third for the Braves with third baseman Bob Horner at the plate. With the count 2 balls and 2 strikes, Rowland breaks for the plate and is hit with a Rick Reuschel pitch that plate umpire Terry Tata calls a strike. Since there were less than two out when this happened, Horner would be called out on strikes, and Office would be allowed to score in conjunction with rule 6.05(n).

I pity the umpire who has to make that call since very few people understand that rule.

There are four sections to rule 6.06, which deals with the illegal action of the batter. The first section, 6.06(a), declares a batter out if *he hits an illegally batted ball.* Using an illegal bat à la Thurman Munson, Ted Simmons, and Graig Nettles, and hitting a thrown ball instead of a pitched ball are two examples of hitting an illegally batted ball.

The following story involves an illegally batted thrown ball. The incident occurred in Sportsman's Park in St. Louis where the Cardinals entertained the Braves. The Braves loaded the bases, and Max West was at the plate. The runner at third took a long lead, as if he was going to break for the plate. Lon Warneke, the Cardinals' pitcher, sensed this, stepped off the rubber, and fired to the plate. West swung and hit the ball off the right field screen for a double. Umpire Tom Gorman called West's hit void because he had hit a thrown ball, not a pitch. As soon as Warneke had stepped off the rubber, his peg to the plate was a throw as an infielder and his toss wasn't a legal pitch.

Adrian "Cap" Anson performed a stunt on August 6, 1891 that would be in violation of 6.06(b), which states, *A batter is out for illegal action when he steps from one batter's box to the other while the pitcher is in position ready to pitch.*

Anson, playing for Chicago from the American League, batted against Charles "Kid" Nichols from Boston. Anson came to bat with runners on second and third, one out, and the score tied, 2-2. As Nichols was about to throw the ball, Anson began jumping from one side of the plate to the other side causing a distraction for Nichols. He repeated the operation several times without pausing in the least.

It was impossible for Nichols to pitch the ball. The Boston team argued about Anson's capers to umpire John McQuaid. The umpire then made a decision that startled everyone in the park. McQuaid allowed "Cap" to go to first base. The arbiter's reasoning was that Anson was entitled to go to first because Nichols refused to pitch. In modern baseball, the pitcher, not the batter, would be protected from such antics.

A popular myth in baseball prohibits batters from batting on both sides of the plate during the same time at bat. Haven't you heard a playground rulesmaker declare, "You can't change sides. You started batting from the right side—you must remain there." Such talk is far from the truth.

Babe Ruth smacked three home runs on May 22, 1930, in his first three at bats in a game against the Philadelphia Athletics. In his fourth at bat, the "Bambino" pulled a burlesque by batting righthanded against right-hander Jack Quinn. Ruth's stunt did not work as he struck out. The Babe batted again in the ninth inning. After watching two called "strikes" batting righthanded, he decided to bat again from the port side. On the next pitch, the immortal Yankee went down swinging.

In 1960, Jimmy Piersall batted on both sides of the plate during the same at bat in a game against the White Sox. The "Waterbury Wizard" took a strike as a righthanded hitter, then switched to the other side of the plate and batted lefty. And just like the Babe did 30 years earlier, Jimmy struck out.

One of the most controversial if not the most controversial play in World Series history took place at Cincinnati on the night of October 14, 1975, in the third game of the fall classic played between the Boston Red Sox and Cincinnati Reds. The play involved rule 6.06(c), which reads as follows: *A batter is out for illegal action when he interferes with the catcher's fielding or throwing by stepping out of the batter's box or making any other movement that hinders the catcher's play at home base. Exception: Batter is not out if any runner attempting to advance is put out, or if runner trying to score is called out for batter's interference.*

This was the situation: With Cincinnati batting in the bottom of the tenth after the Red Sox had rallied from a 5-1 deficit to knot the score at 5-5, Cesar Geronimo was on first with an opening single. Ed Armbrister then pinch-hit for pitcher Rawly Eastwick. Armbrister bunted the ball in front of home plate, and Boston catcher Carlton Fisk charged to field it. Armbrister and Fisk then came together as Armbrister took two steps toward first, backed up, and then started again.

When Fisk picked up the ball, he threw toward second base in an attempt to get the lead runner. But the throw was wild into center field, and the Reds suddenly had runners on second and third base because of the throwing error.

Boston manager Darrell Johnson along with Fisk argued violently with plate umpire Larry Barnett. They claimed that Fisk was interfered with and the rule should be enforced. Barnett said that, "It was simply a collision. . . . It is interference only when the batter intentionally gets in the way of the fielder." Dick Stello, the first base umpire, supported Barnett during the protest.

It was interesting to hear both sides of the play. Fisk said of Barnett,

"He blew it two ways. . . . The first time was when he didn't call interference on the play. The second time was when he didn't call the man out because I probably tagged him after I got the ball."

Armbrister said, "I hit the ball in front of the plate and it bounced high. I started to break for first, and Fisk just came from behind and bumped me, and if he hit from behind, I would say he interfered with me." You can see why baseball needs them, so please, don't kill the umps!

After the argument the Red Sox issued an intentional walk to Pete Rose to load the bases. Merv Rettenmund then struck out, but Joe Morgan proceeded to single home the game-winning run.

To briefly review the situation let's break a couple of things down. *Offensive interference is an act by the team at bat which interferes with, obstructs, impedes, hinders or confuses any fielder attempting to make a play. If the umpire declares the batter out for interference, all other runners shall return to the last base that was in the judgment of the umpire, legally touched at the time of the interference, unless otherwise provided by these rules.* (2.00)

There is no mention in the definition of interference of the word intentional. Umpire Barnett's argument using the word "intentional" was, in my opinion, a mistake. Barnett also revealed that the American League gives umpires a list of special instructions that is a supplement to the rule book. Collisions of this type in the area of home plate are not to be called interference according to A.L. instructions. If this is true, Barnett might be defended. However another rule that supports the Red Sox protest is rule 7.09(l). *It is interference by a batter or a runner when he fails to avoid a fielder who is attempting to field a batted ball or intentionally interferes with a thrown ball etc, etc.* According to this rule, it was Armbrister's duty to avoid Fisk. The word intentional is used in relation to a thrown ball.

In summary, a play of this type is judgment on the part of the umpire to a certain extent. It's easy to sit down with a pen in hand in a quiet room and evaluate the play. Larry Barnett had to make the call before millions of viewers on national television. He believed his call was the correct one and gave some very good reasons. In demand as a banquet speaker in the off-season, Mr. Barnett has become a baseball personality due mainly to this controversial play.

The jury is going to be put out on this one for a long time. That's what makes baseball the great game that it is.

Nick Bremigan offers his opinion on the play. Barnett made the right call. However, at the time the play occurred, the only place where this explanation could be found was ironically in the "Special Instructions to Umpires" for the National League. (Barnett was an A.L. umpire.) It was belatedly thought that everyone should have access to these interpretations, so they were pirated from the "top secret" "Special Instructions to Umpires" book and put into the regular rule book, which anybody can have access to.

I've also talked to N.L. umpire Terry Tata about the play. Terry gave an emphatic "yes" when asked if Barnett had made the proper call.

It's not chic on my part to challenge two major league umpires, but in my mind Barnett believed it was interference (but not intentional) by his statement, "It is interference only when the batter intentionally gets in the way of the fielder."

Since I've been voted down, I guess the play should be referred to as a "simple collision." Amen!

In a game between the Red Sox and White Sox in the 1950s, Frank Malzone, Red Sox third baseman, was called out when he interfered with White Sox catcher Sherm Lollar. The Chicago catcher was attempting to throw out Jackie Jensen, who was trying to steal second. Malzone missed the pitch and his momentum carried him into Lollar. Jensen was safe on the play. The umpire ordered Jensen back to first, and Malzone was called out.

The umpires admittedly missed the next case involving rule 6.06. The incident occurred on July 9, 1969, at Minnesota where the Twins were hosting Kansas City. The Royals were batting with Bob Oliver on first base and Ellie Rodriguez at the plate. Oliver attempted to steal second. In making his throw to second base, Twins' catcher John Roseboro had to push Rodriguez's bat out of the way. Still Roseboro's throw nailed Oliver. Now the fun began.

"At first I wanted to call them both out," said plate umpire John Rice. "Rodriguez for interference and Oliver at second."

Royals' manager Joe Gordon protested. After several huddles, the umps (Bill Kunkel, Larry Napp, and Russ Goetz were the other three) sent Oliver back to first and ruled Rodriguez out.

Rule 6.06(c) says *A batter is out if he interferes with a catcher's fielding or throwing.* There also is an exception, saying the batter is not out if any runner attempting to advance is put out. Rule 2.00, however, says if the umpire declares the batter out for interference, other runners shall return to the last base legally touched at the time of the interference. This might have caused some of the confusion on the part of the umpires.

"What I did was against the rule book," Rice said, after taking eight minutes to make a decision. Rice said the exception should have been invoked.

In other words when a putout is made, this nullifies the interference as stated in 6.06(c).

It is true that Rice made a mistake. But baseball rules are often confusing because they are not consistent. For example, let's assume that Oliver was trying to score from third and Rodriguez interfered with Roseboro. In this case with less than two outs the runner is out. With two outs, the batter (Rodriguez) would be called out. Why not be consistent with the rule? Does the rule punish the offensive team sufficiently if a putout is not made?

Here is another argument: There is a runner on second and one out. The runner attempts to steal third base, and the batter interferes with the catcher, causing the runner to reach third safely. Ruling under 6.06(c): The umpire declares the batter out and the runner would return to second base. There are two outs and a runner is still in scoring position. The next batter then gets a hit and drives in the run from second. Once again I ask, does the rule sufficiently punish the offense?

During the 1955 season in a game played between the Dodgers and Giants, Brooklyn's Sandy Amoros struck out, but the ball got by catcher Wes Westrum when Amoros' bat hit Westrum on the backswing. Amoros reached second base before the dazed Westrum could recover the ball.

If this type of play were to happen today, Amoros would be out as the case book explanation to rule 6.06(c) stipulates, *If a batter strikes at a ball and misses and swings so hard he carries the bat all the way around and, in the umpire's judgment, unintentionally hits the catcher or the ball in back of him on the backswing before the catcher has securely held the ball, it shall be called a strike only (not interference). The ball will be dead, however, and no runner shall advance on the play.* If the situation takes place after a third strike it is ruled as interference under 7.09(a) which states, *It is interference by a batter or a runner when after a third strike he hinders the catcher in his attempt to field the ball.* Thus Amoros would end up in the dugout instead of second base.

The last section of rule 6.06(d) deals with the use of an illegal bat. *Bats that are filled, flat-surfaced, nailed, hollowed, grooved or covered with a substance such as paraffin (a white waxy substance), wax, etc. are illegal.* Anecdotes covered earlier in the text involving Graig Nettles and Ted Simmons would apply here.

There are a few things to keep in mind about batting out of turn. When a player bats out of turn, the player who is supposed to bat is called out. If there is no appeal before a pitch is thrown to the next batter, or before any play is attempted, the man who batted out of turn (the improper batter) is considered to have batted in proper turn and establishes the order that is to follow. Another point to remember is that *if a runner advances, while the improper batter is at bat, on a stolen base, balk, wild pitch or passed ball, such advance is legal.*

Now that we have the basics for rule 6.07 let's explore the rule.

In the seventh inning of the third game of the 1925 World Series between the Pirates and Senators, Earl McNeely ran for Nemo Leibold who had batted for pitcher Alex Ferguson. McNeely then went on to play center field. Sam Rice moved to right, and Fred Marberry went to the mound. Under the rules, McNeely should have batted ninth, but in his place Marberry came up. The Pirates were caught napping, and when they realized the error, it was too late to do anything about it. Sam Rice, the next batter, was already pitched to!

Joe Pignatano played for Forth Worth in the Texas League in 1956. In a game against Shreveport, Pignatano was listed eighth in the batting order but batted seventh on his first trip to the plate. He hit a home run that was protested by Mel McGaha, Shreveport Manager.

It was ruled that the proper number seven hitter was out. Pignatano batted again and hit the first pitch for a home run. In Texas, Joe Pignatano will always be remembered for hitting two successive homers, but one was an out.

On April 17, 1958, Birmingham of the Southern Association managed by Cal Ermer met Chattanooga. When Red Marion, Chattanooga pilot, filled out his lineup card, he listed one batter twice and omitted another. The slipup resulted from the similarity in the last names of Vern Morgan, his third baseman, and catcher Guy Morton. Marion wrote Morgan's name in the second position and again in the number six slot, where he intended for Morton to hit.

In the first inning, Morgan batted second and was retired, but Chattanooga filled the bases with two out, bringing up Morton. He singled to drive in a run. However, Ermer immediately called Umpire Frank Girard's attention to the lineup card, which showed Morgan as the sixth batter as well as second. Girard then ruled Morton batted out of turn, making the third out and nullifying the run. With the aid of this break, Birmingham went on to win 1-0.

To begin with, the umpire should carefully read the lineup cards before the game. If he notices that the same player is listed twice in the batting order, he should have the manager correct the error prior to the start of the game.

In the episode above, since Morgan was listed in both the second and sixth spots, he became the legal number two batter when he batted in that position. With all of the players written on the lineup card in the game, this leaves the number six spot for Morton, the catcher, and he should have been treated as an unannounced substitute, making his hit and RBI legal. This relates to rule 3.08(a-2) which states, *If no announcement of a substitution is made, the substitute shall be considered as having entered the game when if a batter, he takes his place in the batter's box.*

Ermer was alert to the situation, having managed Chattanooga with Morgan and Morton on his team the previous two seasons. Ermer admitted that he had caught himself several times writing down one or the other twice.

Umpires can get confused over the rule like anyone else; as this excerpt shows.

In a game played between the Athletics and White Sox in the early '50s, the following fiasco took place. Philadelphia won the game, 5-1, but the first inning proved to be trouble. You see this was the second game of a double-header, and manager Jimmy Dykes of the Athletics forgot to make a lineup card change for the second game. Here is what happened.

Eddie Joost led off for the A's in the bottom of the first and struck out. Ferris Fain followed with a double to left. Dave Philley then drew a base on balls. Gus Zerniel then doubled to left scoring Fain and advancing Philley to third.

That's when Chicago manager Paul Richards came striding from the dugout, and the rhubarb began. He told umpire Bill Summers that the A's had batted that way in the first game, but before the second game started, manager Jimmy Dykes had revised the batting order, switching Allie Clark to the third spot from fifth and dropping Philley to fifth from third. Dykes did admit that Richards was correct and that he forgot to notify his players between games. So here is what the A's order should have been: Joost, Fain, Clark, Zerniel, Philley, and Michaels. But the improper order was followed: Joost, Fain, Philley, Zerniel, Clark, and Michaels.

After twenty minutes of discussion, with players, fans, and the press box in a great state of confusion, the umpires ruled:

Philley, who batted out of turn, became a legal baserunner when no protest was made before the first pitch to the batter following him.

Zerniel was an improper batter because he followed the wrong man. He was deprived of his double, Fain was returned to second base and Zerniel to the bench to await his next turn in the proper order.

And Cass Michaels, the batter following Philley on the official list, was out because he didn't appear at the plate in his proper turn.

In the case mentioned, Clark should have been the proper batter after Fain batted. However Philley, the improper batter came up. An appeal was not made until Zerniel had batted.

Rule 6.07(c) says, *When an improper batter* (Philley) *becomes a runner or is put out, and a pitch is made to the next batter* (Zerniel) *of either team before an appeal is made, the improper batter* (Philley) *thereby becomes the proper batter and the results of his time at bat become legal.*

Since a pitch was thrown to Zerniel and Philley was on base, this legalized Philley's base on balls. Since Philley was on base and could not bat after Zerniel, Cass Michaels should have taken his turn at bat.

If Richards appealed while Philley was at bat, Allie Clark would have stepped in and inherited the count. If Richards appealed after Philley walked, but before the first pitch was thrown to Zerniel, Philley would be removed from first and Allie Clark would be out. Zerniel would then be the batter.

I think the umpires got lost on this one. The rule sounds a lot more confusing than it really is. From the defensive manager's standpoint, it is suicide to alert the umpire while the improper batter is at bat. If the error is corrected, the proper batter just assumes the count. From the offensive manager's standpoint, it is advisable to put the proper batter up and replace the improper batter if it is possible. The proper batter just inherits the count.

Oriole Manager Paul Richards pulled a reversal to the rule by instructing Jerry Adair to purposely bat out of turn in 1960 in a game against Detroit.

In the eighth inning, Richards let Adair bat when it was pitcher Gordon Jones' turn to bat. When Adair hit a two-run single, Detroit Manager Jimmy Dykes brought the mistake to the umpire's attention.

"Guess I might as well admit," said Richards, "I purposely had Adair bat out of turn. I was hoping the count would get to 3-and-0, and then I could send up Jones to get a walk. I didn't have another pitcher hot, so I didn't want to take out Jones."

In this case Jones was out, and Adair, who normally followed Jones in the order, batted again in his normal spot.

If you want to force a weak hitter to get ahead of the pitcher, this is a pretty good trick.

Rules 6.08 and 6.09 cover the batter's rights to become a runner. *The batter becomes a runner and is entitled to first base without liability to be put out provided he advances to and touches first base when four "balls" have been called by the umpire* (6.08=a) *he is touched by a pitched ball which he is not attempting to hit, unless (1) the ball is in the strike zone when it touches the batter, or (2) the batter makes no attempt to avoid being touched by the ball.* (6.08=b)

In 1876, the first year of the National League, three strikes and nine balls was the rule. The following year, and only for that one season (1877), it required four strikes for a strikeout. The nine ball count, however, stayed until 1880 when it was changed to eight. Then it was dropped to seven, six, five, and finally in 1889 to the present rule of four balls for a walk.

A fourth ball to Gil Hodges of the Dodgers resulted in the final out of the eighth inning in a freak incident at St. Louis on September 5, 1958.

With Junior Gilliam on third base, two out, and a 3-and-1 count on Hodges, Gilliam attempted to steal home against Phil Paine of the Cardinals but was nailed at the plate on the Cardinal right-hander's delivery to catcher Gene Green.

When the Dodgers came to bat in the top of the ninth inning, Steve Bilko, the L.A. first baseman, strolled to the plate, causing some confusion because it was believed that Hodges was the first man up since he was at bat when Gilliam was caught stealing.

However, plate umpire Vinnie Smith disclosed that the pitch which retired Gilliam for the third out also was the fourth ball for Hodges. Although he drew a walk, Hodges had no opportunity to take first base.

A batter is entitled to first base after he receives four balls—that's if the umpires are aware of the count.

It was early in the 1978 season when the Mets and Phillies tangled at the Vet in Philadelphia in what must have been a real yawner.

The Mets' Lenny Randle was batting with a count of three balls and two strikes facing Tug McGraw. The next pitch was called a ball, which entitled Randle to take first base. Apparently everyone in the park must have been napping including the umpires because Randle remained in the batter's box instead of taking his "walk" to first.

With the count of four balls and two strikes, Lenny hit McGraw's next pitch for a triple. Do you believe that happened in a major league game?

The intentional walk has created some interesting situations. Mel Ott, managing the Giants, once ordered Swish Nicholson of the Cubs walked with the bases loaded. Another case in point was Herb Pruett giving Babe Ruth an intentional pass with the sacks full. For those who like baseball firsts, several historians credit Nap Lajoie as the first major leaguer to be intentionally walked with the bases loaded.

Rule 6.08(b), allowing players to be given first base when struck by a pitched ball, first appeared on the books in the American Association in 1884, because John Schappert, who pitched for St. Louis in 1882, supposedly threw at so many hitters. Since that time the rule has caused some interesting situations on all levels of baseball. Hit batsmen have been killed by pitched balls, such as Ray Chapman of the Indians, and several others have been severely injured.

If a pitched ball hits the batter in the strike zone, it is a strike. When Pete Castle played for the Pirates, he attempted to bunt the ball. The ball fell in front of home plate. Castle claimed he was hit by the pitch, but the umpire said it was a bunt. Castle was thrown out at first. Later on, X-rays revealed that Castle had suffered a broken arm as a result of the play.

In that particular play, if the umpire thought that the ball struck Castle in the strike zone, the ball would be dead and the pitch would be ruled a strike. It was quite possible, however, that the umpire believed the ball hit the bat.

The following cases involve a batter making no attempt to avoid being hit by a pitched ball. The rule states, *The batter becomes a runner and is entitled to first base without liability to be put out (provided he advances to and touches first base) when he is touched by a pitched ball which he is not attempting to hit, unless the batter makes no attempt to avoid being touched by the ball.* (6.08=b)

The rule developed after the 1956 season. Baseball people believe that the rule was born because of Minnie Minoso crowding the plate and getting hit so often, as I had previously mentioned.

The 1968 season was a pleasant one for Dodger pitcher Don Drysdale. Drysdale was not only credited with 58-plus consecutive scoreless innings, breaking Walter Johnson's 45-year record, but also achieved a N.L. record for pitching five consecutive shutouts, because of a controversial call by umpire Harry Wendelstedt.

In a game between the Dodgers and Giants at Los Angeles, the Giants had the bases loaded in the ninth and none out with Giants' catcher Dick Dietz at bat with a 2-and-2 count. The next pitch hit Dietz, but Wendelstedt ruled that Dietz had made no effort to get out of the way of the pitch. Instead of permitting a run-scoring hit batsman that would have deprived Drysdale of a chance at both the shutout and scoreless inning records, the umpire ruled the pitch ball three. Dietz eventually flied out, and Drysdale's streak was held intact.

Umpire Hank Soar carried out rule 6.08(b) against Nellie Fox of the White Sox on June 3, 1956, in a game against the Orioles. Fox was hit on the seat of his pants by a curve from Oriole left-hander Johnny Schmitz. Soar ruled that Fox made no effort to get out of the way of the pitch and just called the pitch a ball. Two pitches later, Fox was hit again. This time Soar believed that Fox tried to avoid being hit and allowed Fox to go to first base.

Many years ago only one umpire was utilized in a game. As a catcher, Connie Mack used to take advantage of this. When there were man on base the umpire would stand behind the pitcher. Mack used to tip the bat with his glove, which made several hitters tap weakly to the infield. Today that would be catcher's interference—rule 6.08(c). *The batter becomes a runner and is entitled to first base without liability to be put out (provided he advances to and touches first base) when the catcher or any fielder interferes with him. If a play follows the interference, the manager of the offense may advise the plate umpire that he elects to decline the interference penalty and accept the play. Such election shall be made immediately at the end of the play. However, if the batter reaches first base on a hit, an error, a base on balls, a hit batsman, or otherwise, and all other runners advance at least one base, the play proceeds without reference to the interference.*

It is unlikely that you will attend a game and see the rule enforced. However, if you were at the Tigers-Orioles game on June 19, 1960, you would have seen umpire Ed Hurley invoke this rule against catcher Clint Courtney twice in the same contest. Hurley ruled that Courtney's glove tipped Sandy Amoros' bat in the fourth inning and Steve Bilko's bat in the sixth inning.

In reference to the last part of the rule, let's say that Bilko hit a home run even though Courtney interfered with him. In this case the play would proceed without reference to the interference since all runners including the batter advanced at least one base. If Bilko's shot was an inside-the-park job, he could be thrown out at home and the play would stand as long as all runners including the batter advanced at least one base.

One last note on 6.08(c). A careful look at the rule reveals that the batter is entitled to first base if the catcher or any fielder interferes with him.

Jean McCarthy, baseball coach at Mankato State College in Minnesota, has used this rule to his advantage. McCarthy utilizes rule 6.08(c) to put a batter on first base without throwing four intentional "balls." McCarthy orders his first baseman to position himself about ten feet in front of the plate and just to the first base side of the pitching path. As soon as the first baseman intercepts the pitch, he automatically interfered with the batter's rights to strike the ball. The batter would then be given first base. McCarthy's pitcher has thrown one pitch instead of four, a clever way to alleviate the intentional walk.

The only way a team could be hurt by this method is if a runner on base breaks for the next base on the pitch. Rule 7.04(d) says, *Each runner, other than the batter, may without liability to be put out, advance one base when while he is attempting to steal a base, the batter is interfered with by the catcher or any other fielder.*

Using McCarthy's tactics, "any other fielder" would be the first baseman. McCarthy counteracts this problem by instructing the first baseman to allow the pitch to go to the catcher if he sees a runner breaking from one base to another. Hats off to Coach McCarthy for coaching baseball creatively by the book. A more widespread use of the rule may cause the extinction of the intentional pass.

The last part of rule 6.08 recognizes umpire interference. Although four umpires occupy the field for the full nine innings, the chance of umpire interference is quite remote.

(6.08-d) *If a fair ball touches an umpire or a runner on fair territory before touching a fielder the batter becomes a runner and is entitled to first base without liability to be put out.*

Once again we see where the rule book is redundant. This rule was already spelled out under 5.09(f). It was probably restated to illustrate the runner's rights.

There are several ways that a batter can become a runner. Sections (a-h) of rule 6.09 explain the various ways. *If a batter hits a fair ball he becomes a runner* (6.09=a), a very easy, uncomplicated rule.

Often shots hit down the foul lines become disputed as to whether they are fair or foul. A close check on fair or foul plays in chapter 2 proves this rule is one of the more controversial ones in baseball's playing code.

Rule 6.09(b) has caused many fans to rise to their feet, and it has also caused managers to become gray at an early age. The rule says, *The batter becomes a runner when the third strike called by the umpire is not caught, providing (1) first base is unoccupied, or (2) first base is occupied with two out.*

Because of this rule, several pitchers have registered four strikeouts in an inning. The last pitcher to chalk up four Ks in an inning was Mike Paxton of the Indians when he fanned four in one inning during the 1978 season. Since 1950, Phil Niekro (1977), Bill Bonham (1974), Mike Cuellar (1970), Bob Gibson (1966), Don Drysdale (1965), Lee Stange (1964), Pete Richert (1962), Ryne Duren (1961), Joe Nuxhall (1959), and Jim Davis (1956) each had four whiffs the same frame.

One of the most talked about plays in major league history will be repeated again for the purpose of illustrating the rule. The play of course is the famous Mickey Owen play during the fourth game of the 1941 World Series between the Yankees and Dodgers.

Hugh Casey was pitching for the Dodgers with two out in the ninth leading 4-3. Tommy Henrich was at the plate for the Yankees with the bases empty. Henrich missed a 3-and-2 pitch for what should have been the game-ending out. But Dodger catcher Owen missed the ball, and Henrich ended up on first. The Yankees eventually scored four runs to win the game.

Rule 6.09(c) says, *The batter becomes a runner when a fair ball, after having passed a fielder other than the pitcher, or after having been touched by a fielder, including the pitcher, shall touch an umpire or runner on fair territory.*

Let's say the Seattle Mariners have the bases loaded with Dan Meyer on third, Julio Cruz on second, and Leon Roberts on first. Bruce Bochte, the batter, hits a hard grounder off the glove of Red Sox second baseman Jerry Remy. The ball then hits Roberts going from first to second. In this type of situation, the batter can become a runner and everything is alive and in play.

A fair ball hit over a fence allows the batter to become a runner under rule 6.09(d). However, it sometimes becomes a dispute as to whether the ball is fair or foul.

Leo Durocher, who was never shy with umpires, went into a rage on May 13, 1973, when his Astros were defeated by Cincinnati 2-0. Durocher argued that a home run hit by the Reds' Bobby Tolan was "foul." But first base umpire Augie Donatelli said it was "fair" claiming that the drive curved around the foul pole in fair territory and landed in the second deck in foul territory. Durocher did not believe that something like that could happen. So what appears to be a clear and simple rule can develop into a sticky situation.

On August 5, 1956, Western League umpires Gene Haack and Jack Wagner had to make a decision that was related to rule 6.09(d).

Pueblo first baseman Larry Stankey hit a ball that appeared to be leaving the park in fair territory when the lights went out. After a 51-minute delay the lights were turned on and a search began for the ball. The sphere couldn't be found, and the umpires ruled it a homer. Sioux City protested but withdrew the protest since they won, 7-4.

Wrigley Field in Chicago is tailor-made for rule 6.09(e) with all its vines and shrubbery. The rule says, *The batter becomes a runner when a fair ball, after touching the ground, bounds into the stands, or passes through or under a scoreboard, or through or under shrubbery, or vines on the fence, or which sticks in a fence or scoreboard, in which case the batter and the runners shall be entitled to two bases.*

This rule is commonly carried out in sandlot games but for the most part vines and shrubbery are not a part of most major league fields. The 1945 World Series between the Cubs and Tigers brought this rule to life when Roy Cullenbine of the Tigers hit the ball into the vines at Wrigley Field.

The sixth section of the rule, 6.09(f) is worded about the same as 6.09(e) with the addition that balls that stick in a fence or scoreboard entitle the runners and batter to two bases.

Umpire Lon Warneke became confused over rules 6.09(g) and 6.09(h) on opening day in 1953 at Milwaukee where the Braves hosted the St. Louis Cardinals.

In the tenth inning the Braves' Bill Bruton hit a game-winning homer. The ball bounced out of Enos Slaughter's glove and over the fence. Warneke ruled the drive a double, but Augie Donatelli reversed Warneke's decision.

6.09—(g) *If a "bounding" fair ball is deflected by a fielder into the stands the batter is entitled to advance two bases.* However if a fair "fly" ball is deflected into the stands in fair territory it is a home run. *If a fair fly ball is deflected and goes into the stands in foul territory, the batter is entitled to only two bases if a fair fly ball is deflected at a point less than 250 feet from home plate.* (6.09=h)

It is apparent that Warneke misinterpreted the rules in this case. However when an umpire errs in carrying out a book rule, another umpire can overrule him, as did Donatelli. Speaking of Warneke, he is the only man in baseball history to play and umpire in both the All Star game and the World Series.

On May 10, 1977, at Montreal's Olympic Stadium, Warren Cromartie of the Expos slammed a long drive to center against the Dodgers. Center fielder Rick Monday chased the ball, but was unable to reach it. The ball caromed off the wall, struck Monday on the forehead, and then bounced over the wall. Cromartie was credited with a ground-rule double, and Monday was charged with an Excedrin headache 725!

In the above case, a bounding fair ball was deflected by a fielder into the stands, thus entitling Cromartie to advance to second on the play. Sometimes it just doesn't pay to "use your head." Ask Rick Monday.

Nick Bremigan relates a similar anecdote that was called wrong.

Veteran A.L. umpire Al Smith called this one in Detroit in the early 1960s. A Tiger batter hit a deep fly ball to left center which caromed off the left fielder's glove, hit the fence, came back in and hit the fielder on the head and went over the fence. Smith ruled it a home run, since the ball never struck the ground. As is their practice after a game, the umpires were discussing the play. It soon dawned on them that the hit should have been ruled a ground rule double. Once the ball hit the fence, it became a bounding ball and was no longer a ball "in flight," as defined in rule 2.00. Rule 6.09(g) clearly entitles the batter to only two bases when a bounding ball leaves the playing field. The amazing part about the whole incident was that the defensive team assumed it was a home run and never said a word. The left fielder didn't know the rule.

It should be made clear that a batted ball in flight which caroms off the fielder's glove and keeps on going over the fence in fair territory, as well as a batted ball in flight which hits the top of the fence and keeps on going out are both home runs.

Ron Blomberg of the New York Yankees made baseball history on April 6, 1973, at Fenway Park in Boston when he became the first official designated hitter in major league history at 1:53 P.M. Since that time the designated hitter rule (6.10) has caused many an umpire to scratch his head.

Briefly, I will list a part of the rule. *A hitter may be designated to bat for the starting pitcher and all subsequent pitchers in any game without otherwise affecting the status of the pitcher(s), in the game. A Designated Hitter for the pitcher must be selected prior to the game and must be included in the lineup cards presented to the Umpire-In-Chief. It is not mandatory that a club designate a hitter for the pitcher, but failure to do so prior to the game precludes the use of a Designated Hitter for that game.*

Another part of the rule states, *Once the game pitcher is switched from the mound for a defensive position this move shall terminate the Designated Hitter role for the remainder of the game.*

On Friday evening May 4, 1973, Oakland Athletic manager Dick Williams produced a lineup that included a designated hitter and a designated pinch hitter for a game won, 11-4, over the Cleveland Indians.

Oakland's original lineup listed Deron Johnson as the designated hitter, batting fifth, and Gonzalo Marquez, who throws left-handed, at second base, batting second.

Marquez was really a designated pinch hitter. He sacrificed and reached safely on an error as the A's scored three times off Gaylord Perry in the first inning. But when the A's took the field, Dick Green was at second base and Marquez in the dugout.

Savannah manager Clint Courtney made the designated hitter rule confusing when he pulled the following stunt in a Southern League game played between Savannah and Asheville on April 29, 1973. Courtney started with Mike Walseth as his DH, but had Chuck Sprinkle run for Walseth in the eighth inning. Under the rule, Sprinkle assumed the role of designated hitter. In the ninth, with two men on base and two out, Courtney switched pitcher Wenty Ford to third base and brought Brian Nelson to the mound. After holding up play to consider the situation, the umpires decided correctly that once a pitcher moves to another defensive position, the DH role is terminated. They put Ford into the batting order in fifth place, the DH spot, and listed Nelson eighth in place of third baseman Joe Brookins. Neither came to bat in Savannah's half of the ninth when the Braves rallied for four runs to beat Asheville, 8-7.

Detroit manager Ralph Houk made a lineup card mistake on June 27, 1976, when his Tigers met the Red Sox at Boston. Houk listed both Alex Johnson and Rusty Staub as the Tigers' DH. Boston manager Darrell Johnson brought this to the attention of plate umpire Don Denkinger, who immediately ordered the Tigers to play the game without a DH. The Tigers took the pressure off Houk by beating the Red Sox, 4-2, in 11 innings.

It should be noted that any league may elect to use the designated hitter rule, although the American League is the only league that uses it as of this writing. (a) *In the event of interleague competition between clubs of leagues using the designated hitter rule and clubs of leagues not using the designated hitter rule: the rule will be as follows: (1) In exhibition games, the rule will be used or not used as is the practice of the home team. (2) In All*

Star games the rule will only be used if both teams in both leagues so agree. (3) In World Series Play the rule will be used every other year.

Presently the DH is used in World Series competition on even numbered years.

7.00

The Runner

Running the bases is an art that is not mastered by too many players. Because of this, men like Lou Brock, Maury Wills, and Ty Cobb are distinctive in their own field.

This area of the book deals with the runner from the time he leaves the batter's box. Base running has caused some very sticky problems that I will attempt to cover in this chapter.

The initial rule of this section (7.01) states, *A runner acquires the right to an unoccupied base when he touches it before he is out. He is then entitled to it until he is put out or forced to vacate it for another runner legally entitled to that base.*

A shrewd base runner will sometimes take advantage of this rule. Mickey Mantle demonstrated what could happen if a runner is on first and the first baseman removes the force at second by tagging the bag before throwing to second base.

The scene was the 1960 World Series. The place was Forbes Field in Pittsburgh where the Pirates were entertaining the Yankees.

In the top of the ninth inning of the seventh game, Mantle was on first, and Gil McDougald was on third with one out. Yogi Berra then hit a hard shot to Pirate first baseman Rocky Nelson. The ball was hit so hard that the force of the smash turned Nelson around so that he was facing the outfield. Nelson could not get McDougald going home and felt that he was not in a good position to throw to second for the first-short-first double play. The next thing to do was to tag first base, which he did to retire Berra. As soon as he did this, Mantle was no longer forced to go to second. Mickey alertly slid back into first base and was safe. Mantle's base running gem went for nought when Bill Mazeroski hit his immortal clout in the bottom of the ninth to wrap up the series for the Bucs.

Rule 7.02 says, *In advancing, a runner shall touch first, second, third and home base in order. If forced to return, he shall retouch all bases in reverse order, unless the ball is dead under any provision of rule 5.09. In such cases, the runner may go directly to his original base.*

A controversial call involving umpires John Kibler and Augie Donatelli was the result of a running play by Ken Henderson of the Giants on September 25, 1971, in a game against the Reds. In the top of the eighth inning the Giants were trailing, 6-5. Henderson was on first, and Tito Fuentes was at bat. Fuentes hit a long drive to left center that was caught by George Foster. Meanwhile, Henderson had run all the way to second base before retreating after the catch.

Foster threw to first to pick off Henderson. Umpire John Kibler called Henderson out, even though he got back to first before the throw. Tony Kubek, who was doing the game on NBC Television, emphasized that it was a proper call since Henderson had taken a step with his right foot off second base toward third while his left foot had remained on the bag prior to the catch. When Henderson retreated to first he had stepped off with his left foot from the bag, then allowed his right foot to bypass the second base bag as he broke into a full run.

Donatelli, who was the umpire-in-chief, overruled Kibler's call on Henderson and allowed him to stay at first. The Reds played the game under protest, but won it anyway, 6-5.

According to *The Sporting News,* the slow motion replay supported Kibler's decision.

Harry Hardner played for an amateur team in Milwaukee in 1930. He hit a home run but failed to touch first. After he reached home he went to first for a supposedly five-base hit. I'm not sure how the Hardner play was ruled, but if this were to happen tonight, Hardner couldn't go back and legally touch first base, even if he did retrace his steps because of rule 7.10(b) which declares, *when the ball is dead, no runner may return to touch a missed base or one he has left after he has advanced to and touched a base beyond the missed base.* Once Hardner reached second base he would lose his right to retouch first base—the missed base.

The 7.03 rule has caused some very embarrassing situations. The rule is as follows: *Two runners may not occupy a base, but if while the ball is alive, two runners are touching a base, the following runner shall be out when tagged. The preceding runner is entitled to the base.*

The rule should say "two" or "three" runners because on August 15, 1926, the Brooklyn Dodgers had three men on third base in a game against the Boston Braves at Ebbets Field.

In the seventh inning the Dodgers had Hank DeBerry on third, Dazzy Vance on second, and Chick Fewster on first. Babe Herman hit a drive to right field scoring DeBerry. Vance rounded third and got halfway home when he decided he could not beat the throw home so he retreated back to third, where he found Fewster. Herman decided he was going to try for a triple, and he ended on third joining Vance and Fewster.

The Braves' third baseman, Eddie Taylor, got the throw and started tagging people. Herman got out of the way before he was tagged but was tagged going back to second. Fewster was called out since the base was entitled to Vance. Taylor, who only played one season in the major leagues, took part in one of the most unusual running plays in baseball history.

In a game played between the Los Angeles Dodgers and Houston Astros on July 31, 1973, the Dodgers didn't quite have three men on third, but they had two.

It started when the Dodgers were trailing, 3-1, in the eighth inning and Manny Mota came up with two on and one out after Bill Russell and Dave Lopes had singled.

Mota singled to center, and third base coach Tom LaSorda decided to hold up Russell at third so the Dodgers would have the bases loaded with one out and Willie Davis up.

But Lopes wasn't looking, and he didn't see Russell stop at third. He rounded second and charged to third. Cesar Cedeno's throw to the plate was cut off by pitcher Dave Roberts, who fired to third to Doug Rader. The tag was placed on Lopes, and he became the second out of the inning.

The White Sox and Giants met in the 1917 World Series. In the fifth inning of the second game, the White Sox had Buck Weaver on third and Red Faber on second with two outs. Faber decided to steal third not realizing that Weaver was occupying the base. The throw went to third baseman Heinie Zimmerman who proceeded to tag both Weaver and Faber. The latter was out, since Weaver was the original occupant of the bag. The poor base running didn't hurt the White Sox too much as they took the series in six games.

Ernie Banks and Richie Ashburn got involved with rule 7.03 during the 1960 season when they both played for the Cubs in a game against the Phillies.

In the first inning, Ashburn who was on second, broke for third a little early. Phillie pitcher Chris Short turned and threw to shortstop Ted Lepcio, who threw to third baseman Al Dark. The Phillie third baseman ran Ashburn back to second. Ashburn got back to the bag safely, but then crawled off for a second, and Dark tagged him. Banks, who had meanwhile stolen second base, became confused and stepped back off the bag, and Dark tagged him to complete the double play. If Ashburn had remained on second, Banks would have been out according to 7.03.

The next rule deals with the runner's rights to advance one base without liability to be put out under such circumstances as a balk or if he is forced to advance because of a walk. There is a note to 7.04 which says, *When a runner is entitled to a base without liability to be put out, while the ball is in play, or under any rule in which the ball is in play after the runner reaches the base to which he is entitled, and the runner fails to touch the base to which he is entitled before attempting to advance to the next base, the runner shall forfeit his exemption from liability to be put out, and he may be put out by tagging the base or by tagging the runner before he returns to the missed base.*

Let's explore the possible situations that could arise from this rule. The following play actually took place in a minor league game in the fifties. With the bases loaded and two outs, the pitcher threw a wild pitch to the batter for ball four. All the runners had scored on the play, and the batter made it to second. The first baseman appealed that the batter-runner missed first. Since the appeal resulted in a force out, no runs scored on the play. (See rule 7.12.)

Lee Lacy of the Pirates was a victim of Rule 7.04(b) on July 24, 1979, when the Pirates hosted the Reds. The Pirates had runners on first and third with two out in the bottom of the fourth inning. Omar Moreno, the batter, had a 3-1 count. On the next pitch from Fred Norman, Lacy who was on first took off for second. Johnny Bench picked off Lacy who was called out by umpire Dick Stello.

Moreno stood in the batter's box and watched the play along with the 19,517 fans in attendance. Plate umpire Dave Pallone called the pitch "ball four" a split second after the ball hit Bench's mitt.

Lacy at this point was entitled to second base without liability of being put out even though he was thrown out by Bench. However, Lacy left the second base area thinking he had been thrown out, not realizing that Moreno had walked. When Lacy saw Moreno head toward first, he tried to get back to second base, but Dave Concepcion tagged him for the second time.

An intense rhubarb developed which lasted 34 minutes. Lacy claimed that he was misled by Stello when the arbiter pumped him out at second during an apparent steal attempt. Pirate manager Chuck Tanner was furious.

According to an article written by Charles Feeney to *The Sporting News,* "Stello said he called the play as a second base umpire and never spoke to Lacy twice. Stello however told Tanner, 'a mistake had been made.' "

The rule involved here is 7.04(b) which also claims, *A runner forced to advance without liability to be put out may advance past the base to which he is entitled only at his peril.* Obviously when Lacy left second base, he went at his peril. The game was protested as the Reds won 6-5. But the protest was turned down by N.L. President Chub Feeney, who said, "Since Lacy left second base of his own volition and should have been aware of the possibilities of Moreno receiving a base on balls and because there was no rules misinterpretation by the umpires, the protest is disallowed."

Rule 7.05 lists nine situations in which the runner can advance without liability to be put out. The first section, 7.05(a), covers a fair ball going out of the playing field (home run) that I do not feel its necessary to go into.

The second situation, 7.05(b), gives a runner *Three bases, if a fielder deliberately touches a fair ball with his cap, mask or any part of his uniform detached from its proper place on his person. The ball is in play and the batter may advance to home base at his peril.*

This rule was adopted in 1873. George Wright played shortstop that year for Boston in the National Association. He violated the rule by catching the ball in his cap in a game against the Athletics.

The key word in the rule is "deliberately" as evidenced by the following anecdote. It was July, 1967, and the site was Fenway Park. Luis Aparicio was playing short for the Orioles when the Red Sox batter hit a high pop up to short left field. As Aparicio was getting a beat on the ball, he went to flip his sunglasses down because of the bright sun. Unfortunately, Luis flipped a little too hard, and his entire cap and sunglasses wound up in his glove. And you guessed it—Luis caught the ball in his cap, which was resting in the glove. Umpire Bill Kinnamon ruled the catch legal, stating that rule 7.05(b) only made such a catch illegal if Aparicio had done it intentionally.

Rule 7.05(c) gives a runner *Three bases if a fielder deliberately throws his glove at and touches a fair ball. The ball is in play and the batter may advance to home base at his peril.*

Plate umpire Wally Vanderhoof carried out this rule in an International League game played on April 29, 1958, between Toronto and Richmond.

Richmond's Rance Pless hit a high-bounding ball over the head of Toronto pitcher Eddie Blake. As Blake leaped, his glove flew off. Vanderhoff awarded Pless three bases on the grounds Blake deliberately threw his glove at the hit ball.

Toronto Manager Dixie Walker filed a protest that was rejected on the grounds that it was a matter of the umpire's judgment that Blake intentionally threw his glove. In cases involving sections (b) and (c) of the 7.05 rule, bases are awarded from the time of the pitch.

On July 27, 1947, in the first game of a Boston-St. Louis double-header at Fenway Park, Jake Jones of the Red Sox hit a 60-foot triple.

With two out and none on in the sixth inning, Jones hit a roller outside the third base line. The ball traveled about 60 feet when Fred Sanford, the Browns' pitcher, tossed his glove and struck the ball to keep it from possibly going into fair territory. Hall of Fame umpire Cal Hubbard awarded Jones a triple on the basis of this rule. At the time, National League umpires had an unwritten agreement to ignore the violation in the case of foul balls, but A.L. umpires did not. Finally, in 1954, professional baseball amended the rule to include only fair balls.

7.05—(d) *Each runner including the batter-runner may, without liability to be putout, advance two bases, if a fielder deliberately touches a thrown ball with his cap, mask or any part of his uniform detached from its proper place on his person. The ball is in play.*

Nick Bremigan recalls a play related to the above rule. "Bob Didier was catching for the Richmond Braves at Peninsula in July, 1972. The squeeze was on, but the batter missed the pitch and Didier started chasing the trapped runner back toward third base. As he flipped the ball to the third sacker, he removed his mask with his right hand. The third baseman quickly tossed the ball back to Didier, but the throw was to Didier's right. With mask still in hand, he reached out and stopped the ball with it. Since the mask was 'detached from its proper place on his person . . .' I had no choice but to invoke 7.05(d), and score the runner." The awarding of bases in this rule is made from the time of the throw.

Carl Yastrzemski was accused of violating rule 7.05(e), which says, *Each runner including the batter-runner may, without liability to be put out, advance two bases, if a fielder deliberately throws his glove at and touches a thrown ball. The ball is in play.*

The incident happened on May 22, 1976, at Yankee Stadium. In the bottom of the first inning, Willie Randolph was on first for the Yanks with one out. Bosox pitcher Dick Pole threw wild to first in an attempt to pick off Randolph. As the ball sailed over Carl's head, he leaped for the ball and lost his glove as Randolph went to second on the play.

Yankee manager Billy Martin claimed that "Yaz" intentionally threw his glove at the ball and contact was made. However, first base umpire Bill Deegan ruled that the glove did not touch the ball and the act was unintentional.

If Deegan ruled intent on the part of the Sox first baseman, and the glove made contact with the ball, Randolph would have been given two bases and the ball would have been in play.

As in 7.05(d), the awarding of bases is made from the time of the throw. Concerning sections (b-c-d-e) of the 7.05 rule, there is no penalty if the ball is not touched by a thrown glove, detached cap or mask etc.

The next part of the rule, 7.05(f), gives each runner including the batter the right to advance *Two bases, if a fair ball bounces or is deflected into the stands outside the first or third base foul lines; or if it goes through or under a field fence, or through or under a scoreboard, or through or under shrubbery or vines on the fence; or if it sticks in such fence, scoreboard, shrubbery or vines.*

On July 11, 1919, Cincinnati defeated the Braves, 4-2, in 13 innings. Heinie Groh hit a home run to win the game. In the first inning, Bill Rariden, Cincy catcher, bounced a hit into the scoreboard for a home run. The boy in charge had neglected to close one of the inning spares, and through the opening rolled Rariden's hit. If this were to happen today, Rariden would be given only two bases according to the rule.

Marty Kavanagh of Cleveland was credited with the American League's first pinch-hit grand-slam home run when the ball that he hit rolled through an opening in the fence and could not be recovered in time. It happened on September 24, 1916, as Cleveland beat the Red Sox, 5-3.

The next statute we will study is one of the most important and commonly used rules, and one that very few people really understand. A thorough understanding of rule 7.05(g) will make your next trip to the ball park more enjoyable. *Each runner including the batter-runner may, without liability to be put out, advance two bases when, with no spectators on the playing field, a thrown ball goes into the stands, or into a bench (whether or not the ball rebounds into the field), or over or under or through a field fence, or on a slanting part of the screen above the backstop, or remains in the meshes of a wire screen protecting spectators. The ball is dead. When such a wild throw is the first play by an infielder, the umpire, in awarding such bases, shall be governed by the position of the runners at the time the ball was pitched; in all other cases the umpire shall be governed by the position of the runners at the time the wild throw was made.*

The White Sox and Indians tangled in a July 1, 1956 double-header. A sharp argument developed when Chicago outfielder Jim Rivera fired to the plate to head off a Cleveland runner. "Jungle Jim's" throw went over Sox catcher Sherman Lollar's head. Gene Woodling and Al Smith both scored on the play for the Indians. But umpires John Rice and Bill Summers ruled that Smith, who had been on first base, had not reached second when Rivera uncorked his throw, which landed in the box seats. The umpires ordered Smith to go back to third base. Mel Harder, Indians' coach, was ejected when he violently protested the call.

A foolish but humorous maneuver on the part of Dodger first baseman Johnny McCarthy and Dodger catcher Ray Berres forced the umpires to use 7.05(g) in 1934 in a game against the Boston Braves.

After a Boston hitter had singled, Berres tossed the ball to McCarthy, saying, "Throw it out, John. It's wet." McCarthy tossed the ball into the dugout. The only problem was that "time" was never called, and the umpires allowed the runner to advance two bases to third since a runner gets two bases on an overthrow from a fielder.

Because of an unusual play that happened to umpire Bill Kinnamon in the 1958 Caribbean World Series, an Approved Ruling was added to 7.05(g) which reads: *If all runners, including the batter-runner have advanced at least one base when an infielder makes a wild throw on the first play after the pitch, the award shall be governed by the position of the runners when the wild throw was made.*

Here is what happened: The batter hit a ball safely into short right field, but the second baseman retrieved it, with no outfielder involved in the play. Noticing that the batter who hit the ball had taken a wide turn around first base, the keystone sacker tried to throw behind him, and fired the ball into the dugout. This throw was indeed the first play by an infielder, and at the time, the above ruling did not exist.

Kinnamon had no choice but to award the batter-runner second base. Today, with the rule amended, the batter-runner would be awarded third base.

Notice that the awarding of bases on an overthrow by an infielder is two bases from the runner's position at the start of play if the throw is the "first play" by an infielder. But take the following episode where the overthrow is the "second play" by an infielder.

Say the Cubs are batting with Dave Kingman on third and Larry Biittner on first with one out. Bill Buckner hits a ground ball to Montreal shortstop Chris Speier, who flips to second baseman Dave Cash to start a 6-4-3 twin killing. However, Biittner just beats the throw to second as he was going with the pitch. Cash then throws the ball wild into dead territory.

Since Cash's play is the "second play" in the infield, Biittner would be awarded home since he would get two bases from the point of the throw. On the play both Kingman and Biittner would score.

The awarding of bases is different if a pitcher makes a wild throw and the ball goes dead. Rule 7.05(h) says, each runner may advance *One base, if a ball, pitched to a batter, or thrown by the pitcher from his position on the pitcher's plate to a base to catch a runner, goes into a stand or a bench, or over or through a field fence or backstop. The ball is dead.*

A good example of this occurred in a game between the Washington Senators and Detroit Tigers on May 20, 1956. Senators' southpaw Chuck Stobbs was pitching to Bob Kennedy with the bases loaded. Stobbs's pitch sailed into the seventeenth row along the first base stands at Briggs Stadium in Detroit.

The ball became dead as it entered the stands, and each runner advanced one base. Harvey Kuenn scored from third, while Jim Brideweser and Bill Tuttle each advanced one base.

It should be noted here that if a pitcher steps back off the rubber and his pickoff throw sails into the stands, he is throwing as a fielder, and each runner advances two bases.

An interesting story in conjunction with this rule happened to Nick Bremigan in his first major league assignment in an exhibition contest between the Reds and White Sox. With a runner on first, Reds' pitcher Rawly Eastwick pitched to the batter. He received the ball back from the catcher while standing in front of the mound after his last delivery. Upon receiving the ball, Eastwick immediately turned and threw the little white sphere by the first baseman and into the stands in a vain attempt to pick a White Sox runner off first base. A short argument resulted. It took a few seconds for it to dawn on Reds' skipper Sparky Anderson that the runner was entitled to third base, since the pitcher was off the rubber when he made his throw, and is, therefore, considered an infielder.

It should be understood that when Bremigan awarded the White Sox runner third base, it was the responsibility of the runner to touch second base even though the ball was "dead."

The last segment of rule 7.05 covers a situation that most baseball fans, including myself, have never seen happen and most likely never will. According to rule 7.05(i), *Each runner including the batter-runner may, without liability to be put out, advance one base, if the batter becomes a runner on Ball Four or Strike Three, when the pitch passes the catcher and lodges in umpire's mask or paraphernalia.*

The year was 1948, and Kansas City was playing at Milwaukee in a minor league game. The main characters of this episode were Milwaukee catcher Frank Kerr and plate umpire Harry King.

Kerr called for a pitchout because he sensed the runner on first for Kansas City, Leon Culberson, would be breaking for second. The ball struck the edge of Kerr's mitt and lodged in King's mask. Culberson made it to second and was allowed to stay there, but could advance no farther since the ball was dead.

Two terms that confuse baseball people are "obstruction" and "interference." The two terms are often used interchangeably, which is improper. In general, obstruction refers to an act on the part of the defensive team as opposed to interference, which is an offensive violation.

Obstruction is the act of a fielder who, while not in possession of the ball and not in the act of fielding the ball, impedes the progress of any runner. Obstruction is mentioned in the 7.00 rules because it has a bearing on the advance of a runner or runners.

Rule 7.06 says, *When obstruction occurs, the umpire shall call or signal "Obstruction." (a) If a play is being made on the obstructed runner, or if the batter-runner is obstructed before he touches first base, the ball is dead and all runners shall advance, without liability to be put out, to the bases they would have reached, in the umpire's judgment, if there had been no obstruction. The obstructed runner shall be awarded at least one base beyond the base he had last legally touched before the obstruction. Any preceding runners, forced to advance by the award of bases as the penalty for obstruction, shall advance without liability to be put out.*

Obstruction was called on N.Y. Giant catcher Wes Westrum in a game against the Phillies on August 7, 1956. In the eighth inning of the opening game of a twi-nighter, with New York ahead, 3-2, Richie Ashburn was on second base with one out. Marv Blaylock singled to center, and Ashburn tried to score from second. Ashburn slammed into Westrum as the Giant catcher was reaching for a high throw from Jackie Brandt. Both Westrum and Ashburn went sprawling to the ground beyond home plate.

As they lay there, Westrum called for the ball, which Hoyt Wilhelm had caught while backing up the play. Wilhelm tossed it to him and Wes, still on the ground, turned and tagged Ashburn as the Philadelphian lunged back toward home.

Umpire Vic Delmore yelled "out" as Westrum tagged Ashburn. This started an uproar from Phils' manager Mayo Smith. Smith claimed that Ashburn had been obstructed by Westrum and could not get back to the plate in time to touch it.

The umpires huddled together and decided to rule Ashburn safe. That brought Giant manager Bill Rigney out. After a heated argument, Rigney was tossed out of the game.

Jocko Conlan, who was one of the umpires working the game,

explained, "the runner was safe because of obstruction by the catcher. We didn't call it when he was reaching for the ball and was hit by the runner. But, even though it wasn't intentional, he was obstructing when the runner tried to come back and touch the plate."

Jocko quoted the rule as it appeared in the umpire's manual. "The catcher, without the ball in his possession, has no right to block the pathway of the runner attempting to score. The baseline belongs to the runner and the catcher should be there only when he is fielding a ball or when he already has the ball in his hand."

In a Pacific Coast League game played on August 11, 1959, Spokane manager Bobby Bragan won a disputed protest over a misinterpretation of the obstruction rule. The argument arose in the seventh inning in a game between Spokane and Salt Lake City. With two out and Spokane leading 8-7, umpire Bob St. Clair called Bob Lillis of Spokane out on a play at the plate. Bragan vehemently argued that Daryl Westerfeld, the Salt Lake catcher, had blocked the plate without possession of the ball and thus was guilty of obstruction. When St. Clair refused to change his decision, Bragan protested the game. Salt Lake went on to win, 10-8.

However, the next day, league president Leslie O'Connor upheld the protest. He ruled that St. Clair's decision that the catcher had a right to block the plate while waiting for the ball was a misinterpretation of the rule. The game was ordered replayed from the point of dispute, and Spokane won the replay, 12-7, the following day.

Boston and Washington played a night game on May 21, 1955, in which Boston outfielder Jackie Jensen and Washington pitcher Mickey McDermott were involved in an obstruction play and mild skirmish.

In the top of the twelfth inning, Jensen was on first base with two out. Picked off by McDermott and trapped, Jackie made a break for second, then tried to return to first base. On his way back to first, his progress was obstructed by Mickey Vernon. Obstruction was called by the second base umpire, Ed Runge, but he didn't make any gestures to go with the call.

Jensen was steaming about the obstruction as he charged toward

McDermott, who was waiting to put the tag on him at first base. Jensen pushed McDermott down, and the ball was knocked out of the pitcher's hands.

At first base, umpire Hank Soar called Jensen out for interference. The Senators, believing the side was retired, walked off the field. However, senior umpire Bill Summers said Jensen was obstructed by Vernon and should be given first base. Today Jensen would be given second base, one base beyond the last base legally touched. On the play, Jensen and McDermott got into a scuffle, and both were ejected from the game.

John McGraw, the great ex-New York Giants' manager, used to pull the following stunt, which was an act of obstruction, when he played for Baltimore many years ago. When a runner was on third base and was ready to leave third after an outfield fly, McGraw used to hold the runners belt and slow him down.

The other part of the obstruction rule explains the proper ruling when no play is being made on the runner. *When obstruction occurs, the umpire shall call or signal "Obstruction." If no play is being made on the obstructed runner, the play shall proceed until no further action is possible. The umpire shall then call "Time" and impose such penalties, if any, as in his judgment will nullify the act of obstruction.* (7.06=b)

American League umpire Charlie Berry made a dramatic obstruction call on Boston's Mike Higgins at third base during the 1946 World Series played between the Red Sox and Cardinals.

The Cardinals' Whitey Kurowski was obstructed by Higgins at third base after Dom DiMaggio of the Red Sox had dropped Joe Garagiola's fly ball. Berry waved Kurowski home on Higgins's obstruction. At the time of the obstruction there were two outs, and Garagiola kept running and was eventually tagged out.

Berry said, "The Red Sox didn't see the obstruction at third, and, since Kurowski hadn't scored before Garagiola was out at third, the Red Sox charged umpire Lee Ballanfant at the plate, yelling the run didn't count. I had to break it up and tell them the run counted, due to the obstruction at third base."

The call tied the score 2-2. The Red Sox eventually won the game in the tenth inning on a home run by Rudy York.

In the above case no play was being made on Kurowski, the obstructed runner, so the play was allowed to proceed until no further action was possible.

Nick Bremigan reveals some chicanery on the part of former White Sox manager Eddie Stanky when he managed Chicago between 1966-1968. Stanky had a neat trick that would involve Pete Ward, his third baseman. When an opposing runner was attempting to score from second on a base hit, Ward would move into the path of the runner, and then step aside just before the runner got there. (This would obstruct the runner's path.) There would be no contact, but Ward's actions would cause the runner to break stride just enough to give the Chicago outfielders a chance to nail the runner at home. The umpires finally caught on to Ward's trickery and nailed him a few times. Once they realized the umpires were on to them, Stanky and Ward soon scrapped this caper.

International League umpire Harry Schwarts admitted to pulling a blunder in a game between Rochester and Columbus on April 27, 1960. The blunder related to rule 7.07, which says, *If, with a runner on third base and trying to score by means of a squeeze play or a steal, the catcher or any other fielder steps on, or in front of home base without possession of the ball, or touches the batter or his bat, the batter shall be awarded first base on the interference and the ball is dead.*

Nino Escalcra was at bat for Columbus in the third inning with Julian Javier on third base and two outs. As Bob Keegan began to pitch, Javier broke for the plate. Umpire Schwarts ruled that catcher Dave Ricketts stepped in front of Escalera and voided the tag on Javier. Schwarts permitted Javier to score, but neglected to send Escalera the batter to first. The mistake went unnoticed, another example of ignorance of the rules.

The 7.08 rule is very extensive, carrying eleven different segments. The rule lists the various restrictions on the part of the runner. The first section (7.08=a) says, *Any runner is out when he runs more than three feet away from a direct line between bases to avoid being tagged, unless his action is to avoid interference with a fielder fielding a batted ball; or (2) after touching first base, he leaves the baseline, obviously abandoning his effort to touch the next base.*

Fortunately, Cal Hubbard, the American League supervisor of umpires in 1960 was at Fenway Park in Boston on June 30, 1960, to support plate umpire Red Flaherty.

The score was tied in the last of the eighth with one out in a game between the Tigers and the Red Sox. Pete Runnels tapped to third baseman Chico Fernandez. Don Buddin, who was on third, got in a rundown between third and home. Buddin suddenly stopped, and Tiger catcher Red Wilson, who had the ball, ran past him. Buddin pivoted onto the grass, eluding Wilson's tag, then ran across the plate and scored.

Wilson argued violently with Flaherty claiming that Buddin was out of the baseline. Wilson was ejected, and the Red Sox scored three more runs and won 11-7.

Hubbard supported his umpire explaining that the runner is allowed three feet to either side of the player with the ball in a rundown and that Buddin was within the distance.

Jim Rivera of the White Sox was called out for violating rule 7.08(b). Rivera was on first base when Billy Goodman hit a grounder to the Orioles' second baseman Billy Gardner. Rivera stopped briefly in front of Gardner, hindering the Oriole second baseman. Rivera was called out for interference because his hesitation was ruled an effort to hinder Gardner's vision. The rule states, *Any runner is out when he intentionally interferes with a thrown ball; or hinders a fielder attempting to make a play on a batted ball.*

According to rule 7.08(c) *Any runner is out when he is tagged, when the ball is alive, while off his base.* In making a tag, the fielder must hold the ball securely, both before and after the tag, and he must have the ball in his hand or glove.

Victoria and Corpus Christi met in a Texas League game during the 1958 season. Victoria had the bases full with two outs when J. W. Jones topped the ball to Corpus Christi third baseman Bo Bossard. The ball disappeared into Bossard's shirt. Bossard put his hand on the ball, which was still in his shirt, and tagged Don Miles, the runner going from second to third. A run scored, all runners advanced, and Miles remained on third since it was ruled that Bossard did not make a legal tag.

The next section (7.08=d) is another example of the rule book being repetitious. The rule says, *Any runner is out when he fails to retouch his base after a fair or foul ball is legally caught before he, or his base is tagged by a fielder. He shall not be called out for failure to retouch his base after the first following pitch, or any play or attempted play. This is an appeal play.* A close look at rule 7.02 will show that it strongly resembles the wording in the rule mentioned above. For the sake of continuity in this section, I have discussed a play that affected Reggie Smith while playing for the Red Sox in the 1967 season.

In a game against the California Angels, Smith was on second base when Carl Yastrzemski hit a long drive to left field that was caught by the Angels' Rick Reichardt. Thinking the ball would fall for an extra-base hit, Smith was already around third base as the Angels' outfielder made the catch. Smith returned to second safely, but was called out on an appeal for failing to touch third base on his return to second.

The next rule can also be related to the famous Merkle boner mentioned earlier in the text. Rule 7.08(e) has a great deal of meat in it and warrants a close study to understand it clearly. It reads as follows: *Any runner is out when he fails to reach the next base before a fielder tags him or the base, after he has been forced to advance by reason of the batter becoming a runner. However, if a following runner is put out on a force play, the force is removed and the runner must be tagged to be put out.* (Example—Mickey Mantle in the ninth inning of the 1960 World Series.) *The force is removed as soon as the runner touches the base to which he is forced to advance, and if he overslides or overruns the base, the runner must be tagged to be put out. However, if the forced runner, after touching the next base, retreats for any reason towards the base he had last occupied, the force play is reinstated and he can again be put out if the defense tags the base to which he is forced.*

On opening night in St. Louis in 1974, the following fiasco took place in a game played between the Cardinals and Pirates.

In the tenth inning with the bases loaded and the Cardinals at bat, Lou Brock hit a rope that was trapped by Gene Clines in shallow right field with the scored tied 5-5 and none out.

Clines picked the ball up and quickly threw to catcher Mike Ryan, retiring pinch runner Jim Dwyer at the plate. Neither Dwyer nor third base coach Vern Benson saw first base umpire Lee Weyer's "safe" sign indicating no catch. Because Dwyer did not advance, the runner on second base, Tim McCarver, didn't either and was doubled at third on Ryan's throw to Richie Hebner on the bag.

Meanwhile first base coach Johnny Lewis was urging Jose Cruz to stay put at first. So now we have Cruz and Brock joined at first base.

After receiving Ryan's throw, Hebner threw to second baseman Rennie Stennett. If Stennett had stepped on the bag, Cruz would have been forced for a triple play and an inning-ending out. But umpire Satch Davidson ruled that Stennett was not on the bag when he tagged out a retreating Tim McCarver, who already had been retired.

As in an appeal play, the action was not completed, so the umpires did not call "time" when manager Danny Murtaugh of the Pirates came out to inquire why the side wasn't out. And in the confusion, Cruz tiptoed down to second, after which play was suspended.

Pittsburgh's broadcaster, Bob Prince, maintained that Stennett not only had touched second before tagging McCarver, but that Brock rounding first had passed Cruz. "So we gave you five outs, but got only two," said Prince.

Ted Sizemore then singled, and the Cardinals won, 6-5. Please don't kill the ump! Unfortunately, a majority of umpires' headaches result from the players' ignorance of the rules.

The last part of 7.08(e) is covered with the following play, which Tom Sprague reported to *The Sporting News,* occurring during a California League game played on July 4, 1957. The play centered on a force out in the ninth inning in a game played between Modesto and Stockton.

> Hank Mitchell was on first base for Modesto when Dick Carter hit a line drive to right field. Mitchell rounded second, but turned back and retraced his steps toward first under the mistaken belief that right fielder Bobby Schurr had caught the ball.
>
> En route Mitchell realized that Schurr had actually taken the ball on a rebound off the wall. Before he could return to second, Schurr's throw to second baseman Ben Gonzalez and the relay to shortstop Manny Ortega beat Mitchell to the bag.
>
> However, Ortega did not tag the runner, and umpire Bob St. Clair called him safe. Manager Roy Partee of Stockton argued the

decision and, after a conference between St. Clair and plate umpire Dick McKinney, Mitchell was ruled out on the grounds that the force situation went back into effect when he retouched second base on his way back to first base.

According to the rules, since the runner had left second base on his return to first base, he relinquished his claim to that base, and it is ruled a force out.

The next part of the rule, 7.08(f), is frequently enforced. *Any runner is out when he is touched by a fair ball in fair territory before the ball has touched or passed an infielder,* etc. Often a runner is struck by a batted ball and is called out. On a play of this type, no runners may advance, and no runs can be scored.

The Yankees' Phil Rizzuto, playing in his 52nd World Series game, was called out by umpire Lee Ballanfant for violation of this rule in the seventh game of the 1955 fall classic, which was won by the Brooklyn Dodgers.

In the bottom of the third inning with two out, Rizzuto was on second base and Billy Martin was on first when Gil McDougald topped a bounding ball down the third base line. Had Dodger third baseman Don Hoak fielded it, he probably would have been unable to make a play anywhere. However, the ball struck Rizzuto at the moment he was sliding into third base. The "Scooter" was called out, and the Yanks' rally ended. Thus one of baseball's most basic rules might have had a pivotal effect on the outcome of the series, since the Yankees lost the game, 2-0.

A runner is also out if *he attempts to score on a play in which the batter interferes with the play at home base before two are out. With two out, the interference puts the batter out and no score counts.* (7.08=g)

In a hypothetical situation, Larry Bowa is at bat with one out and Pete Rose on third. The squeeze is on, and Craig Swan is about to pitch the ball. Bowa is judged by the ump to have interfered with Mets' backstop John Stearns immediately after he misses the bunt. Rose would be out because of Bowa's interference.

Passing a runner is taboo in baseball. Home run titles in various leagues have been lost because rule 7.08(h) was violated, which declares a runner out for *passing a preceding runner before such runner is out.*

Lou Gehrig finished the 1931 season tied for the home run title instead of being declared the sole champion because he passed a fellow teammate on the bases in a game at Washington's Griffith Stadium on April 26, 1931. Gehrig hit a shot so fast and hard that the ball popped out of the center field bleachers and into the hands of Washington's center fielder. At the time of the blast, Lyn Lary was on second base with two out. Lary interpreted third base coach Joe McCarthy's sign to slow down as an indication that the ball was caught. Gehrig kept running and eventually passed Lary. Umpire Bill McGowan ruled Gehrig out for the running violation. As a result of the running miscue, Gehrig ended the season with 46 home runs, tied with Babe Ruth. The Yankees also lost two runs on the play and eventually lost the game by a score of 9-7.

Manager McCarthy did not reappear on the coaching lines for the Yankees that season.

On July 9, 1970, Dalton Jones of the Tigers hit a grand-slam homer against the Red Sox but was only credited with a single because he passed runner Don Wert between first and second base.

Passing a runner is not too common a play. However, on the night of June 19, 1974, rule 7.08(h) was violated in two different major league stadiums. A runner passed another runner at St. Louis's Busch Stadium where the Cardinals and Giants met, and the same rule was abused at Pittsburgh's Three Rivers Stadium where the Pirates were hosting the Dodgers.

In the top of the third inning at St. Louis, Garry Maddox led off with a single. Then San Francisco's Ed Goodson hit one of Bob Gibson's pitches deep to the center field fence, where Bake McBride leaped and appeared to make a spectacular catch. Maddox, rounding second, retraced his steps toward first, and Goodson, also figuring he was out, passed Maddox.

However, the ball had plopped out of McBride's glove and over the fence. When the ball reappeared, the umpires permitted Maddox to resume his original run around the bases, but Goodson, though he had hit the ball out of the park, was declared out and limited to a single.

In the first inning of the game at Pittsburgh, which the Pirates won, 7-3, Lee Lacy of Los Angeles was on third, Jimmy Wynn on second, and Ron Cey on first, as Jerry Reuss fired a two-out, full count pitch to Joe Ferguson.

Strike three? Ferguson thought so. So did catcher Manny Sanguillen, flipping the ball toward the mound. And so, unfortunately, did Lacy, jogging toward the Dodgers' dugout.

Strike three? Nope. Ball four.

Wynn, on third by this time, took off for home but was tagged out by Sanguillen, who then relayed it to Richie Hebner at third, who stepped on the bag.

Lacy suddenly realized what was going on and dashed headlong to the plate, where Hebner threw to Sanguillen, who tagged Lacy.

Chief umpire Ed Sudol finally ruled that Wynn was out when he touched home because he technically passed Lacy on the base path. And Lacy was entitled to home because of the bases loaded walk, even though he was near the dugout when Wynn was out. And what's more, the umpire added, Lacy was immune to a tag. So he scored when he slid home, even though Sanguillen tagged him and Wynn who had already made the last out of the inning.

Sudol also explained. "The runner makes his own baseline unless he's chased. The only way Lacy could have forfeited his right to score would have been if he had gone into the dugout."

The Pirates, filing a protest that became merely academic when they won the game, 7-3, insisted that Dodger leadoff man Lacy had left the playing field, but the umpires ruled he had merely left the baselines and had not gone down into the dugout. Lacy's run was legal as he touched first, second, third, and home in the proper order. (4.09=a)

As a result of this play a section (7.08=a-2) was added to the rule book which states: *Any runner is out when after touching first base he leaves the baseline, obviously abandoning his effort to touch the next base.* Part of the case book explanation reads, "Any runner after reaching first base who leaves the baseline heading for his dugout or his positions believing that there is no further play, may be declared out if the umpire judges the act of the runner to be considered abandoning his efforts to run the bases." Even though an out is called, the ball remains in play in regard to any other runners.

The Phillies' Tim McCarver lost a four-bagger on July 4, 1976, the 200th anniversary of our country, when he passed Garry Maddox who was on first base in the second inning of a double-header at Pittsburgh. Maddox went back to first to tag in case the ball was caught. McCarver, running with his head down, passed Maddox and was called out by umpire Ed Vargo. Ed Goodson and Tim McCarver will never forget Garry Maddox.

In plays where a runner passes another runner, one thing to keep in mind is that the back runner is always out. This holds true even when a runner runs by a back runner while retreating for some reason. The theory is that a back runner's position on the basepaths can never pass that of a preceding runner.

The next segment of rule 7.08 prohibits a runner from *running the bases in reverse order for the purpose of confusing the defense or making a travesty of the game.* (7.08=i) This was a trick that was used early in the century to force the defense to make a play to enable the runner on third to score. With runners on second and third, the runner on second would break toward first to tempt the defense to make a play so the man on third base could run home.

Germany Schaefer, who played for the Tigers, once pulled this stunt in a game against Cleveland. Schaefer was on second and Davey Jones was on third with Sam Crawford batting. Schaefer dashed back to first hoping to draw a throw from the Cleveland catcher so that Jones could score from third. However, the catcher did not throw to first. At the time, there was no rule against a play of this type. Schaefer would be out for such an act today. I guess you could say that Germany Schaefer stole first!

It was June 23, 1963, the Polo Grounds, and Jimmy Piersall hit his 100th career home run while playing for the Mets. To celebrate the occasion, Jimmy ran the bases backwards. The incident went unnoticed. Piersall actually made no attempt to confuse the defense. He circled the bases in proper order.

Stan Musial was a victim of rule 7.08(j), but Billy Klaus wasn't. The incidents took place nine years apart. The rule states, *Any runner is out when he fails to return at once to first base after overrunning or oversliding that base. If he attempts to run to second he is out when tagged. If, after overrunning or oversliding first base he starts toward the dugout or toward his position, and fails to return to first base at once, he is out, on appeal, when he or the base is tagged.*

In a game against the Phillies in 1952, Musial was called out on a play at first base. However, the Phils' first baseman Eddie Waitkus dropped the ball, and the umpire changed his call from "out" to "safe." Unaware that the umpire changed his call, Musial trotted to his position in right field. The Cardinals' first base coach yelled to Musial to return to the base, but by the time he started back to the bag, Waitkus picked up the ball and tagged the bag. The Cardinals protested the game, but the protest was rejected.

The White Sox charged umpire Jim Honochick with rules misinterpretation and protested a 10-9 defeat at the hands of the Senators on June 9, 1961.

Billy Klaus hit a grounder to Nellie Fox at second who flipped the ball to first baseman Roy Sievers, who proceeded to drop the ball. Klaus, however, thought that he had been called out. According to the White Sox, Klaus rounded first base and then began heading towards his position. Fox called for the ball and tagged Klaus, but Honochick wouldn't allow it.

Sox manager Al Lopez said, "Honochick and umpire Ed Hurley both said that Klaus was not out because he didn't break for second." However, Lopez protested under rule 7.08(j).

It appears that it was judgment on the part of the umpires as to what Klaus actually did. Under most circumstances, if a runner even fakes going toward second, he is out when he is tagged. If a runner returns to first base after an overthrow, he can walk back to first on either fair or foul territory. It doesn't make a bit of difference which way he turns after he completes his run to first base, as long as he doesn't make any attempt to go to second.

The protest was not upheld.

The Houston Astros and Chicago Cubs played on April 25, 1972, at the Astrodome. Rule 7.08(k) might have been used in this game but wasn't, as we shall see. The rule states, *Any runner is out when in running or sliding for home base, he fails to touch home base and makes no attempt to return to the base when a fielder holds the ball in his hand, while touching home base, and appeals to the umpire for the decision.*

In the bottom of the seventh inning the Astros were batting with a 4-3 lead. Jerry Reuss was on third, and Norm Miller was on first. Jim Wynn then hit a sacrifice fly to apparently score Reuss. According to UPI, "Reuss jumped up and ran back toward the plate, but Cubs' catcher Randy Hundley tagged him."

Frank Pulli, the umpire, ruled that Reuss had touched home plate with his hand after he crossed it. If Reuss did miss home plate and made no attempt to return, Hundley could have touched home plate and appealed to Pulli.

Interference on the part of the runner is covered in rule 7.09(a)-(m). Some sections of the rule are similar to some of the batter's interference rules. Therefore, I will cover only material that is different than anything we have seen.

President Claude Engberg of the Pioneer League upheld a protest citing rule 7.09(c) in a game between Great Falls and Idaho Falls during the 1957 season. The rule says, *It is interference by a batter or a runner when he intentionally deflects the course of a foul ball in any manner.*

The rule was violated by Domingo Carrasquel of Great Falls who was on third base when he picked up a foul grounder off the bat of a teammate and tossed the ball to the Idaho Falls pitcher. The umpires allowed Carrasquel to stay on third instead of enforcing rule 7.09(c) and calling him out.

Engberg ordered the game replayed from the last half of the fourth inning. Great Falls eventually won the game, 3-1. That's what you get for being a nice guy.

Rule 7.09 (e)-(f) (Case Book Comment) was the basis for a protest on September 22, 1954, as the Reds were visiting Milwaukee. *If a batter or a runner continues to advance after he has been put out, he shall not by that act alone be considered as confusing, hindering or impeding the fielders.*

In the top of the ninth inning the Reds had Gus Bell on second and Wally Post on first with one out trailing 3-1. Bob Borkowski, the batter, fanned on a wild pitch by Warren Spahn. Del Crandall, the Braves' catcher, threw to third to try and catch Bell. Borkowski, who had no business going to first since first base was occupied with less than two outs, ran anyway. Third baseman Ed Mathews tossed to first and the ball hit Borkowski in the back and rolled into right field. Bell and Post scored on the play. Borkowski was automatically out for reasons stated above.

The umpires met and discussed the play for 18 minutes before they decided that Borkowski's illegal presence on the base paths had drawn the throw. On that theory the umpires ruled Bell and Borkowski both out and that Milwaukee had won, 3-1.

The Reds protested, and league president Warren Giles upheld the protest and ordered the continuation of the game, starting in the top of the ninth with two Cincinnati outs.

Giles said he overruled the umpires because the standings of five teams were involved. The league president also said that the umpires under game pressure had called it correctly according to interpretation. However, Giles said, he couldn't accept this with a "clear conscience."

As mentioned Borkowski would be out according to 6.05(c). However, the responsibility on a play of this type is placed in the hands of the defense. The mere fact that the batter, although already out, ran to first base and drew a throw, is not cause for a ruling of interference by the batter.

The protested game was played two days later. Johnny Temple singled home Bell and Post to tie the score, 3-3. George Metkovich singled home the winning run for the Braves in the bottom of the ninth.

The set up for the protested game was very unusual. The Reds played Milwaukee in the protested game, and the Cardinals met the Braves for the day's regularly scheduled game. Having three teams in the same park is not too common.

Runners have been tagged out twice on the same play and have not been punished in relation to this rule. Ed Bouchee was involved in a play of this type when the Phillies met the Cubs on May 2, 1960.

The Phils had the bases loaded and one out. Frank Herrera then grounded to Cub third sacker Don Zimmer, who stepped on the bag for a force out on Ed Bouchee. Zimmer then fired to catcher Sammy Taylor trying to nip Johnny Callison at the plate. Taylor forgot that the force play had been removed when Zimmer touched third. Taylor then spotted Bouchee between third and home and threw to Zimmer who tagged Bouchee. The only problem here was that Bouchee had already been forced out. So the Phils scored a run on the play and made one out.

Once again we find the responsibility resting with the defense. In cases like we saw with Borkowski and Bouchee, the defense should know the status of the runners on the bases.

7.09—(f) *It is interference by a batter or a runner when any batter or runner who has just been put out hinders or impedes any following play being made on a runner. Such runner shall be declared out for the interference of his teammate or teammates.*

The scene was Game Four of the 1978 World Series at Yankee Stadium. It was the bottom of the sixth inning. Thurman Munson was on second, Reggie Jackson on first, and the batter was Lou Piniella. Bill Russell was the Dodgers' shortstop and Steve Garvey the first baseman. Joe Brinkman (A.L.) was umpiring second base, and Frank Pulli (N.L.) was at first.

Piniella rapped a hard line drive to Russell who got his glove on it but dropped it. The first question here is, did Russell drop it purposely? If he did, Piniella would be out (Rule 6.05l) and Munson and Jackson would return to their respective bases. However, in Brinkman's opinion, Russell did not drop the ball intentionally so the play proceeded. The Dodger shortstop could have tagged Munson and then stepped on second to force Reggie for an unassisted double play, but he ignored the possibility and just tagged second to force Jackson.

If Russell's act was intentional, this is what he most likely would have done. So give Brinkman an "A" for mind reading.

The scenario continues. Russell, after forcing Jackson, rifled the ball to first to double up Piniella. But the ball hit Jackson in the basepath which caused the sphere to ricochet towards the right field corner in foul territory.

Keep in mind that Jackson was already out when Russell forced him at second. In Pulli's mind Jackson did not violate rule 7.09(f) and "intentionally" interfere. According to Nick Bremigan, "Rule 7.09(f) is a bit misleading in that it seems to indicate that any interference, intentional or not, should be called. Reggie, of course, interfered with Russell's attempt to complete his play, but he was not guilty of interference as the word is defined in baseball. He would have to 'intentionally' interfere, plus the footnote to rule 7.09(f) says, *If the batter or runner continues to advance after he has been put out, he shall not by that act alone be considered as confusing, hindering, or impeding the fielders.* This would give Pulli justification for his ruling."

So I guess we'll also give Pulli an "A" for mind reading. Munson scored on the play and "Sweet Lou" wound up at second.

Bill White, current Yankee broadcaster, was guilty of violating rule 7.09(f) on May 3, 1959, in a game between the Pirates and Cardinals. Pirate catcher Hank Foiles tried to throw out Solly Hemus who was stealing second but was interfered with by White, who had just struck out. Umpire Dusty Boggess ruled Hemus out as a result of White's interference after he had just been put out. Foiles was credited with an unassisted double play.

Speaking of Boggess, the veteran arbiter used to carry around a ball that was autographed by every umpire he ever worked with. It was specified in his will that the ball would be buried with him when he died. His wish was granted.

Gene Mauch was nailed for breaking rule 7.09(f) when he played for the Red Sox in a game against the Orioles on April 22, 1957.

Mauch was batting with Dick Gernert on third base in the seventh inning with one out. Gene grounded to first baseman George Kell, who stepped on the bag and then threw to the plate in an effort to retire Gernert. Mauch, however, deflected Kell's throw to the plate as he threw up his hands. Umpire Ed Rommel also declared Gernert out for Mauch's interference. Kell and catcher Joe Ginsberg were credited with the freak double play.

This rule was enforced as far back as 1883, plus the batter-runner was fined twenty dollars. The violation came about in a game between Detroit and Boston in the early days of the National League. Boston had Ezra Sutton at third with Jack Burdock at the plate. Burdock hit a grounder to Detroit first sacker Martin Powell. As Powell tried to throw to the plate to head off Sutton, Burdock pinned Powell's arms to his body. Umpire George Burnham called Sutton out and fined Burdock twenty dollars.

This brings us to rule 7.09(g), which reads, *It is interference by a batter or a runner when if, in the judgment of the umpire, a base runner willfully and deliberately interferes with a batted ball or a fielder in the act of fielding a batted ball with the obvious intent to break up a double play, the ball is dead. The umpire shall call the runner out for interference and also call out the batter-runner because of the action of his teammate. In no event may bases be run or runs scored because of such action by a runner.*

It was during the first month of the 1957 season when Don Hoak of the Redlegs sent shock waves throughout the baseball world. Because of a loophole in the rules, Hoak engineered a stunt unprecedented in the diamond sport.

In a game against the Milwaukee Braves, the Redlegs were batting with Hoak on second and Gus Bell on first. Wally Post, the batter, bounced a grounder in the direction of Braves' shortstop Johnny Logan. To avert an apparent double play, Hoak startled everyone in sight when he fielded the ball with his bare hands. The guileful Redleg was called out because any runner that is hit by a batted ball in fair territory is out. But did the punishment fit the crime?

At the time there was no provision in the rules to cover such a prank on the part of the base-runner. Hoak's maneuver stimulated the Lords of Baseball to cover such a situation with rule 7.09(g). If that happened today, Post would also be out because of Hoak's actions.

Umpire Ron Luciano carried out this rule against Toby Harrah of the Rangers on April 21, 1974, in a game between the Rangers and Twins. Texas had the bases loaded in the seventh inning with Jeff Burroughs at bat. Burroughs grounded toward the shortstop and the ball hit Harrah. Luciano called Harrah out and also ruled Burroughs out for a double play due to Harrah's interference.

When asked for an explanation both by manager Billy Martin and Harrah, Luciano said, "That's exactly what any good player would have done in that situation, and you're a good player, Toby." How could Harrah argue that?

It is very rare that rule 7.09(h) is violated. The following episode illustrates this seldom enforced baseball law which reads: *It is interference by a batter or a runner when if in the judgment of the umpire, a batter-runner willfully and deliberately interferes with a batted ball or a fielder in the act of fielding a batted ball, with the obvious intent to break up a double play. The ball is dead; the umpire shall call the batter-runner out for interference and shall also call out the runner who advanced closest to home plate regardless where the double play might have been possible. In no event shall bases be run because of such interference.*

Let's assume the Expos have the bases loaded and no outs in a game with the Pirates. With Warren Cromartie on third, Andre Dawson at second, and Ellis Valentine on first, Duffy Dyer bunts a ball to Willie Stargell at first who decides to go for a 3-6-3 double play. Just as Stargell is about to throw to second to begin the DP, Dyer intentionally barrels into Willie to break up the twin killing.

According to the rule, Dyer would be out for his flagrant act and so would Cromartie who had advanced closest to home plate. Dawson would return to second and Valentine to first.

Rule 7.09(i) takes a different twist as it also involves the base coaches. The rule says, *It is interference by a batter or a runner when in the judgment of the umpire, the base coach at third base or first base, by touching or holding the runner, physically assists him in returning to or leaving third base or first base.*

A good example of this baseball statute was enforced during the 1967 season in a Pacific Coast League game between Spokane and

Hawaii. Spokane outfielder Jim Fairey was knocked unconscious by the throw from the Hawaii catcher after he stole third base. The ball rolled into left field after hitting Fairey on the skull. Fairey rolled passed the bag after he was struck by the ball. Third base coach Gordy Coleman lifted him back onto the bag, and Fairey was called out for getting assistance from the third base coach.

It is now illegal for the coach to assist a runner anytime, whether a play is being made on him or not. However, if a runner assists another runner, it is perfectly legal.

Because of this rule interpretation, a dead man once scored a run in a game played in New Jersey many years ago between the University of St. Joseph and the Chatham Stars. According to *Baseball Magazine,* "Chatham was leading 2-0 and two were out in the bottom of the ninth when O'Hara, a weak hitter, doubled to left. He was followed by Robidoux, "a scrappy young Arcadian," who hit a long ball over the center fielder's head. As O'Hara reached third base, he collapsed and died. Robidoux, rounding third, picked O'Hara up and carried him down the base line, touching home plate first with O'Hara and then stepping on the plate himself. The game was tied, 2-2."

The above case might be a dramatic illustration of the rule, but I think it gets the point across.

The next section of the rule, 7.09(j), deals with a coach interfering with a fielder. The rule states, *It is interference by a batter or runner when with a runner on third base, the base coach leaves his box and acts in any manner to draw a throw by a fielder.*

Fred Lieb, probably the oldest sportswriter in the country describes a stunt in *The St. Louis Cardinals* that relates to 7.09(j). The actor involved was Miller Huggins in a game played in 1914 between the Dodgers and Cardinals. According to Lieb, "It was in the seventh inning of a game at old League Park, the score was tied and St. Louis had a runner on third base with two out. Huggins, coaching at third base, suddenly yelled at Ed Appleton, the kid Dodger pitcher, 'Hey, bub, let me see that ball.'

"The startled stripling tossed the ball over to the coaching box. Huggins stepped aside and let the ball roll into foul territory while the winning Cardinal run pranced in from third base."

Dodger skipper Wilbert Robinson, better known as "Uncle Robby," was very angry about the play, but the umpires could do nothing since "time" wasn't called, and there was no rule prohibiting such a ruse. If there was such a rule then as 7.09(j), the Cardinal runner on third base would have been called out for Huggins' actions.

Concerning "Uncle Robby," he is part of a very interesting bit of trivia. He is the only man in major league history to serve as a player, coach, manager, and umpire. "Umpire?", you ask. According to Ted DiTullio of the Society for American Baseball Research, "Robinson served as a fill-in umpire in 1898 when he was catcher with the Baltimore Orioles."

The next segment (7.09=k) is exactly the same as 6.05=k, which we previously covered in relation to the J. C. Martin case in the 1969 World Series. The rule is repeated again to illustrate the interference of the runner.

The final section of the rule, 7.09(m), declares *interference by a batter or runner when a fair ball touches him on fair territory before touching a fielder. If a fair ball goes through, or by an infielder, and touches a runner immediately back of him, or touches the runner after having been deflected by a fielder, the umpire shall not declare the runner out for being touched by a batted ball. In making such decision the umpire must be convinced that the ball passed through, or by, the infielder, and that no other infielder had the chance to make a play on the ball. If, in the judgment of the umpire the runner deliberately and intentionally kicks such a batted ball on which the infielder has missed a play, then the runners shall be called out for interference.*

A protest of this rule by Manager Solly Hemus of the Cardinals was upheld during an exhibition game played in 1959 against the Tigers. In the bottom of the first inning with two out, the Cards had the bases loaded with Gino Cimoli on third, Stan Musial on second, and Joe Cunningham on first. Hal Smith hit a hard grounder to third which bounced off Eddie Yost and into the running path of Musial. Stan "The Man" then kicked the ball and was called out by umpire Bill McKinley. Hemus protested that there was no interference because the ball already had touched an infielder. Hemus won the argument, and the play was ruled a single scoring a run. When is the last time you saw a manager win an argument?

Hal Smith was involved in another incident that had a bearing on 7.09(m) two years earlier in which umpire Vinnie Smith came out smelling like roses. It took place in a game between the Cardinals and Pirates on July 28, 1957. Smith hit a ball in the bottom of the first that went by Pirate third baseman Gene Baker and struck Ken Boyer, who was running to third. Many people thought that Boyer should have been safe because he was hit by the sphere after it skipped past Baker. However, umpire Smith stated that, in his opinion, shortstop Dick Groat was behind Boyer and could have made a play. Therefore, Boyer was called out under rule 7.09(m). A check on the rule supported Smith's call.

If you read the rule carefully you will notice that a runner is not out if he is hit with a batted ball if no fielder has a chance to make the play. If Vinnie Smith believed that Groat could not have made a play, Boyer would have been safe.

Here is a conceivable situation that would cause a real explosion. Let's say the Angels are batting with the bases loaded and one out in the bottom of the ninth inning in a game against the Royals. The Angels have Don Baylor at third, Bobby Grich on second, and Rod Carew on first. Rick Miller is the batter with the score tied, 4-4. Kansas City has the infield in on the grass. Miller hits a shot to the left of Fred Patek at shortstop and strikes Grich going to third. However, umpire Bill Haller properly rules that the ball is in play since no fielder was in position to field the ball. Good luck, Mr. Haller!

There are five appeal plays in baseball: (1) batting out of turn; (2) failure of the batter-runner to return to first base immediately after overrunning or oversliding; (3) failure of a runner to retouch his base after a fly ball is caught; (4) missing a base while advancing or returning; (5) failure to touch home. The first two situations have been covered. I will review the other three in the remaining part of this chapter.

In making an appeal play, the first question a player should ask himself is, "Is the ball dead or is the ball still in play?" If the ball is still in play, the player can simply tag the base or the runner and properly notify the umpire. If the ball is dead via an overthrow or a home run, for example, the ball must be returned to the pitcher. The pitcher must then wait until the umpire puts the ball in play. He then should step back off the rubber and throw to the appealed base. It should be noted that he can appeal from the rubber and doesn't have to step off.

During a Senators-Indians game in 1960, a Cleveland player missed first base by a foot and a half on his way to second. However, the first baseman for Washington did not know how to properly appeal the play, and the Cleveland runner ended up on second.

President Calvin Griffith of the Senators was so angry over his player's ignorance of the rules, he ordered 25 rule books for his team.

Concerning appeal plays, *When the ball is dead, no runner may return to touch a missed base or one he has left after he has advanced to and touched a base beyond the missed base.* (7.10=b)

Bob Stevens reported the following play to the *Sporting News.* Read the rule carefully and make your decision whether the play was properly handled. The play in question occurred in a game between the Giants and Pirates in Pittsburgh on July 18, 1967, and involved umpire Augie Donatelli, Pittsburgh third baseman Maury Wills, and Giant base runner Jim Ray Hart.

According to Stevens, "With Hart on first base, Ollie Brown almost tore Wills's hands off with a searing line drive. Wills stopped it, then dropped it. Donatelli ruled Wills had possession of the ball long enough for the out on Brown.

"Hart took off for second, Wills recovered the ball and threw it into the stands back of first base for an error.

"Giant Manager Herman Franks ran out to Donatelli protesting Wills did not have possession and that Brown was safe. By then Hart was in the argument at third base, too, having touched and rounded second base.

"Donatelli told Franks to 'get off the field, Herman, the play is still in progress. I award Hart third base for the overthrow but Brown is out.'

"Franks thought he was being chased for arguing until coach

Charlie Fox pointed out that wasn't so. He said to Franks, 'But Hart still has to go back and touch first base. He didn't tag up after the catch.'

"Herman said, 'Oh, okay,' and walked off the field.

"Fox then told Hart to return to first base and tag up. Hart started to cross the diamond and through the mound until Fox yelled at him to touch second base on the way back. Jim Ray made the half arc turn, stepped on second and walked casually back to first base as the crowd screamed its approval.

"The screams turned to boos, however, when Jim Ray calmly toed first base and then swept majestically on up to second base, and around and into third without a challenge being made by Pittsburgh.

"The public address announcer finally informed the angry crowd of the overthrow rule—two bases—and peace was restored." Donatelli, an umpire, could not coach Hart on his return to first base.

In reference to this play, Nick Bremigan explains, "This play was ruled 100 percent correctly. Hart was allowed to do all this when the ball was dead. He had no choice, as it was not his fault the ball was dead, and he was around second base when the defense caused the ball to become dead. Hart never reached second base legally the first time he touched and rounded it, because he had not tagged up at first base. The award starts from his original base in this case, because it requires him to tag up before legally advancing."

Have you ever heard of a run scoring while an umpire held the ball? Well it happened in a Western League game played between Sioux City and Lincoln in 1957. The play that will be discussed is also related to 7.10(b).

Artie Burnett scored a run for Sioux City in the fourth inning as Bob Rikard doubled off the center field wall. However, Burnett did not touch home plate.

Base umpire Tom Dunne called time and asked for the ball when it was returned to the infield, not realizing Burnett had missed the plate. Lincoln catcher Harry Dunlop called for the ball so he could tag the plate or Burnett, who had headed for the dugout. While umpire Dunne was examining the ball, Burnett returned to home plate because of the prodding of his teammates. Plate umpire Jack Wagner then called Burnett safe, allowing the run to score. Wagner ruled that the action of play was not stopped when Dunne, unaware of the situation, called "time" to examine the ball.

A close look at the rule (7.10=b) reveals that Burnett should not have been allowed to retouch since the ball was dead under rule 5.10(e) which stipulates, *The ball becomes dead when an umpire calls "Time." The umpire-in-chief shall call "Time" when the umpire wishes to examine the ball, to consult with either manager, or for any similar cause.*

The fifth game of the 1911 World Series between the Philadelphia Athletics and New York Giants went 10 innings, but if an appeal had been made on a runner missing home plate, the game might have gone until darkness ended it.

The Giants scored the winning run in the last of the tenth inning as Fred Merkle hit a sacrifice fly to score Larry Doyle. As Doyle came in prancing and shouting, he leaped over home plate into the arms of his joyous teammates. Bill Klem, the plate umpire, noticed that Doyle had missed the plate, but the A's did not appeal, and the Giants won the game, 4-3. The A's won the series, which ended on October 26, 1911, a rather late date, especially without television.

Considering the case just mentioned, rule 7.10(d) says, *Any runner shall be called out, on appeal, when he fails to touch home base and makes no attempt to return to that base, and home base is tagged. Any appeal under this rule must be made before the next pitch, or any play or attempted play. If the violation occurs during a play which ends a half-inning, the appeal must be made before the defensive team leaves the field, etc.*

Notice the rule states that an appeal must be made before "any play or attempted play." Personally I would have to challenge the fairness of the rule.

Let's say the Oakland A's are batting with Larry Murray on first and Mitchell Page at bat. Page doubles to right center field advancing Murray to third. However, Page misses first base en route to second. The Red Sox then decided to appeal. As the Sox are about to appeal, Murray breaks for home and is tagged out by Boston catcher Bob Montgomery. Since the Red Sox made a play they now forfeit their right to appeal Page who missed first base. Thus, Oakland still has a runner in scoring position. It's quite possible that Page made it to second because of his short cut around first.

My question is, "Why shouldn't Boston be allowed to appeal at first base also?"

There is a note that is attached to rule 7.10 which says, *Appeal plays, may require an umpire to recognize an apparent "fourth out." If the third out is made during a play in which an appeal play is sustained on another runner, the appeal play decision takes precedence in determining the out. If there is more than one appeal during a play that ends a half inning, the defense may elect to take the out that gives it the advantage. For the purpose of this rule the defensive team has "left the field" when the pitcher and all infielders have left fair territory on their way to the bench or clubhouse.*

On August 22, 1957, the Red Sox and Indians were almost involved in a four-out inning, a situation unprecedented in major league baseball, with the exception of that opening day technicality at Ebbets Field several years ago.

According to Cal Hubbard, who was the supervisor of the American League at that time, here is how it happened.

"The Red Sox had one out in the top of the ninth, Gene Mauch at second and Pete Daley at first when the batter, Mike Fornieles, lifted a sinking liner to short center.

"It appeared to be a base hit to everyone in the park and especially to the base runners who were off with the crack of the bat. But aided by a strong wind blowing in from center, Chico Carrasquel, the Indians' shortstop, managed to make a spectacular catch while on the dead run.

"When he turned around after the catch, he saw Daley scrambling around at second, trying to reverse his field. Mauch wasn't in Chico's line of vision, for he had kept on running and by now was at home plate.

"Chico now had the choice of walking over to second and tagging it to double Mauch, or he could throw to first and double Daley. Since he didn't see Mauch, he probably forgot about him momentarily, so he threw to first, doubling Daley for the third out to retire the side.

"The Indians ran off the field, and the Red Sox took their positions.

The moment Mike Fornieles, the Bosox hurler, made the first pitch in the bottom of the ninth, plate umpire Hank Soar turned toward the official scorer in the press box and shouted, 'The run counts.' The scoreboard was changed to add this marker.

"Of course, the Red Sox didn't need it, for it merely raised the score to 11-0. So the Indians didn't make an issue of it, but it wouldn't have made any difference if they had."

Explained umpire Soar, "Mauch crossed the plate before the appeal was made on Daley at first base for the third out. I couldn't count the run at that moment, though, because Mauch had left his base too soon and therefore had scored illegally, you might say.

"The Indians had the right to appeal Mauch's run, but their time of appeal ran out at the next pitch, according to the rules." (According to the rules at that time.)

Thus, even though there already were three outs, the Indians any time before the next pitch could have touched second base, appealing that Mauch had left too soon, and the umpires would have had to call him out.

"The fourth out, in this case," explained umpire Charley Berry, whose crew worked the game, "takes precedence over the third out. The scorecard wouldn't show the extra out because the original third out would be ignored and the new one substituted for it."

Later on, some of the Indians felt that the umpires should have indicated in some way that Mauch had scored.

Soar said, "We couldn't without tipping off that he left his base too soon. On an appeal, it's up to the team to call our attention to the play, not for us to call their attention to it." The rule now states that the appeal cannot be made once the pitcher and the infielders have left fair territory on their way to the bench or clubhouse.

The remote possibility of a five-out inning, which actually occurred in a Virginia high school tournament championship game, is born out of this rule.

Assume that the Orioles have the bases full with one out in a game against the Red Sox. On the pitch to Rick Dempsey, all runners are off and running. Dempsey hits a fly to Fred Lynn. Two outs! Lynn then throws to first to double up Mark Belanger. Three outs! Carl

Yastrzemski, the Sox first baseman, then throws to second, realizing that Ken Singleton never tagged and didn't return. Four outs! Rick Burleson then throws to third to catch Al Bumbry, who never tagged or returned. Five outs! According to the rule, the defense "may elect to take the out that gives it the advantage." A five-out inning?

The last rule that I will go into in this chapter is rule 7.12 which states, *Unless two are out, the status of a following runner is not affected by a preceding runner's failure to touch or retouch a base. If upon appeal, the preceding runner is the third out, no runners following him shall score. If such third out is the result of a force play, neither preceding nor following runners shall score.*

The following appeal plays voided a run since the third out was the result of a force play. The Indians and Red Sox met at Fenway Park. Cleveland had Minnie Minoso on first and Bobby Avila on third with two outs. Rocky Colavito stroked the ball off the left field wall scoring Avila. Minoso, in his zest to reach third, missed second base. Nearing third, Minnie turned and started back toward second. Boston's Billy Klaus tagged Minoso as he slid into second, then told the umpire that Minoso had missed the bag originally. The appeal was upheld, and Avila's run was scratched.

Failure of a player to abide by this rule cost outfielder Wally Post of the Reds a hit and also cost the Redlegs a run in the first inning of a night game played on June 4, 1956. Post was facing Saul Rogovin of the Phils with Johnny Temple on third, Frank Robinson on second, and Gus Bell on first. Wally hit a shot to left field that struck in front of Del Ennis and bounced out of Ennis' hands. Del threw to third sacker Willie Jones to catch Bell coming into third, but the throw was too late.

Rogovin then appealed that Robinson had missed third. Umpire Jocko Conlan upheld the appeal, and the play went into the books as a force out, since there were already two outs when the play began.

"Can't anybody here play this game?" That was the popular cry in the early sixties when the Mets were in their hapless embryonic stage. Mets' fans will long remember the legendary story when Marvelous

Marv Throneberry's triple against the Cubs went for nought when the Cubs appealed that he not only missed first base, but also second. The base-running comedy took place at the Polo Grounds on June 17, 1962, in the first game of a double header.

Following Throneberry's slapstick running exhibition, Charlie Neal homered. Ironically, the Mets lost 8-7 without the benefit of Marv's run that would have scored on Neal's blast. Fittingly the game ended when Throneberry went down swinging for the final out.

A very odd force play ended a Dodger rally on September 12, 1957, when the Dodgers faced the Braves at Milwaukee.

In the top of the fourth inning, the Dodgers had the bases loaded with one out. Charlie Neal was on third, Roy Campanella occupied second, and Danny McDevitt was the runner on first.

Jim Gilliam then hit a low liner to right field off pitcher Bob Trowbridge. Braves' outfielder Andy Pafko came in to make the catch. Second base umpire Hal Dixon signaled that the ball had been caught. A fifth umpire, Ed Sudol, who was used down the right field line that night, signaled "no catch."

The ball was returned to Red Schoendienst, who allegedly tagged Campanella and then stepped on second base to force McDevitt, who was on first base. The umpires called it a double play and nullified Neal's run, since the third out was the result of a force.

If Schoendienst had tagged second before tagging Campanella, who was on the bag, the force would have been removed and the run would have counted.

Notice that an appeal must be made before the next pitch or any attempted play. If a pitcher balks when making an appeal, it is considered a play. It should also be noted that time is not out when an appeal is being made.

Ex-major leaguer Danny Litwhiler has coached baseball at Michigan State University for several years. A few years ago his team was involved in a rare appeal play in the NCAA tournament.

The Michigan State runner missed first base on a triple. Litwhiler instructed his runner on third to break for home when the pitcher threw to first to make the appeal. As the pitcher came set, the runner on third broke for home, causing the pitcher to balk. The umpire waved the runner home, but after five minutes of arguing, the umpire ruled the Michigan State runner out at first. Litwhiler correctly argued that the balk constituted a play and therefore nullified the appeal.

Dick Cole submitted the following play, which took place when he played for the Pirates. With runners on second and third, the Pirate pitcher threw the ball to first base appealing that the runner on second missed first base. The throw to first was wild and sailed over the first baseman's head into the stands. The play nullified the right to appeal again and also allowed the runners to score, helping to pin a 3-2 defeat on the Pirates.

8.00

The Pitcher

The pitcher, like the batter and the runner, also has certain rights and restrictions. Every pitcher displays different characteristics on the mound. A large majority of pitchers are very slow and deliberate. The great Dizzy Dean was once punished by the umpires because of time-consuming tactics that will be discussed in this chapter.

Hurlers like Jim Kaat and Randy Jones waste very little time on the mound. It appears that this style is becoming more popular. A pitcher like the Tigers' Mark Fidrych exhibits a style unparalleled with his talking antics on the mound.

There are basically three areas in the 8.00 rules with which a pitcher must concern himself: (1) the spitter, (2) delaying the game, and (3) the balk rules. In the next few pages, cases involving violations in these areas will be covered.

The spitball has been forbidden since 1920, but each season brings about the spitball problem. In 1968 the major leagues wanted to crack down on pitchers who threw the spitter. An edict was adopted forbidding a pitcher to go to his mouth or lips with his pitching hand. The first violation drew a warning from the umpire, the next an ejection from the game. The rule caused so many early departures during the exhibition season that the penalty for going to the mouth was reduced to a call of a ball.

In the next three anecdotes, you will see how the rule has been tampered with and interpreted by various umpires, managers, and players.

Rule 8.02 says, *The pitcher shall not (1) bring his pitching hand in contact with his mouth or lips while in the 18 foot circle surrounding the pitching rubber.* The rule, of course, is intended to eliminate the immortal "spitball." However, rule 8.02 did lead to a walk given up by Rusty Staub, playing first base for the Astros during the 1968 season. The incident happened during a game with the Dodgers at Los Angeles.

Staub walked over to the mound to give Astros' pitcher Larry Dierker a short rest. Rusty asked Dierker for the ball. He then spit on it and rubbed it. At the time Dierker was pitching to Dodger pitcher Bill Singer with a count of three balls and one strike.

Umpire Shag Crawford called "ball four," charging Staub with spitting on the ball. Singer was awarded first base and eventually went on to score. Staub was probably the only first baseman to ever give up a walk.

On March 23, 1968, the Cubs and Indians played an exhibition game in Tucson, Arizona. Leo Durocher, Cub manager, instructed Jim Ellis, Cub pitcher, to go to his mouth if he wanted to create an intentional walk. In the eighth inning Ellis gave Don Nelson an intentional pass with a count of 3-and-1 by going to his mouth for an automatic ball.

Plate umpire Emmett Ashford gave Nelson first base. The trick became known as the "Lip" pass.

The first umpire to eject a pitcher from a game for throwing a spitter was Cal Hubbard. The ejection came in 1944 when Nelson Potter of the St. Louis Browns was given the thumb for throwing the wet pitch. This did not happen again until 1968 when N.L. umpire Ed Vargo tossed out Phillies' pitcher John Boozer.

The situation took place on May 1, 1968, at Shea Stadium, where the Mets were hosting the Phillies. Boozer relieved Woodie Fryman in the seventh inning. As Boozer was about to take his eight warm-up pitches, plate umpire Vargo yelled "ball," claiming that Boozer went to his mouth. Manager Gene Mauch argued that the rule did not apply when a pitcher is warming up.

Mauch instructed Boozer to go to his mouth again and the umpire quickly called "ball two." Once again Mauch ordered Boozer to go to his mouth, and the umpire then called "ball three." Vargo then ejected both Mauch and Boozer.

Mauch was actually ejected when he protested the first called ball since it is automatic ejection when a manager protests a called ball or strike.

Dick Hall then relieved Boozer and faced Bud Harrelson with a count of three balls and no strikes.

N.L. president Warren Giles did not uphold Mauch's protest, but instructed his umpires not to call a ball when the ball was dead, as when the pitcher is taking his preparatory pitches. I guess you could say that Mauch lost the battle but won the war.

You could also say that Harrelson was perhaps the first batter in baseball history who went to the plate with a three ball count to his advantage before a pitch was even thrown to him. After Hall got two strikes on Harrelson, the Met shortstop grounded out.

There are other restrictions placed on the pitcher which are listed in rule 8.02. A pitcher shall not: *(a) (1) Bring his pitching hand in contact with his mouth or lips while in the 18 foot circle surrounding the pitching rubber. PENALTY—For violation of this part of this rule, the umpires shall immediately call a ball. However, if the pitch is made and a batter reaches first base on a hit, an error, a hit batsman, or otherwise, and no other runner is put out before advancing at least one base, the play shall proceed without reference to the violation. Repeated offenses shall be subject to a fine by the league president. (2) Apply a foreign substance of any kind to the ball. (3) Expectorate on the ball, either hand, or his glove. (4) rub the ball on his glove, person or clothing; (5) deface the ball in any manner; (6) deliver what is called the "shine" ball, "spit" ball, "mud" ball or "emery" ball.*

Because the 1968 edict was successful in combating the spitter, pitchers went to the "vaseline" ball or "grease" ball to compensate for the rule change. Although Gaylord Perry has received the majority of the publicity in relation to throwing illegal pitches, several other pitchers have made their bread and butter by loading the ball with a foreign substance.

If a pitcher is found with any foreign substance on his person, or in his possession, the penalty is automatic ejection. If no foreign substance is found, the umpire should declare the first illegal pitch thrown a ball. The second such pitch thrown by the pitcher disqualifies him from the game. Starting with the 1974 season, the umpire was given complete authority in ruling on such a pitch. However in 1968, umpires were not given such freedom.

Umpire Chris Pelekoudas called an illegal pitch on Cubs' pitcher Phil Regan by the abnormal flight of the ball. A controversy developed which led N.L. president Warren Giles to declare that umpires must find evidence of a foreign substance before calling a pitch illegal.

On June 25, 1973, Yankee manager Ralph Houk took the rules in his own hands when he raced out to the mound and yanked Indians' hurler Gaylord Perry's cap off his head as he suspected Perry of wrongdoings. Nothing was found and the game continued.

An interesting story emerges concerning the rule change in 1974 involving the penalty for violating rule 8.02(a) sections 2 to 6 and Gaylord Perry, who was pitching for Cleveland that year.

Nick Bremigan explained that the rule change was new for that year. Umpire Marty Springstead was working the season opener that year in Cleveland, and Perry was the pitcher. The American League office instructed Springstead to invoke and enforce the new rule if the opportunity arose, to show baseball's new get-tough policy regarding these types of pitches. That is not to say that the office told Springstead to call it whether it happened or not; but to call it if Springstead honestly felt that Perry threw a loaded pitch.

Prior to 1974, umpires were reluctant to call this violation because of the severity of the penalty (ejection from the game for the first offense), as well as the necessity of securing proof of the violation. There is always the legal aspect for an umpire to consider also. In the 1970s, it seems baseball was played in the courts as much as on the field. Many pitchers who have the reputation for violating sections of this rule, as well as 8.02(d), threaten to take baseball and umpires to court if they enforce this rule against them. The rule change in 1974 made the initial penalty less severe, and deleted the necessity of any umpire securing proof of the violation, in the hopes that umpires would be more willing to enforce the rule.

In that Opening Day game in 1974, Springstead did indeed invoke this rule against Perry. A rhubarb ensued, of course, and Perry went on to lose the game. He won his next fifteen consecutive decisions, and came into Oakland 15-1 early in July. He needed a win to tie an A.L. record for most consecutive wins by a pitcher, and was slated to face Vida Blue and the Oakland A's on July 8, 1974, in Oakland. It was a Monday night, but over 47,000 people showed up in Oakland that night to witness the confrontation, even though the Bay Area was experiencing rare June showers. The plate umpire that night was a rookie named Nick Bremigan.

The game went into the tenth inning tied 3-3. In the bottom of the tenth, Perry was still in there, but struggling. The A's got runners on first and third with two outs, when they sent up a rookie hitter by the name of Claudell Washington, who stroked a single to left, thus dashing Perry's hopes of tying the record.

Midway through the game, an unusual situation developed. Gaylord Perry always goes through all kinds of antics on the mound. Most of them are designed to get the other team thinking and upset, although nothing illegal is usually taking place. A majority of the advantage a pitcher who has a reputation of loading up the ball gains is psychological. The offensive team gets to looking for illegal actions on the part of the pitcher and gets themselves "psyched out." The batters start to concentrate more on the mannerisms of the pitcher than on the reason they carried the bat up to home plate in the first place. Perry knows this and is a master at it.

Perry had a habit of really loading up his pitching hand with resin. This is fine, as long as he wipes the resin off before the delivery. Several times this particular evening, Perry overloaded his pitching hand with resin, but didn't wipe it off. The result was that resin flew off his hand as he delivered the pitch, and it looked like the ball was coming out of a cloud of dust, which was quite deceiving to the batter.

The Oakland batters complained, and Bremigan went to the mound on three separate occasions to warn Perry to stop this. Perhaps he knew he had a rookie behind the plate, and decided to see just how much he could get away with. In any event, it is probably the only time in history that Gaylord Perry was warned for throwing a pitch that was too dry.

Assuming that the offensive team hits a pitch such as a "spit" ball, the offense may elect to take the play unless all runners including the batter-runner advance one or more bases in which case there would be no option—the offensive team must take the play. The ball is not necessarily dead.

An example of this would be Gaylord Perry being caught for serving up a "wet" one. On the pitch, Eddie Murray of the Orioles hits safely. In this situation, the Orioles would have to take the play since Murray advanced one base. If this happened Perry would be warned for the first offense and ejected if he did it a second time in the same game.

8.02(b) *The pitcher shall not have on his person, or in his possession, any foreign substance. For such infractions of this section the penalty shall be immediate ejection of the game.*

During the 1979 season umpires Nick Bremigan and Don Denkinger were ordered by the American League office to talk to Twins' pitcher Mike Marshall and manager Gene Mauch concerning Marshall's alleged scuffing of baseballs. When approached by the umpires, Marshall commented, "Put it in writing and I'll give it to my lawyer."

8.02(c) *A pitcher shall not intentionally delay the game by throwing the ball to players other than the catcher, when the batter is in position, except in an attempt to retire a runner.*

8.02—(d) *The pitcher shall not intentionally pitch at the batter. If, in the umpire's judgment, such violation occurs, the umpire shall warn the pitcher and the manager of the defense that another such pitch will mean immediate expulsion of the* *pitcher. If such pitch is repeated during the game, the umpire shall eject the pitcher from the game.*

The most barbaric baseball beast is the pitcher who intentionally throws at a batter. A hitter who is going well at the time or has delivered a key hit his previous time at bat is a natural target for such pitching madness. He must painfully concern himself with the moundsman's retributive justice.

In the 1976 season, Cardinals' chucker Lynn McGlothen admittingly threw at the Mets' Del Unser and severely bruised his right elbow, which sidelined him for a week. McGlothen was retaliating against Unser's game winning home run in the 17th inning the night before. After he smacked Unser, he proceeded to hit Mets' pitcher Jon Matlack, which triggered a wild melee between the two teams.

McGlothen received a $300 fine and a five-day suspension for his blatant actions.

Since 1978, umpires are allowed to remove the pitcher and the manager from the game, which was the case early in the '78 campaign at Shea Stadium when pitcher Jerry Koosman and manager Joe Torre both got the "boot."

Another pitching edict is covered in rule 8.03. *When a pitcher takes his position at the beginning of each inning or when he relieves another pitcher, he shall be permitted to pitch not to exceed eight preparatory pitches to his catcher during which play shall be suspended. . . . If a sudden emergency causes a pitcher to be summoned into the game without any opportunity to warm up, the umpire-in-chief shall allow him as many pitches as the umpire deems necessary.*

An amusing story relates to 8.03 involving Jimmy Dykes when he managed the White Sox. In this particular game the opposition brought in a relief pitcher. After the pitcher threw seven warm-up pitches, Dykes shouted, "Next one is the last and let's get going." Umpire George Moriarty wasn't about to let Dykes tell him how to run the game. He allowed the pitcher to take about 15 or 16 warm-ups.

Baseball critics have charged that the game is too slow. The responsibility of a fast-moving game is for the most part in the hands of the pitchers. A study of the game has shown that pitchers have the ball in their possession without throwing a pitch approximately one-half of the game.

In 1943 the average time to complete an American League game was one hour and fifty-eight minutes. In 1955 the average time was two hours and thirty-one minutes. As an incentive to umpires to keep the game moving, the American League gave a cash prize in the early 1930s to the umpire with the lowest average time for the games in which he worked. The prize was won by Bill Dinneen. However, it was soon realized that it was the pitcher, not the umpire, who determined the length of a game.

The American League experimented with speedup tactics during the 1956 exhibition season by eliminating the traditional four intentional pitches. Batters were ordered to go to first base immediately when the defensive team declared an intentional walk.

National League president Warren Giles said at the time that if the intentional walk is wiped out, you are depriving the fan of booing four times. I agree!

Upon completion of the 1956 season, rule 8.04 was born. The rule was inaugurated to avoid unnecessary delays. It declares that, *When the bases are unoccupied, the pitcher shall deliver the ball to the batter within 20 seconds after he receives the ball. Each time the pitcher delays the game by violating this rule, the umpire shall call "Ball."*

In the fifth inning of a contest between the Astros and Giants during the 1972 season, umpire Bill Williams called an automatic "ball" on Astros' pitcher Larry Dierker when he failed to deliver a pitch in 20 seconds.

Bill Veeck had a Pitchometer put on the scoreboard in Chicago to time the pitcher between pitches. Many pitchers rejected the idea as a distraction.

As stated, the rule only applies when the bases are empty. The second base umpire carries a stopwatch to help enforce the rule. As soon as a runner reaches a base, the stopwatch goes in the umpire's pocket. There are several factors to consider in the proper deployment of this rule. For example, the clock does not start until the pitcher receives the ball back from the catcher; the clock stops and starts over if the batter voluntarily steps out of the batter's box on a pitch that has been fouled off; or the clock doesn't start until the pitcher has a new ball, *and* the batter gets back into the box. Veeck's pitchometer is now confined to use in determining the velocity of pitches which is the way it should be.

In closing it is safe to say that the amount of time a pitcher holds the ball plus his control are important factors in determining the time a game takes to be completed. Billy Pierce of the White Sox and Jim Archer of the Athletics proved this on August 11, 1961. Neither pitcher issued a single walk or allowed a count to reach 3-and-2. The White Sox won, 1-0 on Luis Aparicio's home run. The time of the game was one hour and thirty-two minutes.

The balk rule was instituted before the turn of the century mainly to protect the runner from trickery or deceit on the part of the pitcher. A few things should be understood about balks: (1) There can be a balk only when one or more runners are on base; (2) each runner is entitled to advance one base on a balk; (3) the batter is not awarded first base on a balk; (4) the ball is in play when a pitcher balks; (5) the batter can swing at a pitch that is called a balk, and, if each runner including the batter advances at least one base, the balk is nullified; (6) if the pitcher does something that would be considered a balk and the bases are empty, it is simply no pitch.

When an umpire notices a balk, he uses a clenched fist signal with his left hand. During the 1956 American League winter meeting, it was suggested that the umpires should drop a handkerchief such as a football official would. However, the idea was not acceptable to A.L. prexy William Harridge.

The balk rules are probably the least understood by players and fans. The balks which are covered in this section are often times confusing even to the more knowledgeable baseball minds.

Rule 8.01 explains the legal pitching delivery. According to the rule there are two legal pitching positions, the "Windup Position," which is used when the bases are empty, and the "Set Position," which is commonly used with a runner or runners on base. Before a pitcher begins his delivery to the plate, he is required by this rule to take his sign from the catcher while standing on the 24″ by 6″ whitened rubber.

Section (a) deals with the windup position. *The pitcher shall stand facing the batter, his entire pivot foot on, or in front of and touching and not off the end of the pitcher's plate, and the other foot free. From this position any natural movement associated with his delivery of the ball to the batter commits him to pitch without interruption or alteration . . .* etc.

Phil Paine was pitching for the Cardinals in 1958 in a game against the Cubs. In the eighth inning Paine was pitching to Sammy Taylor with Walt Moryn on second base. Because a pitcher is committed to pitch the ball once he begins a full windup, a pitcher will pitch from the set position with a runner on base so he doesn't give the runner too big a lead, which would enable him to steal a base.

Paine thought he could catch Moryn sleeping by starting in a windup position and cutting it short. At that point he would wheel and throw to second to pick off Moryn or catch the runner breaking early to third.

Moryn, alertly observing the full windup, broke early for third but was thrown out by Paine after he altered his windup.

Paine's stunt was an obvious violation of the pitching rule, since he did not throw to the plate from the windup position, and he was charged with a balk.

Section (b) covers the set position. *Set Position shall be indicated by the pitcher when he stands facing the batter with his entire pivot foot on or in front of and in contact with and not off the end of the pitcher's plate* etc.

American League umpire Nester Chylak enforced this rule and called a balk on the Pirates' Steve Blass during the 1971 World Series played between the Pirates and Orioles. Chylak charged Blass with pitching with his foot on the side of the rubber.

From the set position a pitcher *may deliver the ball to the batter, throw to a base or step backward off the pitcher's plate with his pivot foot.*

If a pitcher steps in front of the rubber when he is in his set position, it is a balk when there is a runner or runners on base.

Pitching to Ron Cey of the Dodgers, the Mets' Craig Swan balked when he stepped in front of the rubber with his pivot foot. Second base umpire Ed Vargo made the call at Shea Stadium on the night of June 17, 1976.

In the following pages I will attempt to cover the balk rule, 8.05, as it is stated in the rule book.

8.05—(a) *It is a balk when the pitcher while touching his plate, makes any motion naturally associated with his pitch and fails to make such delivery.*

There were two All-Star games played in 1961, the first one being at windy Candlestick Park in San Francisco. In that game Stu Miller was charged with a balk when he failed to make a delivery because the wind blew him off the mound.

Danny Murtaugh, the manager of the N.L., appealed that it was an "act of God," but the umpires upheld the balk ruling.

It wasn't long ago that pitcher Steve Hamilton threw the so called "folly floater." The pitch was outlawed in 1970 and even called a balk under rule 8.05(a). Before Hamilton, the pitch was known as the "ephus" pitch, popularized by National Leaguer Rip Sewell.

The 1975 World Series played between the Boston Red Sox and Cincinnati Reds will go down in history as one of the greatest ever played. Prior to the opening game of the series, there was a great deal of publicity regarding Luis Tiant's motion and his herky-jerky moves.

N.L. umpire Nick Colosi nailed Tiant with a balk in the top of the fourth inning with one out in game one of the fall classic. The balk was called on Tiant because he moved his left leg forward and threw to first. It had nothing to do with his hands which Reds' skipper Sparky Anderson had questioned before the start of the series.

The violation would relate to rule 8.05(a) since Tiant apparently made a motion associated with his pitch and failed to pitch to the batter.

8.05—(b) *It is a balk when the pitcher, while touching his plate, feints a throw to first and fails to complete the throw.*

When a pitcher while on the rubber makes a motion to first base or home plate, he must throw the ball and step in the direction of his throw. Pitchers will often times step toward second base or third base and not throw the ball. Fans cry "balk," but the pitcher hasn't done anything illegal. Stepping toward the base is specifically covered in the next segment.

Stu Miller, Bob Friend, Steve Busby, and Jim Kern share the distinction of being the only hurlers who have committed balks in

All-Star game competition. Busby's balk came during the 1975 All-Star Game at Milwaukee. The balk was called because of a violation of rule 8.05(c), which states, *It is a balk when the pitcher, while touching his plate, fails to step directly toward a base before throwing to that base.*

In the top of the third inning, Joe Morgan was batting with no count and Lou Brock on first. Busby pivoted toward first in an attempt to pick off Brock but did not step in that direction. A balk was called advancing Brock to second.

In the 1979 All-Star classic, Jim Kern of the Texas Rangers joined this select group by being charged with a balk when he threw to first without stepping in the direction of the base.

Rule 8.05(d) almost came alive in the 1975 midsummer classic. It states, *It is a balk when the pitcher, while touching his plate, throws, or feints a throw to an unoccupied base, except for the purpose of making a play.*

Mets' hurler Jon Matlack threw to an unoccupied base in the bottom of the seventh inning with one out, but did so for the purpose of making a play. Matlack fired to first baseman Steve Garvey to pick off the speedy Claudell Washington. While the ball was in flight to first base, Washington took off for second. Garvey promptly threw to Larry Bowa and caught Washington. Although the base was momentarily unoccupied, Matlack threw to the base for the purpose of making a play. In this situation first base was technically an "occupied base," since a runner is considered as occupying a base until he has advanced to and is occupying the next base.

It is also a balk *if the pitcher makes an illegal pitch.* (8.05=e)

There are several ways a pitcher can throw an illegal pitch. Among them are a quick pitch and pitching while not on the rubber.

Umpire Ken Burkhart called a balk on Giants' pitcher Billy O'Dell prior to his release to the plate in a game against the Cubs on April 24, 1960. On the balk Tony Taylor scored from third. In the confusion the balk was incorrectly counted as a ball, and the count became 1-and-1 instead of 0-and-1 on George Altman, the Cubs' batter. Altman eventually walked, completing his turn at bat on three balls.

If the pitcher balks with the bases empty it would simply be called a ball. However, since Taylor was on third, a ball should not have been called. Giant skipper Bill Rigney protested the play but lost the argument. A close check on rule 8.01(d) will support Rigney's argument.

A quick pitch is one made with obvious intent to catch a batter off balance. It is also considered an illegal pitch. Jim Kaat of the Yankees has been accused of this a number of times.

One of the famous quick return pitches in baseball history occurred during the 1928 World Series as the Cardinals played the Yankees. The Yankees had won the first three games but were behind in the fourth game by a score of 3-1 in the seventh inning. With Babe Ruth at bat, Cardinal pitcher Bill Sherdel threw a pitch over the plate for an apparent third strike that Ruth insisted was a quick pitch.

The umpire agreed with Ruth and ordered Sherdel to rethrow the pitch. Sherdel ran the count to two balls and two strikes. On the next pitch the "Babe" connected for a home run over the right field roof in St. Louis. Lou Gehrig, the next batter, also hit a four-bagger to tie the score. The Yankees eventually won the game, 7-3, giving Waite Hoyt his second win of the Series.

During a 1956 spring training game, Tommy Byrne pitching for the Yankees threw a pitch behind his back to Pee Wee Reese with no runners on base. Plate umpire Larry Napp ruled the pitch illegal.

Frank Lary, Detroit Tiger pitcher in 1958, had to retire a batter twice because he made an illegal pitch. Lary struck out the White Sox Dick Donovan, but his pitch was ruled illegal because he delivered the pitch with his foot off the rubber. Jim Honochick, umpiring at third base, made the ruling.

Lary, who was already in the Tiger dugout, was recalled to pitch again to Donovan, who flied out on his second life at the plate. If on the illegal pitch Donovan had reached first base on a hit, an error, a base on balls, or had gotten hit by the pitch, the illegal pitch would have been nullified. Since he struck out, the illegal pitch was called a ball. It would have been a balk with any runners on base.

Yankee pitcher Luis Tiant, with all his twisting and unsteady movements on the mound, has been accused of violating rule 8.05(f), which reads, *It is a balk when the pitcher delivers the ball to the batter while he is not facing the batter.* It sometimes appears that Luis is facing the center field bleachers prior to his delivery. However, when he pitches the ball, he is facing the batter, which is in compliance with the rules.

The next segment of the balk rules (8.05=g) tells us that *it is a balk if the pitcher makes any motion naturally associated with his pitch while he is not touching the pitcher's plate.*

If a pitcher lifts his foot up off the rubber in the act of making a pivot, it is legal, even though his foot is temporarily off the rubber.

On May 15, 1973, Nolan Ryan, California Angels' pitcher, hurled a no-hitter against the Kansas City Royals at Anaheim, California.

Royals' manager Jack McKeon protested that Ryan was lifting his foot off the rubber. Umpire John Rice said that Ryan was lifting his foot while making his pivot, which is considered legal.

The pitcher gains no momentum or advantage by doing this. He merely lifts his right foot to turn it to fit into the hole in front of the rubber which is legal. Phil Regan who pitched for the Tigers, Dodgers, Cubs and White Sox from 1960-1972, was called several times for violating this rule, as he would use this motion to gain momentum as he moved forward to pitch.

What would a baseball book be without a Dizzy Dean story? "Diz" violated balk rule 8.05(h) which says, *It is a balk when the pitcher unnecessarily delays the game.*

In the sixth inning of a game between the Giants and Cardinals at St. Louis on May 19, 1937, umpire George Barr called a balk on Dean because he did not come to a full stop after his stretch. (8.05=m) Diz was so upset about the call that in his next game on May 23 against the Phillies, he intentionally carried out long delays between each pitch. Umpire Beans Reardon called a balk on Dean for delaying the game.

8.05—(i) *It is a balk when the pitcher, without having the ball, stands on or astride the pitcher's plate or while off the plate, he feints a pitch.*

One of the oldest pranks in baseball is the hidden ball trick. Runners unaware of where the ball is are often caught napping.

Pitchers must be very careful where they are on the mound when an infielder tags a napping runner. If they are on or astride the rubber without the ball, it is a balk as stated in the rule.

Umpire Ken Burkhart invoked this rule on August 12, 1961, against Giants' pitcher Jack Sanford in a game against the Reds. Giants' shortstop Jose Pagan concealed the ball in his glove and was ready to tag Cincinnati catcher Johnny Edwards if he stepped off the bag at second base. Sanford put his foot on the rubber without the ball in his possession. Burkhart called a balk, and Edwards was allowed to go to third base.

Giants' pitcher Juan Marichal and Cards' chucker Dick Hughes had balk rule 8.05(j) called against them during their pitching careers. The rule reads, *It is a balk when the pitcher, after coming to a legal pitching position, removes one hand from the ball other than in an actual pitch, or in throwing to a base.*

Marichal was nailed on August 2, 1960, in a game between the Giants and Phillies. Umpire Frank Secory claimed that Marichal brought his hands together and then pulled them apart while crouching to get a sign from catcher Hobie Landrith. Since Marichal didn't throw to the plate when he separated his hands, it was ruled a balk.

Hughes had the same problem when the Cardinals and Giants met on June 18, 1967. The Cardinal pitcher was pitching to Willie Mays at the time. According to Hughes, Mays and catcher Tim McCarver weren't ready. Plate umpire Chris Pelekoudas called the balk over the objections of Hughes and Cardinal manager Red Schoendienst.

The next balk rule is a rare one. I am sure it has been called, but I have no data concerning a balk of this type. The rule says, *It is a balk when the pitcher, while touching his plate, accidentally or intentionally drops the ball.* (8.05=k)

I have called the next balk, but have never seen it enforced in a major league game. Rule 8.05(1) reads, *It is a balk when the pitcher, while giving an intentional base on balls, pitches when the catcher is not in the catcher's box.* This sometimes happens on a pitchout when a catcher because of his eagerness pops out of the catcher's box before the pitcher delivers the ball.

The only time a catcher is confined to his catcher's box before a pitch is during an intentional base on balls. He is not confined on a pitchout. The rule was designed to prevent the catcher from standing 30 or 40 feet up the baseline while the pitcher is issuing an intentional pass, as that would be considered farcical.

Balks are fairly common, but most games are completed without a balk being called. However, on May 4, 1963, Bob Shaw of the Milwaukee Braves balked five times in a game played between the Braves and Cubs. During the game a total of seven balks were called. The other two were called against Denny Lemaster of the Braves and the Cubs' Paul Toth.

The balks against Shaw were called because he didn't come to a stop in his set position, which is an infringement of rule 8.05(m). *It is a balk when the pitcher delivers the pitch from Set Position without coming to a stop.* Three of Shaw's balks came in the same inning.

Umpire John Stevens enforced the rule against Tiger pitcher Paul Foytack on May 1, 1960, in a game between the Tigers and White Sox. Luis Aparicio was thrown out at second by Tiger catcher Red Wilson, but the putout was nullified because of the balk. Aparicio was allowed to stay on second base because of the pitching violation. Tiger Manager Jimmy Dykes created a ruckus and was ejected from the game.

Nick Bremigan discusses the thinking behind the rule. "Back in 1971, the Rules Committee felt pitchers weren't coming to a complete stop before delivering the pitch to the batter. So they amended the rule for the 1972 season to read that a pitcher had to stop for one full second before delivering. This led to so many balks being called during the first month of the season, that they amended the rule to read as it does now.

"What is a stop? According to the laws of physics, any moving object must stop before it can reverse direction. Applying this law to pitching, it is considered a stop if a pitcher's arms are coming down to complete his stretch, and then start his delivery. The stop may not be noticeable, but a complete stoppage of all motion is not required. A mere change of direction is all that is required."

As stated in the beginning of this section, the ball is not necessarily dead when a balk is called, if the batter reaches first on a hit, an error, a base on balls, a hit batsman, or in any other manner, and all other runners advance at least one base, the play proceeds without reference to the balk.

The following play illustrates this aspect of the rule. The odd play occurred on May 6, 1957, in a game between the Tigers and Orioles. Connie Johnson was pitching for the Orioles. The Tigers had runners on second and third with the score tied, 1-1. As Johnson began his delivery to Charlie Maxwell, Tiger coach Billy Hitchcock rushed to the plate demanding umpire Ed Runge call a balk. At this point Maxwell hit the pitch for a single to score two runs.

Runge raised his left arm to indicate the balk, but the ball was not dead. Since all runners, including Maxwell, the batter, advanced at least one base, the balk call was nullified.

As mentioned, all runners including the batter must advance at least one base for the balk to be nullified. The following episode illustrates a case where all runners did not advance one base on a balk.

On April 19, 1977, the Yankees hosted the Toronto Blue Jays. In the bottom of the fourth inning, New York had Jim Wynn on third with two out when third base umpire Dave Phillips called a balk on rookie Blue Jay hurler Jerry Garvin.

While Phillips was calling the balk, Lou Piniella hit a long drive to center that bounced off Gary Woods's glove for a double. But for some reason Wynn stayed on third and did not advance the one base necessary to negate the balk.

"Sweet Lou" was ordered to bat again, and Wynn was advanced home because of the balk. Phillips explained to an outraged Billy Martin, the Yankee skipper, that if Wynn had scored, the play would have stood.

The last rule in this chapter, 8.06, pertains to the visit of the manager or coach to the pitcher. *(a) This rule limits the number of trips a manager or coach may make to any one pitcher in any one inning; (b) A second trip to the same pitcher in the same inning will cause this pitcher's automatic removal.*

Let's take a look at part (b) of this rule. This baseball edict limiting the number of conferences a manager may have with a pitcher provided an unusual sidelight to a Sally League game between Columbia and Charlotte on the night of July 9, 1956.

Columbia catcher Robbie Robertson headed for the dugout in the sixth inning with two Charlotte runners on base, and two out. Robertson claimed he was going to repair his shinguard. When he returned to the field, he went out to the mound and talked with pitcher Bill Riale.

Charlotte skipper Rollie Hemsley protested, insisting that Robertson had gone to the dugout to get instructions for the pitcher from manager Hank Biasatti. The umpires upheld Hemsley's protest, and, since Biasatti already had visited Riale once that inning, the Columbia manager was given a choice of removing his pitcher or taking himself out of the game. Biasatti decided on the latter and departed. Riale went on to win, 3-0.

Part (c) of the rule says, *The manager or coach is prohibited from making a second visit to the mound while the same batter is at bat, but (d) if a pinch-hitter is substituted for this batter, the manager or coach may make a second visit to the mound, but must remove the pitcher.*

Orioles manager Earl Weaver protested that Yankee coach Whitey Ford made an illegal second visit to the mound while Sam McDowell was pitching to the same batter. The incident took place in April 1974. The details of this case are not clear, but the protest was not upheld.

Umpires must be very alert as to the proceedings of an inning. Sometimes a long inning or a heavy rhubarb can make players, managers, and umpires forgetful of certain situations. In relation to the rule under discussion, Nick Bremigan spared Angels' fireballer Nolan Ryan a trip to the showers.

Bremigan recalled, "The scene was Met Stadium in Minnesota, where the Twins were hosting the Angels in a day game during the 1975 season. Nolan Ryan was pitching for the Angels, and Dick Williams was their manager. In the bottom of the sixth, Ryan was struggling, and Williams went out to the mound to talk with his starting pitcher. He left Ryan in and returned to the dugout. According to rule 8.06, this meant that Ryan would have to pitch to the next batter before Williams could come out again to visit his pitcher.

"Ryan worked the count to 1-2 on the next batter. On his next pitch, Ryan thought he had a strike out, but plate umpire Jerry Neudecker ruled it a ball. Ryan charged down off the mound to confront Neudecker, who immediately charged Ryan and told him to get back onto the mound. Williams came out to get Ryan and Neudecker apart. Ryan went back to the mound, while Williams and Neudecker engaged in a short discussion. A manager is expected to come out and stick up for his player in such a situation, so there was nothing wrong yet.

"Following his discussion with Neudecker, Williams decided to stop by the mound to try to settle Ryan down. Neudecker had his back turned and didn't see this, but I saw it from second base and proceeded to charge toward Williams yelling for him to get away from Ryan. He was somewhat startled, but I soon made him realize that he couldn't talk to Ryan. Williams knew the rule and didn't argue the point; he had merely forgotten in all the excitement. Thus, a potential protest was averted. It should be emphasized that all umpires share in the responsibility for vigilance concerning this rule and the one involving substitutions in rule 3.00."

9.00

The Umpire

Marty Springstead, Steve Palermo, Frank Pulli, Lee Weyer, and Terry Tata are just some of the men who make their living calling balls and strikes in the major leagues. Chances are you wouldn't recognize these men if you saw them enter or leave the ball park. To reach the major leagues an umpire serves an arduous apprenticeship in the minor leagues. He is expected to exercise good judgment and have a strong command of the playing code.

9.01—(a) *The umpires shall be responsible for the conduct of the game in accordance with the rules and for maintaining discipline and order on the playing field during the game.*

Former National League umpire George Magerkurth was a heavyweight prizefighter before he became one of the men in blue. Magerkurth was aware that the umpire was responsible for maintaining discipline. One day he became so furious over an argument with Billy Jurges, he decked Jurges with one punch after Jurges spit in his face. A melee developed around Magerkurth with the ump getting in some good punches.

Jurges was plastered with a fine for spitting at the umpire, and Magerkurth was fined $250 and suspended for ten days for losing his dignity as a big league ump.

It is important that an umpire display good moral character. Emmett Red Ormsby who umpired in the American League for 19 years got a break to advance himself in the minor leagues because an umpire was caught carrying a deadly weapon on the field.

Ormsby was umpiring in the old Three-I League when an umpire in the Western League dropped a gun he was carrying in his pocket as he ran across the diamond to call a play at third. The umpire was fired, and Ormsby was elevated to the Western League.

If you get an umpire upset enough he might just pull out a gun and hold up the crowd! Such was the case during the summer of '78 in Vicksburg, Mississippi when ump R. B. Williams threatened to kill the crowd while umpiring a softball game. The belligerant ump claimed that spectators at the park started at him with bats after he engaged in a heated argument with them. The rebel arbiter claimed he used the pistol in self-defense. Nobody was hurt, but Mr. Williams was arrested.

Just as the United States Constitution has its so-called "elastic clause," so does the rule book. Rule 9.01(c) gives *each umpire the authority to rule on any point not specifically covered in these rules.*

Sam Jethroe, Loren Babe, Vic Davallilo, and Elio Chacon were all involved in the following play when they were in the minors. With Jethroe on first for Toronto and none out, Babe grounded to Davallilo, the Cubans' second baseman, who threw to shortstop Chacon for a force. Chacon then fired to first base, but the ball disappeared. No one knew what happened to the white sphere until Jethroe reached inside his shirt, where it was resting snugly.

The only thing that could be done in a situation like this was to call "time." There was no intentional interference on this play. The ball was dead and the batter remained at first base. The incident happened on August 15, 1957, at Toronto.

Dizzy Trout was pitching for the Detroit Tigers in a game against the White Sox several years ago. Tiger hurler Virgil Trucks describes a stunt pulled by Trout. According to Trucks, "Trout was pitching to Luke Appling who proceeded to foul off about 14 pitches. On the 15th pitch, Trout kept the ball and threw his glove up to Appling. Luke did not swing as the glove was low and outside. The umpire almost threw Trout out of the game." I would imagine that this would be an illegal pitch, but that's why we have rule 9.01(c).

What do you call if a batter hits a ball that does not leave the playing field and disappears? In an International League game between Memphis and Syracuse on July 30, 1976, Memphis center fielder Art Gardner hit a drive off the center field wall in the bottom of the third inning and raced around the bases for an apparent inside-the-park home run. While Gardner was circling the bases, Syracuse outfielder Rick Bladt searched the outfield for the ball. The umpires had Gardner return to second and called the missing-baseball play a ground-rule double.

Ever heard of a guy named Johnny Bates? Playing for Mobile in 1917, he hit a fly ball that sailed about two hundred feet in the air over second base. To the amazement of everyone in the park, the ball got stuck in the fuselage of a passing plane. The umpire ruled the stow away clout a home run using the following logic. "When last seen, the ball was traveling out of the park in fair territory."

John "Ziggy" Sears was a National League umpire from 1935 to 1945. In a game played between the Cardinals and Reds in 1935, Ziggy got himself into a little trouble. John P. Carmichael of the *Chicago Daily News* tells the story:

> With Joe Medwick of the Cards on first base, the batter fouled off a pitch from Johnny Vander Meer. The batboy returned the sphere to Sears, working behind the plate, and Ziggy, believing Vandy was ready to fire again, held the ball rather than sticking it in his pocket.
>
> When Vander Meer cut loose again, the ball was high and got away from catcher Gilly Campbell, and Medwick took off for second. Campbell turned around and barked at Sears: "Give me a ball." . . . And Ziggy, not thinking, handed him the spheroid he was holding.

Medwick kept going around second and a horrible light began to dawn on Sears. "Throw that ball down," he barked at Campbell. "It's not in play. Go get the other one against the stands." Gilly reacted in part. He dropped the ball, but didn't go after the original. Medwick scored while the fans rolled in their seats from unrestrained laughter.

Out came Bill McKechnie, manager of the Redlegs. "Did the hitter foul that?" he asked. The embarrassed Sears said no. "I was just caught dreaming," he said truthfully. "The ball I gave Campbell doesn't count. The run does."

Then just to make sure, Sears walked out to where Bill Klem was umpiring at first. "What would you say?" asked Ziggy. Klem was succinct. "You're the umpire-in-chief," he said. "You rule on it. . . ." So the decision stood.

The next case is not covered in the rules. The ruling on a problem of this type is a matter for a league president or commissioner to contend with. However, the umpires were caught in the middle, as they usually are. Sportswriter Jerry Holtzman reported the story to *The Sporting News*:

An official protest was lodged by the White Sox during their May 15, 1960, double-header in Cleveland. The White Sox contended that the Indians had used an ineligible player in the seventh inning of the second game.

It all came about when Indian manager Joe Gordon sent outfielder Pete Whisenant to the plate as a pinch hitter for Gary Bell with two out in the seventh when the Indians were trailing, 3-2. Whisenant actually never did bat, for Gordon immediately withdrew him for another pinch hitter when White Sox manager Al Lopez countered with a pitching change bringing in righthander Gerry Staley.

The White Sox protested on the grounds that Whisenant made his appearance (though he didn't bat he was still in the game and therefore listed in the box score) at 6:35 P.M. (EDT) exactly 35 minutes after the Indians had officially traded him to the Senators for infielder Ken Aspromonte.

White Sox Vice President Hank Greenberg contended that the

use of Whisenant had a direct bearing on the game since when Whisenant appeared, Lopez immediately removed southpaw Frank Baumann and brought in Staley. Gordon then withdrew Whisenant in favor of Tito Francona a lefthanded hitter who grounded out.

As we have seen, umpires can rule on anything not specifically covered in the rules. Sometimes a play will arise where several rules are involved, but yet not one of them properly covers the problem at hand. Nick Bremigan discusses a mind-boggler that happened in 1977 at Minnesota where the Twins hosted the Indians.

For some reason the American League is extremely reluctant to put interpretations in writing. This play involves rules 4.09(a), 4.09(b), 6.08(a), 7.08(a-2), and 7.10—how's that for a knotty problem?

Cleveland and Minnesota were tied in the bottom of the 11th inning, but the Twins had the bases loaded with two outs and Butch Wynegar batting. The count was 3-1. Pitcher Jim Kern uncorked a wild pitch back to the screen for ball four, and the winning run raced across the plate. Wynegar and the rest of the Twins began jumping around celebrating their victory, and as a result, Wynegar never went down to touch first. Indians' manager Jeff Torborg pointed this fact out to plate umpire Vic Voltaggio, and Voltaggio quickly told him that a passed ball takes precedence in this situation. But does it?

The pitch happened to be both ball four with the bases loaded and a wild pitch on which the runner would easily have scored even if it hadn't been ball four. But which takes precedence? If we rule that the base on balls takes precedence, then according to 4.09(b), the game isn't over until the runner scores *and* Wynegar touches first. Also note that 6.08(a) allows the batter to go to first base without liability to be put out, *provided he advances to and touches first base*. Another consideration: If the base on balls takes precedence, then if Wynegar is put out for not touching first base, the run does not count since this is the third out (4.09=a). And, how is Wynegar put out? Does the defense have to appeal with the ball (which is "God only knows where" by now), or can the umpires rule Wynegar out for abandoning his effort to run the bases (7.08=a-2), without the defense appealing?

Let's look at it the other way. Torborg bought Voltaggio's explanation that the passed ball takes precedence, and the run scored because of the passed ball rather than because of the walk. That's logical in this play, because the ball went all the way back to the screen, and the Cleveland catcher didn't even attempt to retrieve it. But, how far past the catcher does a passed ball have to go before a runner would have scored on it? No one can answer that question in a matter of feet or inches. Let's say the pitch had only gone 10 feet behind the catcher. Would the runner have scored? Who knows—it didn't happen! Or let's say fifteen feet, or twenty one feet six inches? The point is, if we say that the passed ball takes precedence, then we have to come up with some kind of interpretation concerning just how far the ball has to get by the catcher before we can rule that the runner would have scored on the passed ball, regardless of the base on balls. Obviously, we can't do that.

To this day, the A.L. will put nothing in writing to cover an interpretation of this situation. I personally feel the base on balls must take precedence for two reasons: 1) the pitch was a ball before it became a passed ball; 2) the impossibility of determining how far a passed ball must get by the catcher before the runner would have scored because of it rather than because of the base on balls. That doesn't assure that I interpreted it correctly.

Although the odds are one million to one against a batter hitting a pennant flying from a flagpole in center field, Winston Brown of Boise of the Pioneer League achieved the feat in a game with Salt Lake City, setting up a puzzling problem for president Claude Engberg during the 1957 season.

The ball on Brown's drive entangled itself with the pennant and then dropped back on the playing field, but the umpires allowed a home run, helping Boise to a 4-3 victory. Manager Cliff Dapper of Salt Lake City protested the game.

Salt Lake City contended that the pennant—Boise's banner for its 1956 championship—was part of the flagpole. Under the ground rules at Boise, any ball hitting the flagpole remained in play if it rebounded to the field.

Engberg, after polling all his umpires and after making a personal visit to Boise from his home in Salt Lake City, overruled Salt Lake

City's protest. He said in his decision: "While I can find no precedent for ruling on this protest, the fact that flags are not attached to the flagpole at all times made the contention that a flag is part of a flagpole questionable. Had a ball been hit in the spot earlier in the season (before Boise raised the pennant) it would have been a home run. I can see no reason why it should not be a home run with the flag flying."

A rare "ball" penalty was called in a Pacific Coast League game between San Diego and Hollywood on May 5, 1956, by umpire Al Mutart.

San Diego manager Bob Elliott removed pitcher Pete Mesa from the game in the eighth inning as Hollywood had the bases loaded and nobody out. Elliott signaled for Tom Herrera to come in from the bull pen. Mutart notified the reliever that Elliott wanted him to pitch. When Herrera insisted on taking an extra warm-up pitch before coming in, Mutart called "ball one" on the next hitter, Joe Duhem, even though there was no pitcher on the mound. Elliott was so infuriated by the umpire's decision that he made some unkind remarks to Mutart. The San Diego manager was then ejected from the game. Duhem proceeded to whack a bases-loaded home run, and Hollywood went on to win, 7-2.

Baseball had its own "Watergate" during the 1898 season in a game between the Philadelphia Phillies and Cincinnati Reds at Philadelphia. Frederick Lieb and Stan Baumgartner report the incident in *The Philadelphia Phillies.* It was not mentioned how the umpire ruled on the problem, so I'll let you be the judge on this one.

> Tommy Corcoran, Cincinnati Reds infielder, was coaching at third base and kicking dust around, when the spikes of his shoes caught in something which at first seemed to be a thick vine. Tommy looked down at his feet and on closer inspection found it was no vine, but a wire. He gave it a good yank and several yards of wire came out of the ground.
>
> Corcoran halted the game, kept tugging away at the wire, and with players of both teams at his heels, traced the wire across the field right into the Phillies locker room. There they found Morgan

Murphy, a reserve catcher who rarely did any catching, sitting with a telegraph instrument beside an open window. Murphy tried to hide the instrument, along with a pair of strong opera glasses that completed his equipment. But the cat was out of the bag. It eventually was learned that Murphy spied on opposing catchers and relayed their signals, via the wire, to the Philadelphia third base coach. A sort of a buzzer was under the dirt, and by keeping his foot on it, the coach knew one buzz meant a fastball, two a curve, three a change of pace. The coach signaled his information to the batsman, who usually knew what to expect.

Rule 9.01(d) reads as follows: *Each umpire has authority to disqualify any player, coach, manager or substitute for objecting to decisions or for unsportsmanlike conduct or language, and to eject such disqualified person from the playing field. If an umpire disqualifies a player while a play is in progress, the disqualification shall not take effect until no further action is possible in that play.*

Red Sox catcher Sammy White was ejected during a play on August 28, 1956, as the Boston Red Sox entertained the Detroit Tigers at Fenway Park in Boston. Red Wilson of the Tigers circled the bases while the Red Sox were protesting a decision.

Wilson hit a ground ball through the box that was fielded by Milt Bolling behind second base. Bill Tuttle, who was on second at the time, tried to score on the play. Bolling threw to White in an attempt to head off Tuttle. Umpire Frank Umont called Tuttle safe, which caused White to go into a frenzy. White disgustedly heaved the ball into center field and was immediately ejected by Umont. During all the confusion, Tiger coach Jack Tighe instructed Wilson to keep running. The ball was retrieved back to the infield by Ted Williams, but the ball went unnoticed by the Boston players. Meanwhile, Wilson circled around the bases and came into score.

Cal Hubbard, A.L. umpire supervisor at the time, said, "As long as there is a chance for a continued play on the runner at first base, Umont can't call time. In fact, if Wilson had been sent back to first, Detroit would have had grounds for a real protest."

Red Sox manager Mike Higgins argued the play but didn't get any satisfaction, as the decision stood.

Sometimes an ejection can work in reverse, as was the case in St. Louis on August 30, 1958, when the Cardinals met the Cubs. Umpire Frank Secory ejected Cubs' outfielder Lee Walls and manager Bob Scheffing in the third inning after they argued with Secory over a controversial pitch from Sal Maglie.

The Cubs argued that Walls had been hit by a Maglie pitch. Chuck Tanner then went to bat for Walls, inheriting an 0-and-1 count. He took the next pitch for strike two and then hit a three-run homer.

National League umpire Bruce Froemming enforced rule 9.01(e) when he umpired in the Northern League in 1960. The rule gives the umpire *authority at his discretion to eject from the playing field (1) any person whose duties permit his presence on the field, such as ground crew members, ushers, photographers, newsmen, broadcasting crew members, etc. and (2) any spectator or other person not authorized to be on the playing field.*

Froemming ordered four sportswriters and business manager Graydon Stromme of Duluth to leave the press box under threat of forfeiting the game to Winnipeg. The umpire set a ten-minute time limit. Froemming allowed the game to continue after a few reporters vacated the press box. The press box is not part of the playing field, but Bruce evidently got away with it.

The next baseball maxim, 9.02(a), declares that *Any umpire's decision which involves judgment, such as, but not limited to, whether a batted ball is fair or foul, whether a pitch is a strike or a ball, or whether a runner is safe or out is final. No player, manager, coach or substitute shall object to any such judgment decisions.*

Take a good look at the last sentence of this rule. I think it is rather amusing. Can you imagine telling the managers prior to the game that they are not allowed to question any judgment decisions made by the umpire?

If a manager thinks the umpire made an improper call, he may request the umpire to appeal to the other umpires for their opinion. However, the umpire does not have to do so if he feels strongly that his decision is correct. Half swings are a menace to umpires. This is probably the most often appealed play in baseball from one umpire to another. *Appeals on a half swing may be made only on the call of "ball" and when asked to appeal, the home plate umpire must refer to a base umpire for his judgment on the half swing. Should the base umpire call the pitch a strike, the strike call shall prevail.* (9.02=c)

A few years ago the plate umpire did not have to appeal to the field umpires on half swings or even full swings for that matter. On July 17, 1961, the Cards' Ken Boyer took a deliberate swing to protect Bill White, who was stealing second in a game against the Cubs. Plate umpire Ed Vargo didn't realize that Boyer had swung and called the pitch a ball. Cubs' head coach Elvin Tappe argued, but Vargo held firm in his decision. Shag Crawford was umpiring first and Mel Steiner was working third base, but neither one could do a thing since they were not appealed to by Vargo.

Rule 9.02(c) also says, *If a decision is appealed, the umpire making the decision may ask another umpire for information before making a final decision. No umpire shall criticize, seek to reverse or interfere with another umpire's decision unless asked to do so by the umpire making it.*

Beans Reardon was the plate umpire on June 8, 1938, in Chicago where the Cubs hosted the Giants. Reardon was caught in the middle of a chaotic play in the fifth inning of that game. Here are the details.

Carl Hubbell singled home a Giant runner who was on second base. The play at the plate was close and Beans signaled safe. The call set off an explosion on the part of the Cubs. While the Cubs were arguing with the arbiter, Hubbell broke for second base. Clay Bryant, the Chicago pitcher, saw him take off and alertly grabbed the ball from catcher Bob Garbark, who was part of the arguing circle around the plate. Bryant then threw the ball into center field, trying to catch Hubbell going to second. Hubbell eventually landed on third base.

Reardon ordered Carl to go back to first claiming he had called "time" when the argument began. Now the Giants joined the Cubs in the quarrel, insisting that time had not been called. Getting nowhere with Reardon, the Giants appealed to the other umpires, Larry Goetz and Babe Pinelli. The latter two umpires agreed that time was not called and allowed Hubbell to go to third.

Then the argument shifted into a Reardon vs. Pinelli and Goetz phase. Although Reardon was most likely boiling that he was overruled without appealing for help, he allowed Hubbell to go to third, being outnumbered two to one. In my opinion Goetz and Pinelli committed a cardinal sin among umpires, in that they overruled a decision without being appealed to.

In the next three episodes we find other games where the umpires reversed their decisions after consulting with their brother umpires.

The Yankees played at the Polo Grounds before the original Yankee Stadium was constructed. In a game against the St. Louis Browns in 1922, with two out in the top of the ninth inning and the Yankees ahead 2-1, the Browns' Johnny Tobin grounded to Yankee first baseman Wally Pipp, with Chick Shorten on second and Pat Collins on first. Pipp tossed to Yankee chucker Sam Jones, covering first base. Umpire Ollie Chill waved Tobin out, and the Yankee players along with the large crowd of 49, 152 assumed the game was over.

However, Lee Fohl, coaching at first, had noticed that Jones did not have possession of the ball as he juggled it before holding it securely. Fohl took it up with plate umpire Brick Owens, who told Chill in his opinion Tobin was safe. In the meantime, the tying Brown run had scored from second. After a 20-minute delay, Chill reversed his original decision the game was resumed, and the Browns won, 7-2. So here we have a game that was temporarily won but eventually lost.

Out of necessity, umpires sometimes have to break up a victory party and order the team back on the field. Baltimore was playing in Cleveland in July of 1977. The umpires were Vic Voltaggio, Larry Barnett, Marty Springstead, and Jim Evans. With the score tied in the bottom of the ninth, Cleveland had a runner on first with two outs. The runner was moving on a 3-2 pitch to the batter, who hit a ground ball to Rich Dauer at second base. The runner from first kept on running and rounded second on his way to third. Dauer bobbled the ball around for a while, finally secured it and threw it by Tony Muser at first and into the Indians' dugout. The umpires were not thinking, and allowed the runner from first (who was running close to third at the time the ball went into the dugout) to score, and everybody started leaving the field. While the Indians' players were jumping around celebrating their "victory," it finally dawned on crew chief Marty Springstead that the runner should only be awarded third and the batter-runner second, in accordance with rule 7.05(g) which was covered earlier. Dauer threw the ball before the batter-runner got to first, so the Approved Ruling under 7.05(g) could not be invoked, since all runners, *including the batter-runner,* had not advanced at least one base each. It was clear that the runner from first was well past second when Dauer threw the ball, but he still can only go to third. Springstead had to bring the Indians back out to continue the game. Baltimore proceeded to get out of the jam, and went on to win the game in extra-innings. Weaver tried to claim the credit for catching Springstead in a situation where he misapplied a rule, but Springstead had the situation well in hand before it ever dawned on Weaver that he hadn't lost the game.

Senators' manager Ted Williams and coach Nellie Fox protested a decision on April 13, 1969, when the Senators played at Baltimore.

Ken McMullen hit a liner to Oriole outfielder Don Buford, who appeared to have made a shoestring catch. However, umpire Emmett Ashford ruled that Buford had trapped the ball.

Ashford consulted with the other umpires after listening to a loud protest by the Orioles. The umpires decided that the ball was caught, and Ashford reversed himself, to the dismay of Williams and Fox.

There are times when an umpire is too embarrassed to change his decision. Such was the case with the great Bill Klem, while he was umpiring a Dodgers-Cardinals game at St. Louis several years ago.

Rogers Hornsby hit a ball that sailed over the head of Dodger center fielder Hi Meyers. The Dodgers' center fielder retrieved the ball and threw it to Jimmy Johnston at third, who then threw to Hank DeBerry at the plate to nail Hornsby, who was trying to let out an inside-the-park home run. As Klem was going through his out motion, a ball fell to the ground. Klem changed his out call to safe, thinking that Hornsby had knocked the ball from the grasp of DeBerry.

The Dodger catcher showed Klem that he did not lose the ball. Klem, however, wouldn't change his decision. He was too embarrassed. The ball that lay on the ground had evidently fallen from one of Klem's pockets.

The last segment of the rule, 9.02(d), says, *No umpire may be replaced during a game unless he is injured or becomes ill.*

American League umpire Charlie Berry was working third base on September 3, 1960, at Baltimore. Berry finished the game behind the plate after Larry Napp was carried off the field after being struck by foul balls three different times.

Jocko Conlan walked off the field during a Dodgers-Reds game in 1955. Conlan, umpiring behind the plate, called a strike on the Dodgers' Jackie Robinson on a pitch that almost hit the dirt. Jocko had been suffering from an attack of arthritis and was having difficulty bending over to follow the pitch. Conlan said, "Robinson seemed so honestly shocked over the call, I figured I must have missed it. I didn't want any more like it."

Personally I was horrified when plate ump Lou DiMuro was leveled by the Yankees' Cliff Johnson (since traded to Cleveland) during the 1979 season in a game at Milwaukee. After Johnson crossed the plate, he crashed into DiMuro sending Lou to the hospital for several days. It isn't often that an umpire must leave a game. When he does, you can be sure it is for a good reason.

Rule 9.03 reads, *(a) If there is only one umpire, he shall have complete jurisdiction in administering the rules. He may take any position on the playing field which will enable him to discharge his duties (usually behind the catcher, but sometimes behind the pitcher if there are runners). (b) If there are two or more umpires one shall be designated umpire-in-chief and the others as field umpires.*

Major league umpires work in teams of four men. Minor league umpires and most amateur baseball umps work in teams of two men. Once in a great while umpires are given the chore of working a game alone. In the late nineteenth century and early twentieth century, games were handled by one man. Players, managers, and groundskeepers were well aware of this difficult responsibility. To gain an edge, trickery was often used to take advantage of the one umpire.

Tom Murphy, the old Baltimore Orioles groundskeeper, used to let the grass grow high in the outfield and plant extra baseballs to be used by Oriole outfielders in case of an emergency. Jim Price, the Baltimore sportswriter of the 1890s, tells this story about the planted baseballs.

"The St. Louis Browns were playing at Baltimore, and with Joe Quinn on first, Tommy Dowd hit a sharp drive to left center. Kelley cut across the path of the ball, apparently scooped it up, and threw to McGraw to catch Quinn at third base. Just as the single umpire was about to call Quinn out, Brodie, who had been chasing the real ball to the fence, threw it in from deep center, and gave away another of Baltimore's inside plays. After an argument, the umpire forfeited the game to St. Louis."

When the majors used only one umpire, he sometimes observed the action from behind the mound. Tommy Connolly, a Hall of Fame arbiter, who later became chief of the American League umpires, handled the Chicago White Stockings-Cleveland game on opening day April 24, 1901, by himself. Connolly worked before a crowd of 9,000 people.

The 9.04 rule explains some of the duties of the umpire-in-chief, who is usually referred to as the plate umpire. His main responsibilities are to take charge of the game and call and count balls and strikes.

Bill Stewart was the plate umpire the night Johnny Vander Meer pitched his second consecutive no-hitter. The Reds' Vander Meer pitched his first no-hitter on June 11, 1938, against the Boston Braves, and his second one came on June 15, 1938, against the Brooklyn Dodgers.

In the ninth inning of his second no-hitter against Brooklyn, the Dodgers had the bases loaded with two outs. The batter was Leo Durocher, who had a count of one ball and two strikes. Vander Meer said, "On the next pitch I hit the outside of the plate with a fastball for a strike, and umpire Bill Stewart called it a 'ball.' On the next pitch Durocher popped out to center field for the final out."

When the game ended, Stewart was the first to congratulate Vander Meer. "If Leo got a hit, according to Vander Meer, Stewart said, I was the blame as I missed the pitch and the batter should have been struck out on the previous pitch."

When a batter swings at a pitch and misses, it makes the plate umpire's job that much easier, since nobody can object the umpire's call of a strike. At least this is the case most of the time.

Don Heffner tells this story concerning an umpire's decision when he managed in the minors. Heffner said, "The first year I managed in the minors, I was stunned by the quality of umpiring that the minors had to contend with. Of course, that's where umpires get their experience. This particular night this kid on the opposing team took a full swing at the ball and missed, and the ump said 'ball three' instead of 'strike three' as there was a two strike count on the batter. I went charging out to home plate and asked what in the hell was going on? The ump still maintained it was a 'ball.' I was so exasperated I finally turned to this young kid who had struck at the ball with a full swing, and said, 'You look like an honest young man, tell the truth, did you or didn't you take a cut at that pitch? He looked uncomfortable for a second, and said 'Yes, I swung at the ball.' The umpire then said loud and clear 'strike three,' and the kid walked back to the dugout ending the game."

Rule 9.04(b) gives the field umpire the authority in calling, *Time, balks, illegal pitches, or defacement or discoloration of the ball by any player.*

Readers are advised to refer to chapter 3 (3.12) to find cases related to 9.04. You will recall that Ted Kluszewski and Don Money were each deprived of home runs because field umpires Ed Hurley and Jim McKean called "time" during the play.

Aside from watching for balks, illegal pitches, etc., field umpires must be ready to rule on obstruction and interference plays that occur. The field umpires working first and third bases must also be ready to help the plate umpire on half swings.

9.04—(c) *If different decisions should be made on one play by different umpires, the umpire-in-chief shall call the umpires into consultation, with no manager or player present. After consultation, the umpire-in-chief shall determine which decision shall* *prevail based on which umpire was in best position and which decision was most likely correct. Play shall proceed as if only the final decision had been made.*

The Dodgers and Cardinals met at St. Louis on May 12, 1969, when umpires John Kibler and Ed Vargo got their wires crossed, as they each made the opposite call on the same play. The play involved the Dodgers' Bill Sudakis at second base. Sudakis tried to take second on a fly ball hit to short center. Cardinal shortstop Steve Huntz and second baseman Julian Javier left second base unprotected as they chased the ball. Cardinal center fielder Curt Flood got to the ball and fired to third baseman Mike Shannon covering second. After a discussion, Kibler's out call prevailed.

9.05— *When a player is ejected, the umpire must report to the league president within twelve hours after the end of a game all violations of rules and other incidents worthy of comment. This also includes the disqualification of any trainer, manager or coach.*

The history of baseball has seen several different reasons for disqualifications of players and managers. Most ejections are the result of vile language and protests on the part of players and managers. Some ejections are the result of demonstrations on the part of managers or players.

Casey Stengel was once given the thumb because he brought a flashlight onto the field claiming it was too dark to play. Connie Ryan actively protested against playing in the rain by kneeling in the on-deck circle wearing a raincoat. Ryan performed this stunt in the bottom of the fifth inning in a game against the Dodgers on September 29, 1949. Umpire George Barr ran Ryan from the game.

Protests over ejections have taken on many different forms. Pirate manager Bobby Bragan, unhappy over his ejection from the July 31, 1957 game at Milwaukee, returned to the field and offered umpires Frank Secory, Stan Landes, and Bill Baker a sip of his orange drink.

It's not often that a player or manager who gets ejected from a game is unaware that he has been given the thumb, but it happened to Twins' pilot Gene Mauch on April 17, 1977, in a game against

Oakland. Mauch was run out of the game by the colorful Ron Luciano after he complained the A's pitcher Jim Umbarger had balked when he picked off Jerry Terrell in the first inning.

In the second frame, when Oakland was making a pitching change, Bill Haller said to Mauch, "Who's managing your team?" "I am," responded Mauch. Haller then informed Mauch that Luciano had ejected him from the game. Oakland manager Jack McKeon proceeded to protest the game. The protest was not necessary since the A's won, 10-2.

I guess each umpire has their favorite ejection story and Nick Bremigan has his.

"Steve Boros pulled a real classic when he was managing in the minor leagues in the late 1960s. He was managing the visiting team this particular night, and was getting soundly beaten 10-1. He felt he was getting a raw deal from the umpires in the game, and got ejected after an argument in the sixth inning. While wandering around outside his clubhouse after showering, he noticed a big sign on the door of the umpires' room which appropriately read "Umpires." The wheels began turning. He snatched the sign and proceeded to go out to the scoreboard, which was above the left field fence. The home team had scored four more times before Boros got there, making the score 14-1. A strange thing occurred when the base umpire looked up at the scoreboard in the eighth inning; the line score read: Visitors 1, Umpires 14. I wonder how that happened????"

10.00

The Official Scorer

The official scorer is an integral part of the game. Fans and players anxiously await the decision of the scorer concerning a controversial hit or error. The scorer is usually a sportswriter from one of the local newspapers in the several major league cities. Three official scorers are assigned to a World Series game because of its importance.

In the next few pages I will attempt to cover various plays and situations that affect the official scorer. My intent of bringing in the official scorer in the text is to illustrate the difficult and responsible job of the person and to also show the important part he plays in the game.

One of the first things the scorer does when the game ends is to compute the *number of at bats* a player is charged with. (10.02=a)

Charles T. Pick of the Boston Braves took the collar in 11 at bats in the 26-inning game that was mentioned earlier in this book.

George Kell went hitless in 10 at bats for the Philadelphia A's in a 24-inning affair in 1945. That's an unbelievable statistic for a player who completed his 15 years in the majors with a .306 average.

Sam White, Eugene Stephens, and Tom Umphlett each batted three times in the seventh inning of that June 18, 1953, Red Sox game, with Stephens collecting three hits. Pee Wee Reese batted three times in an inning for the Dodgers on May 21, 1952.

The *number of runs a player scores* in a game is also listed. Mel Ott (Giants), Johnny Pesky (Red Sox), and Frank Torre (Braves) have each scored six runs in a game at one time or another.

Red Rolfe of the Yankees scored 30 runs in 18 consecutive games in 1939. Babe Ruth led the league in runs scored eight different seasons.

The number of *safe hits* and *runs batted in* is also computed. Rennie Stennett of the Pirates collected seven hits on September 16, 1975, against the Cubs. Cecil Travis of the Washington Senators banged out five base hits in his first major league game on May 16, 1933. The game lasted 12 innings. Ty Cobb collected five hits in one game on fourteen different occasions. Tiger shortstop Cesar Gutierrez had seven hits in seven times at bat in a 12-inning victory over the Indians on June 21, 1970. John Burnett of the Indians collected nine hits in an 18-inning game against the A's on July 10, 1932. Burnett's hits went for nought as the Athletics won the game, 18-17.

George Brett of the Kansas City Royals had six consecutive three-hit games early in the 1976 season.

To the ballplayers, RBIs are often given more importance than batting average and home runs, a reason why Hack Wilson's record 190 RBIs in 1930 is so highly respected. *Credit the batter with a run batted in for every run which reaches home base because of the batter's safe hit, sacrifice bunt, sacrifice fly, infield out or fielder's choice; or which is forced over the plate by reason of the batter becoming a runner with the bases full (on a base on balls, or an award of first base for being touched by a pitched ball, or for interference or obstruction).* (10.04=a)

The rule as written sometimes creates the rarity of an RBI on an error. In 1958, Cy Kritzer reported the following play to *The Sporting News:*

> On June 15, 1958, Columbus and Buffalo met in the second game of a double-header.

Bill Causion was on first base for Columbus and running on the pitch with two out in the first inning when Paul Pettit doubled.

Joe Astroth, Buffalo catcher, stood just in front of the plate while awaiting the relay from shortstop Bobby Morgan. As he leaped for the ball, he tripped Causion, causing him to stumble past home plate and miss touching it. After catching the ball, Astroth raced back to tag Causion for the out.

However, umpire Harry Schwarts ruled "obstruction" against Astroth, and so the run scored despite the heated protests. Astroth was charged with an error for his act of obstruction. The official scorer also ruled that Pettit deserved a run batted in because Causion would have scored whether or not Astroth had obstructed him.

Jim Bottomley of the St. Louis Cardinals batted in 12 runs in a game against the Dodgers on September 16, 1924.

Tony Lazzeri of the Yankees had 11 ribbys on September 16, 1924.

Fred Lynn batted in 10 runs with three homers, a triple, and a single in a 15-1 Red Sox win at Detroit on June 18, 1975.

The number of *doubles, triples,* and *home runs* are also handled by the scorer at the conclusion of the game. Several players have doubled four times in a game. In recent years Billy Williams of the Cubs performed the feat on April 9, 1969. Cub pitcher Hank Borowy doubled twice in the same inning on May 5, 1946. White Sox pitcher Ted Lyons did likewise on July 28, 1935.

On July 12, 1931, the Cardinals played the Cubs in a double-header. There were 32 doubles hit in the twin bill, as 23 of them were hit in the second game.

In the triples' department, Ernie Banks of the Cubs was the last National Leaguer to connect for three triples in a game when he did it on June 11, 1966.

Al Bumbry of the Orioles was the last American Leaguer to whack out three triples in a contest, having his big day on September 22, 1973.

Since 1900, Bill Dahlen (1900), W. Curtis Walker (1926), Al Zarilla (1946), and Gil Coan (1951) have each unloaded two triples during the same inning—a real long shot.

On May 6, 1934, the Red Sox rapped four triples in a row when Carl Reynolds, Moose Solters, Rick Ferrell, and Bucky Walters made contact against the Tigers. Cookie Rojas batted 621 times in 1968 without hitting a triple all year.

Ten players have hit four home runs in one game. The last man to accomplish this was Mike Schmidt of the Phillies in 1976. Until Schmidt's big day against the Cubs, Willie Mays held the distinction of being the last man to hit four round-trippers in one game. Mays did his thing on April 30, 1961.

Mays also has the distinction of hitting 22 extra-inning home runs during his career. Babe Ruth hit 16 in overtime and Frank Robinson 15.

Relief artist Hoyt Wilhelm hit a home run in his first time at bat in the major leagues. Wilhelm's blow came on April 23, 1952, playing for the Giants at the Polo Grounds. Wilhelm never hit another home run during his 21-year playing career.

Dodger pitcher Clem Labine came to bat 31 times in 1955 and had but three hits, but every hit was a home run.

Boston Braves' pitcher Jim Tobin belted three consecutive home runs in one game on May 13, 1942. Tobin became the first pitcher in major league history to hit a home run as he pitched a no-hit game, which he did against the Dodgers on April 27, 1944.

Speaking of home runs, the 1945 Washington Senators hit only one home run all season in their own ball park, an inside-the- park job by Joe Kuhel. You might think that the Senators had a poor year because of their week home run output in their home park. However, the Senators had a fine record, being nosed out for the pennant by the Tigers on the last day of the season.

The 1908 White Sox hit only three home runs that season. It was good enough for a third-place finish.

Frank Howard hit 10 home runs in 20 at bats during an amazing stretch in 1968.

Mel Ott hit 511 career home runs, and not one was ever hit in Shibe Park in Philadelphia.

On June 8, 1961, the Athletics hit three consecutive triples, a remarkable feat. On the same day, the Milwaukee Braves, not to be outdone, hit four home runs in succession and still lost the game to the Reds, 10-8. Home runs were hit consecutively by Ed Mathews, Hank Aaron, Joe Adcock, and Frank Thomas.

The Braves hit four home runs the same inning again on June 8, 1965, against the Cubs. Joe Torre, Eddie Mathews, Hank Aaron, and Gene Oliver each connected with a four-bagger in the tenth inning of that game.

On May 31, 1958, Aaron, Mathews, and Wes Covington hit home runs on successive pitches off Ron Kline of the Pirates.

A player named Eugene Mercantelli played for Waco, Texas in 1930 under the name of Gene Rye. On August 6, 1930, Rye hit three home runs in the eighth inning against the Beaumont, Texas team.

Jay "Nig" Clarke hit eight home runs for Corsicana in a Texas League game against Texarkana on June 15, 1902. The game was won by Corsicana, 51-3. Clarke played nine years in the major leagues and banged out a career total of six home runs.

On July 10, 1929, the Phillies and Pirates hooked up in a home run derby. A four-bagger was hit in every inning of the game.

Bob Nieman of the St. Louis Browns hit two consecutive home runs in his first two times up in a major league game on September 14, 1951, against the Red Sox. Oakland shortstop Bert Campaneris hit two homers in his first major league game on July 23, 1964, playing for the Kansas City Athletics in his first and third at bats.

The *total bases on safe hits* is also totaled. (10.02=a-8) Joe Adcock had a game base total of 18 on July 31, 1954. Adcock racked up the 18 bases on four home runs and one double.

Rule 10.02(a-9) deals with the number of *stolen bases* during the game. In 1912, on September 11 and September 22, Eddie Collins of the Philadelphia Athletics stole six bases in one game. The Twins' Rod Carew stole three bases in one inning on May 18, 1969. Vic Power of the Cleveland Indians was the last man to steal home twice in the same game. Power accomplished the trick on August 14, 1958, yet only stole three bases all year.

In 1953 Hank Aaron played in the Class A Sally League. In one game he stole four bases and got picked off four times.

The Washington Senators stole eight bases in the first inning against the Detroit Tigers on July 19, 1915. The Tiger catcher was Steve O'Neill.

On June 28, 1907, 13 Washington Senators stole bases on Wesley Branch Rickey, catcher for the New York Highlanders.

The Mets' Tommie Agee created somewhat of a knotty problem for the official scorer on May 27, 1970, when he stole home in a game against the Cardinals at Shea Stadium. The rule in question was 10.08. *A stolen base shall be credited to a runner whenever he advances one base unaided by a hit, a putout, an error, a force-out, a fielder's choice, a passed ball, a wild pitch or a balk, etc.*

Here are the details. Agee stole home while the Cardinal's Steve Carlton committed a balk. Defying the rule, the official scorer, Dick Young, credited Agee with a stolen base. According to the rule, the balk had to nullify the steal.

Young consulted with N.L. president Charles Feeney to confirm his decision that Agee should be given a stolen base since Agee had home stolen in the opinion of the official scorer and umpire Andy Olsen. Young believes that the official scorer should have the option of awarding a stolen base in cases like this one.

Three weeks later Agee was officially granted the stolen base. I guess you can call that a delayed steal.

Rule 10.02(a-10) concerns itself with *sacrifice bunts.* Odd but true, Harmon Killebrew never laid down a sacrifice bunt in his major league career, which included 8,147 career at bats.

Al Benton, who pitched to both Babe Ruth and Mickey Mantle, had two sacrifices in the same inning, a major league record. Benton accomplished this playing for the Tigers in the third inning on August 6, 1941.

10.02—(a-1) *A player is not charged with a time at bat when: (1) he hits a sacrifice bunt or sacrifice fly; (2) he is awarded first base on four called balls; (3) he is hit by a pitched ball; (4) he is awarded first base because of interference or obstruction.*

On April 15, 1961, the Tigers were retired in the fifth inning against the White Sox without having an official time at bat. Rocky Colavito and Norm Cash each drew walks to open the inning. The next batter, Steve Boros, laid down a sacrifice bunt, advancing the runners to second and third. Dick Brown was then intentionally walked with first base open. With Chico Fernandez at bat, the Tigers' signals became mixed up. Colavito, who thought the squeeze was on, broke for the plate and was tagged out. Cash, attempting to go to third base on the play, was tagged out in a rundown for the third out.

The Cardinals had nine players bat in a rally and only two were charged with an at bat in a game against the Dodgers in 1960. Dodger pitcher Danny McDevitt walked the first two Cardinal batters, Ken Boyer and Daryl Spencer. Ellis Burton, pinch-hitting for Carl Sawatski, sacrificed off Dodger pitcher Ed Roebuck, advancing the runners. Curt Flood then drew an intentional pass. With Julian Javier at bat, Boyer scored on a wild pitch. Javier eventually walked to reload the bases. Ernie Broglio was then charged with the first Cardinal at bat of the inning when he singled home two runs. Joe Cunningham proceeded to hit a sacrifice fly for another run. Bill White then walked, causing the first eight Cardinals to be charged with only one at bat. Bob Nieman then made the last out.

The first part of this rule excludes a batter from a time at bat when he hits a sacrifice fly. Harry Steinfeldt (Cubs—1909), Bob Meusel (Yankees—1926), Ernie Banks (Cubs—1961), and Russ Nixon (Red Sox—1965) each had three sacrifice flies in one game in the years indicated.

Sacrifices are covered in the 10.09 rules. For the purpose of the next two stories, I will bring out 10.09(c) sections (1 and 2). *Score a sacrifice fly when; before two are out, the batter hits a fly ball or a line drive handled by an outfielder, or an infielder running in the outfield which (1) is caught, and a runner scores, or (2) if in the scorer's judgment the runner could have scored after the catch had the fly been caught. NOTE: Score a sacrifice fly in accordance with 10.09(e-2) even though another runner is forced out by reason of the batter becoming a runner.*

Here is a twist to the sacrifice fly rule. In a game played between the Indians and Tigers during the 1957 season, official scorer Harry Jones found himself confronted with an unusual play and, after a careful study of the rules, granted Roger Maris, who was then playing for the Indians, a sacrifice fly, although the book at the time didn't actually specify one. "The intent was there, though," decided Jones.

The situation was this: With Al Smith on third and Joe Altobelli on first, Maris hit a long fly to right. Al Kaline went back to the fence for the ball, but dropped it. Smith tagged up and scored. Altobelli also had tagged up, and Kaline's throw to the infield forced him at second.

Had Kaline caught the ball, it would have been a simple decision, a sacrifice fly. Or, had Altobelli reached second safely, it would have been an obvious sacrifice fly. In 1957, there was nothing in the rules concerning a sacrifice fly even though another runner is forced out by reason of the batter becoming a runner.

In the play described above, no error could be charged against Kaline because of the force out at second. At the time, Jones felt that the Rules Committee apparently hadn't anticipated such a situation. It seemed to Jones that this was a fly ball which scored a runner from third and therefore should be ruled a sacrifice fly.

On one swing Red Sox pitcher Frank Sullivan hit into a double play, got a run batted in, and was not charged with a time at bat. The rare play happened on April 17, 1956, as the Red Sox and Orioles clashed.

Sullivan flied to right fielder Dave Philley with the bases loaded in the third inning. Jim Piersall scored from third, but Sammy White was thrown out trying for second.

Another way a batter is not charged with a time at bat is to *walk.* Jimmie Foxx walked six times in one game on June 16, 1938, playing for the Red Sox. Roger Maris of the Yankees received four intentional passes on May 22, 1962, in a 12-inning game.

Getting *hit with the pitch* also absolves a batter from a time at bat. Ron Hunt was struck by pitches 243 times. In 1971, Hunt was plunked 50 times. Minnie Minoso had 189 lifetime bruises. Frank Thomas of the New York Mets was hit twice the same inning on April 29, 1962, in the first game of a double-header. The Reds' Willard

Schmidt was also decked twice during the third inning on April 26, 1959.

Rick Manning of the Indians went down swinging five consecutive times on May 15, 1977 during a nine-inning game. Dodger shortstop Bill Russell also whiffed five times in a regular game on June 9, 1971.

Five players, Carl Weilman (1913), Don Hoak (1956), Rick Reichardt (1966), Bill Cowan (1971), and Cecil Cooper (1974) all have the dubious distinction of striking out six times in an extra-inning game.

Who said you had to be in the game to strike out? Just ask Doe Boyland who came up with the Pittsburgh Pirates at the end of the 1978 season.

Boyland had been removed for pinch hitter Rennie Stennett when the count was one ball and two strikes. Rennie struck out, but because Doe left him with the handicap of two strikes, playing rules hold that Boyland be responsible for the strikeout. Rule 10.17(b) states, *When the batter leaves the game with two strikes against him, and the substitute batter completes a strikeout, charge the strikeout and the time at bat to the first batter.* Case closed!

The following records for each fielder are covered under the 10.02(b) section. The number of *putouts, assists, errors, double plays* participated in, and *triple plays* participated in are listed as guidelines for the official scorer to follow.

It is rare that a player gets credit for both a putout and an assist in getting out one batter, but this rarity occurred on May 11, 1958, at Yankee Stadium, where the Yankees played the Washington Senators. Truman Clevenger, Washington pitcher, was struck by a line drive hit by Elston Howard in the seventh inning. The ball caromed off Clevenger's leg into foul territory near first base. First baseman Norm Zauchin fielded the ball and tossed it to Clevenger covering first base. Credit Clevenger with both an assist and a putout on the same play.

First basemen usually have a large number of putouts because of their position. For instance, Ernie Banks of the Cubs had 22 putouts in a nine-inning game on May 9, 1963. Several first sackers including the likes of Bill Skowron, Gene Tenace, Norm Cash, Earl Torgeson,

Rudy York, and Dolph Camilli have gone through an entire game at different times without registering a putout. As defined, *A putout shall be credited for each fielder who (1) catches a fly ball or a line drive, whether fair or foul; (2) catches a thrown ball which puts out a batter or runner, or (3) tags a runner when the runner is off the base to which he legally is entitled.* (10.10)

Senator catcher Luke Sewell was credited with two putouts on the same play on April 29, 1933, at Yankee Stadium where Washington met the Yankees.

In the bottom of the ninth inning with the Senators leading, 6-4, the Yankees had Lou Gehrig on second and Dixie Walker on first. Tony Lazzeri then hit a long drive deep to right field over the head of "Goose" Goslin. Goose relayed the ball to Joe Cronin, who in turn fired the ball to Sewell, who tagged Gehrig at the plate. Walker kept running from first on the play and was called out by umpire George Hildebrand on another tag by Sewell, giving him two putouts on the play.

In a game played between the Boston Braves and Chicago Cubs in 1924, the Braves had three men thrown out at the plate in one inning. Gabby Hartnett, Chicago catcher, made all three putouts.

Outfielder Earl Clark of the Boston Braves was credited with 12 putouts on May 10, 1929, an unusual statistic for an outfielder. On May 27, 1977, Lyman Bostock, then with the Twins, had a busy day, snaring 12 putouts.

A fielder is credited with a putout if he catches a foul fly, as stated in the rule. Johnny Mostil, who played center field for the White Sox in the twenties, is the only major league center fielder ever to have caught a foul ball.

The Cardinals and Pirates played at Busch Stadium in St. Louis on August 27, 1958. In this game Cardinal shortstop Gene Freese was charged with an error and credited with a putout on the same play.

In the first inning the Pirates' Roberto Clemente hit a grounder to Freese. The Cardinal shortstop threw the ball over the first baseman's head for an error. Catcher Gene Green hustling down the line to back up the throw got the ball and tossed it to Freese to nail Clemente attempting to go to second.

10.11—*An assist shall be credited to each fielder who throws or deflects a batted or thrown ball in such a way that a putout results, or would have resulted except for a subsequent error by any fielder. Only one assist and no more shall be credited to each fielder who throws or deflects the ball in a run-down play which results in a putout, or would have resulted in a putout, except for a subsequent error.*

It is not often that an outfielder is credited with an assist. However, Don Buford of the Orioles, and the San Diego Padres' Al Ferrara each had two assists in one inning during the 1970 season.

Outfielder Walt Berger of the Boston Braves was the last flychaser to chalk up four assists in one game. Berger pulled off four assists on April 27, 1931.

On June 20, 1911, Springfield outfielder Lou Barbour registered three assists in one inning in a game against Hartford in the old Connecticut League.

The Reds defeated Philadelphia, 10-3, on July 22, 1906, without a single assist to their credit.

Jack McCarthy of the Cubs chalked up three assists in one game as an outfielder on April 26, 1905. McCarthy accomplished this feat by throwing out three Pirate runners at home plate, each of whom became the second out of a double play.

An unusual scoring play occurred on August 4, 1958, as the Milwaukee Braves met the Pittsburgh Pirates. The Pirates' Ramon Mejias lined to right center in the ninth inning but was called out for failing to tag first when the Braves appealed. Bill Bruton who retrieved the ball, relayed it to Johnny Logan at second. Logan unaware that Mejias missed first, threw the ball to pitcher Juan Pizarro on the mound. Pizarro then tossed the ball to Frank Torre at first to appeal the missed base. On the play, Bruton, Logan, and Pizarro were given assists, and Torre was credited with a putout.

According to 10.11(d), *Do not credit an assist to a fielder whose wild throw permits a runner to advance, even though the runner subsequently is put out as a result of continuous play. A play which follows a misplay (whether or not it is an error) is a new play, and the fielder making any misplay shall not be credited with an assist unless he takes part in the new play.*

This rule came alive in 1967 in a game between the Red Sox and White Sox. Boston's Jose Tartabull singled to right field scoring Lee Stange who was on second.

Walt "No Neck" Williams fielded the ball and threw to Tom McCraw, the cutoff man. McCraw then tossed to shortstop Ron Hansen in an effort to cut down Tartabull, who had rounded first base deliberately to draw the throw away from the plate. Hansen then threw the ball wild to first in an attempt to catch Tartabull. As the ball was about to roll into the Boston dugout, No Neck flew in from nowhere and stopped the ball. Williams then threw to Hansen at second in time to erase Tartabull.

Scoring on the unusual play went 9-3-6-9-6. Scorer Larry Claflin was able to give Williams only one assist on the play. Hansen, who nearly had an error, was saved by Williams and got a putout and an assist on the play.

Cincinnati shortstop Tom Corcoran came up with 14 assists on August 7, 1903. Bob Reeves, Washington Senator shortstop, had 13 assists in a game on the same date 24 years later.

On July 25, 1959, the White Sox and Orioles hooked up in a 17-inning duel. Oriole center fielder Willie Tasby didn't have a single fielding chance, though he played the entire game. During the game there were 154 fielding chances—100 putouts and 54 assists. The Orioles had 29 assists, and the White Sox had 25.

Dick Williams played all three outfield positions for the Orioles on August 30, 1958, in a game against the Red Sox and didn't have a single putout or assist as Baltimore beat Boston, 7-2.

Any misplay in fielding is an error in the game of baseball. *An error shall be charged for each misplay (fumble, muff or wild throw) which prolongs the time at bat of a batter or which prolongs the life of a runner, or which permits a runner to advance one or more bases.* (10.13)

The official scorer must make judgment on errors and tally up the total at the end of the game. (10.02=b-3)

In the butterfingers department, several players have committed three or more errors in a game. Cub shortstop Len Merullo had four miscues on September 13, 1942. On June 20, 1914, Ray Chapman booted four at the shortstop position for the Indians.

Since 1900, three infielders have been charged with five errors in a game. Second baseman Charles Hickman of the Washington Senators (September 29, 1905), and Nap Lajoie of the Philadelphia Athletics (April 22, 1915) each had five fumbles in a game. Third baseman Dave Brain of the Boston Braves committed five miscues at the hot corner on June 11, 1906.

Detroit had 12 errors in one game against Chicago on May 1, 1901. Chicago returned the favor committing 12 muffs when they played Detroit on May 6, 1903.

The Reds and Cubs combined for 25 errors in a double-header played on October 8, 1900.

It isn't very common to see a major league team commit three errors in a ball game, never mind three miscues during the same play. The comedy of errors occurred on the night of May 12, 1976, at Yankee Stadium in a game between the Yankees and Tigers.

With the Yankees leading, 5-1, Jim Mason and Mickey Rivers singled with one out in the fourth inning. Roy White lifted a fly ball to center field where Ron LeFlore dropped it, but recovered in time to throw Mason out at the plate as he tried to score from second.

However, catcher John Wockenfuss, thinking it was the third out, rolled the ball toward the mound, and the speedy Rivers kept running and scored. Pitcher Bill Laxton retrieved the ball but threw wildly past third base, and White came home with what proved to be the winning run.

When it was all over, LeFlore, Wockenfuss, and Laxton were each charged with an error.

Section (e) of the 10.13 rule states, *An error shall be charged against any fielder whose failure to stop, or try to stop, an accurately thrown ball permits a runner to advance, providing there was occasion for the throw. If such throw be made to second base, the scorer shall determine whether it was the duty of the second baseman or the shortstop to stop the ball, and an error shall be charged to the negligent player. NOTE: If in the scorer's judgment there was no occasion for the throw, an error shall be charged to the fielder who threw the ball.*

With a left-handed batter at the plate, it is the shortstop's responsibility to cover second base on a steal. During the 1958 season, shortstop Reuben Amaro of the Cardinals was charged with an error when he failed to cover second to receive a throw by catcher Hobie Landrith allowing Del Crandall of the Braves to steal second.

The number of double and triple plays participated in (10.02=b-(4)-(5), comes next in the official scorer's report.

Double plays and triple plays are dealt with in rule 10.12. *Credit participation in the double play or triple play to each fielder who earns a putout or an assist when two or three players are put out between the time a pitch is delivered and the time the ball next becomes dead or is next in possession of the pitcher in pitching position, unless an error or misplay intervenes between putouts.*

Unassisted double plays are infrequent accomplishments for any fielder, especially the pitcher. Ex-Cub pitcher Warren Hacker played with Buffalo in the International League in 1960 when he turned in an unassisted double killing against Richmond.

With Richmond runners on first and third, Hacker fielded Fritz Brickell's bouncer, sprinted to the third base line to tag Ken Hunt, who had been on third, and then outlegged and tagged out Jesse Gonder, who was trying to go from first to third.

There have been five unassisted triple plays in American League history, and the Cleveland Indians have been involved in all of them, three times as the victim. The National League has seen three unassisted triple plays in its history.

The first play of this type was executed by Neal Ball of the Cleveland Indians on July 19, 1909, in a game against the Red Sox. With Boston runners on first and second, Ball caught Amby McConnell's liner, touched second, retiring Heinie Wagner who was on his way to third base, and then tagged Jake Stahl as he came up to second. Ball also hit a home run that game, making him the only man to hit a home run in the same game in which he pulled an unassisted triple play.

More recently Ron Hansen pulled off an unassisted triple killing on

July 30, 1968, as a Senator shortstop against the Indians. Hansen caught Indians' Joe Azcue's line drive, stepped on second to retire Dave Nelson and tagged Russ Snyder coming from first.

The triple play most written about took place in the 1920 World Series when the Dodgers met the Cleveland Indians.

In the fifth inning of that game, the Dodgers had runners on first and second with nobody out. The hit and run was on with pitcher Clarence Mitchell at bat. Both runners took off as soon as pitcher Jim Bagby released the ball. Mitchell hit a line shot to second baseman Bill Wambsganss, who stepped on second to double up Pete Kilduff, and then spun around and tagged Otto Miller, who broke from first. This was the only unassisted triple play in World Series history.

Here is a 7-5-4-6 triple play that took California Angels' speedballer Nolan Ryan off the hook on June 27, 1972. The odd play helped Ryan and the Angels whip the Twins, 3-1.

This is what happened. Harmon Killebrew had opened the Twins' fourth inning with a single and moved to third on Steve Braun's double. Next, Jim Nettles flied to Jim Spencer in left. One out!

Killebrew faked a start from third, and Braun apparently thought he was running and also started to go. Third baseman Ken McMullen cut off Spencer's throw and relayed the ball to second baseman Sandy Alomar, who tagged the trapped Braun. Two out! Next Alomar fired to shortstop Leo Cardenas, covering third, and Cardenas tagged Killebrew who was, for some unexplained reason, standing a few feet off the base. Three out. Triple Play!

What might have been the most unusual triple play in baseball history took place at Fenway Park in Boston where the Sox met the Indians on September 7, 1935. The Red Sox had the bases loaded in the last of the ninth, none out, and Joe Cronin at bat against Oral Hildebrand. Cronin hit a line drive to Odell Hale, the Tribe's third baseman. The ball caromed off his forehead to shortstop Bill Knickerbocker on the fly. One out! Knickerbocker then threw to Roy Hughes at second. Two out! Hughes then fired to Hal Trosky at first. Three outs! Amen.

Cleveland outfielder Charlie Jamieson participated in two triple plays in 1928, a rare statistic for an outfielder. The first one came on May 23 against the White Sox and the second on June 19 against the Yankees.

In a most unusual back-to-back performance, the Detroit Tigers executed triple plays in two consecutive games against the Red Sox on June 6 and 7, 1908.

On his final at bat in the majors, Mets' catcher Joe Pignatano hit into a triple play in a game against the Cubs at Wrigley Field on the last day of the 1962 season.

The 1979 season saw the Red Sox and the Oakland A's each pull off three triple slayings.

10.03—(a) *In compiling the official score report, the official scorer shall list each player's name and his fielding position or positions in the order in which the player batted, or would have batted if the game ends before he gets to bat.*

Unusual names and spelling have always been a headache for official scorers. Things became confusing in Lubbock, Texas on May 3, 1956, when the Beaumont Exporters and the Lubbock Hubbers met in a Big State League game. In that game there were five players named Smith in the box score. To make matters worse, three of them were named George Smith.

Bob Uecker, sports announcer and television personality, was part of a weird batting order during the 1956 season playing for the Eau Claire (Northern League) Braves. Uecker's team came to the plate in the exact reverse order, 9-8-7-6-5-4-3-2-1, of the players' position numbers as used in most scoring systems. Uecker was the catcher and batted in the number 8 position.

Bert Campaneris of the A's played all nine positions in a game against the Angels on September 8, 1965. The Angels won 5-3, in 13 innings. Cesar Tovar also completed the same stunt in 1968.

The three Alou brothers—Felipe, Matty, and Jesus—played in the Giant outfield at the same time on September 15, 1963.

The official scorer had to list Stan Musial as a pitcher after he pitched to the Cubs' Frank Baumholtz on the last day of the 1952 season. Musial threw one pitch, which was hit to third sacker Billy Johnson.

Art Hoelskoetter played 299 games for the Cardinals from 1905 to 1908; 77 were at third base, 16 were at short, 77 were at second, 28 were at first, 49 were as a catcher, 15 were as a pitcher, and 20 were in the outfield. How's that for versatility?

Unlike Hoelskoetter, Luis Aparicio played in 2,599 games in 18 years and never played an inning at any position except shortstop.

Official scorers have listed some very historic names. Such handles as Davey Crockett, John Kennedy, Ethan Allen, Albert Schweitzer, and John Paul Jones have filled major league box scores at one time or another. For poetic justice, a player named Walt Whitman also made his living playing the diamond sport.

The number of passed balls allowed by each catcher (10.02=e) is part of the official scorers report.

Rule 10.15(b) says, *A catcher shall be charged with a passed ball when he fails to hold or to control a legally pitched ball which should have been held or controlled with ordinary effort, thereby permitting a runner or runners to advance.*

Yankee catcher Bill Dickey handled 751 chances for the Yankees in 1931 without a passed ball. Pirate catcher Al Todd was perfect in 712 chances in 1937.

On the negative side, J. C. Martin, who had the misfortune of handling knuckleball artist Hoyt Wilhelm, holds the modern record for passed balls in a season, 33 in 1965 for the White Sox.

Wilhelm also had a negative statistical effect on Angels' catcher Tom Egan and Giant backstop, Ray Kaat. Egan was charged with five passed balls on July 28, 1970. In 1954, Kaat was once charged with four passed balls in one inning, on the shaky receiving end of Wilhelm.

The number of runners left on base (LOB) is a statistic (10.02=g) that haunts managers throughout the season. It is not a good day when a team leaves 10 runners on base. When a team leaves 20 men on base, as the Yankees did when they played the Red Sox on September 21, 1956, it is a disaster. The Yankees stranded their runners in a nine-inning game.

The Twins and Seattle Pilots hooked up in an 18-inning affair on July 19, 1969. Combined they had an unbelievable 44 runners LOB. The Twins had 23 and the Pilots 21.

10.02—(h) *Names of batters who hit home runs with the bases full* is also on the official scorer's checklist. Lou Gehrig had 23 grand-slam home runs during his career, a record that might never be broken. Seven players have hit two bases-filled home runs during the same game. The last one to do it was Frank Robinson on June 26, 1970, when he was a member of the Baltimore Orioles.

"Frosty" Bill Duggleby, a pitcher for the Philadelphia National League team, hit a grand-slam home run in his first major league at bat ever on April 21, 1898.

Pitcher Tony Cloninger of the Braves collected nine ribbys on July 3, 1966 against the Giants, as he hit two grand-slam homers.

Horace Clarke, who labored at second base for several seasons with the Yankees, has the distinction of hitting his first two major league home runs with the bases loaded. That's not bad for a guy with only 27 career home runs.

The All-Star game was first played in 1933 at Chicago's Comiskey Park. There has never been a grand-slam home run hit in the annual affair.

In 1938, Rudy York hit three grand-slam home runs during the month of May.

On September 16, 1974 during a double-header between the Braves and Reds, three grand-slam home runs were hit, one by Cesar Geronimo (Reds, first game), one by Darrell Evans (Braves, first game), and another by Johnny Bench (Reds, second game).

Jimmie Foxx and Roy Sievers hold the rare distinction of having hit pinch-hit grand-slam home runs in each league.

There have been 73 grand-slam homers hit in extra innings since 1900. Four players did it twice: Cy Williams, Roger Maris, Tommy

Davis, and Cookie Rojas. No player ever hit a grand-slam later than the 16th inning. Clyde Vollmer hit a grand-slam in the 16th frame playing for the Red Sox in 1951.

Jim Palmer has pitched over 3,000 innings of baseball during his magnificent career. And would you believe he has never given up a grand slam home run!

On the negative side, pitchers Ned Garver, Milt Pappas, Lindy McDaniel, and Jim Brewer have each given up nine grand slams during their careers.

The official scorer also logs the *names of batters who ground into force double plays and reverse force double plays.* (10.02=i)

There has been little statistical research regarding the double play. The National League started compiling grounded into double plays (GDP) in 1933 and the American League only since 1940.

It might surprise you, but Hank Aaron holds the career record for GDPs with 320. Hank is followed by Brooks Robinson, who never was noted for his blinding speed. It should also be noted that 14 of the top 15 players who lead in career totals for GDPs were right-handed hitters. The only left-handed swatter was Stan Musial.

The Reds' Ernie Lombardi led the N.L. in GDPs four different times. Jackie Jensen (Red Sox) and George Scott (Red Sox-Brewers) led the A.L. in grounding into twin killings three times.

Pitching strategy at Fenway Park with its "Green Monster" appears to be related to the fact that the Red Sox have had players lead the A.L. in GDPs 13 different times. Jensen's GDP total of 32 in 1954 is a major league record.

Leon "Goose" Goslin of the Tigers hit into four consecutive twin killings on April 28, 1934, in a game against the Indians. Joe Torre, playing for the Mets, grounded into four consecutive DPs against the Astros on July 21, 1975. Burleigh Grimes hit into two double plays and one triple play in the same game playing for the Dodgers in 1925.

Augie Galan of the Chicago Cubs batted 646 times without hitting into a double play in 1935. Dick McAuliffe of the Tigers had 570 at bats in 1968 without hitting into a double play.

The next item is the *names of runners caught stealing.* (10.02=j)

Ty Cobb stole a total of 892 bases during his career. But would you believe he holds the mark for the number of times caught stealing during a season, being nailed 38 times in 1915.

The scorer must record *the number of outs when the winning run is scored, if the game is won in the last half-inning,* (10.02=k), *the names of the umpires* (10.02=m), *and the time required to play the game* (10.02=n).

In reference to the names of the umpires (10.02=m), Bill McGowan, former A.L. umpire, was listed by the official scorer in 2,541 consecutive games. McGowan umpired in the American League from 1925 to 1954. The "Iron Man" umpire had his consecutive string of games over a period of 16½ years.

Babe Pinelli umpired in the big show from 1935-1956. According to an article written by Larry Gerlach to the 1979 Society For American Baseball Research Journal, Pinelli in a letter to the Baseball Hall of Fame Historian, stated he did not miss a regulation game in his 22 years of service. Babe was the plate umpire the day Don Larsen pitched his perfect game against the Dodgers in the 1956 World Series. Remarkably this was Pinelli's last plate assignment ever as he retired from baseball following the 1956 season.

Concerning *the time of a ball game,* the Giants-Phillies game on September 28, 1919, was completed in 51 minutes. On the other hand, it took the Mets and Giants 7 hours and 23 minutes to finish a 23-inning game on May 31, 1964.

The next chore on the scorer's agenda is to compute the score by innings for each team. (10.02=l)

If you think that the Red Sox 17 run inning in 1953 was something special, you should have been in Tarboro, North Carolina on June 2, 1951. Tarboro had a Class D minor league team that played Wilson that night. Tarboro exploded for 24 runs in one inning. Twenty-five men went to bat before an out was made, with a total of 29 men batting in the inning, as Tarboro won the game, 31-4.

Hopscotching through section 10.00, we come across rule 10.07(d). *When a batter, after making a safe hit, is called out for having failed to touch a base, the last base he reached safely shall determine if he shall be credited with a one-base hit, a two-base hit or a three-base hit. If he is called out after missing home base, he shall be credited with a three-base hit. If he is called out for missing third base, he shall be credited with a two-base hit. If he is called out for missing first base, he shall be charged with a time at bat, but no hit.*

Cleveland's Rocky Colavito lost credit for a hit and saved Kansas City Athletics' outfielder Bob Cerv from an error when he missed first base after hitting a hard line drive to left field. Colavito attempted to take second base when he saw Cerv's throw to the infield go awry. Having seen Colavito miss first base, A's first sacker Dick Williams called for the ball. Umpire Larry Napp ruled Colavito out for missing the base. The running error not only cost Rocky a hit, but allowed Cerv to be credited with an assist instead of being charged with an error. The game was played on April 19, 1959.

Sections (f) and (g) of the 10.07 rule deal with game-ending hits. *Subject to the provisions of 10.07(g), when the batter ends a game with a safe hit which drives in as many runs as are necessary to put his team in the lead, he shall be credited with only as many bases on his hit as are advanced by the runner who scores the winning run, and then only if the batter runs out his hit for as many bases as are advanced by the runner who scores the winning run. NOTE—Apply this rule even when the batter is theoretically entitled to more bases because of being awarded an "automatic" extra-base hit under various provisions of Playing Rules 6.09 and 7.05.*

Toronto's Stan Jok apparently hit a bases loaded home run to defeat Rochester, 6-2, in the last inning on September 6, 1957. However, thirty minutes after the game ended, umpire Walter Vanderhoof decided Jok's game-winning hit, which hit the scoreboard, had not left the park and was only a single, making the final score 3-2.

10.07—(g) *When the batter ends a game with a home run hit out of the playing field, he and any runners on base are entitled to score.*

Under the old rule a batter received credit only for the number of bases that was needed to drive in the winning run, regardless whether the hit was a home run or a single. Babe Ruth lost a home run under this rule in a game between the Indians and Red Sox at Fenway Park on July 8, 1918. With no score in the bottom of the tenth, Amos Strunk singled for the Red Sox and Ruth followed with a home run into the right field bleachers. According to the rule at the time, this wasn't a home run. Ruth was credited with a triple, and the game ended with the Red Sox winning, 1-0. Had Strunk been on third base when Ruth hit the home run, the Babe would have only received credit for a single.

In 1919, Frank Baker of the Yankees hit a ninth-inning home run at the Polo Grounds with the score tied and the bases loaded. Baker was credited with only a single and one run batted in.

Rule 10.02(c) sections (1-15) and 10.02(d) sections (1-3) deal with statistics concerning the pitcher that must be compiled by the official scorer.

In the next few pages I will cover some of the pitching statistics contained in the official scorer's report. Such things as earned runs, strikeouts, bases on balls, and wild pitches will be touched on. Cases concerning how a winning and losing pitcher is determined will also be covered.

The scoring of one-hit and/or no-hit games has been a touchy issue. Because of this problem, some newspapers have been reluctant to have their writers serve as official scorers. Newspapers in certain cities have even gone as far as to ban any sportswriter on their staff from being the official scorer in major league games.

The *number of hits allowed* (10.02=c-4) is often the result of decisions made by the official scorer.

John Drebinger of *The New York Times* was the official scorer at Yankee Stadium on August 25, 1952, as the Yanks entertained the Tigers. In the third inning of that game, Yankee shortstop Phil Rizzuto hit a slow roller to Detroit shortstop Johnny Pesky, who charged the ball but had trouble getting it out of his glove. Drebinger scored the play an error. Dan Daniel of *The New York World Telegram* challenged Drebinger's decision, claiming you couldn't call a ball that got stuck in a fielder's glove an error. The error was then changed to a hit.

The call became more serious as the game went on, since Virgil Trucks was pitching a one-hitter in the sixth inning for the Tigers.

Finally Drebinger called Pesky on the special telephone that connects the press box with the dugout. Pesky said he should have been charged with an error, admitting that he allowed the ball to squirt out of his hand.

On the basis of Pesky's testimony, the call was reversed back to an error, and Trucks went on to pitch a no-hitter.

Only nineteen times in baseball history has a pitcher gone 8 2/3 innings of pitching no-hit baseball and then lose it by giving up a hit to the last batter. Among the more popular figures that this has happened to are Johnny Morrison, Bill Bevens, Billy Pierce, Ken Holtzman, Tommy Bridges, Whitlow Wyatt, Herb Pennock, Grover Cleveland Alexander, and Ken Brett. The latter's almost no-hitter took place in a game between the White Sox and Angels during the 1976 season that ended in a controversial note involving official scorer Don Merry of *The Long Beach Independent Press-Telegram.* The play in question was as follows.

The Angels' Jerry Remy bounced the ball to the left side of Sox third sacker Jorge Orta. According to Brett, "Orta took two or three steps and his glove hand wasn't extended. The ball was hit slowly and it went right under his glove." Merry said, "He just never got to the ball, there's no way I can give him an error if he doesn't get to the ball." Brett believed he was robbed by the call. Veteran baseball writer Jerome Holtzman of *The Chicago Sun-Times* said, "It was a terrible call."

An error, the rules state, shall be charged when in the scorer's judgment, the fielder could have handled the ball with ordinary effort. Holtzman said, "The book says ordinary effort, but I think with two outs in the ninth inning of a no-hitter, a fielder should be expected to give more than ordinary effort."

Phil Pepe reports the story behind a no-hitter pitched in 1917 in his book *No Hitter.* According to Pepe, "On May 5, 1917, Ernie Koob of the St. Louis Browns set down the Chicago White Sox in a tainted no-hitter. Koob actually was touched for an infield single in the first inning, but when the game ended with that being the only hit off him, the official scorer called a meeting of the writers covering the game. It was agreed to change the hit to an error on the third baseman."

It's a rarity to have a no-hitter pitched on any day during the baseball season. But how about two no-hitters on the same day. It happened in the year 1898. Ted Breitenstein of Cincinnati pitched one on the morning of April 22, 1898, and Jim Hughes of Baltimore duplicated the feat the same afternoon.

Alva "Bobo" Holloman in his first big league start for the St. Louis Browns, hurled a no-hitter on May 6, 1953, against the Philadelphia Athletics. Since 1893, he is the only man to accomplish this feat.

In chapter 9, Johnny Vander Meer's back-to-back no-hitters were discussed. Johnny pitched one more no-hitter that is never mentioned. His last no-hitter came while pitching for Tulsa in the Texas League. The opposing manager that day was Harry Craft. A strange thing about this story is that Craft was the center fielder who made the last putout in the game when Vander Meer pitched his second consecutive no-hitter against the Dodgers.

On May 2, 1917, the Cubs and Reds met at Wrigley Field, at that time called Weeghman Park. On that day, Cincinnati pitcher Fred Toney and Chicago hurler "Hippo" Vaughn each pitched nine innings of scoreless no-hit baseball. The Reds scored in the top of the tenth to ruin Vaughn's no-hit bid, but Toney retired the Cub batters in order in the bottom of the tenth for a ten-inning no-hitter.

Sandy Koufax and Nolan Ryan have each tossed four no-hitters, a well-known baseball fact. But did you know that White Sox catcher Ray Schalk has caught four no-hitters? Schalk, elected to the Hall of Fame in 1955, caught the four no-hitters from 1914 to 1922.

On the other side of the coin, Harley Parker surrendered 26 hits on June 21, 1901, pitching for the Reds against Brooklyn. Horace Lisenbee, Philadelphia Athletics' pitcher, also gave up 26 hits in a game against the White Sox on September 11, 1936. Merle Adkins, pitching for the Red Sox July 8, 1902, surrendered 12 hits in one inning. Phillies' hurler Reggie Grabowski gave up 11 hits in the ninth inning on August 4, 1934.

The number of *runs, earned runs,* and *home runs* allowed (10.02=c-

5-7) must also be contained in the official scorer's report.

On May 18, 1912, Detroit chucker J. Travers was shelled for 24 runs by the Philadelphia Athletics.

Frank "Lefty" O'Doul pitched for the Red Sox on July 7, 1923, in a game against the Cleveland Indians. Pitching in the sixth inning of that game, O'Doul gave up 13 runs in Boston's 27-3 loss. O'Doul gave up pitching a couple of years later and turned to the outfield. He eventually led the N.L. in batting twice.

In contrast to Travers and O'Doul, the Chicago Cubs' Ed Reulbach shut out Brooklyn twice the same day on September 26, 1908, pitching 18 innings of scoreless baseball.

Cardinal pitcher Bob Gibson, who once played for the Harlem Globetrotters, had an earned run average (ERA) of 1.12 in 1968, but Ferdinand Schupp achieved an ERA of 0.90 pitching for the Giants in 1916.

Gibson turned in his 1.12 ERA over a stretch of 305 innings, while Schupp's record was based on only 140 innings of pitching. "Gibby" broke Walter Johnson's 1.14 ERA title for pitchers with over 300 innings in a season. If it were not for a farce game, Johnson would still hold the record he established in 1913.

The Senators and Red Sox played a season-ending game at Washington on October 4, 1913. The meaningless game developed into a comedy that saw the Senators use eight different pitchers, three of whom were nonpitchers. Johnson played center field for the first eight innings. In the ninth inning with the Senators leading, 10-3, Johnson came in to pitch with a man on first. He then grooved a few pitches giving up a single to Steve Yerkes and a double to Clyde Engle. Johnson then returned to the outfield and was eventually charged with two runs, as Engle and Yerkes both scored. The Senators held on for a farcical 10-9 victory. When the league records were issued in 1913, the A.L. statistician paid no attention to Johnson's pitching stint in the farce game. He credited Johnson with a 1.09 ERA, which lasted in the record book for many years. It wasn't until several years after "The Big Train" retired that a game by game check of his career revealed that the two men (Engle and Yerkes) he had put on base in the joke game had scored and had to be charged as earned runs, thereby increasing his ERA to 1.14. The game cost Johnson the ERA record 55 years later when Gibson logged that nifty 1.12 ERA for the Cardinals.

Rule 10.23(b) says, *The individual pitching champion shall be the pitcher with the lowest earned-run average, provided that he has pitched at least as many innings as the number of games scheduled for each club in his league that season.* (162 innings)

To compute a pitcher's earned run average, you multiply the total earned runs charged against his pitching by 9, and divide the result by the total number of innings he pitched.

Grover Cleveland Alexander and Sandy Koufax led the N.L. in the ERA department five different years. In 1955 the Pirates finished the season in the N.L. cellar. However, pitcher Bob Friend compiled a league-leading 2.83 ERA pitching for the hapless Bucks. Friend finished the season with a 14-9 record that year.

In 1916, the St. Louis Browns staff had an earned run average of 6.24. Imagine if they played their home games in Fenway Park!

Joe Cleary, who pitched to nine men for the 1945 Senators, struck out one batter for his only out. He gave up five hits and three bases on balls. The luckless Washington chucker was charged with seven earned runs and was credited with pitching one-third of an inning. Cleary's career ERA mark stands at 189.00. Believe it or not!

Concerning earned runs, *An earned run is a run for which the pitcher is held accountable . . . an earned run shall be charged every time a runner reaches home base by the aid of safe hits, sacrifice bunts, a sacrifice fly, stolen bases, putouts, fielder's choices, bases on balls, hit batters, balks or wild pitches (including a wild pitch on third strike which permits a batter to reach first base) before fielding chances have been offered to put out the offensive team. For the purpose of this rule, a defensive interference penalty shall be construed as a fielding chance. (1) A wild pitch is solely the pitcher's fault, and contributes to an earned run just as a base on balls or a balk.* (10.18)

What first appeared to be an unearned run for the Cardinals was turned into an earned run in their June 30, 1958 game against the Dodgers in St. Louis because of a wild pitch.

The Cardinals had Don Blasingame on second and Stan Musial on first with one out, when Ken Boyer hit back to the pitcher. Musial was forced at second, but as Don Zimmer threw wildly to first, Blasingame scored and Boyer ended up at second.

After Gene Green walked, both runners moved up on a Johnny Klippstein wild pitch. Had the error not occurred, Blasingame would have scored on the wild pitch since he would have been on third.

Sections (c) and (d) of this rule led to a controversial scoring decision by Dick Young that was later reversed by N.L. prexy Chub Feeney. Rule 10.18(c) declares, *No run shall be earned when scored by a runner whose life is prolonged by an error, if such runner would have been put out by errorless play.*

And section (d) says, *No run shall be earned when the runner's advance is aided by an error, a passed ball, or defensive interference or obstruction, if the scorer judges that the run would not have scored without the aid of such misplay.*

The play in question took place on July 30, 1974, at Shea Stadium, where the Mets hosted the Pirates. Jack Lang reported the details to *The Sporting News.*

> In the disputed play, there was one out in the Mets' half of the sixth, with Jerry Grote on first base. Cleon Jones, playing with bad knees at the time, hit a routine grounder to second baseman Rennie Stennett, who flipped to shortstop Mario Mendoza for what appeared to be the start of a certain double play.
>
> However, Mendoza dropped the perfect throw and both Grote and Jones were safe. Ed Kranepool followed with a three-run homer. At the end of the inning, Young surprised the press box with the ruling that all three runs off Bruce Kison were "unearned."
>
> Young reasoned that had Mendoza held the ball, a double play surely would have been made. No one questioned the fact. He also pointed out that nowhere in the playing rules or scoring rules is there anything in writing which says an official scorer "cannot assume a double play."

In reversing Young's decision and ruling two of the three runs earned, Feeney pointed out that if scorers are given such latitude where they can begin assuming what might have happened instead of following what actually does happen on the field, inconsistencies in scoring would pop up every day.

Young said, "I only wish he had contacted me and talked to me first before he reversed my decision. I was there, I saw what happened and I called it the way I saw it. I used common sense in my decision, which is what scoring is all about."

According to Feeney, "Official scorers have no right to assume a double play, particularly if the first out is not made."

Pitchers who commonly give up home runs are known to serve the "fat pitch" or the "gopher." Hall of Famer Robin Roberts gave up 502 homers in his career. Pitching for Los Angeles in the A.L. on July 31, 1963, Paul Foytack gave up four home runs in one inning. Ben Wade showed his generosity to enemy batters by yielding four round-trippers in the same inning on May 28, 1954, while pitching for the Brooklyn Dodgers. The last pitcher to be whacked for six home runs in one game was George Caster of the Philadelphia A's, on September 24, 1940.

Bases on balls are probably the pitcher's worst enemy. Henry Mathewson, Christy's brother, gave up 14 free passes pitching for the Giants on October 5, 1906. Bill Gray walked 8 men in one inning on August 28, 1909. The Senator pitcher walked 7 of the 8 in succession in a game against Chicago. Bruno Haas of the A's walked 16 Tigers in his major league pitching debut on May 9, 1916. Tommy Byrne passed 16 batters pitching for the St. Louis Browns in a 13-inning game in 1951. Conversely, Bill Fischer, who pitched for the Athletics and Tigers in 1961, went 84 1/3 consecutive innings without giving up a single walk.

Hit batsmen is another statistic that the official scorer takes into account. White Sox pitcher Tommy John hit four batters in one game on June 15, 1968. Since 1950, three pitchers have hit three batters in one inning. They are Tom Morgan (Yankees—1954), Steve Ridzik (Giants—1956), and Raul Sanchez (Cincinnati—1960).

Walter Johnson, Warren Spahn, Christy Mathewson, Lefty Grove, Rube Waddell, Sandy Koufax, and Bob Gibson rank high among the great strikeout artists in the twentieth century. Tom Seaver, Steve Carlton, and Nolan Ryan each have registered 19 strikeouts in a nine-inning game. Seaver's performance came on April 22, 1970, while Carlton struck out 19 Mets and lost on September 15, 1969. Ryan fanned 19 Red Sox batters on August 12, 1974. Tom Cheney of the Senators struck out 21 Oriole hitters in a 16-inning game played on September 12, 1962. Bob Feller racked up 348 strikeouts in 1946. Barney McCoskey of the A's was the only regular player in the A.L. that was not struck out by Feller during the season.

Emil Levson, Cleveland pitcher, proved that you don't have to be a strikeout king to win games. On August 26, 1926, Levson beat the Yankees twice on the same day (5-1 and 6-1) and never registered a strikeout during his 18 innings of pitching. This was the last time anyone has pitched two complete games in one day in the major leagues.

10.15—(a) *A wild pitch shall be charged when a legally delivered ball is so high, or so wide, or so low that the catcher does not stop and control the ball by ordinary effort, thereby permitting a runner or runners to advance.*

(1) A wild pitch shall be charged when a legally delivered ball touches the ground before reaching home plate and is not handled by the catcher, permitting a runner or runners to advance.

The Senators' immortal Walter Johnson was once charged with four in one inning on September 21, 1914. The Dodgers' Don Sutton threw three wild ones in the fourth inning in a game against the Giants on September 11, 1970.

During his 16 seasons in the major leagues, Dick Hall was charged with only one wild pitch.

Johnny Miljus, pitching for the Pirates in the 1927 World Series against the Yankees, let go with two of the costliest wild pitches of all time in the fourth game of the series.

Babe Ruth was the Yankee batter in the bottom of the ninth with runners on first and second and the score tied, 3-3. With Ruth at the plate, Miljus let go with his first wild one, allowing the runners to each advance one base. Miljus then purposely passed the Babe with first base open. The Pirate hurler then struck out Lou Gehrig and Bob

Meusel in succession, but still had to face Tony Lazzeri. In his eagerness, Miljus put too much on the ball and tossed it over the catcher's head. The wild pitch allowed Earl Coombs to cross the plate with the winning run and give the Yankees the Series.

The number of *balks* committed is also listed. We already saw where Bob Shaw balked five times during the same game. The Yankees' Vic Raschi was charged with four balks on May 3, 1950. Jim Owens of Cincinnati joined Shaw in 1963 by balking three times in one inning. The hapless Mets' staff balked 20 times in 1963.

The next segment of the 10.02 rule, 10.02(d), requests the scorer to give the following additional data: *(1) Name of the winning pitcher, (2) Name of the losing pitcher, (3) Names of the starting pitcher and the finishing pitcher for each team, (4) Name of pitcher credited with save.*

The Cards and Cubs clashed in a double-header on May 10, 1959. In the first game, Elmer Singleton was credited with the Cubs' win and Lindy McDaniel took the loss for the Cardinals. In the second game the situation reversed itself with McDaniel gaining the victory and Singleton the defeat.

The same thing happened on May 31, 1943, as the Indians and Senators hooked up in a twin bill. The Senators' Alex Carrasquel won the opener and lost the second game while Pete Center of the Indians lost the opener but won the second game.

Cy Young is the record-holder for most games won with 511 career victories. Cy also holds the record for most games lost, with 315.

Elroy Face had a winning percentage of .947 in 1959 with a record of 18-1 pitching for the Pirates, a record for highest winning percentage in a season. Elroy also leads all pitchers in major league history in giving up 21 extra-inning home runs during his career.

The Braves' Warren Spahn helped to make rule 10.03 (e-2) come alive. The rule says, *If a regulation game is forfeited, include the record of all individual and team actions up to the time of forfeit. If the winning team by forfeit is ahead at the time of forfeit, enter as winning and losing pitchers the players who would have qualified if the game had been called at the time of forfeit. If the winning team by forfeit is behind or if the score is tied at the time of forfeit, do not enter a winning or losing pitcher. If a game is forfeited before it becomes a regulation game, include no records. Report only the fact of the forfeit.*

Spahn was the starting pitcher for the Braves when they met the Giants in New York on September 26, 1942. In the bottom of the eighth inning with the Giants winning, 5-2, several youngsters who had been admitted to the Polo Grounds for bringing scrap metal as a contribution to the war effort swarmed all over the field and caused so much confusion that umpire Ziggy Sears forfeited the game to the Braves. According to the rule it was impossible for Spahn to be the winning pitcher, since the Braves were behind at the time the game was forfeited.

The 1942 season was Spahn's first season with the Braves. Because of the forfeited game, the official averages show he had no victories, no defeats, and no ties, yet was credited with one complete game.

Rule 10.19(a-g) is a very long and detailed rule explaining the winning and losing pitcher. I will just bring out a few key sections to illustrate certain points. The first section, 10.19(a) says, *Credit the starting pitcher with a game won only if he has pitched at least five complete innings and his team not only is in the lead when he is replaced but remains in the lead the remainder of the game.*

Frank Yeutter of *The Philadelphia Bulletin* was the official scorer on August 22, 1957, at Philadelphia where the Phillies met the Cardinals. Yeutter in a capricious interpretation of the rules, ignored the rule stated above in awarding the decision of the game to Billy Muffett. However, N.L. president Warren Giles overruled Yeutter's controversial decision.

Here is the story: Cardinal starter Larry Jackson was knocked out of the box in the sixth inning without retiring a single batter, but he departed with a 6-3 lead. Muffett pitched excellent ball the rest of the way and was given the win by Yeutter. The official scorer claimed that he conferred with Philadelphia and St. Louis writers, plus Jackson and manager Fred Hutchinson of the Cardinals, and all agreed that the victory should go to Muffett. A few days later, Giles reversed the decision of the official scorer and declared Jackson the winning pitcher under a strict interpretation of 10.19(a).

The rule leaves much to be desired. The following case, which occurred during the 1976 season, well illustrates the weakness of the rule.

Oakland pitcher Mike Torrez pitched eight innings of four-hit shutout ball. Paul Lindblad relieved Torrez in the top of the ninth with the Athletics leading the Twins, 1-0. Lindblad gave up two runs and four hits in the ninth inning. In the bottom of the ninth, Oakland scored four runs to gain the victory. Lindblad, although pitching ineffectively, was credited with the win.

The official scorer used rule 10.19(c-4) in making his decision on June 21, 1972, in a game between the Angels and Orioles. In the seventh inning of that game, Lloyd Allen relieved Angel starter Rudy May. Allen faced two men and gave up a hit that scored a run. After the Angels scored four runs in the seventh to go ahead, 6-3, Allen was relieved by Eddie Fisher, who yielded one hit over the last two innings. Technically Allen should have been given the win since the Angels went ahead while he was pitching, but in the eyes of the official scorer, Fisher was more effective. Rule 10.19(c-4) states, *Normally the winning relief pitcher shall be the one who is the pitcher of record when his team assumes the lead and maintains it to the finish of the game. EXCEPTION: Do not credit a victory to a relief pitcher who pitches briefly or ineffectively if a succeeding relief pitcher pitches effectively in helping to maintain his team in the lead. In such case, credit the succeeding relief pitcher with the victory.*

Preacher Roe cashed in on a victory by throwing just one pitch while pitching for the Pirates against the Dodgers on May 5, 1946.

Roe was brought in from the bull pen in the top of the sixth inning and replaced Nick Strincevich with the score tied, 3-3. On Roe's first pitch, the Dodgers' Bob Ramazzotti broke for the plate from third and was tagged out by Billy Salkeld.

The Pirates scored in the bottom of the sixth to go ahead, 4-3. The game was called after six innings by umpire Beans Reardon giving Roe the win after throwing one pitch. Rule 10.19(c-2) says, *Whenever the score is tied the game becomes a new contest insofar as the winning and losing pitcher is concerned.* Since the score was tied, 3-3, when Roe entered the game, Preacher became the pitcher of record.

The Yankees and Dodgers met in the 1947 World Series. Dodger relief pitcher Hugh Casey was the winning pitcher of the fourth game of the Series, accomplishing the victory by only throwing one pitch. Casey relieved Hank Behrman in the top of the ninth inning with the bases loaded and the Yankees leading, 2-1. The Yankees' Tommy Henrich hit Casey's first pitch back to the mound. The Dodger pitcher threw to catcher Bruce Edwards who touched the plate and then tossed to first to double up "Old Reliable." The Dodgers then scored two runs in the bottom of the ninth on Cookie Lavagetto's drive over Henrich's head in right field, scoring Al Gionfriddo and Eddie Miksis. The hit broke up Yankee pitcher Floyd "Bill" Bevens' bid for a no-hitter. Bevens pitched eight and two-thirds innings without permitting a hit. Bevens almost pitched a no-hitter while walking nine Dodger batters that day.

In the 1954 All-Star game, Dean Stone of the Washington Senators was declared the winning pitcher without retiring a batter. Stone, who relieved Chicago's Bob Keegan in the eighth inning with two outs, faced Duke Snider. Red Schoendienst was on third and Alvin Dark on first with the N.L. leading, 9-8. Stone worked Snider to a one ball, one strike count when Schoendienst tried to steal home, but was tagged out by A.L. catcher Yogi Berra.

In the bottom of the eighth, the A.L. scored three runs to go ahead, 11-9. Virgil Trucks then replaced Stone in the ninth to preserve the win for Stone who never retired even one batter.

Because of rule 10.18(g) a relief pitcher can walk a batter who eventually scores the winning run and still not be the losing pitcher. According to the rule, *When pitchers are changed during an inning, the relief pitcher shall not be charged with any run (earned or unearned) scored by a runner who was on base at the time he entered the game, nor for runs scored by any runner who reaches base on a fielder's choice which puts out a runner left on base by the preceding pitcher.*

This is what happened at Cincinnati when the Phillies beat the

Reds, 3-2, on May 13, 1967. In the eighth inning with the score tied, 2-2, the Phillies' Gary Sutherland led off the inning with a double to left center off Reds' hurler Bill McCool. Ted Abernathy came in to relieve McCool.

Richie Allen then grounded out to first, sending Sutherland to third. Abernathy walked pinch hitter Bill White, putting runners at the corners. Tony Gonzalez was then sent in to run for White.

Cookie Rojas tried to squeeze Sutherland home, but Sutherland was called out at the plate.

On the out Gonzalez took second base. Johnny Callison then singled to left center scoring Gonzalez, who became the winning run. Because of the inning's proceedings, the run and the defeat were both charged to McCool.

Also included in rule 10.18(g) are the following words: *When a pitcher puts runners on base, and is relieved, he shall be charged with all runs subsequently scored up to and including the number of runners he left on base when he left the game, unless such runners are put out without action by the batter, i.e., caught stealing, picked off base, or called out for interference when a batter-runner does not reach first base on the play.*

Jim Stump was victimized by this part of the rule pitching for Charleston in an American Association game against Denver on May 9, 1958.

Stump entered the game in the third inning with Charleston ahead, 4-3, and Denver runners on first and second.

Gordon Windhorn then singled home the tying run that was charged to starting pitcher Bob Bruce. Jim McManus moved to second on the hit.

While pitching to John Blanchard, Stump picked off McManus at second. McManus was the last runner chargeable to Bruce. So when Denver scored five additional runs that inning and stayed ahead to win, Stump was charged with the loss since the go-ahead run (Windhorn) was his responsibility. Had it not been for the pickoff, the go ahead run would have been charged to Bruce and the defeat with it.

On June 29, 1958, Billy Muffett of the Cardinals had a workless appearance against the Phillies.

In the bottom of the eighth inning, the Phillies were trailing, 4-3, with runners on first and third and nobody out. Muffett came in to relieve Morrie Martin. Before Muffett could throw a pitch, the game was suspended under the Sunday curfew law.

N.L. president Warren Giles ruled that a new pitcher could pick up in the playout, since Muffett had gone to Omaha but was recalled in time for the July 29 playout. However, Jim Brosnan resumed the game for the Cardinals, who won the game, 4-3.

As a consequence, Muffett appeared in the box score of the game without having thrown a ball, without having disposed of a batter, without having seen the side retired, and without having been on the mound at the conclusion of the game.

Regarding the starting and finishing pitcher, Warren Spahn led the N.L. nine different years in games completed. From 1890 to 1911, Cy Young completed 751 games out of 818 started.

Relief specialist Hoyt Wilhelm finished 635 games during his playing career.

As stated in rule 10.19(f), *No pitcher shall be credited with pitching a shutout unless he pitches the complete game, or unless he enters the game with none out before the opposing team has scored in the first inning, puts out the side without a run scoring and pitches all the rest of the game. When two or more pitchers combine to pitch a shutout a notation to that effect should be included in the league's official pitching records.*

Starting pitcher Babe Ruth was ejected from a game on June 23, 1917, while pitching for the Red Sox in a game against the Senators. Ruth was given the thumb by umpire Clarence Owens after walking the first batter. Babe was relieved by Ernie Shore. The runner on first, Ray Morgan, was caught stealing while Shore was pitching to the second batter. Shore then retired the next 26 batters to complete a "perfect" game.

On the final day of the 1975 season, four Oakland hurlers—Vida Blue, Glenn Abbott, Paul Lindblad, and Rollie Fingers—combined for a no-hitter against the Angels.

The Orioles' Steve Barber (8 2/3) and Stu Miller (1/3) combined to pitch a no-hitter against the Tigers on April 30, 1967 and lost, 2-1.

On July 28, 1976, John "Blue Moon" Odom and Francisco Javier Barrios pitched a combined 2-1, no-hit victory, tarnished by 11 walks. Odom pitched the first five innings and gave up 9 walks. Barrios finished the last four frames and gave up 2 walks.

According to rule 10.20 a pitcher is credited with a save when he meets all three of the following conditions: *(a) He is the finishing pitcher in a game won by his club; and (b) He is not the winning pitcher; and (c) He qualifies under one of the following conditions: (1) He enters the game with a lead of no more than three runs and pitches for at least one inning; or (2) He enters the game with the potential tying run either on base, or at bat, or on deck (that is, the potential tying run is either already on base or is one of the first two batsmen he faced); or (3) He pitches effectively for at least three innings. No more than one save may be credited in each game.*

Until the early '70s a pitcher was credited with a save as long as he came in relief and protected his team's lead. Because of this shoddy rule, several pitchers were credited with cheap saves. For instance, on May 22, 1969, George Stone was credited with a save pitching for the Braves. When Stone entered the game, the Braves were winning, 14-3, and eventually won, 15-3. Stone pitched a total of 1 2/3 innings, picking up the save.

The system used today for crediting saves was suggested as far back as 1959 by Lou Boudreau, who was then a Chicago Cubs' announcer. John Hiller picked up 38 saves in 1973 coming in relief for the Tigers. Clay Carroll racked up 37 saves for the Reds in 1972.

Overall "Sparky" Lyle (A.L.) and Dave Giusti (N.L.) lead their respective leagues in career saves.

Determining the American League batting champions in 1910 and 1953 became a thorn to the official scorers and a much talked about controversy over the years. Rule 10.23 reads; *To assure uniformity in establishing the batting, pitching and fielding championships of professional leagues, such champions shall meet the following minimum performance standards: (a) The individual batting champion shall be the player with the highest batting average, provided he is credited with as many or more total appearances at the plate in league championship games as the number of games scheduled for each club in his league that season, multiplied by 3.1 in the case of a major league player, or multiplied by 2.7 in the case of a National Association player. However, if there is any player with fewer than the required number of plate appearances whose average would be the highest if he were charged with the required number of plate appearances or official at bat, then that player shall be awarded the batting championships.* Example: If a major league schedules 162 games for each club, 502 plate appearances qualify (162 times 3.1 equals 502).

Ty Cobb and Nap Lajoie went head to head for the batting crown in 1910. In the last game of the season, Lajoie playing for the Indians, batted nine times in a double-header against the Browns, hitting safely his first eight times at bat. Many of his hits were slow rolling taps or bunts down the third base line where St. Louis third sacker John Red Corriden persisted in playing an unusually deep position.

On Lajoie's final appearance he hit a ground ball to shortstop Bobby Wallace who muffed the chance. The official scorer, a woman named Elisa Green Williams, called it an error. A few minutes later a Browns' coach, Harry Howell, tried to entice her to change her decision. Resisting the temptation of being granted new clothing, the scorer held to her guns, which cost Lajoie the championship to Cobb by a fraction of a point.

Commissioner Ban Johnson banned Browns' manager Jack O'Connor and Coach Harry Howell from baseball for life. Corriden, a rookie third baseman, was sent back to the minors. Cobb emerged the batting champ with a mark of .3848, while Lajoie finished at .3841.

On the last day of the 1953 season, Mickey Vernon of the Washington Senators edged Al Rosen for the batting title. The Senators played the Athletics in the finale of the '53 season. Late in the game, Vernon hit a line drive which Elmer Valo of the Athletics caught. Vernon came back to the bench with an average of .337. Word arrived from Cleveland that Rosen was through for the day, and if Vernon didn't hit again, the batting championship was safe for him by a margin of .0011.

There was an outside chance that Vernon would have to bat again and possibly lose a point. Then his teammates decided to come to the rescue. Mickey Grasso doubled but got picked off second base. Kite Thomas singled and was thrown out at second as he leisurely attempted to stretch the single into a double. With those tactics, Vernon's batting title was well in hand.

A close check on the rules reveals that a player has to have 502 plate appearances to qualify for the batting title. For instance, a player who walks three times and gets one hit is credited with four appearances with only one official at bat.

Fireworks were in vogue in 1976 especially on the last day of the regular season when George Brett of the Royals nosed out teammate Hal McRae for the A.L. batting title in a game against the Twins. Going into the ninth inning McRae was hitting .3326 and Brett .3322. Brett hit an apparent catchable fly to left field. But the ball fell in front of Minnesota outfielder Steve Brye and skipped past him, as Brett circled the bases with an inside-the-park home run and a .3333 batting average.

McRae lamented that Brye deliberately let the ball drop. He said, "I was surprised. I saw the guy come in and go back, then come in and stop. He played it so well it went for a home run."

McRae following Brett in the batting order saw his batting title hopes vanish when he grounded out finishing the season with a .3321 average.

In defense Brye stated, "I just messed up. I played the ball too cautiously. I didn't want it to get by me. If I had gone for a shoestring catch and missed, the same thing would have happened."

The Brett-McRae-Brye triangle created so much attention that everyone seemed to forget about Rod Carew who was in a Twins uniform that day and also in contention for the title. If Carew had one more hit and Brett one less, Rod would have won the batting championship with a .33223 average to McRae's .33206 and Brett's .33178. In conclusion, if anyone had the right to be disenchanted it was Carew.

Before 1951, the rules required only that a player appear in 100 games. Taffy Wright of the Washington Senators appeared in exactly 100 games in 1938 for a league-leading .350 average but was denied the title. Since Wright came to bat only 263 times, the league ruled that even under the existing rules Wright had not come to bat enough times and ruled that the 1938 batting champion was Jimmie Foxx, who had a .349 batting average in 149 games with 565 at bats.

In 1954, the rule required 400 times at bat to qualify for the batting crown. That year Ted Williams officially came to bat only 386 times, walking another 136 times. The "Splendid Splinter" ended the season with a .345 average to lead the league in that category, but was 14 at bats shy of the qualifying figure. The title went to Bobby Avila of Cleveland with a .341 average. Under present rules, Williams' 522 plate appearances would have qualified him for the batting championship.

The 1931 National League batting championship was decided by a very close margin. Charles Hafey of the Cardinals won the title with a percentage of .3489. The Giants' Bill Terry came in a close second with a batting percentage of .3486 and Jim Bottomley of the Cards came across the line third at .3482.

Check any baseball record book and you will find that in 1945 George "Snuffy" Stirnweiss of the Yankees won the A.L. batting championship by the margin of one decimal point, finishing the season with an average of .309, while Tony Cuccinello of the White Sox batted .308. However, a close mathematical study reveals that Stirnweiss who had 195 hits in 632 at bats was credited with a .30854430 batting average. Cuccinello (124 for 402) pulled up second with a .30845771 average. Unbelievably, Stirnweiss edged Cuccinello by .00008659 of a point. They don't come any closer than that. In 1945, as in 1954, a player had to have at least 400 at bats to qualify for the title.

The final aspects of the official scoring rules that I will briefly touch are some of the guidelines for cumulative performance records mentioned in sections (a) and (b) of rule 10.24. *(a) A consecutive hitting streak shall not be terminated if the plate appearance results in a base on balls, hit batsman, defensive interference or a sacrifice bunt. A sacrifice fly shall terminate the streak.*

Mike "Pinky" Higgins had twelve consecutive hits playing for the Red Sox in 1938. The Tigers' Walt Dropo batted safely twelve consecutive times in 1952.

(b) A consecutive game hitting streak shall not be terminated if all the player's plate appearances (one or more) result in a base on balls, hit

batsman, defensive interference or a sacrifice bunt. The streak shall terminate if the player has a sacrifice fly and no hit.

Joe DiMaggio's 56 game hitting streak may stand forever. During the streak, Philadelphia Athletics' pitcher Johnny Babich planned on ending the streak by getting "Joltin' Joe" out once and then walking the "Yankee Clipper" the rest of the night. However, DiMaggio singled his first time up against Babich, and the hitting streak was kept alive. Concerning DiMaggio's marathon 56 game streak, did you know that "Joltin' Joe" collected 56 singles and scored 56 runs?

This concludes our look at the rules of our national pastime and many of the great moments and oddities that have occurred in baseball history because of the wording or interpretation of these rules. It is my hope that it has been both entertaining and informative, and that a better understanding of the rules will make it more enjoyable for you to watch or play the game.

The task of learning the playing rules of baseball is monumental indeed. From the day they take the field under the warm March Florida sun, to the day they depart amidst the picturesque autumnal foliage, umpires are expected to exercise good judgment one hundred per cent of the time. To say it takes a special kind of man to cope with petulant, boorish behavior throughout the extensive season, would be fitting.

Unfairly labeled as sightless villains with stone age intelligence, umpires have been the scapegoat target of leather-lunged players, managers, and fans throughout the annals of baseball. Sportswriter Furman Bisher once said of umpires, "They're submerged in the history of baseball like idiot children in a family album."

The popular credo "Nice Guys Finish Last" has served to enhance impugnent behavior on the part of baseball's participants. For some of baseball's constituents, the security of a macho profile has often been manufactured at the expense of the men in blue.

Hopefully, those who have taken the time to read this text have not only enriched their portfolio of baseball knowledge, but have come to realize the difficult chore umpires must face. It was not my intention to create public affection for umpires—just appreciation.

Index